LABOR MARKETS
IN
LATIN AMERICA

Sebastian Edwards *and*
Nora Claudia Lustig, *editors*

LABOR MARKETS IN LATIN AMERICA

Combining Social Protection with Market Flexibility

BROOKINGS INSTITUTION PRESS
Washington, D.C.

Library of Congress Cataloging-in-Publication data

Labor markets in Latin America: combining social protection with
  market flexibility / Sebastian Edwards and Nora Claudia Lustig, eds.
    p.   cm.
  Includes bibliographical references and index.
  ISBN 0-8157-2106-4 (cloth: alk. paper)
  ISBN 0-8157-2107-2 (pbk.: alk. paper)
    1. Labor market—Latin America.   2. Manpower policy—Latin
America.   3. Labor laws and legislation—Latin America.
I. Edwards, Sebastian, 1953–   . II. Lustig, Nora.
HD5730.5.A6LC   1997
331.12'098—dc21   97-22909
                                                                      CIP

9 8 7 6 5 4 3 2 1

The paper used in this publication meets the minimum requirements of the
American National Standard for Information Sciences—Permanence of Paper
for Printed Library Materials, ANSI Z39.48-1984.

Typeset in Times Roman

Composition by Harlowe Typography
Cottage City, Maryland

Printed by R. R. Donnelley and Sons Co.
Harrisonburg, Virginia

Foreword

DURING THE PAST decade, Latin American governments implemented economic reforms that affected almost every sector. Nonetheless, in most countries labor markets remain highly regulated. As of 1997, only a handful of Latin American nations had reformed their labor markets in any significant way, while most continued to rely on labor legislation enacted several decades earlier. This legislation has favored employment protection while taxing employers heavily. Some analysts, business leaders, and policymakers argue that the social protection provided through labor market regulation limits the market's ability to adjust wages and unemployment and is the principal cause of large pockets of "precarious" employment—that is, employment that does not receive any of the benefits and protection awarded by current legislation. Others believe that dismantling existing labor regulations will worsen social conditions and increase poverty and income inequality. Given the importance of this debate, remarkably little empirical research is available on the relationship between labor market regulations and labor market performance in Latin America. The main purpose of this book is to help fill this gap.

Part one of *Labor Markets in Latin America* examines the relationship between labor market institutions and economic performance in general and as applied to Latin America. Unions and collective bargaining arrangements, minimum wages and poverty, and unemployment insurance schemes are discussed. Part two offers an overview of current labor market regulations and the status of labor reform in the region as a whole, as well as in-depth analyses of the experiences of Argentina, Brazil, Chile, Colombia, and Mexico.

The chapters in this volume are the product of the project on labor market reform in Latin America jointly sponsored by the Brookings Institution and the World Bank. The papers were originally presented at a conference cosponsored by the Brookings Institution, the Instituto and

Universidad di Tella, and the World Bank. The conference took place at the Instituto and Universidad di Tella, in Buenos Aires, Argentina, on July 6 and 7, 1995. The editors are grateful to Adolfo Canitrot (director of the Instituto di Tella) and Gerardo della Paolera (rector of the Universidad di Tella) for their help in organizing the conference.

The authors greatly benefited from the comments given by the discussants at the conference: Hildegart Ahumada, Luis Beccaria, Juan Luis Bour, Victor Elías, William Experton, José María Fanelli, Edgardo Favaro, Pablo Gerchunoff, Osvaldo Giordano, Daniel Heymann, Gustavo Márquez, Ernesto May, Patricio Millán, Guillermo Mondino, Silvia Montoya, Luisa Montuschi, Fernando Navajas, John Pencavel, Alberto Petrecolla, Pablo Sanguinetti, Osvaldo Schenone, Jorge Streb, Federico Sturzenegger, Juan Carlos Torre, and Carlos Zarazaga; as well as the anonymous referees that reviewed the chapters. The editors wish to thank Gary Burtless and Richard Haass for their comments on earlier versions of the introduction and Rebecca Harris and Fernanda Torres for their research assistance on the introduction.

Many staff members at Brookings and the World Bank contributed to the project. The editors are grateful to all of them. In particular, they want to thank Jennifer Abner and Fernando Losada at the World Bank.

At Brookings Janet Herrlinger prepared the manuscript for publication and helped coordinate production of the book. Tanjam Jacobson and Theresa Walker edited the manuscript, Carlotta Ribar proofread it, and Julia Petrakis compiled the index.

Funding for this project was provided by the John D. and Catherine T. MacArthur Foundation and the World Bank. Their support is gratefully acknowledged.

The views expressed in this study are those of the authors and should not be ascribed to any of the persons or organizations mentioned above, or to the trustees, officers, or other staff members of the Brookings Institution, the Instituto and Universidad di Tella, and the World Bank.

Michael H. Armacost
President

July 1997
Washington, D.C.

Contents

Tables

Figures

LABOR MARKETS
IN
LATIN AMERICA

CHAPTER ONE

Introduction

Sebastian Edwards
Nora Claudia Lustig

DURING THE PAST decade, the Latin American economies have under-
gone a remarkable transformation. Nations that for decades pursued
protectionist policies and scorned the market system have implemented
reforms aimed at achieving macroeconomic stability, in the process de-
regulating business practices and opening their markets to foreign competition. The progress of these reforms has been uneven. While in some
countries (Chile is the premier example) they have advanced far, in others
(such as Brazil) they have proceeded slowly and selectively. In yet others
(Ecuador, for instance) they have barely begun.

Although reform programs have affected almost every sector, labor
markets remain highly regulated in most countries. In the mid-1990s the
vast majority of Latin American nations continued to rely on labor legislation enacted in the 1950s and 1960s or even earlier, favoring employment
protection, with lifelong job security in the public sector, and taxing labor
heavily. As of 1997, only a handful of countries had reformed their labor
markets in any significant way.[1] It is no exaggeration to say that the labor
market has been forgotten in Latin America's economic reform.

The persistence of high unemployment rates, unimpressive wage performance (with the exeption of Chile), and a large informal sector (see

The authors are very grateful to Gary Burtless, René Cortázar, and Richard Haass for
their comments on an earlier draft.
1. See Edwards (1995).

1

Table 1-1. *Urban Unemployment Rates, Selected Latin American Countries, 1989–96*

Country	1989	1990	1991	1992	1993	1994	1995	1996[a]
Argentina	7.6	7.5	6.5	7.0	9.6	11.5	17.5	17.0
Brazil	3.4	4.3	4.8	5.8	5.4	5.1	4.6	5.9
Chile	7.2	6.5	7.3	4.9	4.1	6.3	5.6[a]	...
Colombia	10.0	10.5	10.2	10.2	8.6	8.9	8.9	11.1
Mexico	2.9	2.7	2.7	2.8	3.4	3.7	6.3	5.9

Source: For all countries except Chile, data for 1989–94 are from CEPAL (1995, p. 52, table A-4), and for 1995–96, from ECLAC (1996, p. 14, table 3). For Chile, all data are from CEPAL (1995).
a. Preliminary.

tables 1-1 and 1-2) has generated a heated debate about the role played by prevailing labor market institutions in explaining these trends.[2] While some analysts, business leaders, and policymakers argue that the social protection provided through labor market regulation limits market response to high unemployment and is causing large pockets of precarious employment, others argue that any measure aimed at dismantling existing labor regulations will worsen social conditions and increase poverty and the inequality of income distribution.[3]

Advocates of labor market reform argue that the experiences of certain East Asian countries strongly support their views.[4] They point out that East Asian economic success has largely resulted from a significant degree of labor market flexibility that has allowed small and medium-sized firms to adapt rapidly to new market conditions, remain competitive internationally, and take advantage of technological advances.[5] On the

2. According to one estimate, the proportion of workers in the informal sector rose from 25.6 to 31.9 percent between 1980 and 1992; Tokman (1994, table 1, p. 178).

3. The intensity of this debate could be observed in Argentina in 1996, when the Menem administration's proposal for labor market reform faced fierce opposition not only from unions and their leadership, but also from other nongovernmental organizations, including the Catholic church; see, for example, the newspaper *El Clarín*, December 5, 1996.

4. See, for example, Krueger (1990). Other factors, however, have also been important in explaining the better performance of East Asian labor markets. See, for example, Cortázar, Lustig, and Sabot (forthcoming).

5. The extent of labor market regulation in Latin America contrasts sharply with the extreme flexibility in the East Asian countries. Consider, for example, the pattern of ratification of conventions of the International Labour Organisation (ILO), which can be interpreted as a government's willingness to intervene in labor markets. The number of ILO conventions ratified by Latin American and East Asian countries up to December 1993 is as follows (although, in Latin America, many are not observed): Argentina, 67; Brazil, 73; Chile, 41; Colombia, 50; Mexico, 76; Peru, 66; Hong Kong, 0; Indonesia, 10; Malaysia, 11; Singapore, 21; South Korea, 3; Thailand, 11. In comparison, note that the

Table 1-2. *Average Remunerations, Selected Latin American Countries, 1989–96*

Average indexes: 1990 = 100

Country	1989	1990	1991	1992	1993	1994	1995	1996[a]
Argentina	95.5	100.0	101.3	102.7	101.0	102.0	100.8	100.7
Brazil								
Rio de Janeiro	111.9	100.0	79.3	79.5	85.7	87.1	91.8	104.0
Sao Paulo	111.7	100.0	88.3	85.3	94.6	98.0	102.0	105.2
Chile	98.2	100.0	104.9	109.6	113.5	118.8	123.6	130.6
Colombia	101.3	100.0	97.4	98.6	103.2	104.1	105.5	106.3
Mexico	96.5	100.0	106.5	114.3	124.5	129.1	111.5	97.0

Source: For 1989 through 1991, CEPAL (1995), p. 53, table A.5). For 1992 through 1996, ECLAC (1996, p. 15, table 4).
a. Preliminary.

other hand, those analysts who oppose reform maintain that regulations provide a remedy for market failure, help to avoid employer abuses, and improve social conditions. Moreover, many argue that labor regulations are often ignored by employers and that most Latin American labor markets are de facto very flexible and competitive.

Given the importance of this debate, it is remarkable how little empirical research is available on the relationship between labor market regulations and labor market performance in Latin America.[6] The papers in this volume are intended to fill that gap. In particular, they look at the relationship between existing labor market regulations and institutions, labor market outcomes, and the economy's ability to adapt to global competition and changing market conditions. In so doing, they describe existing labor regulations and the status of labor reform in Latin America, demonstrate how such regulations affect employment generation, wages, and social conditions, and suggest how existing legislation ought to be changed.

The volume is divided into two parts. The first examines the relationship between labor market institutions and outcomes in a broad context and as it applies to Latin America. Topics analyzed include unions and efficient collective bargaining arrangements, minimum wages and poverty, and optimal unemployment insurance schemes. The second part provides an overview of existing labor market regulations and the status

United States has ratified 11 conventions, while many European countries have ratified most of them, for example: France, 114; Germany, 73; Spain, 124; Sweden, 84.
    6. Of the studies available, see Marquez (1995).

of labor reform in the region as a whole, as well as in-depth analyses of the experiences of Argentina, Brazil, Chile, Colombia, and Mexico.

Unions and Efficient Collective Bargaining Arrangements

In the next chapter, John Pencavel examines the consequences of alternative ways of structuring collective bargaining in developing countries. The analysis has significant relevance for Latin American countries, an increasing number of which are struggling with reform of existing legislation in this area.

Pencavel argues that, because of the prevalence of self-employment, unions are bound to have a smaller presence (as measured by the proportion of unionized workers) in developing countries than in more advanced ones. Nevertheless, in many Latin American countries unions have traditionally been highly politicized and powerful and have endorsed populist policies, even, on occasion, those that helped to bring on economic crises.

Moreover, when unions act as pressure groups for the redistribution of income in favor of their members, they lobby the government to obtain legislation that favors their general interests. The specific nature of these pressures depends on the institutional and political characteristics of the country in question, including the degree of democracy. Pencavel points out that most unions have supported public policies that restrict competition at various levels. Unions tend to support protectionism, barriers to entry, state ownership of enterprises, and wide-ranging government regulations. According to Pencavel, union gains come at the expense of other workers' incomes, not, as is often thought, from firms' profits.

This last point is supported by Pencavel's analysis of the effects of unions on wages and employment. Using a three-sector model characterized by a unionized sector, a sector in which wages are administratively determined, and a sector in which wages are determined by market forces alone, he finds that high wages in the union sector result in wage increases for some other high-skilled workers, a reduction in employment in the unionized and administered wage sectors, and reduction in wages in the competitive sector. Thus in his model union activity is damaging to non-unionized workers.[7]

7. It should be noted, however, that this is not a general result. See, for example, Carruth and Oswald (1981).

Pencavel also argues that unions can have beneficial effects as *participatory* institutions. In principle at least, unions can help to make the production process run more smoothly by making labor contracts (which are usually quite vague) more explicit. There are potential efficiency gains to union participation in the determinion of actual working conditions. The situation is not so simple, however, as unions can also interfere with the efficient use of resources; for example, when they shield and protect inefficient and ineffective workers.

In the final section of the chapter, Pencavel considers how to design collective bargaining rules in order to minimize the damage and maximize the benefits of union activity. He argues that one basic principle should be to restrict collective bargaining to the enterprise level. In this way, the potential costs of noncompetitive actions would be reduced. Moreover, in order to preserve competition, it is important to allow for the existence of multiple unions in each firm and to give workers the freedom to decide which, if any, should represent them. In the case of labor disputes, Pencavel argues that the government should adopt a neutral stance. With monopolistic firms—in the public sector in particular—strikes can become costly because of the lack of substitutes for the goods or services that are being withheld. Under these circumstances, the most efficient strategy might be a procedure known as final offer arbitration, using a third party as the arbitrator.

Minimum Wages and Poverty

In the third chapter, Nora Claudia Lustig and Darryl McLeod examine the relationship between changes in real minimum wages and changes in poverty levels for a cross-section of developing countries. There are a number of reasons why, in principle, minimum wages should have little or no impact on poverty in the developing world. The coverage of minimum wage laws is very incomplete and enforcement is weak, their beneficiaries are usually not the poorest populations, and while governments may be able to change nominal minimum wages, they may be unable to affect real minimum wages, because of the impact of the former on inflation. Moreover, conventional analysis holds that if minimum wages have any impact on the poor, it is likely to be negative. This type of analysis rests on variations of the Harris-Todaro model of migration, according to which when increases in the minimum wage raise real wages in the covered (or formal) sector of the economy, displaced labor will search for employment in the uncovered (or informal) sector, driving down wages in that sector.

However, several authors have shown that this result depends on a constellation of elasticities—most important, on the labor demand elasticity to wages in the covered sector. As a rule, the more inelastic this is, the less likely are wages in the uncovered sector to fall. Furthermore, general equilibrium analysis has shown that in small open economies, a rise in covered sector wages always raises wages in the uncovered sector as well. In open economies, wage increases in the covered sector cannot be passed along to prices, and as profits fall, capital rather than labor leaves the covered sector, driving up employment and wages in the uncovered sector. In closed economies, the result can go either way, depending on certain key parameters. Lustig and McLeod conclude that theoretical analysis reveals that "the impact of change in statutory minimum wages on poverty in developing countries is really an empirical issue."

Accordingly, they examine the relationship between minimum wages and poverty by regressing changes in poverty rates on changes in the minimum wage and other variables that could affect poverty levels. They use a cross-section of twenty-two developing countries, including nine countries outside Latin America (five in Asia and four in Africa), between 1970 to the early 1990s. The regression results show that real minimum wages and poverty are inversely related: that is, an increase in real minimum wages is accompanied by a fall in poverty, and a decline is accompanied by a rise. On average, the estimated elasticity is about -0.7, ranging from -0.64 to -1.29. These results are consistent with the findings of other authors who carried out similar analysis for Latin America alone.[8]

Moreover, Lustig and MacLeod find that real minimum wages seem to affect poverty independent of average wages and per capita income growth. Also, controlling for unemployment in the regression increases the minimum wage coefficient, implying that these factors are inversely related. Thus, contrary to the "new economics" of the minimum wage, the results do not rest on an unconventional relationship between unemployment and real wages. Finally, inflation seems to affect poverty

---

8. See, for example, Morley (1992).

primarily by reducing minimum (unskilled) wages, but it appears that real minimum wages capture more than this effect.

The inverse relationship between minimum wages and poverty is found across different poverty measures (headcount ratio, poverty gap, and calorie intake), poverty lines (extreme and moderate), and population groups (urban and rural). Moreover, it persists when observations are classified into cases of positive and negative growth and when Latin American observations are distinguished from Asian ones. Lustig and McLeod conclude that their results are robust but suffer from the short-comings inherent in cross-section regression analysis. Hence their find-ings "should not lead to a flat endorsement of minimum wage increases as an effective policy measure to reduce poverty." However, they should caution those who would eliminate minimum wages in the name of the poor: while the results "do not demonstrate that raising minimum wages is consistently an effective instrument to reduce poverty, eliminating or reducing minimum wages in developing countries may hurt the poor."

Designing an Optimal Unemployment Insurance Scheme

Using modern contract theory, in the fourth chapter Hugo Hopenhayn and Juan Pablo Nicolini develop the properties of an optimal unemploy-ment insurance program. They also compare their optimal program with that introduced in Argentina in 1992, apparently in response to the sharp rise in domestic unemployment observed since 1991.

Hopenhayn and Nicolini present a model with a risk-averse agent (the worker) and a risk-neutral principal (the government) in order to gener-ate the properties of an optimal unemployment insurance contract. "The key feature of the [model's] environment is that the probability of finding a new job depends on the effort exerted by the agent, which is not observable by the principal." In other words, the government must design a program that will not produce contrary incentives—for example, that it might be more attractive for a worker to collect unemployment benefits than to seek a new job. A perfectly insured worker has no incentive to search for a new job. But to provide no unemployment insurance is not optimal either. Thus there is a trade-off between insurance and incen-tives, and a well-designed program must find the right balance. The formal model leads the authors to two conclusions. First, in an optimal unemployment insurance program, benefits should decrease with the duration of unemployment. Second, the unemployment tax paid on subsequent reemployment should increase with the duration of the preceding period of unemployment.

Using a simple numerical example to compare the tax and benefit rates implied by an optimal contract with the existing unemployment insurance program in Argentina, Hopenhayn and Nicolini find that the optimal program could save about 17 percent of the government's budget when the tax side is incorporated, but only 4 percent when the benefit schedules alone are compared. Hence they argue that "step-wise decreasing sequence of benefits in Argentina's current unemployment insurance program approximates the optimal contract very well," given that adopting the optimal contract would yield only small savings. However, the results also suggest that adopting a reemployment tax contingent on length of unemployment could represent an important saving for the government.

An Overview of Labor Market Regulations and Reforms in Latin America

In the fifth chapter, Alejandra Cox Edwards provides a detailed review of labor legislation in the region as of the mid-1990s. In particular, she discusses collective bargaining rules, hiring restrictions and dismissal costs, payroll and social security taxes, workers' compensation, and training programs.

Cox Edwards concurs with Pencavel and argues that, by and large, the laws governing collective bargaining in the most important countries in the region reduce competition, force a large number of unrelated firms—often in different sectors—to abide by the same type of contracts, and discourage the creation of employment. She argues that there is an urgent need to reform this legislation to introduce greater competition and make union leaders more accountable. However, in order for this type of reform to be successful, it is necessary to liberalize goods markets as well. She points out that if goods markets are truly competitive, all parties involved in collective bargaining will have incentives to minimize the costs of labor conflicts.

As Cox Edwards shows, Latin American labor legislation has a long history of protecting job security. This goal has been pursued by restricting the hiring of temporary workers and imposing substantial costs on dismissal, in the form of mandated severance payments whose magnitude tends to grow with the length of employment. Although, in principle, severance payment schemes would not necessarily have distortionary effects if they merely represented an income smoothing mechanism, in practice, they are often viewed by employers as equivalent to a tax on dismissals, and so discourage job creation. Existing severance payment schemes also discourage voluntary quits because such workers lose their right to compensation. As the author points out, the legislation is trying to achieve two objectives with one instrument: to penalize wrongful dismissals and to provide unemployment insurance. While these objectives are valid, the chosen mechanism may be ineffective (for example, firms often find ways to reduce the severance payment) and costly in terms of the rigidities it introduces to the labor market. The existing schemes are also "unfair": the more irreversible the hiring practices, the greater the penalties to new entrants to the labor force.

Of the ten countries in Cox Edwards's sample, practically all impose restrictions on temporary contracts.[9] The most frequent restriction (found in Argentina, Brazil, Ecuador, Nicaragua, and Peru) is that contracts are limited to a maximum term of two years and cannot be renewed. However, although all countries require some type of compensation in the case of severance either without "just cause" or due to "economic cause," some have begun to change the forms of payment in order to reduce the rigidities introduced by the classical case, when the cost is not internalized by the firm at the time of hiring. Some countries (for example, Bolivia and Brazil, and more recently, Colombia and Peru) have begun to transform their former severance payment schemes into deferred compensation plans. In Bolivia the compensation is the same for all workers, whether they quit or are laid off, after five years on the job. In Brazil, Colombia, and Peru the severance payment system has been replaced with a time-of-service fund.[10]

Cox Edwards argues that if the severance payment system is reformed to become a contribution-defined fund, a national unemployment insurance scheme would not be necessary. Workers would make contributions

9. See table 5-2.

10. Nevertheless, as evidenced by Lora and Pagés (1996), problems remain because practically all of these schemes include a supplementary indemnification in the case of layoffs without just cause. Since neither economic distress nor the need to restructure are considered just causes, employers facing economic difficulties or new opportunities will have to face this additional cost.

to such a fund and could access it in case of unemployment, regardless of the cause of a layoff or whether it was the worker's decision. A contribution-defined fund would be superior to national unemployment insurance because it is difficult to fund the latter without some form of cross-subsidization. Usually, all workers are subject to the same payroll tax, regardless of their employment histories. However Nicolini and Hopenhayn have argued that an optimal unemployment insurance program could address this problem.[11]

Cox Edwards points out that payroll taxes in Latin America are notably high, ranging from 20 to 40 percent of gross wages—although in practice they may be much lower, because of the nontaxable portion of income and the rate of noncompliance. These high labor tax rates may deter employment creation in the more modern (that is, technologically sophisticated) sector of the economy.

Furthermore, payroll "contributions" currently are not linked to workers' benefits. Social security systems—covering pensions, health care, and work-related accidents—are a case in point. Traditionally, Latin American countries have had pay-as-you-go, defined benefit social security systems. According to Cox Edwards, the contributions gradually came to be perceived as a tax, and the benefits as entitlements. Most systems did not fare well in terms of cost incidence and equity. Because of the threat of insolvency, in particular, and the implied increase in labor costs, Latin American social security systems have been undergoing very important reforms since the early 1980s. As of December 1995, seven countries (Argentina, Chile, Colombia, Costa Rica, Mexico, Peru, and Uruguay) had introduced pension reforms. Although these vary from country to country, the general trend is toward systems with a large defined contribution component.

Labor training programs provide a potential safety net for the unemployed. Cox Edwards argues that in most Latin American countries, labor training programs became, in effect, a payroll tax in the formal sector, and also had a low degree of accountability. Again, benefits and contributions have not been closely related. Aware of these problems, several countries have begun to introduce reforms that deprive the programs of their traditional funding (Bolivia, Colombia, and Costa Rica) and have increased the participation of entrepreneurs in management (Peru) or program development (Brazil). In the view of Cox Edwards, it

11. See Nicolini and Hopenhayn (1995).

would be more effective policy for the governments to increase the coverage of secondary education, which in most countries remains well below 40 percent. In addition, the subsidies embedded in labor training should be transferred to the demand side; that is, to the workers rather than the labor training institutes. This would encourage competition and innovation among the providers and potentially improve the equity of the programs, because the funds could be targeted to the most needy. At present, investment is concentrated in the training of individuals with complete secondary schooling, far from the poorest workers.

Argentina

In the sixth chapter, Carola Pessino identifies four major trends in Argentina's labor market following the introduction of the Convertibility Plan in 1991: stagnating employment growth, growing labor force participation, a rising open unemployment rate, and increasing wage differentials.[12] In addition to a rise in open unemployment, there has been an increase in involuntary part-time work. During the first two years of the plan, high GDP growth was accompanied by rising open unemployment and slow growth in employment. In the latter part of 1993 employment actually suffered an absolute decline, and during 1993 and 1994 employment growth was achieved through a rise in underemployment (that is, in the proportion of workers who are involuntarily employed for less than thirty-five hours a week). The trend was for employment to shift from manufacturing into the service sector. Unemployment grew worse during the 1995 recession, a by-product of the Mexican crisis in an economy operating with a fixed exchange rate and a currency board.

Pessino argues that although there was a significant increase in labor force participation due to the incorporation of women (the "added worker effect"), most of the rise in unemployment can be attributed to a weak labor demand growth rather than an increase in the labor supply. She maintains that the underlying causes of the disappointing performance of labor markets in Argentina can be traced to three factors: the liberalization of the economy, the Convertibility Plan, and labor market regulations.

12. Argentina's open unemployment rate tripled despite the remarkable expansion of the economy, which, cumulatively, grew by 30 percent between 1990 and 1994.

Economic liberalization has done away with many traditional jobs and rendered the skills of a number of workers obsolete. Since in 1994 Argentina was, so to speak, halfway through the economic transition, the process of employment destruction in declining sectors was still overriding the process of employment creation. Hence part of the observed low net employment creation and high unemployment is bound to disappear in the medium term, as economic reform bears fruit.

Moreover, the combination of trade liberalization and the Convertibility Plan has made capital relatively cheap and labor costs relatively expensive, particularly when wages are measured in dollars. According to government estimates, the relative price of capital declined by about 40 percent in the early 1990s. However, although the relative price of labor is high in dollar terms, in terms of purchasing power the wages of the unskilled are low. Hence it is unlikely that the labor market imbalance can be fully corrected by lowering wages. Even employers may be reluctant to lower wages further because of the potential negative impact on productivity (the "efficiency wage" factor).

Given that the Convertibility Plan is not likely to be abandoned, because of its high payoff in the area of price stability, and that wages probably will not fall much further, because of the efficiency wage considerations mentioned above, the existing disequilibrium in the labor markets has to be addressed by other means: reforming labor market regulations. According to Pessino, labor mobility is hampered because of expensive severance payment schemes, high fixed costs to hiring, and restrictions against moving workers to other functions within the same firm. Moreover, very high payroll taxes—which produce an approximately 55 percent wedge between net and gross wages—reduce labor demand. Finally, existing collective bargaining agreements are an obstacle to labor mobility and, in some sectors, impede the downward wage adjustments needed to keep more workers on the job.

In examining the trends in unemployment, Pessino finds some interesting patterns. First, the rise in unemployment, contrary to conventional belief, is not explained by a disproportionate increase in female or teenage unemployment, despite the recorded increase in labor force participation by these two groups. In fact, unemployment has hit the more stable portion of the labor force. In terms of sectors, unemployment rose more pronouncedly in manufacturing—that is, the sector most affected by trade liberalization—than in services. In terms of skills, the author's empirical work reveals that unemployment did not increase proportionately with lower levels of skills or educational attainment. Although the less educated and those with unfinished degrees were hit hardest at first, later the more educated—except for those with completed tertiary degrees—were most affected.

In her empirical analysis of the determinants of unemployment, Pessino finds that the probability of unemployment decreases as the number of years of schooling increases. Also, the probability of unemployment initially rises and then declines as employment experience increases. These results seem to confirm that the obsolescence of skills has been one cause of unemployment in Argentina.

Brazil

In the seventh chapter, Edward Amadeo and José Márcio Camargo investigate the consequences of labor market regulations in Brazil. In particular, they ask, first, what is the actual—as opposed to legislated—degree of labor market flexibility? And second, how do labor market regulations—minimum wages, mandated benefits, and severance payments—affect the country's international competitiveness? These important questions go to the heart of the policy debate over labor market reform policy in Latin America and also in other parts of the world. Brazil is generally recognized as one of the more severely distorted Latin American countries, in terms of labor market regulations. Yet a number of analysts have argued that since these regulations are largely ignored by employers, the Brazilian labor market is flexible and internationally competitive. From their analysis of a significant body of empirical evidence, Amadeo and Camargo conclude that this is indeed the case.

The authors rely on the "wage curve" methodology suggested by David Blanchflower and Andrew Oswald to analyze the aggregate degree of labor market flexibility in Brazil.[13] This approach is based on the existence of an internationally stable relationship between unemployment and real wages. A steeply sloping curve indicates a high degree of labor market flexibility, since it suggests that increases in unemployment prompt a major wage rate response. Amadeo and Camargo argue that

13. See Blanchflower and Oswald (1990).

although the slope of the wage curve in Brazil has varied significantly in the last two decades, throughout most of the period it has been significantly greater than in the countries of the Organization for Economic Cooperation and Development (OECD). This suggests a high degree of real wage rate flexibility in Brazil, and provides some evidence of a very dynamic labor market.

Amadeo and Camargo then address the cost of labor in Brazil and its impact on international competitiveness, labor market flexibility, and the informal sector. They divide their analysis into three main parts. First, they compare the extent to which Brazilian workers consider social security and other mandated contributions to be deferred payments rather than pure taxes on labor. Second, they discuss whether Brazilian firms act as perfect competitors when making hiring decisions, and hence whether the existence of an informal sector is evidence of binding distortions. Third, they investigate the extent to which dismissal costs reduce international competitiveness and labor market flexibility.

Using survey data, Amadeo and Camargo conclude that the typical Brazilian worker "appropriates" a percentage of total hourly compensation roughly similar to that of workers in the average OECD country. In that respect, mandated benefits do not impose a higher tax burden in Brazil than in other nations. The authors develop a model in the tradition of the efficiency wages literature to argue that, in the presence of different preferences, some workers would choose to be employed in the informal sector, even if mandated benefits were not perceived as taxes but were considered to be deferred compensation. After analyzing the available Brazilian data—evidence on wage rate differentials, in particular—they conclude that the presence of a large informal sector is not evidence that the existing structure of benefits has introduced costly distortions. In fact, the massive informal sector—covering approximately 30 percent of the labor force—reflects the fact that many workers prefer informal labor relations.

In order to determine whether existing regulations on dismissals affect the flexibility of the labor market in Brazil, Amadeo and Camargo look at turnover and unemployment frequency. They find that although the legal costs of dismissal are roughly similar in Brazil, France, and Germany, Brazil has a higher frequency of unemployment and also a lower rate of long-term unemployment. Moreover, they find that the degree of employment flexibility in Brazil is not that different from that of the United States.

Chile

In the eighth paper, René Cortázar analyzes Chile's path toward labor reform over the period 1973–94. He follows a political economy approach—emphasizing the role of ideology and government preferences—and discusses the ways in which public policy shaped the behavior of some of the key labor variables in Chile. This chapter not only provides a concise history of labor policies and outcomes in the country that pioneered reform in Latin America, but also presents some important lessons in the design of modern labor legislation, which could prove useful to policymakers in the region, as well as in other parts of the world.

Cortázar divides Chile's recent labor history into three periods. The first, 1973–79, corresponds to the more authoritarian phase of the military regime. The second, 1979–89, is characterized by the relaxation of some of the constraints on collective bargaining and unionization. It was at this time that the bases of Chile's current labor legislation were defined. Possibly the most important policy initiatives during this period were the labor market reform of 1980 and the social security reform of 1981. The third phase, 1990–94, covers the return to democratic rule, including the labor policies implemented by President Patricio Aylwin's administration.[14]

Cortázar describes the first period as characterized by a desire to reduce the importance of unions (in fact, collective bargaining was forbidden until 1979) and to exercise administrative control over the growth rate of wages. He presents some statistical evidence, based on simple regressions, to argue that during this period wage increases were dictated almost exclusively by government actions. Moreover, he points out that during the early years of General Augusto Pinochet's regime, the government deliberately underestimated the rate of inflation in order to grant lower wage adjustments.

Cortázar argues that external pressure—mostly from the United States—prompted the military regime to revise its labor policies in the late 1970s. The changes centered on two main initiatives: a labor law that envisaged a new—significantly more restrictive, in historical terms—role for unions, and major reform of the social security system. The labor law

---

14. René Cortázar served as minister of labor during the four years of the Aylwin administration.

allowed the creation of unions in almost every firm. Membership, however, was voluntary. Collective bargaining had to take place at the firm level, and striking workers could be replaced. Labor mobility was encouraged, and severance payments were significantly reduced.[15] The reform of the social security system replaced a pay-as-you-go regime with a fully funded defined contribution scheme administered by private companies. Although it was opposed quite actively when it was first proposed, this system has since become famous throughout the world, as an increasing number of countries have tried to emulate it.[16]

Cortázar ends his chapter with an analysis of the labor reform implemented by the Aylwin administration, the first democratic regime after Pinochet's. He points out that President Aylwin's reform was aimed at achieving "growth with equity." The minimum wage was increased, collective bargaining rules were relaxed, public sector workers were allowed to form unions, the maximum severance payment was increased, and the social security system was amended in order to increase the benefits of the poor. He argues that this policy of "continuity and change" has been largely successful, as real wages have increased rapidly (mostly reflecting increases in productivity), unemployment has declined steadily, macroeconomic balance has not been threatened, and poverty has been reduced by more than 25 percent.

To reform collective bargaining rules, however, is not a simple task. Cortázar provides one account of the political and policy restrictions faced by Aylwin's government when it redefined these rules in a democratic setting. As he describes, during this period labor policy and institutions in Chile resulted from the strategic interaction of different actors—such as the government, labor unions and the business sector—each with its own set of preferences, incentives, and restrictions.

Colombia

In the ninth chapter, Eduardo Lora and Marta Luz Henao analyze the reform of Colombia's labor legislation in 1990. This initiative was part of a major attempt to modernize the Colombian economy undertaken by President César Gaviria's administration in 1990–94. It constitutes a par-

15. See the chapters by Pencavel and Cox Edwards in this volume for further detail on these issues.

16. See, for example, "Retirement Revolution," *Economist*, November 23, 1996, p. 95.

ticularly important episode in the recent Latin American structural reforms because, in contrast to the other countries in the region, Colombia implemented its labor reform very early in the transformation process. In fact, Law 50—as the legislation that reformed Colombian labor market relations is known—was enacted on December 28, 1990, less than six months after President Gaviria had taken office and before the reform of international trade, infrastructure provision, or the rules governing direct foreign investment and exchange controls.[17] Some authors—in particular, the architects of the reforms—argue that this unique labor-first sequencing of structural change explains why trade reform did not generate employment dislocations in Colombia.[18]

Lora and Henao first detail key aspects of the Colombian labor reform of 1990, including hiring conditions, severance payments, costs of dismissal, minimum wages, and the rules regulating collective bargaining, as well as social security, which was reformed under a different piece of legislation in 1993. They discuss the main features of the old legislation and those of the new law and argue that, by and large, the Gaviria reform was aimed at introducing greater flexibility to the labor market, reducing the extent of the informal sector, and reducing the uncertainty associated with costs of dismissal.

The authors show that the degree of unionization in Colombia has been traditionally low, peaking at 13.5 percent of urban employment in the mid–1970s and then dipping to 7 percent in 1993. The 1990 reform reduced the costs of forming unions and thus encouraged, at least in principle, the degree of unionization, but also greatly reduced the social and economic costs of labor conflicts.

Lora and Henao then analyze the effects of the 1990 labor reform on wages, employment, and the international competitiveness of the export sector. From the results of simulations using a twenty-one-sector computable general equilibrium model of the Colombian economy, they argue that changes to the legal aspects of labor relations have had very little effect on how the labor market functions. Costs other than wages increased from 38 to 53 percent of wages in the manufacturing sector, and from 43 to 53 percent in the retail sector. On the positive side, there

17. It has not escaped the attention of perceptive observers that Law 50 was approved on Saint Innocent's Day, which is celebrated throughout Latin America with pranks and jokes—some of them in bad taste—in much the same spirit as April Fool's Day in the United States.

18. See, for example, Hommes, Montenegro, and Roda (1994).

has been a significant reduction in uncertainty regarding labor/costs, mainly as a result of changes in the severance payment system.

The authors show that there was an important reduction in the degree of labor market informality between 1988 and 1994. On the basis of results obtained from their computable general equilibrium model, they conclude that this was the result both of the labor reforms and of a reduction in the real minimum wage. They also show that after the reforms, the importance of temporary employment increased significantly. This is not surprising, since one of the most important purposes of the reform was to facilitate the hiring of temporary workers. Overall, Lora and Henao conclude that the 1990 labor reform in Colombia was a step in the right direction, but a timid step.

Mexico

Enrique Davila begins the final chapter by stating that the gap between the cost incurred by the employer and the benefit derived by the worker under current Mexican labor legislation "can constitute an important obstacle to employment growth in the formal sector of the economy and to the adequate functioning of the social security institutions." He argues that one of the major objectives of the recent reform of the Mexican social security system, enacted in 1996 and effective from 1997, is precisely to reduce this gap between costs and benefits.

Mexico has been undergoing significant economic liberalization since 1985. Nevertheless, Davila points out, open unemployment has been rather low. In part, this is explained by the way in which unemployment is measured in Mexico. Following the International Labour Organisation's recommendations, the "employed population consists of those who had worked at least one hour in the week before they were surveyed. Those who did not work but were certain to return to a job or business, and those who were going to begin a new job in the next four weeks are also included. The open unemployed are those who did not work but were available to engage in some economic activity and actively sought to do so in the two months prior to the time of the survey."

In part, though, the low open unemployment figures also result from the logic of the job hunting process at the individual level. In a country without unemployment insurance and in which a large fraction of workers lack legislative protections such as severance payments and have very little in savings, workers cannot afford a long search for a job. In Mexico, the problem is not unemployment, but the low quality and remuneration of available jobs.

Davila investigates whether minimum wages, an inherent element of labor market legislation in Mexico, are binding. By comparing minimum wages with the wages of unskilled workers (corrected for hours worked and the personal characteristics of workers), he finds that in 1976 the minimum wage was twice as large as the average wage received by uneducated workers in establishments employing between one and five persons; that is, the minimum wage was binding. But by 1987 the minimum wage was no longer binding for a large portion of the labor force, and by 1992 it was not binding at all. Thus at current levels the minimum wage does introduce distortions in the labor market.

In regard to the costs of dismissal, Davila argues that existing labor legislation makes dismissal costs so high that the probability of receiving the full indemnification is low. Moreover, the law gives the worker the right to opt for reinstatement, reducing the flexibility of labor markets. Even in the case of justified dismissals, the "abundance of subjective terms in the language of the law provides a large margin of discretion to labor authorities. This, in turn, encourages drawn out settlements and creates legal insecurity for economic agents." Davila recommends eliminating the option of reinstatement and offering the worker, in its place, a no-fault indemnification. The employer would have to deposit the indemnification in an account subsidiary to the employee's social security investment account from the day of the dismissal or resignation. The former employee could withdraw amounts until the funds ran out, or he or she found a new job.

Under existing social security legislation—before the 1996 reforms take effect—contributions can equal up to 30.5 percent of base salary. These contributions cover disability, old age, old age severance, and life insurance; retirement insurance; sickness and maternity insurance; occupational hazard insurance; day care center insurance; and the government housing program. Davila shows that the existing rules for old age pension are not equitable and produce distortions. In particular, the fact that in order to receive a pension, workers must continue to contribute until the age of retirement (sixty-five), discriminates against female and unskilled workers. Unskilled workers, for example, are more likely to engage in the uncovered sector at least part of their working lives. Davila reports figures that confirm this hypothesis, showing a "drastic fall in the percentage of contributing women and contributing men of low education levels with increasing age." Moreover, he contends that the financial sustainability of the existing pension system is based on two undesirable factors: the loss of claims of those who stopped contributing before the age of retirement and the confiscation of part of the claims due to inflation.

Davila explains the advantages of a fully funded system with individual accounts; as proposed by the 1996 reforms, such a system permits significant improvement in the link between benefits and costs, hence creating a better incentive structure. And it does not discriminate against those who are unable to contribute throughout their working lives. Davila also suggests that introducing uniform contributions, unrelated to salary levels, for sickness and maternity insurance will avoid unjustified (in terms of equity, for example) cross-subsidies and discourage opportunistic behavior, such as joining the system after starting a family, at an advanced age, or after developing a serious health problem.

However, the question remains whether any of the reforms proposed or adopted will bring fundamental changes to what Davila has identified as the main problems of labor market performance in Mexico: the low quality and low remuneration of a large portion of the available jobs.

Concluding Thoughts

In the mid-1990s, labor market regulations and institutions in most Latin American countries remained quite restrictive. Theoretically, legislation on union activity artificially raised the bargaining power of unions beyond market conditions, restricted a worker's right to choose union membership, and encouraged long and costly collective bargaining. Regulations favoring job security restricted the hiring of part-time workers and imposed substantial costs on dismissals. Payroll taxes were excessively high (20 to 40 percent of gross wages) and reduced the pace of job creation in the more modern sector of the economy.

Furthermore, the chapters on Argentina, Colombia, and Mexico argue that labor market regulations appear to have had a negative effect on market flexibility and employment generation in the formal sector, and possibly to have worsened the fate of workers in the informal sector, most of whom are poor. However, the chapter on minimum wages (chapter 3) suggests that some forms of intervention may benefit the poor, even if their impact on employment is shown to be negative. Moreover, the evidence from Brazil indicates that legal restrictions did not significantly affect the actual performance of labor markets, because of the high rate of noncompliance. Finally, the case of Chile serves to illustrate that providing greater social protection in some areas is compatible with good labor market outcomes: the reintroduction of labor rights and protective legislation with the advent of democracy was accompanied by very rapid GDP growth, rising real wages, and lower unemployment.

Overall, labor regulations in Latin America should be revised to phase out unwarranted restrictions and reduce labor costs. Such changes can be introduced without compromising social protection in any fundamental way. Rules on collective bargaining should encourage negotiations at the enterprise or plant level, and firms should not be forced to comply with stipulations that ignore their particular economic or financial conditions. Workers, if they so desire, should be allowed to be represented by more than one union at a given plant or firm. In addition, individual workers should be free to choose which, if any, union to join, and the current restrictions on a worker's right to work should be relaxed. Last, governments should play a neutral role in collective bargaining and strike resolution. In the case of private or state monopolies, third party arbitration might be the most efficient policy.

In order to make legislation on hiring and firing practices congruent with greater job flexibility while preserving the goal of social protection, several changes need to be introduced. The economic distress of a firm must be accepted as a just cause for layoffs. The old severance payment scheme should be converted into deferred compensation plans. Severance compensation should be similar for all workers, whether they quit or are laid off, and should not necessarily be a direct function of seniority. The legislation should allow for enterprises to make appropriate provisions to absorb the costs implied by the reformed compensation schemes. Also important, companies should be allowed to move workers within plants without penalty.

Finally, reforms to reduce payroll taxes are desperately needed. One way to accomplish a reduction in nonwage labor costs is by reforming the social security system. An existing publicly managed, pay-as-you-go, defined benefit system could be converted to one with a substantially smaller public pillar, coexisting with a mandatory, privately managed, fully funded component. Under such a reformed system, social protection could be preserved by providing workers with some form of a publicly funded minimum pension and access to subsidized health care. Several countries in the region have already begun introducing such reforms, with Chile the pioneer. But because these reforms are so new, in most cases their actual impact cannot yet be assessed.

Labor reform has proved to be particularly difficult in political terms. The key to success might be to introduce the reforms as implying greater choice rather than more restrictions. For example, under the new legislation, decentralized collective bargaining should not be obligatory but offered as an alternative. In order to encourage decentralization, it would suffice to allow individual firms to decide whether to follow sector- or industrywide collective contracts. It is also important that reforms preserve the notion of reciprocity. For example, it may be worthwhile to maintain a small severance payment scheme, so that laying off workers is not seen as totally without cost to the employer. Such measures may make labor reform politically more palatable and hence more feasible. Selling it purely on the grounds of efficiency is unlikely to generate the support to make labor reform happen or, if it does, make it sustainable.

References

Blanchflower, David, and Andrew Oswald. 1990. "The Wage Curve." *Scandinavian Journal of Economics* 92 (2): 215–35.

Carruth, Alan A., and Andrew J. Oswald. 1981. "The Determination of Union and Non-Union Wage Rates." *European Economic Review* 16(2–3): 285–302.

CEPAL (Comisión Económica para América Latina y el Caribe). 1995. *Balance Preliminar de la Economía de América Latina y el Caribe*. Santiago, Chile: United Nations.

Cortázar, Rene, Nora Claudia Lustig, and Richard Sabot. Forthcoming. "Economic Policy and Labor Market Dynamics in Latin America." In *Efficiency- and Equity-Enhancing Reforms in Latin America*, edited by Nancy Birdsall, Carol Graham, and Richard Sabot. Brookings.

ECLAC (Economic Commission for Latin America and the Caribbean). 1996. *Economic Panorama of Latin America, 1966*. Santiago, Chile: United Nations.

Edwards, Sebastian. 1995. *Crisis and Reform in Latin America: From Despair to Hope*. Oxford University Press.

Hommes, Rudolf, Armando Montenegro, and Pablo Roda. 1994. *Una Apertura Hacia el Futuro*. Bogota, Colombia: Ministerio de Hacienda y Crédito Público, Departamento Nacional de Planeación and Fondo Nacional de Desarrollo Económico.

Krueger, Anne O. 1990. *Perspectives on Trade and Development*. Harvester and Wheatsheaf.

Lora, Eduardo, and Carmen Pagés. 1996. "La Legislación Laboral en el Proceso de Reformas Estructurales de América Latina y el Caribe." Washington: Interamerican Development Bank, Office of the Chief Economist (September).

Marquez, Gustavo. 1995. *Reforming the Labor Market in a Liberalized Economy*. Johns Hopkins University Press.

Morley, Samuel. 1992. "Structural Adjustment and Determinants of Poverty in Latin America." In Nora Lustig, ed., *Coping with Austerity: Poverty and Inequality in Latin America*. Brookings.

Nicolini, Juan Pablo, and Hugo Hopenhayn. 1995. "Optimal Unemployment Insurance." Paper prepared for the Conference on Labor Markets in Latin America. Brookings and World Bank, Buenos Aires, Argentina, July 6–7.

Tokman, Víctor. 1994. "Informalidad y Pobreza: Progreso Social y Modernización Productiva." *El Trimestre Económico* 61(1): 177–99.

Part One

LABOR MARKET REGULATIONS, MARKET FLEXIBILITY, AND SOCIAL PROTECTION

CHAPTER TWO

The Legal Framework for Collective Bargaining in Developing Economies

John Pencavel

THIS IS AN ESSAY in both positive and normative economics. The positive aspect describes the activities of labor unions in an economy. Given these activities, the normative component advocates the appropriate framework for the law on collective bargaining. The type of economy I have in mind is a developing economy, such as that of Latin America, Africa, or Southeast Asia. With such a wide sweep of countries, it would be remarkable if labor unions operated, or should operate, in these economies in just the same way. Local circumstances have an impact on the manner in which institutions work, so there is real value to a detailed study of a country's institutions that recognizes the wider historical and cultural context in which they fit. Therefore the price of attempting a statement about the operation of unions that is designed to be so widely

The basic arguments in this paper were first presented in a manuscript prepared in Santiago, Chile, in May 1979. This is an expanded version of that paper. Its preparation has been supported by the World Bank, although the opinions expressed are not necessarily those of the World Bank. This version has benefited from comments on earlier drafts from Ben Craig, Alejandra Cox Edwards, Gary Fields, Hafez Ghanem, Paul Glewwe, David Lindauer, Julie Anderson Schaffner, Roberto Steiner, Michael Walton, and two anonymous referees.

applicable is that it will undoubtedly not describe accurately each and every situation.

At the same time, there is also value to generalization and to determining what statements can be made about the typical or representative situation. The difficulty is that most developing economies lack the sort of scientific studies on which informed conclusions about the operation of unions should depend. The consequence is that a statement made today about labor unions in these economies must rely in large part on two types of information: one consists of inferences from theoretical models whose value in other circumstances has been shown to be useful; and the other consists of inferences from empirical studies of labor unions in developed economies. Of course, both of these sources of information may be unreliable.

It may be that the type of theoretical reasoning that has worked well to describe the behavior of many different types of markets in developed economies does not operate as satisfactorily for drawing inferences about labor markets in less rich economies. Or it may be that the particular findings from the study of labor markets in developed countries do not extend to developing economies. This is why it is important to emphasize that the arguments that follow in this chapter rest on considerably less assured foundations than I should like. Although the statements and arguments sound confident and unambiguous, they rest on fragile underpinnings.

In fact, studies of labor markets in developing economies usually yield inferences remarkably consonant with orthodox models, provided these models are appropriately amended to take account of the particular circumstances of time and place.[1] Hence, although the detail and rigor of the studies may not always match those conducted on the more developed economies, there is good reason to believe that the type of reasoning applied to developed economies will apply to the developing countries, too.

In this essay, I first draw attention to some general features of labor markets in developing countries as they bear on the issue of collective bargaining and unionism. With these features in mind, I then discuss the wage effects of labor unions. I do so in the context of a three-sector model, where the wages of union workers and the wages of certain non-

---

1. See, for instance, the assessment of Rosenzweig (1988).

union workers interact with one another. The employment ramifications of these interactions are felt, in part, by workers in the low-wage competitive sector. I proceed to examine other activities of unions at the place of work and consider whether their participation in the exchange of labor services enhances or reduces productivity. The role of the union as a distributional pressure group on government is evaluated in the following section. Out of this argument emerges a rough assessment of who benefits and who loses from unionism.

With a better understanding of the effects of labor unions, I move on to an unabashedly normative analysis of the appropriate structure of the law with respect to collective bargaining. In other words, given the arguments in the earlier sections about the operation of labor unions in an economy, I address how the law on collective bargaining *ought* to be designed. This is a topic that is well suited to the perspective of the economist, although in recent years economists have shied away from making such statements.

The Context of Collective Bargaining in Developing Economies

Limits to the Extent of Unionism

One very important difference between the highly developed economies and the less developed economies is that, as a rule, the structure of the developing economies cannot sustain as high a level of unionism as the more developed economies. This is because unions are agents of employees and in less developed economies a larger fraction of workers are not employees but are self-employed and unpaid family workers. Moreover, given the costs of organizing workers in geographically dispersed rural areas, the locus of unionism is in urban areas and, within urban areas, in what is sometimes called the "formal" sector, the prototype being large conspicuous enterprises.

The consequence is that the fraction of the economy's labor force that is potentially unionizable in less developed countries is smaller than in highly urbanized, more highly developed economies. Indeed, the fraction of workers in developing economies covered by collective bargaining agreements is typically less than one-quarter, often substantially less than

this.[2] The workers represented by collective bargaining are more likely
to be those employed by the state and large private sector employers,
sometimes described as among the elite of the economically active population. Even in countries such as Mexico, where the union movement
has a long and vigorous history and where petroleum, transport, textile,
mining, and government employees are unionized, unskilled and poorly
educated workers are outside the unions.

Patronage and Obstructionist Regimes

In this setting, states have adopted different postures with respect to
unionism and collective bargaining. It is useful to distinguish two types
of posture: there is the *patronage* regime, where the state nourishes
unionism and collective bargaining, and there is the *obstructionist* regime, where the state undermines and subverts unionism and collective
bargaining.

In patronage regimes, collective bargaining is explicitly endorsed as a
proper system for organizing labor markets and the state facilitates the
extension of unionism to formerly unorganized enterprises. The activities
of unions are supported by measures that restrict the discretionary behavior of employers of nonunion and union labor alike. Examples of such
regimes are provided by India, Bangladesh, and certain African and West
Indian countries (many of them former British colonies). Firms are often
required to pay substantial severance pay to workers laid off from their
jobs, there are mandatory employer-financed fringe benefits, and firms
may not close their plants without government permission.[3] As the visible
manifestation of an import-substitution policy, unionized firms often enjoy substantial protection from foreign competition. In these countries,

2. For instance, Joshi and Little (1994) estimate the formal sector of India's economy
as constituting about 9 percent of total employment and they estimate unionism as representing between one-fifth and one-third of all formal sector employment. About 20 percent
of manufacturing employment is estimated to be in the formal sector, with unionism covering between 30 and 45 percent of this. As a percentage of the nonagricultural labor force
(note the different base), Frenkel (1993) estimates union densities at 17 in Singapore, 19 in
Hong Kong, 33 in Taiwan, 24 in South Korea, 14 in Malaysia, and 6 in Thailand.

3. In India, companies get around the law by paying workers enough money to induce
them to leave voluntarily, in which case government permission is not needed to close down
a plant. Although there has been talk of changing the law, labor unions oppose change out
of fear that mass closures would result.

close ties exist between political parties (sometimes including the governing party) and labor unions.

By contrast, obstructionist regimes strictly regulate, if not suppress, collective bargaining. Each union must obtain the sanction of the state to operate as a collective bargaining agent, the unionization of large sectors of the economy is prohibited, the content of collective bargaining agreements is restricted, and strikes are often illegal. In some cases, union members and leaders are routinely intimidated by the "security" forces. Some of these features are found in certain countries in Southeast Asia and North Africa.

Some countries exhibit a mixture of these two types of regime. In much of Latin America, employer-financed severance payments and fringe benefits are mandatory and alliances between unions and political parties are common. At the same time, the state may intervene heavily in union affairs and in the collective bargaining process.[4]

In Brazil, for instance, the executive branch of government not only determines whether a union may represent a group of workers, it also fixes its dues and the allocation of its expenditures. Union representation requires the sanction of the Ministry of Labor, and, until the 1988 constitution, the state had the power to seize union funds whenever the public good was served by that action, the minister of labor being the individual making the determination. The state determined eligibility to union positions, a substantial power in an economy where many labor grievances and disputes were handled by an elaborate system of labor courts on which state-sanctioned union representatives were guaranteed a seat.[5] The result was a system whereby the union leaders were often more dependent on the favor of the ruling political party than on the support of the workers whom they were supposed to represent. Until 1988, the right to strike was severely restricted and yet, in many years, Brazil experienced frequent strikes, a consequence, in part, of the fact that workers' participation in strikes was subsidized. When some of a union's original strike demands had been met, employers were obliged to pay employees for the workdays lost through strikes.[6]

---

4. See Cox Edwards (1992).
5. The system was inherited from Getulio Vargas's authoritarian "*Estado Novo*" of the late 1930s and early 1940s.
6. On labor laws and industrial disputes in Brazil, see Amadeo and Camargo (1993) and Sandoval (1993).

Politicization

Both patronage and obstructionist regimes share the feature that unions are highly politicized. To the unions, it appears as if the discretionary activities of local or national political leaders assume much greater importance than the economic realities in the workplace. Because the state figures routinely in defining their effective environment, the unions' relations with the state and political leaders become more important than their dealings with the employers of the workers they represent. Resolving questions with politicians naturally tends to remove the issues from the particular context and circumstances of a single firm, with the result not only that the ultimate agreements may bear little relation to the economic circumstances of each firm, but also that the dissonance between the rank-and-file union members and the union leaders is increased.

Indeed, the union movement is often the route to political power: many leading politicians in developing countries have embarked on their career by gaining influence within the union movement.[7] Labor unions and their leaders are apt to exert disproportionate influence on economic policy in developing countries because (along with the military) "they are among the few interest-group power centers that have organizational structure, leadership, and a more or less clear idea of objectives."[8] In Mexico, for instance, the union leadership has been closely tied to the government since the 1920s and, although the connection today is weaker than for many decades, it remains the case that leading figures in the union movement occupy important positions in the executive branch of government.

When the links between the political process and unionism are so strong, the conditions are ripe for what has been called the macroeconomics of populism, the attempt to use macroeconomic policy tools to engineer a redistribution of income. The political system is seen as the agent delivering economic outcomes, so that it is natural for union leaders

7. For instance, Essenberg (1981) reports that in Bombay, a survey of forty-five labor unions indicated that the union leaders were not drawn from the rank-and-file of the workers they represented but were "outsiders," pursuing their personal political goals by allying with one or more labor unions. Only seven leaders spent their time on a single union; most leaders were devoting their time to between two and five unions. The survey was taken in 1958, but Essenberg claims that "the situation has not changed appreciably since the survey was taken" (p. 96).

8. Essenberg (1981, p. 94).

to believe that if political power can only be captured, macroeconomic policy can be steered to deliver higher incomes for wage earners. The experience of populism has been appalling for wage earners; short-term real wage gains end up as drastic real wage losses.[9] Though a highly politicized collective bargaining system is neither a necessary nor a sufficient condition for the macroeconomics of populism, the risks of macroeconomic instability are greater in a system where workers see their welfare as emanating from the political system. What is needed is a system of collective bargaining that directs the efforts of unions toward the ultimate lasting source of their members' welfare, namely, the production unit with which they are associated.

To deal with the politicized nature of unionism below, I propose an alternative framework for collective bargaining in these economies. First, I describe the activities of unions, starting with their wage-making activities.

The Wage-Making Activities of Unions

The Union Sector

A primary concern of labor unions is to raise the wages of the workers they represent. Analytically, to an economist, because they act as wage-makers rather than wage-takers, this role identifies unions as monopolies.[10] If a union raises wages higher than they would otherwise be, if the union's other activities do not offset the higher costs thus imposed on the firm, and if the pay of workers in competitive firms is not raised correspondingly, the wage-making activities of the union cannot persist in the long run, unless the firm's product markets possess some monopolistic features.

In other words, in a competitive industry where some workers are unionized and some are not, unionized firms tend to lose business to their nonunion competitors and, ultimately, the unionized firms are driven from the industry. Though this process sometimes takes years or

9. See the essays in Dornbusch and Edwards (1991).

10. A union is sometimes labeled a monopoly for other reasons. For instance, in the United States, once a union is certified by the National Labor Relations Board, it has an *exclusive* area of operation in representing workers in the specified bargaining unit and the employer must recognize the union as the *sole* bargaining agent. This sense of the union as a monopoly arises from particular features of U.S. law and not from the economic setting.

decades to manifest itself, there are many examples, and it means that unions constantly have to organize new workers simply to maintain their market share. This is because, other things equal, unionized firms tend to shrink in size while their lower-cost competitors expand. This "Red Queen" feature of unionism implies that far-sighted unions should care about the rules governing the unionization of new workers because the cheaper it is to organize new firms, the easier it is for unions to maintain their presence in an economy.[11]

The tendency for unionism to decline in importance operates more slowly in industries where virtually all firms are unionized or where the unionized firms possess some product market power. In the latter case, by pushing up wages, the union shares monopolistic rents with the firm. Even in this case, however, the lower return on capital than would obtain in the absence of the union will tend to discourage the entry of new capital into the monopolistic industry. The feature also works less rapidly in public sector labor markets, where firms may be monopolies by statute or where competitive pressures are attenuated.

This reasoning would suggest, therefore, that unions tend to be found in industries where firms have some product market power, unless unions are able to offset their wage leverage with productivity-enhancing activities or to use the authority of the state to confer analogous cost disadvantages on nonunionized establishments.[12] And indeed, across countries, it is the monopolistic product markets (whether the monopolies are public or private) that are most hospitable to unionism. For instance, the incidence of unionism in the public sector usually exceeds that of the private sector.[13] Moreover, union density tends to be lower in agriculture, financial services, and trade, where competition in the product market is

---

11. "Now, *here*, you see, it takes all the running *you* can do, to keep in the same place. If you want to get somewhere else, you must run at least twice as fast as that." (The Red Queen in Lewis Carroll, *Through the Looking Glass and What Alice Found There.*)

12. For instance, many countries have rules requiring nonunion firms to pay higher wages than they would otherwise pay. Sometimes these rules prescribe that nonunion firms pay their workers the wage that collective bargaining has established in neighboring or related firms.

13. For instance, in Malaysia in 1985, private sector union density lay in the range of 7 to 10 percent, while among government employees the percentage was about 43; see Arudsothy and Littler (1993). The Organisation for Economic Co-operation and Development (1991) estimates that, averaged over eighteen developed economies, union membership in the late 1980s constituted 61 percent of public sector workers and 41 percent of private sector workers.

keen, than in manufacturing and transport, where firms may enjoy some product market power.

The above reasoning rested on the presumption that the wages of unionized workers exceed those of nonunion workers. This is often, but not always, the case. There are a number situations in which such wage differentials do not exist; for instance, if wages determined through collective bargaining in the unionized sector are extended to nonunion workers as well. Indeed, in some economies, the pay of only a few workers is unaffected directly by collective bargains.[14]

Even without this type of automatic extension to the nonunion sector of wages negotiated by labor unions, the pay of union workers may not differ from the pay of nonunion workers who are otherwise similar. As an example, consider Julie Schaffner's sophisticated analysis of wage differentials among urban male Peruvian workers in 1985.[15] She finds that unionized workers tend to be paid more than nonunion workers, but that this is principally because union workers are employed in larger establishments and there exist substantial wage differences by size of establishment. Once wage differences across size of establishment are taken into account, the take-home pay of union and nonunion workers differs trivially.[16] In other words, among workers with approximately the same skills and employed in similar types of firm (here measured by the size of plant), there are very small union-nonunion wage differentials.

This result is not unusual. Hwang-Joe Kim reports union-nonunion wage differentials among South Korean production workers of 2.2 percent for men and 2.8 percent for women in 1988, after controlling for differences in skills among workers and their place of employment.[17] Analogously, in his analysis of earnings differentials among urban Malaysian workers in 1975, Dipak Mazumdar states that once differences in

---

14. For instance, Jimeno and Toharia (1993) estimate that at least 75 percent of employees in Spain are covered by at least one collective bargaining agreement, although the fraction of employees who are members of labor unions is probably between 10 and 15 percent (International Labour Office 1985).

15. Schaffner (1993).

16. Schaffner's regression equations are fitted to a sample of about 1,100 male workers and also include variables measuring a worker's labor market experience, his schooling, whether he works in Lima, and whether he is the head of his household. Note that Schaffner's result cannot be interpreted as evidence that unions in large establishments have greater wage-making powers than those in small establishments. Among establishments of the same size, union-nonunion wage differentials are small.

17. Kim (1993). Without controlling for these other factors, the union-nonunion wage differentials were 30 percent for male and 8 percent for female production workers.

schooling, experience, establishment size, and other characteristics are taken into account, "the unionization variables generally turned out to be of little importance."[18]

Usually, the explanation for the absence of a positive union-nonunion wage differential is that wage increases secured by unionized workers spill over to raise the wages of certain nonunion workers, which suggests that a simple division between a unionized sector and a nonunionized sector is not a fruitful perspective on labor markets. A more useful characterization is one that distinguishes at least three sectors, only one of which is unionized. In addition to the unionized sector, there is another relatively high-wage sector that is influenced by wage-setting practices in the unionized sector. I label this high-wage nonunion sector the *administered wage sector*. The third sector is a *competitive wage sector*.

The Administered Wage Sector

Firms in the administered wage sector may be required by law to pay union-negotiated (or close to union-negotiated) wages. Or these firms may choose to pay higher wages to discourage the unionization of their work forces. Or, to reduce turnover, firms in the administered wage sector may select wages closely related to those in the union sector. For all these reasons, the wages in the unionized sector and the administered wage sector are closely related.[19]

The administered wage sector is likely to consist of skilled workers and, especially, workers with specific skills; that is, workers embodying skills of value to a single firm. Here a situation of bilateral monopoly

18. Mazumdar (1981, p. 160). There is a great variety of experience and I do not mean to suggest that union-nonunion wage differentials in developing economies are always nonexistent. Far from it. For instance, Teal (1994) measures union-nonunion earnings differentials in Ghanaian manufacturing industry in 1992–93 of the order of 30 percent. As another example, Standing (1992) measures wage differentials for production workers in Malaysian manufacturing in 1988 of 20 percent for industrial unions (that is, unions organized on an industrywide basis) and 15 percent for company unions. My point is simply that the absence of union-nonunion wage differentials should not be interpreted as evidence that labor unions have not had an impact on earnings.

19. Nonunionized employers may imitate not only the wages of unionized workers, but also other features of the union-negotiated employment contract. For instance, Mazumdar (1993) reports that in Malaysian manufacturing industry nonunion employers typically fix wages for the two- or three- or four-year period that characterizes the contract length of unionized workers and adjust wages automatically with seniority, in just the way that union contracts stipulate.

obtains, even in the absence of labor unions. The specific skills embodied in workers create an asset that is of greater value to one firm than to all other firms. The wage paid to a worker with specific skills will be no less than the value of the worker's general skills (that is, what this worker is worth in his or her next best job) and no more than it would cost an employer to hire and train a replacement. The turnover of specifically trained workers imposes particular costs on the firm. Also, it is specifically trained workers whose association with the firm is likely to be of long duration and, therefore, to whom an investment in unionism is likely to be particularly attractive. Hence firms employing workers with specific skills are likely to be in the administered wage sector and are likely to be concerned with relative wages.

Other types of firm in the administered wage sector include foreign multinationals, which are sensitive to being characterized by their shareholders or by local politicians as "exploiting" their workers. Such firms are likely to have monopolistic power and they use some of their monopoly profits to enjoy a "quiet" life.[20] Workers in large firms with government contracts or in those firms that lobby the government are likely to be in the administered wage sector, as are public sector workers (such as police officers, fire fighters, nurses, and teachers), where explicit rules about the comparability of their pay may link wages directly to those of unionized workers. Governments sometimes want to provide an example of how employers ought to behave, and as a consequence, set public sector wages and working conditions that compare favorably with those that the most successful of unionized employees have negotiated.

The Competitive Wage Sector

There are some labor markets that are neither unionized nor characterized by the administered wage setting described above. In these markets, either workers possess few skills or those skills that they have are general. This means that turnover is typically high, but because the workers who leave have few or easily replaceable skills (that is, the firm does not have to undertake expensive in-house training), turnover is not as costly to the firm and administered wage policies to discourage turnover are not required. The threat of unionization is small. As a first approximation, these markets resemble textbook auction-type labor mar-

20. "The best of all monopoly profits is a quiet life." Hicks (1935, p. 8.)

kets. Workers predominantly have low skill levels and, in view of the small degree of specific training, shocks to the demand for output are transmitted to the labor market through variations in their employment and wages. Such labor markets are typically found in agriculture and in many urban services. Employment is often irregular and volatile.

Wage increases engineered by·unions in the unionized sector are imitated by wage increases in the administered wage sector, but employment in these sectors is discouraged. Some of the workers who would otherwise work in the high-wage sectors seek employment in the competitive wage sector, which puts downward pressure on wages in the competitive wage sector. If minimum wage regulation acts as an effective floor for wages in the competitive wage sector (which requires not merely the existence of the law but also its enforcement), then unemployment may be evident. If a worker cannot, or chooses not to, be fully employed in the competitive sector and at the same time seek and be available for work in the unionized and administered wage sectors, then "wait" unemployment may arise; that is, workers find it profitable to wait for job openings rather than be employed at lower wages in the competitive wage sector.[21]

Summary

According to this analysis, therefore, unions raise the wages of their members and also raise the wages of some other high-wage workers. This has a very important implication: *the wage gains of unions (over what would have existed in the absence of unionism) are not equivalent to the wage gaps between unionized and nonunionized workers.*[22] The impact of unionism on the wage structure is not measured by the wage differential between union and nonunion workers. Employment in the unionized and administered wage sectors falls below what it would otherwise

21. Consider Sri Lanka's unemployment as an example. According to Glewwe's (1985, pp. 205–06, 236) analysis of urban labor markets in Sri Lanka in the 1970s, "unemployment is primarily a characteristic of young, relatively well-educated, unmarried adults with no previous work experience who can rely on the [income] support of other household members. . . . These young people are searching for jobs that are commensurate with their educational background . . . and it appears that they are searching for the better paying jobs, which are primarily government jobs." Glewwe estimates that urban males earn at least 45 percent higher wages if employed by the government (holding constant their age, schooling, ethnic background, marital status, and certain household characteristics). Because it is the relatively well-off who are experiencing unemployment, Myrdal (1968) characterizes this as a "bourgeois problem."

22. On the distinction between wage gains and wage gaps, see Lewis (1986, chap. 2).

be. In the competitive wage sector, this lower employment translates into lower wages, or unemployment, or both. The benefits of unionism are thus extended to some other high-wage workers, but they are enjoyed at the cost of lower wages and lower employment among unskilled workers. The implications of this model of the wage-setting activities of unions for the appropriate posture of the law with respect to collective bargaining are considered later. First, I consider other activities of unions in the workplace.

Unions as Participatory Institutions

The wage-making activities of unions discussed above concern the price at which labor is transacted, but what is to be exchanged? What services are to be undertaken by the workers? What are the workers supposed to do? And what constitutes the employers' part of the bargain?

Although there are many instances where workers are paid partly, if not entirely, on the basis of what they produce (that is, piece rates or payment by results), an employer usually purchases a worker's time. What a worker is to do during this time is rarely specified with any precision. In this sense, labor contracts are routinely incomplete—so much so that chaos results when workers "work to rule" (that is, work to the specific terms of their contracts). Similarly, management's part of the bargain is normally not fully specified. Even if it were possible to provide a lengthy statement of what services workers were to supply and what management was to do in return, a substantial margin would remain for disputing whether a contract had been violated.

In such circumstances, because the nature of the transaction—what work is to be done, how it is to be done, and the precise meaning of its terms and conditions—is often so difficult to determine prior to exchange, labor services have "experience characteristics." That is, only by actually working on a job for a while can a worker learn what is required of him or her and allow management to assess the quality of work performed. When a satisfactory match has been made, subsequent contracting is facilitated and the cost of transacting falls with the duration of employment, so long-term contracts develop. In this way, the contract is apt to become singular: the worker's current job involves the use of skills that are specific to the job and this makes the worker's earnings in this job greater than those that he or she could earn in the next best opportunity;

for its part, management considers a new employee to be an imperfect substitute for the existing employee. The labor contract becomes defined by previous practice, so that understandings that arise out of convention replace what for other contracts would be the specifications of a written agreement.[23]

The role of a labor union in this context differs in various circumstances. In most cases, the union tries to make the labor contract more explicit and it does so by engaging in the process of spelling out what the exchange of labor services is to consist of. For example, even oral collective bargaining agreements in relatively poor economies specify the employees' hours of work and the frequency of wage payment. As economies grow richer, so the content of collective bargaining agreements embraces more issues, such as the procedures an employer will follow to change employment, the assignment of workers to particular tasks, and the conditions under which employees will be dismissed. In other words, in these instances, a labor union *participates* with management in determining what labor services are to be exchanged and under what conditions.

Because it involves workers or their agents in explicitly determining their labor contracts, industrial relations scholars have sometimes conjectured there may be efficiency gains from participation. As Sumner Slichter writes: "The very fact that the workers have had an opportunity to participate in determining their working conditions is in itself favorable to efficiency. . . . Efficiency depends upon consent. Even though the specific rules and policies adopted in particular instances may not be ideal, the process of joint determination of working conditions at least offers the possibility of achieving greater efficiency than could be obtained under rules and conditions dictated by one side."[24]

For instance, in many jobs a worker may be better informed about the potential for productivity improvements within a department than the supervisor. The worker will be more willing to provide that information if he or she is confident that any change in organization will benefit him or her. The presence of an agent of the worker—that is, the union—may make the worker less suspicious that the information revealed will benefit only management. There is evidence that participation by workers in a firm's decisionmaking sometimes raises productivity, and if the union involves the workers in efficiency-enhancing activities, then unionism is associated with a more productive organization.

23. This argument is drawn from Pencavel (1991).
24. Slichter (1941, p. 575).

Another perspective on this attribute arises from the recognition that working conditions in some enterprises have the character of public goods, in that their consumption by one worker does not reduce their consumption by another worker. The pace at which an assembly line moves is an obvious illustration: each employee's work effort adjusts to the rate at which the assembly line moves, and the pace of work is "consumed" in equal amounts by all employees. Job safety is another work characteristic with public goods attributes. Workers will select their work pace and safety by job shopping, but in the presence of costly mobility, there is the potential for savings in transaction costs if an agent of the workers—a union—can efficiently communicate workers' preferences. In this sense, labor unions tend to arise as instruments to help determine the optimal production of working conditions.[25]

There are also arguments to suggest that unionism harms productivity. For instance, a union may protect indolent or careless workers from disciplinary action. Or a union may increase the costs of technological change (and especially, labor-saving technological change) and thereby retard an organization's development. Or a union may successfully negotiate capital-to-labor ratios that oblige the firm to use more workers per machine than relative input prices would call for.

The point here is not to argue that unions necessarily either harm or enhance productivity—this will vary in different circumstances and calls for empirical investigation—but simply to point out that unionism usually alters the nature of the employment relationship. Collective bargaining allows workers to participate in determining features of their work and their work environment, and these may have implications for their productivity.

Unions as a Pressure Group on Government

Although a union's proximate concern is with the representation of its members at their places of work, it is common for unions to act in concert and thus to act as a pressure group on government. This is natural, as many of the factors that affect their members' welfare are determined by the legislative, executive, and judicial acts of government. So, as the

25. See Duncan and Stafford (1980).

agents of their members, they concern themselves with activities beyond the workplace.

The form that this pressure takes depends on the nature of the existing government. Thus over the past decade or so, unions in Poland and South Africa have been in the forefront of organizations pushing these illiberal regimes toward more representative and civil government. In other instances, unions have collaborated with authoritarian governments, as in the case of the unions' support of the military officers who seized power in Argentina in 1943.[26]

In open societies (that is, those characterized by representative government and respect and support for individual freedoms), labor unions are often among the most active of organizations pressing their interests upon governments. In countries such as Argentina, Singapore, and Venezuela, links between the government and labor unions have been strong, and the unions have constituted a prominent pressure group.[27] Their pressure group activities take the form of endeavoring to secure changes in the legal system and in government policy that advance the position of unions as organizations. These cover not only immediate issues regarding the formation of labor unions and the conduct of collective bargaining, but also questions such as the pay of nonunion workers, the private ownership and regulation of industry, international trade in goods and services, and macroeconomic policy.

As a generalization, most labor unions have supported government policies that have impeded the working of markets. This has involved not only supporting minimum wage regulations and working against free trade in international transactions, but also advocating greater government regulation, even state ownership, of industry. In macroeconomic policy, unions have tended to support a goal of minimizing unemployment and have been tolerant of inflation. Indeed, in Latin America especially, when union-negotiated wage settlements have tended to result in increased unemployment, unions have often encouraged government to apply expansionary policies to curtail the rise in unemployment.

26. Of course, what started out in 1943–45 as union support for the military junta ended up, by the late 1940s, as control by the Peronist government of the union movement.

27. There is a great variety of forms of influence across countries. Thus in some of these countries the unions may constitute an element of a larger political coalition, while in others they form an independent pressure group, regardless of the party in power. See Nelson (1994).

The success of labor unions naturally varies from society to society, but it is routine for unions to characterize their activities as designed to enhance the welfare of workers in general, and to portray those whose incomes are classified as profits, rents, interest, and dividends as the opponents of their efforts. This is often a successful characterization, because union agents are habitually called on by government to serve on commissions and councils as representatives of the interests of all workers.

No doubt there are circumstances when the activities of unions in this regard do have the effect of raising the welfare of many workers. However, there are other occasions when the pressure group activities of unions on government enhance the welfare of union workers but damage the welfare of nonunionized workers. In these instances, the conflict is not between people receiving their incomes in the form of wages and people receiving their income in the form of profits or dividends; the conflict is *among* wage earners.

For instance, unions customarily support measures that impede the flow of goods and services across economies. They are not well known as advocates of free trade. Impediments to free trade benefit those people (wage earners as well as recipients of dividends and profits) whose incomes derive from the production and sale of those goods for which consumption increases as a consequence of tariffs or quotas; and they harm those people whose incomes derive from the production and sale of those goods for which consumption decreases in response to protectionist measures. In other words, the classifications of winners and losers from tariffs and other protectionist measures typically do not divide neatly into workers and owners of physical capital, nor into people in one country and people in another country; rather, workers and owners of physical capital figure on both sides of the balance sheet, as do foreigners and natives.

An illustration of the communality of employees' and employers' interests in capturing the power of the state over international trade is illustrated by Paul Schultz's study of male income differentials in Colombia in 1970.[28] After accounting for differences in labor market experience and schooling, he finds that employees' incomes are significantly higher in those industries effectively protected from foreign imports. The elas-

---

28. Schultz (1982).

ticity of incomes with respect to an index of effective protection is about 0.34 in manufacturing industry and even larger if all industries are examined.

When the same equations are fitted to male *employers*, once more a highly significant association exists between the income of these employers and the effective protection from imports enjoyed by the industry in which they work. Thus the quasi rents earned in protected sectors benefited both employees and employers in these sectors, at the expense of other sectors of the economy. Indeed, the gains of employers exceed those of employees.[29] Schultz concludes that "the structure of effective protection in Colombia in 1970 increased the inequality in personal income distribution, induced a misallocation in factors of production among sectors, and stimulated rent-seeking activity that is commonly associated with a deadweight loss to the society."[30]

Although there may well be particular instances in which a union raises the pay of its members by diverting income that would otherwise be paid out in the form of profits or dividends, this cannot be the typical situation. Consider the opportunities for the transfer of incomes in a particular economy, for example, Colombia. Suppose all property and entrepreneurial income earned in 1985 in Colombia were appropriated and distributed among all wage earners without any attempt to compensate people, such as the retired, whose consumption derives largely from such income. This radical action would have raised the average earnings of workers by 15 percent, and this would have been a once-and-for-all bonus. As another example, the same operation for Peru in 1980 yields a wage increase of a little less than 11 percent.[31] The capacity to transfer much income in this manner is limited by two factors: first, only a relatively small fraction of national income takes the form of profits, dividends, and interest; and second, there are a large number of workers

29. This point is important because it has sometimes been argued that the activities of labor unions as a pressure group on government should be encouraged, so that they offset the pressure of employers. The flaw in this argument is that the interests of labor unions and employers often coincide. Protection from foreign trade is a case in point. The suitable posture would seem to call for discouraging the pressure group activities of *all* parties.

30. Schultz (1982, p. 110).

31. I selected 1985 for Colombia and 1980 for Peru simply because I was able to locate estimates of the number of wage earners for those years. In these calculations, I exclude the self-employed from the transfers and do not consider the expropriation of the profits of unincorporated businesses, which includes the income of the self-employed. In other words, the operation involves transferring income from major enterprises to employees, leaving the self-employed neither losers nor gainers.

among whom to allocate the confiscated income. Consequently, collective bargaining is less a struggle between labor and capital for the division of national income, and more a competition among different groups of workers and between workers as a whole and the population receiving income in the form of transfers through the state.[32]

Even if unions were able to effect a significant shift in the distribution of income away from entrepreneurial income and toward wage income, there remains the question of the impact of this redistribution on economic growth. There is little convincing empirical research on this issue, so speculation must take the place of a solid body of evidence. But the natural conjecture suggested by writing on rent-seeking activities is that gains achieved by a distributional coalition, such as a labor union, discourage the allocation of resources to additional output.

There are at least two reasons for this outcome. The first arises from the fact that economic growth does not usually proceed uniformly across all sectors of the economy. Typically, sectoral differences in productivity growth will call for change in relative prices, and this will entail alterations in expenditures on the output of the sectors. Hence resources need to be reallocated to maintain efficiency if the economy is fully to exploit the increase in productivity. If there are impediments to resource mobility across sectors, economic growth will be impaired. Labor unions typically frustrate resource mobility: by raising wages, which tends to discourage the employment of labor in covered employments; and also by lobbying government for support on behalf of those sectors whose output has suffered from reductions in demand.

Second, labor unions may harm economic growth insofar as they garner resources at the expense of entrepreneurial income. This reduces the rate of return on physical capital investment in such industries, discouraging investment and retarding economic growth. In other words, current gains achieved by distributional coalitions such as labor unions are appropriated, in part, at the expense of the next generation.

In short, in closed societies, labor unions have sometimes been a progressive force toward more liberal and representative government. In

32. One does not have to rely on the speculative numbers in this paragraph to make the point. There are episodes of populist government policies that illustrate the limits of aggressive redistributive policies. For instance, in Chile, in his first year of government, Salvador Allende's redistributive policies succeeded in raising real wages by 17 percent, and the share of labor income in GNP rose from 52.3 percent in 1970 to 61.7 percent in 1971. During the following year, 1972, real wages fell by 10 percent and they fell again in 1973, by 32.1 percent. For other examples, see Sachs (1990).

open societies, labor unions constitute a pressure group on government that, by imposing impediments on market processes, tends to increase the incomes of unionized workers at the expense, primarily, of nonunion workers, consumers, and future generations.

The Legal Framework of Collective Bargaining

The purpose of this section is to draw upon the above review of labor union activities to sketch the appropriate legal framework for dealing with unionism and collective bargaining. Throughout, I assume as desirable a representative government and respect for individual freedoms— in short, an open society—and ask how such a society should define the rights and responsibilities of unions and collective bargaining.

The Dilemma

Along with other associations of men and women, labor unions raise a dilemma for an open society: on the one hand, the principle of freedom to form associations and clubs is an integral element of a liberal society; but on the other hand, if, in the name of this principle, such associations secure too many privileges, a new source of coercive power is created, with the accompanying risk of the abuse of that power.[33]

In determining the rules of the game within which labor unions operate, societies have wrestled with the problem of finding the proper balance between, on the one hand, upholding the principle of free associations and, on the other hand, granting entitlements that result in resource inefficiencies at best, and in challenges to the authority of the democratic state at worst. It is toward finding that balance that the arguments in this section are directed.

According to the reasoning provided in the sections above, the wage gains of labor unions may well be extended to some nonunion workers. However, these tend to be workers who are already paid relatively high

---

33. Dicey (1914, pp. 467–68) provides a classic statement of this dilemma: "Some forms of association force upon public attention the practical difficulty of so regulating the right of association that its exercise may neither trench upon each citizen's individual freedom nor shake the supreme authority of the State. . . . How can the right of combined action be curtailed without depriving individual liberty of half its value; how can it be left unrestricted without destroying either the liberty of individual citizens, or the power of government?"

wages. For example, in those countries where public sector workers are not unionized, their wages are often tied to those of unionized workers, so wage increases for teachers, police officers, fire fighters, and hospital workers often imitate those negotiated by union workers. By contrast, low-wage workers tend not to be unionized, and their wages do not rise when union workers secure wage increases. For instance, in many developing countries, many workers in urban areas are employed in small enterprises, and there are large wage differentials by size of firm and size of plant.[34] Workers employed in small enterprises are much less likely to be unionized, and their wages are not tied to the wages of unionized workers in the large establishments.

In their participatory activities at the enterprise level, unions have the potential to be either socially productive or unproductive organizations. On the one hand, there are clear instances in which unions interfere with the use of the most productive methods, sustain defective or careless work, and increase the costs of responding to changes emanating from product markets and production technology. In addition, a labor union tends to represent more fully the interests of workers currently employed in a firm and is less inclined to promote the interests of those people currently unemployed and seeking work in that firm. Labor unions have devised many ways of making it more difficult for firms to lay off workers, but they have spent much less energy and thought on facilitating the hiring of new workers.

On the other hand, by involving individuals in determining the shape of their work environment, a union may help workers identify more fully with the success of the enterprise. By acting as an agent for the workers' interests and concerns and shaping the working environment accordingly, a union may make an enterprise not merely more pleasant, but also more productive. Moreover, it is likely to be less costly and more effective if complaints about arbitrary and capricious treatment against individual employees are dealt with at the plant rather than through the law courts or through market processes, and the presence of a labor union makes the effective representation of workers' grievances much more meaningful than do workers' committees that are the creations of employers. Furthermore, some labor unions operate as classical friendly societies, providing financial support to their members to cover contingencies such as unemployment or illness, as well as retirement.

34. See, for instance, Mazumdar (1989) and Schaffner (1993).

Finally, in their activities as a pressure group on government, labor unions represent a classic distributional coalition, acting to increase their wealth at the expense of the wealth of the poorly organized. Their activities in this regard usually take the form of hampering market processes and introducing resource inefficiencies, especially by retarding economic growth. It is sometimes argued that the pressure group activities of unions are desired to offset the pressure group activities of employers. This presumes that the interests of employers are opposed to the interests of unions. In fact, as Schultz's analysis of incomes in Colombia indicated in the section above, employers and employees may have common interests in increasing rents to their firms and industries, before dividing these rents between each other. The appropriate stance calls for inhibiting the pressure group activities of both employers and unions.

In short, this evaluation suggests that unionism may yield benefits at the level of the enterprise, but that union wage activities at the microeconomic level and pressure group activities on government produce resource inefficiencies that should be mitigated. This assessment would call for a legal framework that neither encouraged nor discouraged unionism, but contained the activities of unions to the domain where they have potential as a productive force, namely, the enterprise.[35]

Enterprise-Level Collective Bargaining

If collective bargaining takes place at the enterprise or plant level, the ability of the union to effect monopoly wage increases is tempered (because the competitive pressures on the firm from the product market are at their most severe), and yet the potential exists for the union to act as a participatory organization for the workers. Of course, even with collective bargaining limited to the enterprise, the discipline on monopolistic wage behavior is diminished if product markets are not competitive and if the nonunion labor market is uncompetitive. That is, if the state so encumbers the nonunion labor market with wage constraints (such as those implied by incomes policies or minimum wage statutes), restrictions on the hiring and firing of workers, and regulations on employment practices that its flexibility is substantially diminished, it will operate much less effectively as a constraint on monopolistic wage practices in the

---

35. By enterprise, I mean a plant or group of plants under a single ownership. The proposition that collective bargaining be limited to the enterprise level has a long history. One statement of this proposition is found in Lewis (1951).

unionized sector of the labor market. The appropriate posture with respect to the law on collective bargaining, therefore, calls for policies that foster competitive and flexible nonunion labor markets.

Not only does a competitive nonunion labor market discipline the monopolistic wage practices of unionism, but the corollary also applies: the more regulated and noncompetitive the nonunion labor market, the more inclined an authoritarian government will be to contain union activity by engaging in explicitly coercive antiunion activities. Other things equal, governments are more likely to adopt coercive policies toward unions (such as arresting union leaders and violently suppressing strikes) when the operation of nonunion labor markets has been restricted such that they do not constitute an effective check on the activities of agents in the union sector.[36]

If collective bargaining takes place at the level of the enterprise, its content may be determined by the parties themselves, and there is no need for legislation to prescribe what the parties may or may not contract over. If management is willing to make agreements with the union concerning capital-to-labor ratios, entry into apprenticeship programs, and the conditions under which temporary workers are hired, then the law should not forbid it. The fact is that in a competitive product market, the costs of these agreements will fall, in large part, on the firm and union, and this will deter such agreements.

Similarly, there is no need for the law to prescribe one and only one union at a given enterprise. Although there may well be instances in which, by virtue of the production technology, a small group of workers possesses considerable bargaining power (that is, the amount of specific capital in these workers is such that there is a wide range of wages compatible with equilibrium), this does not create sufficient reason to mandate that all workers join together in a single union for collective bargaining. These instances are unlikely to be sufficiently frequent to

36. Of course, there are many other factors affecting the disposition of governments toward coercive antiunion activities, so the other things equal condition in this statement is rarely satisfied. However, many (certainly not all) of the authoritarian military governments in Latin America that have pursued aggressive antiunion policies have also adopted labor market policies that, in practice, place constraints on the flexibility of both union and nonunion labor markets. For instance, the military coup in Brazil in 1964 brought to power a regime that actively persecuted unions and also introduced extensive wage regulations, embracing the labor markets of the entire formal sector. Indeed, as a rule, the military governments of Latin America have combined an antiunion posture with heavy-handed intervention in the operation of all labor markets.

warrant ignoring workers' preferences for separate associations. If management has a strong preference for a single union, in order to minimize bargaining costs, then it is up to management to provide adequate incentives for the unions to join together as one organization for the purposes of collective bargaining. Moreover, facilitating the formation of other unions provides a check on the likelihood that an established union will be managed to serve the interests of a small oligarchy. In countries that are moving from authoritarian governments toward more open systems, the inherited labor unions were often created by the *ancien régime* to help control the society. A policy of facilitating the formation of new unions at the enterprise level dispenses with the need to identify and dismantle those old unions that do not serve the interests of their members.

There is a concern that policy permitting the formation of more than one union at each enterprise will lead to disputes and rivalry among unions. This is, indeed, a possibility, and the question is whether that rivalry will serve the workers' interests. The claim that it will not serve the workers' interests offers as evidence the situation on the Indian subcontinent, where the strength of unions is sapped through disputes among themselves rather than through bargaining with employers. The evidence, however, is not fully convincing. This situation reflects the highly politicized nature of unionism on the Indian subcontinent, where links between unions and political parties are close and formal. The political process and political parties are viewed as the mechanism for workers to enhance their welfare; workers do not see their place of work as the source of improved wages and working conditions. In such a highly politicized environment, the unions are simply manifestations of competition among political groups for support. The appropriate response is not to mandate one bargaining agent per enterprise, a situation that would invite the development of an entrenched and unresponsive oligarchy of union leaders and aid state control of collective bargaining, but to end the notion that improvements to the welfare of workers originate in the political system.[37] Once the state leaves the determination of wages and

37. It is common in sub-Saharan Africa for the law to prescribe one and only one union in a given sector of an economy. The purpose of mandating such a system is to facilitate the control of the union movement by the state. As Panford (1994, p. 37) writes: "The imposition of single unions may violate workers' rights where they restrict workers' choices and force them to join only state approved unions. . . . Workers have only two choices. They either join organizations sanctioned by the state or they cannot join any unions at all."

conditions of work to employers and workers, competition among democratic unions for the support of workers becomes something to be desired.

Confederations of Unions

With enterprise-level bargaining, the locus of collective bargaining is decentralized. This is sometimes regarded as a defect because a confederation of unions lacks the power and authority that it would have in a more centralized system. It is argued there are occasions when such a central union confederation can help to devise and implement major stabilization programs. This argument offers as evidence the part played by the union confederation in Israel in the mid-1980s in contributing to the design and political acceptance of the stabilization programs in that country.[38]

It is certainly easier to secure popular acceptance of a radical reform package if an economy's major organizations endorse and support it. To this extent, the argument has merit: the reform package has a greater probability of success if a powerful and authoritative labor confederation backs it. However, this argument should examine the prior steps: What is the likelihood of a union confederation supporting a stabilization package? How are the components of that package altered to secure the confederation's support? And have the confederation's activities contributed to the conditions that necessitate a major stabilization program? There are many instances in which union confederations have contributed to the failure of promising stabilization reforms, Argentina's Austral plan in 1985 being one example. And Israel's union confederation—mentioned above as contributing to the success of the country's stabilization programs—is a classic example of an organization that is closely allied to the political system and that uses the political process to extract rents for itself.

---

38. The literature comparing the labor markets of developed economies in terms of their ability to respond effectively to shocks such as oil price increases has sometimes concluded there are benefits to a system where confederations of unions bargain with confederations of employers. This conclusion rests on the suppositions that the wages of all employees are covered by collective bargaining contracts and that there is no nonunion sector. The labor markets of Sweden and Austria provide the prototypes. This literature is reviewed in Moene and Wallerstein (1993). Such arguments are of little relevance to developing countries, where there is almost always a substantial fraction of the labor force whose wages are not covered by collective bargaining contracts.

Israel's trade union confederation, the *histadrut*, is unusual in being an owner of some firms, a health service provider, and a pension fund manager, in addition to acting as the principal agent for the union movement. There are some independent unions that are not affiliated with it. These many activities dilute its voice as a representative of unionized workers, although it has regularly engaged the confederation of employers in discussions over prices and wages and it routinely negotiates with the government over economic policy affecting investment. Collective bargaining is highly politicized and confrontational. "From a cross-national perspective, strike activity in Israel is high. . . . The 'political' shape of strikes—typically brief but broadly based—also stands out, and is symptomatic of the high concentration of labor disputes in the public sector (including state-owned transport, communication, and utilities). . . . In Israel, a corporate labor organization enters into social contracts with the state, while at the same time members of marginalized social groups form an exposed underclass in the labor market, with clearly inegalitarian consequences."[39]

In a frank characterization of the fundamental goals of the confederation, a representative of the holding company for all *histadrut* enterprises has stated: "Relations between the manufacturers and the *histadrut* are characterized not by conflict of interest but rather by dialogue. Both sides have the same interest. . . . There aren't two separate world views, but rather a single view shared by both. The community of interests is very great, and both view the government as a foreign element— both as a cow to be milked and also as a body to be feared lest it hand down undesirable decrees."[40] This is a remarkably clear and candid statement of the cartels' conception of the state ("a cow to be milked"), of the mutual interests of the confederation of employers and unions, and of the fallacy of envisaging a union confederation as a necessary counterbalance to the pressure group activities of employers.

It can be argued that the *need* for monetary stabilization is enhanced by the presence of large rent-seeking organizations such as union confederations. Each cartel seeks to increase its share of national income at the expense of others and, to forestall the unemployment and resource misallocation that would naturally result, monetary authorities are apt to engineer a general increase in prices. If this process is repeated, the

39. Shalev (1992, p. 246).
40. Quoted in Grinberg (1991, p. 73).

economy experiences inflation, the proximate cause of which is the monetary authorities' loss of control. But this loss of control is attributable to their attempt to conceal the resource misallocation resulting from rent-seeking activities by cartels. Elements of this scenario are to be found in the experiences of Israel in the 1970s and 1980s and of many Latin American countries. Ultimately, attempts are made to restore control through a stabilization program and, as a major actor in the economy, the union confederation will usually be invited to cooperate in determining its structure and in gaining acceptance for it. It is somewhat incongruous that the confederation is applauded for its cooperation in helping to end a process that it helped to initiate.

In some countries, the state has encouraged the formation of a powerful confederation of unions so that the state itself may control the union movement. For instance, this was the unabashed goal of the first post-colonial governments in Ghana, where labor unions were designed to be agencies of the state, mobilizing the workers to serve the interests of the government.[41] The term "responsible trade unionism" was concocted and, to ensure "responsibility," the government played a heavy role in the selection of union officials, in the organization of new workers, and in the determination of the incidence and form of industrial disputes. To help the state control workers, not merely must unions be state approved, but in some sectors of the economy, union membership is mandatory![42] In this way, more effective control may be exercised over workers than if they were not unionized. Of course, the state has not always been successful in controlling workers in this way and, when it has lost control, industrial disputes have assumed huge political significance. However, for many countries in sub-Saharan Africa (such as Kenya, Zambia, and Nigeria, as well as Ghana), the state has seen a central union confederation as a necessary component of a union movement that it seeks to control. This is a further reason to encourage the devolution of labor union authority and to avoid conferring prerogatives on centralized confederations of unions.

---

41. In introducing the 1958 Industrial Relations Bill, the minister of labor stated: "The government . . . agrees with the view . . . that the needs of the workers and of the nation as a whole would best be served by a strong centralized trade union organization whose central body is recognized by government and is given certain powers and duties; and over which . . . the government will be able to exercise some supervision to ensure that those powers are not abused."

42. See the discussion in Panford (1994, pp. 46–47).

Enterprise-level collective bargaining makes it more difficult for union confederations to pursue aggressive rent-seeking policies, reduces the degree to which collective bargaining is politicized, and diminishes the ability of authoritarian governments to act arbitrarily.

Disputes

The paragraphs above have concerned the procedures for maximizing the likelihood that unions will act as a source for social and productive efficiency and for minimizing their resource misallocation effects. In addition to the costs of settlements, one should consider the costs of reaching settlements. Here, the guiding principle should be to design procedures such that, insofar as possible, the costs of bargaining are borne by the parties to the contract themselves and not by those unrepresented in the negotiations. When production in a single firm in a competitive industry is interrupted in a management-union dispute, the costs of the dispute tend to fall on the parties themselves and not on consumers, who have alternative sources of supply.

In a dispute in private industry under competitive conditions, the state should occupy as neutral a position as possible. This implies it should not provide loans or payments to either party during a strike or lockout, so the firm remains liable for its tax payments during the period of the work stoppage, while workers are not eligible for unemployment compensation. There is no reason why workers involved in a strike or lockout should not be eligible for temporary (or, indeed, permanent) work elsewhere. Analogously, the employer should have the option of hiring temporary (or, again, permanent) workers in an attempt to resume production. There is no need for government to mandate either that strikers be paid wages during an interruption in production (as is common in Latin America) or that strikers not be paid. Again, this is a matter for the parties to the dispute to determine, and not for the state to regulate one way or the other. In general, the state should take a "hands off" stance.

This hands off posture is sometimes difficult to maintain, because the costs of a dispute can appear considerable. The media are inclined to report huge costs of a strike or lockout, even though these numbers are typically manufactured by one side in the dispute in order to put leverage on the other. Often they are derived by multiplying the daily gross revenues of the firm before the strike or lockout by the number of days of interrupted production. But if consumers are able to purchase the goods from inventories or from alternative suppliers, then these costs are borne by the parties and should not occasion concern. The union and management can avoid these costs immediately, by reaching agreement. Moreover, in such popular characterizations of disputes, these costs are not contrasted with the alternative costs of reaching agreement on terms currently being demanded by one side or the other. The tacit comparison is usually with an outcome assuming there were no bargaining with the two sides reaching immediate agreement on some unstated compromise.

In fact, when the commodity is durable, inventories can be run down and the firm can often make up for production "lost" during a strike or lockout through additional production before or after the dispute has been resolved. This argument may not apply to a nonstorable good or service (such as the services provided by the police or fire fighters), but these tend to be produced under monopolistic conditions, which I discuss below.[43]

Private Monopolies and the Public Sector

The prescriptions regarding collective bargaining and disputes above relate to the private sector of the economy or, more precisely, to those firms producing under competitive conditions. The public sector poses special problems because the product markets of services produced in the public sector tend to be monopolistic. Although rudimentary price theory suggests that the wage gains of unions are likely to be greater when product markets are monopolistic, these wage premiums are insufficient cause to deny public sector workers the right to form associations to represent their interests, if they so wish.

The principal problem posed by public sector unionism is that disputes tend to be more costly for consumers, because there are no ready substitutes for the services whose production is interrupted. For instance, the services of police officers cannot be stored and consumed from inventory, and the use of substitutes is difficult to arrange and organize. Similar arguments, to a greater or lesser extent, can be made with respect to the work performed by fire fighters, teachers, hospital workers, and utility (gas, electricity, and water) and public transport workers. The

---

43. Naturally, the violence and intimidation that sometimes accompanies strikes (be it initiated by management or the union) should not be tolerated. "Sympathetic" action by other management or workers represents the extension of collective bargaining beyond the single enterprise and therefore would be unlawful.

critical element here is not that the state often has a controlling interest in the production of these services; the critical element is that these services tend to be produced by a (public or private) monopoly, so that the possibility of substitution by consumers is substantially reduced. This implies that for these services, a larger part of the costs of a strike or lockout are borne by parties not represented in collective bargaining negotiations.

In these circumstances, in the public sector and for private sector monopolies, it is natural to seek alternatives to strikes and lockouts.[44] Arbitration by third parties is the obvious policy. Among alternative arbitration mechanisms, "final offer" (or "pendulum") arbitration has much to recommend it. Under final arbitration, the arbitrator is constrained to choose either management's "final" offer or the union's "final" offer.[45] The reason for the preference for final offer arbitration over conventional arbitration (according to which the arbitrator may fashion any agreement he or she wishes) does not lie in the fact that wage agreements tend to differ from one system to the other. On the contrary, there is little powerful evidence to suggest that conventional and final offer arbitration produce different outcomes.

However, with each party fearing the imposition of a very unfavorable outcome, final offer arbitration tends to encourage the parties to reach an agreement on a contract, and it is generally believed that the parties themselves can usually devise a better agreement than that dictated by a third, probably less well-informed, party.[46] That is, if the parties are risk averse, the fear that one party's offer will appear more reasonable to the final offer arbitrator induces the other party to moderate its position, so that agreement between the parties becomes more likely. In other words, under final offer arbitration, if the system is working well, then after both

44. In New York state, in the event of public sector workers going on strike, each striking worker loses one day's pay (in addition to the pay lost through being on strike) for each day on strike. This penalty is applied by the state government and has been routinely enforced.

45. Of course, final offer arbitration need not be restricted to monopolies. In the competitive sector of the economy, private employers and their unions may choose to avoid strikes by having their unresolved disputes settled by arbitration. Many of the so-called new-style deals introduced in Britain in the 1980s involved agreements characterized by a single union in each establishment and by no-strike clauses. Final offer arbitration was a common method of resolving disputes in these enterprises.

46. Moreover, a contract that both parties have framed is more likely to be honored and made to work than a contract in which one party has had less say in its design.

parties have become familiar with its operation the arbitrator will be called upon infrequently.[47]

The parties in the dispute are aided if they know what criteria guide the arbitrator's choice between management's and the union's last offers, so it would help if the law were explicit on this issue. In particular, recent movements in the general cost of living and in labor productivity in the particular enterprise are valid criteria for the arbitrator to apply. The arbitrator should be more inclined toward increasing wages when hiring workers of the sufficient quality has become difficult than when such workers are abundant.

Conclusion

It is important to emphasize that, ultimately, an increasing standard of living for workers requires growth in productivity. As argued above, the opportunity to raise workers' earnings by redistributing income from profits, dividends, and interest is meager and certainly cannot form the basis of a persistent rise in earnings. If growth in productivity is essential for raising the living standards of workers, the direction of causation needs to be stressed: in the economy as a whole, increases in productivity are associated with changes in the demand for and supply of labor that lead to increases in real wages; economywide wage increases do not cause increases in productivity.

The increase in the standard of living of workers in developed economies over the past century has not been achieved by engineering distributional reallocations of a fixed income, but by the benefits of a growing national income being distributed among the population. Or, to draw on more recent evidence, the growth in living standards of workers in South Korea, Taiwan, Hong Kong, and Singapore in the last thirty or so years has been achieved by expanding the production potential of these econ-

47. I have written "the" arbitrator in this paragraph although, in practice, the system usually operates with several arbitrators acting together. There are a number of different mechanisms for selecting arbitrators and they usually involve both the union and management deleting from a longer list names not preferred to each party. For a description of the various arbitration systems operating for public sector workers in different states in the United States, see Lester (1984).

omies, not by movements around a given production frontier.[48] As Gary Fields and Henry Wan Jr. have argued, a comparison of the economic performance of East Asia with that of the Caribbean and certain countries in Latin America indicates that government policies mandating or encouraging high-wage policies discourage the economic growth that is the ultimate, durable source of improvements in workers' living standards.[49] Therefore, the question to ask is how will the policies of labor unions contribute to the growth in national income and to the growth of workers' standards of living in the future.

The answer is that unions have the potential to help raise productivity in the workplace by participating with management in the search for better ways of organizing production. It is important also that workers not feel alienated from the economic and social system and to believe they have a stake in it. Process matters: even if outcomes are identical, employees value the fact that they or their agents help to shape their working environment. The labor union has been the primary vehicle for accomplishing this situation. Devising a regulatory system such that the potential benefits of unionism are accomplished without incurring resource inefficiencies is the purpose of the above section.

The predicament is that productivity growth is often accompanied by distress for those workers suffering from technological displacement or from the shifting patterns of consumer expenditure. It is natural to sympathize with defensive actions by labor unions to protect the immediate interests of such workers. The trouble is that the cost of such protection is paid out of the living standards of future workers, workers whose interests are not explicitly represented in any organization or union. There are policies that can be adopted to mitigate the drop in living standards for individuals whose worth in the labor market has unexpectedly deteriorated, but

48. I hasten to add that this point should not be interpreted to mean that I applaud and recommend the policies that governments in countries such as South Korea and Singapore have applied to unionism. On the contrary, it should be evident that the policies I have argued for are inconsistent with coercive practices toward unions and intrusive government mandates in the labor market. The South Korean and Singaporean cases simply illustrate that free and active labor unions are not *necessary* for an improvement in workers' material living standards, and that the increases in workers' real incomes have been achieved by expanding these economies' wealth.

49. See Fields (1984) and Fields and Wan (1989). These policies include not merely encouraging centralized collective bargaining and the application of such union-negotiated wages to nonunion workers, but also aggressive minimum wage laws, rents to government employees in the form of higher wages than those needed to attract the required quantity and quality of workers, and pressure on multinational firms to pay high wages.

these should not include ensuring that such individuals continue to produce goods that consumers would prefer not to buy.

References

Amadeo, Edward J., and Camargo, Jose Marcio. 1993. "Labour Legislation and Institutional Aspects of the Brazilian Labour Market." *Labour* 7(1): 157–80.

Arudsothy, Ponniah, and Littler, Craig R. 1993. "State Regulation and Union Fragmentation in Malaysia." In *Organized Labor in the Asia-Pacific Region: A Comparative Study of Trade Unionism in Nine Countries*, edited by Stephen Frenkel, 107–30. Cornell International Industrial & Labor Relations Report 24. Ithaca, N.Y.: ILR Press.

Cox Edwards, Alejandra. 1992. "Labor Market Legislation and Economic Reforms in Latin America and the Caribbean." Mimeo. Washington: World Bank, Human Resources Division.

Dicey, A. C. 1914. *Lectures on the Relation between Law and Public Opinion in England during the Nineteenth Century*, 2d ed. London: Macmillan.

Dornbusch, Rudiger, and Sebastian Edwards, eds. 1991. *The Macroeconomics of Populism in Latin America*. University of Chicago Press.

Duncan, Greg J., and Frank P. Stafford. 1980. "Do Union Members Receive Compensating Wage Differentials?" *American Economic Review* 70(3): 355–71.

Essenberg, Bert. 1981. "The Interaction of Industrial Relations and the Political Process in Developing Countries." *Labour and Society* 6 (1): 91–101.

Fields, Gary S. 1984. "Employment, Income Distribution, and Economic Growth in Seven Small Open Economies." *Economic Journal* 94 (373): 74–83.

Fields, Gary S., and Henry Wan Jr. 1989. "Wage-Setting Institutions and Economic Growth." *World Development* 17(9): 1471–83.

Frenkel, Stephen, ed. 1993. *Organized Labor in the Asia-Pacific Region: A Comparative Study of Trade Unionism in Nine Countries*. Cornell International Industrial and Labor Relations Report 24. Ithaca, N.Y.: ILR Press.

Glewwe, Paul W. 1985. "An Analysis of Income Distribution and Labor Markets in Sri Lanka." Ph.D. dissertation, Stanford University.

Grinberg, Lev Luis. 1991. *Split Corporatism in Israel*. State University of New York Press.

Hicks, J. R. 1935. "Annual Survey of Economic Theory: The Theory of Monopoly." *Econometrica* 3 (January): 1–20.

International Labour Office. 1985. *The Trade Union Situation and Industrial Relations in Spain*. Geneva: International Labour Office.

Jimeno, J., and L. Toharia. 1993. "Spanish Labour Markets: Institutions and Outcomes." In *Labour Market Contracts and Institutions: A Cross-National Comparison*, edited by J. Hartog and J. Theeuwes. Amsterdam: North-Holland.

Joshi, Vijay, and I. M. D. Little. 1994. *India: Macroeconomics and Political Economy, 1964–1991*. Washington: World Bank.

Kim, Hwang-Joe. 1993. "The Korean Union Movement in Transition." In *Organized Labor in the Asia-Pacific Region: A Comparative Study of Trade Unionism in Nine Countries*, edited by Stephen Frenkel, 133–61. Cornell International Industrial & Labor Relations Report 24. Ithaca, N.Y.: ILR Press.

Lester, Richard A. 1984. *Labor Arbitration in State and Local Government: An Examination of Experience in Eight States and New York City*. Research Report 124. Princeton University Industrial Relations Section.

Lewis, H. Gregg. 1951. "The Labor-Monopoly Problem." *Journal of Political Economy* 49(4): 277–87.

———. 1986. *Union Relative Wage Effects: A Survey*. University of Chicago Press.

Mazumdar, Dipak. 1981. *The Urban Labor Market and Income Distribution: A Study of Malaysia*. Oxford University Press.

———. 1989. "Government Intervention and Urban Labor Markets in Developing Countries." Mimeo. Washington: World Bank, Economic Development Institute (January).

———. 1993. "Labor Markets and Adjustment in Open Asian Economies: The Republic of Korea and Malaysia." *World Bank Economic Review* 7(3): 349–80.

Moene, Karl Ove, and Michael Wallerstein. 1993. "Bargaining Structure and Economic Performance." In *Trade Union Behavior, Pay-Bargaining, and Economic Performance*, edited by R. J. Flanagan, Karl Ove Moene, and Michael Wallerstein. Oxford University Press.

Myrdal, Gunnar. 1968. *Asian Drama: An Inquiry into the Poverty of Nations*. Pantheon.

Nelson, Joan M. 1994. "Organized Labor, Politics, and Labor Market Flexibility in Developing Countries." In *Labor Markets in an Era of Adjustment*, edited by Susan Horton, Ravi Kanbur, and Dipak Mazumdar, 347–75. Washington: World Bank, Economic Development Institute.

Organization for Economic Cooperation and Development. 1991. "Trends in Trade Union Membership." *Employment Outlook* (July): 97–134.

Panford, Kwamina. 1994. *African Labor Relations and Workers' Rights*. Westport, Conn.: Greenwood Press.

Pencavel, John. 1991. *Labor Markets under Trade Unionism*. Oxford: Blackwell.

Rosenzweig, Mark R. 1988. "Labor Markets in Low-Income Countries." In *Handbook of Development Economics*, vol. 1, edited by H. Chenery and T. N. Srinivasan, 713–62. Elsevier Science Publishers.

Sachs, Jeffrey D. 1990. "Social Conflict and Populist Policies in Latin America." In *Labour Relations and Economic Performance*, edited by Renato Brunetta and Carlo Dell'Aringa, 137–69. London: Macmillan.

Sandoval, Salvador A. M. 1993. *Social Change and Labor Unrest in Brazil since 1945*. Boulder, Colo.: Westview Press.

Schaffner, Julie Anderson. 1993. "Employer Size, Wages, and the Nature of Employment in Peru." Unpublished manuscript. Stanford University (September).

Schultz, T. Paul. 1982. "Effective Protection and the Distribution of Personal Income by Sector in Colombia." In *Trade and Employment in Developing*

Countries, vol 2, edited by Anne O. Krueger, 83–148. University of Chicago Press.

Shalev, Michael. 1992. *Labour and the Political Economy in Israel.* Oxford University Press.

Slichter, Sumner H. 1941. *Union Policies and Industrial Management.* Brookings.

Standing, Guy. 1992. "Do Unions Impede or Accelerate Structural Adjustment? Industrial versus Company Unions in an Industrialising Labour Market." *Cambridge Journal of Economics* 16(3): 327–54.

Teal, Francis. 1994. "The Size and Sources of Economic Rents in a Developing Country Manufacturing Labor Market." Unpublished paper. University of Oxford, Centre for the Study of African Economies (June).

CHAPTER THREE

Minimum Wages and Poverty in Developing Countries: Some Empirical Evidence

Nora Claudia Lustig
Darryl McLeod

INCREASED EMPHASIS on job creation in developing countries has focused attention on institutional rigidities, such as minimum wage laws. In particular, many Latin American governments seeking to become more competitive in the international arena are targeting labor market rigidities as impediments to reform and job creation. Interestingly, some governments are moving in the opposite direction, as their major OECD trading partners in the North seek to impose "fair labor standards" as a

The authors benefited from comments and suggestions by George Akerlof, Gary Burtless, Susan Collins, Alejandra Cox Edwards, Sebastian Edwards, Albert Fishlow, Richard Freeman, Edward Leamer, Martin Rama, Martin Ravallion, Jaime Ros, and Jacques van der Gaag, as well as by participants at the Brookings and World Bank conference "Labor Markets, Growth, and Poverty in Latin America," Buenos Aires, July 1995, and the Brookings Economic Studies Program Work in Progress seminar series. The authors are especially grateful to Shihua Lu for excellent research assistance and to Marcelo Cabrol, Moo-Ho Han, and Esen Raifoglu for their invaluable assistance in gathering and compiling the data. They also want to thank Dan Dougan and Michael McLean for their help in this task. The views expressed are those of the authors and should not be interpreted as those of any of the above, or of the trustees, officers, or other staff of the Brookings Institution or the World Bank. All errors and omissions remain the responsibility of the authors.

condition of further market access.[1] Korea, for example, passed a new minimum wage law in 1988. These labor market reforms raise the question of whether minimum wage laws help or hurt the poor in developing countries. This chapter analyzes the impact of change in statutory minimum wages on poverty.

Our main empirical finding is that minimum wages and poverty are inversely related: that is, an increase in real minimum wages is accompanied by a fall in poverty. Similar results are obtained using a variety of poverty measures (headcount ratio and poverty gap), poverty lines (low and high), and population groups (urban and rural). The inverse relationship is also found when observations are classified by positive and negative growth, and when Latin American observations are distinguished from those for Asia.

Although the recurrent result is that minimum wages and poverty are inversely related, one cannot conclude that a rise in the minimum wage is the most cost effective way to reduce poverty. We do not estimate the efficiency losses that may result from higher minimum wages. Also, this empirical exercise is subject to all the caveats associated with cross-section analysis. Even if minimum wages can reduce poverty, they may not be the most efficient way to achieve this objective.[2] The paper is organized as follows. We briefly review the relationship between minimum wages and wages in the informal sector in labor market models with covered and uncovered sectors. We then present our main econometric results. Finally, the last section adds some concluding remarks on the policy relevance of these results.

Minimum Wages and Poverty: Theory

Debate over the distributional implications of minimum wages laws has been rekindled by the "new economics" of the minimum wage. Card and Krueger for example, argue that raising minimum wages sometimes

1. An example of this sort of pressure in Latin America was the proposal that Mexico raise its minimum wage at the rate of productivity growth, put forward by some pro-labor members of the U.S. Congress as one of the conditions for the passage of the North American Free Trade Agreement.
2. See, for example, the discussion in Saint-Paul (1994). In the case of Latin America and the Caribbean, Rama (1995) finds that the cost of minimum wages in terms of economic performance is not significant.

increases employment.[3] Whereas many believe minimum wages reduce poverty in developed countries—albeit at a cost—this not the conventional wisdom for developing countries. Rather, the dominant view is the one outlined by the recent *World Development Report* on labor markets, "Minimum wages may help protect the most poverty-stricken workers in industrial countries, but they clearly do not in developing nations."[4] Several arguments in support of this view are commonly cited. First, coverage of minimum wage laws in developing countries is limited to a small formal sector and because the informal sector is large these laws are difficult to enforce. Second, poverty lines are lower in developing countries and workers who benefit from minimum wage increases are usually not the poorest of the poor. Third, a large fraction of the poor work in the uncovered or self-employed sector. Also, high inflation rates make it hard to set real minimum wages.

Most of the arguments focus on variations of the Harris-Todaro model.[5] Under certain assumptions, the presence of a large uncovered sector means that an increase in formal sector wages pushes more unemployed into the informal sector, driving down informal sector wages. However, as Edward Gramlich—and, more recently, Daniel Hamermesh and David Card and Alan Krueger—emphasizes, this argument depends on a particular constellation of elasticities.[6] If formal sector labor demand is inelastic, a boost in formal sector wages may also drive up wages in the informal sector.[7] However, as Jeffrey Williamson and others have emphasized, many of the empirical predictions of the Harris-Todaro model do not seem to be borne out by empirical studies of developing country labor markets.[8] Hence it does not provide a solid basis for analysis of the impact of minimum wages in developing countries.

3. Card and Krueger (1995).

4. World Bank (1995, p. 75). The International Labor Organization has a different view: "minimum wages are a potentially important labour market policy instrument for reducing poverty" (Rodgers, 1995, p. 48). For more on this issue, see Lipton (1995, p. 130).

5. For early examples of formal models of the impact of minimum wages, see Mincer (1976) and Welch (1974).

6. Gramlich (1976); Hamermesh (1993); Card and Krueger (1995).

7. "Demand link" models present another alternative. In this case, the change in the distribution of income generated by raising the minimum wage may cause incomes in the uncovered sector to rise. This result largely depends on change in demand patterns of covered sector workers induced by the minimum wage increase. (Fiszbein, 1992.) The idea that the covered and uncovered sectors are linked not only through the labor market but also through the goods market was initially developed by Tokman (1978), among others; see also Cole and Sanders (1985).

8. Williamson (1989).

In fact, there are some a priori reasons why minimum wage legislation should have a greater impact on the poor in developing countries. Unskilled wages are a more important component of the poor's income in less developed countries than in developed countries, where a large portion of the poor are unemployed, on welfare, or retired. Because in developing countries the minimum wage and poverty lines are closer to one another, a minimum wage increase may lift workers out of poverty. In the United States, on the other hand, minimum wage earnings are generally not enough to lift the poor out of poverty.[9]

Moreover, the general equilibrium analysis models of Alan Carruth and Andrew Oswald and by Edward Leamer show that in small open economies a rise in formal sector wages always raises both covered and uncovered wages, while reducing the capital rental rate.[10] The intuition behind this result is straightforward: a rise in union or minimum wages in the formal sector cannot be passed along in higher prices. Therefore, profits fall, leading to a migration of capital, rather than labor, out of the formal sector. Capital moves to the informal sector, driving up wages and employment in that sector.[11] In addition, scattered evidence suggests that in some cases—Brazil, Costa Rica, and Mexico, for example—formal and informal wages move together, contrary to predictions from conventional analysis, which would lead one to expect that they were inversely related.[12]

9. The ratio of minimum wages to poverty lines (expressed as a percentage) for some of the developing countries used in this study is shown in table 3-4.

10. Carruth and Oswald (1981); Leamer (1995). Although Carruth and Oswald's model is intended to analyze the impact of unions, their analysis also applies to minimum wage legislation.

11. Note in the Harris-Todaro model and in the demand link general equilibrium models, the effects of minimum wage changes do *not* depend on the existence of a nonstandard relationship between minimum wages and employment in the covered sector. In contrast to some of the models posited by the "new economics" of the minimum wage (see, for example, Card and Krueger, 1995, p. 236), in these models higher real wages in the formal sector unequivocally lead to lower levels of formal employment. Conversely, a nonstandard result does *not* require that the poor work in minimum wage jobs. One does need to assume, however, that the government can affect the real value of the minimum wage through statutory changes in the nominal minimum wage, and that the minimum wage is enforced at least in part of the economy. In closed economies, the reverse is likely to be true: covered sector wages may move inversely with wages in the uncovered sector, although the outcome depends on key parameters in the model.

12. On Mexico, see Maloney (1996), and on Brazil and Costa Rica, World Bank, (1990, p. 110). See also the studies listed in note 13.

In sum, the conventional wisdom holds that minimum wage laws are likely to harm uncovered and rural workers in developing countries. Most of these arguments appeal to a particular case of the Harris-Todaro model, in which higher formal sector wages force workers back into the informal sector, pushing down informal incomes. But theoretical results from small open economy models suggest otherwise. Also, to the extent that minimum wage laws affect unskilled wages, they are more likely to reduce poverty in developing countries than in industrialized countries.

The preceding discussion reveals that the impact of change in statutory minimum wages on poverty in developing countries is really an empirical issue. Most of the available econometric work focuses on the relationship between minimum wages and the wages of the unskilled workers. The existing studies often find the relationship to be positive.[13] However, they usually focus on urban workers, whereas the stronghold of poverty in developing countries is in rural areas. In addition, estimating labor market parameters is very data-intensive and is therefore difficult to carry out for a large number of countries simultaneously. An alternative approach is to estimate the determinants of poverty, including the minimum wage as one of the explanatory variables. We chose such a course. Specifically, we analyze the relationship between minimum wages and poverty by regressing change in poverty rates on change in the minimum wage and other variables that could affect poverty levels, for a cross-section of developing countries.

Minimum Wages and Poverty: Empirical Evidence

The preceding discussion shows that higher minimum wages can thus reduce poverty, as long as (1) higher minimum wages result in higher uncovered sector wages; (2) the rise in uncovered sector wages is large enough to push some of the population out of poverty; and (3) the number of the beneficiaries (that is, those who are no longer poor) exceeds the number of those who become poor because the increase in minimum wages leaves them unemployed or earning less in the uncovered or "subsistence" sector.[14]

13. See, for example, Marquez (1981), Reyes-Heroles (1983),Wells and Drobny (1982), and Cicchelli-Velloso (1990). See also Freeman (1993, p. 128), Shaheed (1995), International Labor Organization (1988), and Bell (1995).

14. The underlying assumption is that the conventional poverty line is below the statutory minimum wage and is higher or equal to Hamermesh's (1993) "subsistence wage."

Available studies for Latin America show that a rise in the minimum wage may reduce poverty (and vice versa), at least in the short run. Samuel Morley, for example, who looks at the relationship between minimum wages and poverty in a cross-section of Latin American countries, finds a negative correlation between minimum wages and poverty.[15] The coefficient loses significance, however, when the relationship is analyzed for periods of recession only. Also using a cross-section of countries, Alain de Janvry and Elisabeth Sadoulet find that the coefficient is negative (that is, higher minimum wages imply lower poverty levels) in most cases. In contrast to Morley, in the case of urban poverty they find that the coefficient is significant only during a recession. These studies, however, use observations for Latin America alone. Our empirical analysis includes a number of developing countries outside this region.

Poverty and Minimum Wages: A Cross-National Analysis

Research in this area has historically been limited by inconsistent and infrequent poverty statistics for developing countries. Although the lack of poverty data remains a serious problem, the availability of consistent poverty statistics has greatly improved recently, as several research groups at the World Bank and the International Labour Organisation (ILO) have compiled comparable poverty rates for a number of developing countries. We use the poverty data compiled by these studies to assemble a sample that includes twenty-two countries and over forty time intervals.[16]

Using this sample, we regress the *change* in the standard headcount and other poverty measures on key determinants of poverty, including real wages and per capita income growth. This approach avoids the problems inherent in comparing the level of poverty across countries; for example, the lack of comparability across poverty lines and the need to include a number of state variables. Among our independent variables are several structural variables, such as the stock of human capital and the share of the labor force in agriculture, that can be measured in a similar way across countries. In contrast to previous studies, we include sixteen nonoverlapping sample intervals from nine countries outside

15. Morley (1992).
16. See table 3A-1.

Latin America: five in Asia and four in Africa, as well as sample intervals from thirteen Latin American countries.[17]

By restricting each sample to nonoverlapping intervals, we exclude a number of observations. However, by using alternative criteria to select nonoverlapping groups, some of these observations can still be utilized. In every case, our choice of countries and time intervals is dictated by the availability of consecutive survey-based poverty measures using identical poverty lines.[18] The lack of real minimum wage series also imposes limitations on the sample size: about ten observations of change in poverty had to be dropped because there were no data on minimum wages.

We first examine the impact of real wages and real per capita income growth, separately, on poverty. The regression equations 1.1, 1.2, and 1.3, reported in the first three columns of table 3-1 and in figures 3-1, 3-2, and 3-3, reveal the expected positive correlation between per capita income growth, real (minimum and average) wages, and poverty. The results for per capita income and minimum wages are repeated in the regression in table 3-2 discussed later. Comparing regressions 1.2 and 1.3, the explained variance and statistical significance are clearly higher for change in real minimum wages than for either of the other two real wage variables tested: average real wages collected in the ILO's *Year Book of Labour Statistics* and the real manufacturing earnings series reported in the World Bank's CD-ROM *World Tables 1994*. Note, however, that since the three wage series were often not available for a given country, the regressions reported in table 3-1 are based on slightly different samples.[19]

Equation 1.4 adds minimum wages and average wages to the per capita income growth equation 1.1. Both the real minimum wage and growth coefficients remain highly significant, but the average wage coefficient drops dramatically in significance. When we control for change in per

17. The main sources of our poverty data (presented in table 3A-5) are two compilations recently assembled by the World Bank and the ILO. The main source of minimum wage data is International Labour Organisation (1988). Average wages come primarily from International Labour Organisation (various years) and CEPAL (1994). Because the two sets of average wage data differ slightly for some high inflation countries, both series were tested, yielding very similar results. All the series used in the regressions are available from the authors upon request.

18. See figures 3A-1 and 3A-2.

19. Ideally, one should use wages for unskilled workers. However, not enough observations are available for use in a regression.

capita income or in minimum wages, the average and manufacturing wage coefficients become insignificant.[20] Although heteroskedasticity is potentially a problem in regression 1.3, as the White test indicates, we find it generally true that the impact of average wages on poverty cannot be separated from that of per capita income and minimum wages. In over one-third (eighty-nine) of our observations in the full sample (including overlapping periods) poverty rises over a given interval, and in 134 cases it falls. Similarly, real minimum wages rise in about two-thirds of our observations and fall in seventy cases. This implies that our estimates do not simply represent trends in these two key variables.

These results suggest minimum wages affect poverty more than average wages and that they are less correlated with change in national income.[21] This is consistent with the fact that minimum wage laws mainly affect unskilled wages and therefore may be a more important determinant of the income of poor workers. The lack of correlation with national income can also be explained by the fact that real minimum wages are a target of government policy.[22] When we control for per capita income growth, real minimum wages remain highly significant but the magnitude of the effect on poverty drops substantially. Also, the variance explained by equation 1.4 is substantially higher than that explained by the previous regressions.

Although real minimum wages seem to affect poverty independent of average wages and per capita income growth, this correlation may result from other government policies or employment opportunities that are moving in consonance with minimum wages. Minimum wage changes may thus indicate a broad commitment by government to reduce poverty, using a variety of policy measures. We find little evidence to support this hypothesis. As discussed below, the impact of low wages on poverty persists even after controlling for available government spending variables. Also, when time series on social spending are available, they are not positively correlated with real minimum wages. In fact, the correla-

20. Regressing poverty changes on real manufacturing earnings and education expenditures yields a real wage coefficient of -0.85 with a t statistic of -1.65, but the adjusted $R2$ is only about 0.1, even with the education variable.

21. See table 3A-2 for a three-way classification of countries and periods according to the direction of change in poverty, minimum wages, and per capita income.

22. Variations on equation 1.4 (not reported here) confirm these suppositions. Both average wage measures become insignificant when per capita income growth or minimum wage changes are added to the regression.

Table 3-1. *Poverty and Real Wages: Headcount Poverty Measures*[a]

Poverty line and independent variable	(1.1)	(1.2)	(1.3)	(1.4)	(1.5)	(1.6)[b]	(1.7)	(1.8)[b]	(1.9)[b]	(1.10)[b]
Poverty line[c]	High	High	High	High	High	Low	High	Low	High	High
Per capita income	**−1.90** (−5.77)	... ...	... ...	**−1.08** (−2.53)	−0.63 (−1.85)	**−1.93** (−3.50)	... ...	... ...	... ...	**−0.72** (−2.13)
Real minimum wage	... ...	... ...	**−0.97** (−6.03)	**−0.78** (−4.08)	**−0.64** (−4.24)	**−1.09** (−4.00)	**−0.71** (−4.68)	**−1.29** (−4.00)	**−0.81** (−3.68)	**−0.61** (−3.64)
Real average wage	... ...	**−0.69** (−2.07)	... ...	0.15 (0.66)	... ...	... ...	... ...	... ...	... ...	... ...
Real public spending	... ...	... ...	... ...	... ...	... ...	... ...	−0.20 (−1.06)	−0.54 (−1.54)	−0.24 (−1.06)	... ...
Terms of trade	... ...	... ...	... ...	... ...	**−0.36** (−2.56)	... ...	**−0.44** (−3.00)	... ...	**−0.42** (−3.11)	**−0.40** (−2.44)
Human capital stock[d]	... ...	... ...	... ...	... ...	−0.36 (−1.23)	... ...	−0.46 (−1.49)	... ...	−0.55 (−1.72)	−0.42 (−1.65)
Unemployment[e]	... ...	... ...	... ...	... ...	... ...	... ...	... ...	... ...	**1.36** (2.41)	... ...

Inflation	...	...	...	...	...	...	...	...	...	0.01
	...	...	...	...	...	...	...	...	...	(0.40)
Education expenditure[f]	...	...	**−0.02**	...	**−0.77**	**−1.28**	**−0.77**	**−1.25**	...	...
	...	...	(−3.07)	...	(−2.21)	(−2.56)	(−2.09)	(−2.17)	...	...
Addendum										
Intercept	0.01	−0.02	**−0.02**	−0.01	0.02	**0.06**	0.02	0.04	0.01	0.00
	(0.58)	(−1.5)	(−3.07)	(−1.05)	(1.25)	(3.10)	(1.08)	(1.71)	(0.55)	(0.15)
White F test[g]	0.68	0.53	2.25	0.92	0.48	0.85	1.25	0.29	0.91	0.48
Probability value	0.62	0.60	0.13	0.50	0.88	0.55	0.32	0.93	0.56	0.89
Adjusted R^2	0.47	0.12	0.55	0.67	0.74	0.71	0.72	0.61	0.71	0.69
Number of observations	39	26	30	24	30	23	30	23	20	30

a. The dependent variable is the log annual change in poverty assessed by the headcount measure; that is, the growth rate of the poor less that of the total population. All variables are expressed as annual log changes, except where noted. t statistics are shown in parentheses. Boldface indicates coefficients significant at the 5 percent level.

b. t statistics are calculated using White consistent errors.

c. The high and low poverty lines are typically $50–$60 per month and $30 per month in 1985 purchasing power parity dollars, respectively.

d. Human capital growth is proxied by the log change in average years of secondary education per adult.

e. The unemployment variable is the change in the unemployment rate divided by the number of years in the interval.

f. Average education expenditure is expressed as a percent of GDP. This is often important as a state variable.

g. This is the F statistic for White's heteroskedasticity test without cross-terms. A high F or a low probability value suggests that the null hypothesis of homoskedastic errors should be rejected.

Figure 3-1. *Change in Headcount Ratio and Minimum Wage*[a]

Headcount ratio[b]

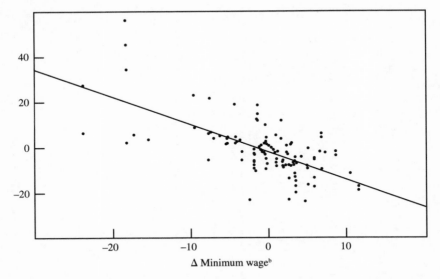

Δ Minimum wage[b]

a. All observations for high and low poverty lines, including overlapping periods.
b. Annual log change.

tion is often negative.[23] Changes in agricultural output and prices also affect poverty, especially in low-income countries.

To allow for these potential interactions, we test a number of measures of public spending and agricultural income.[24] Unfortunately, there are few consistently reported series on social spending targeted at the poor. When time series are not available, we use time-invariant averages as "state variables" to capture each country's ongoing commitment to particular programs. Regressions 1.5 to 1.8 are typical of those including a broader range of policy and state variables. Our social spending state variables include total current spending, spending on social programs, and spending on social security. The most relevant state variable seems to be the share of education expenditure in GDP (which we express as a percentage). A related but time-varying measure is annual change in years of secondary education per adult. This measure of human capital does better than either total years of education or years of primary

23. These results are available directly from the authors upon request.
24. Domestic agricultural terms of trade are not available for most countries, so we use external terms of trade with change in real agricultural value added.

Figure 3-2. *Change in Headcount Ratio and per Capita GDP*[a]

Headcount ratio[b]

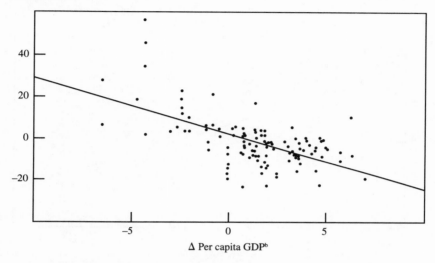

Δ Per capita GDP[b]

a. All observations for high and low poverty lines, including overlapping periods.
b. Annual log change.

education per adult, although the *level*—rather than the change—of primary education per adult sometimes affects the rate of decline when
poverty is severe. Change in total real government consumption is the
only broadly available indicator of government spending on social programs. The other public spending measures we test are not statistically
significant.[25]

Change in agricultural value added, or its GDP share, has no consistent impact on the rate of change in poverty levels, so regressions including this variable are not reported. Change in external terms of trade,
however, does affect households near the high poverty line.[26] When the
terms of trade variable is included in regressions 1.6 and 1.8 (where the
sample is based on low poverty lines), it turns out not to be significant
(and hence it is left out of the reported regressions). Since severe poverty
mostly occurs in rural areas, this suggests that in commodity exporting
nations, changes in terms of trade affect the urban poor and the upper

25. Recall that comparable annual measures of social spending are very difficult to
obtain for developing countries.
26. Data on domestic terms of trade are not available for the required countries and
periods.

Figure 3-3. *Change in Headcount Ratio and Average Wage*[a]

Headcount ratio[b]

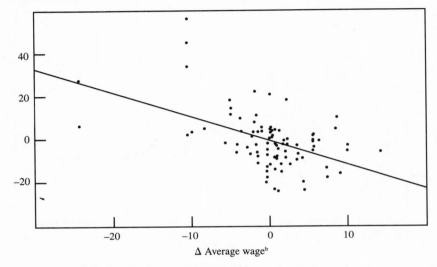

Δ Average wage[b]

a. All observations for high and low poverty lines, including overlapping periods.
b. Annual log change.

strata of the rural poor. This is consistent with the findings of Martin Ravallion and M. Huppi which suggest that, in Indonesia, the upper strata of the poor benefit the most from higher rice prices.[27]

Controlling for other factors such as human capital investment and per capita income growth reduces the poverty-minimum wage elasticity from almost 1.0 to the range of 0.6 to 0.8. Still real minimum wages remain an important (and statistically significant) determinant of poverty. Observe that the poverty-minimum wage elasticity is always higher for the low poverty line sample. This seems counterintuitive, but seems to be an artifact of how we measure the change in poverty.[28]

Since minimum wages affect unemployment, controlling for change in unemployment is a strictly counterfactual exercise. For the subsample of

27. Ravallion and Huppi (1989).
28. See appendix 3A. If we use the annual difference in the headcount rather than the log change, much of the difference between the high and low poverty line disappears. Note also that the coefficients are consistently higher in the low poverty line regressions, suggesting that the metric of the dependent variable is a factor. The coefficient on per capita income, for instance, increases from 0.63 for the high poverty line sample in equation 1.5 to 1.93 for the low poverty line regression 1.6.

countries for which unemployment rates are available, this variable is associated with higher poverty. Controlling for unemployment increases the minimum wage coefficient to -0.81 in equation 1.9 (from the lower levels in regressions 1.5 and 1.7), implying that these variables are inversely related (that is, when the unemployment variable is not kept constant "artificially," raising the minimum wage has a smaller impact on poverty). This inverse relationship between unemployment and minimum wages can be confirmed by regressing unemployment on minimum wages as shown in table 3-3.

Eliana Cardoso argues inflation is an important determinant of poverty.[29] However, the coefficient for inflation is not statistically significant in regression 1.10. When the minimum wage variable is dropped from this equation, inflation does have a significant negative impact on poverty. Together, these results suggest that inflation affects poverty by reducing minimum or unskilled wages.[30] If nominal minimum wages change infrequently or by small amounts compared to inflation, real minimum wage movements may be dominated by change in the price level. If this were the case, the two variables would be inversely correlated, potentially creating a problem of multicolinearity and making it hard to separate the effect of the two variables. Neither of these problems is apparent in our samples. Adding inflation in equation 1.10 has little effect on the coefficients on minimum wages or other variables. Also, replacing minimum wages by inflation in regression 1.5 (not shown here) reduces the R^2 from 0.71 to 0.47. This suggests that real minimum wages are capturing more than the effect of inflation on poverty.

The Impact of Minimum Wages by Growth Phase, Region, and Sector

Previous studies have found asymmetric poverty dynamics in recessions and recoveries. Morley, for example, finds evidence that raising minimum wages mitigates poverty only when the economy is growing.[31] We find more symmetrical effects. Because our sample includes eight intervals in which per capita income declined, we are also able to test the regional aspects of poverty and real wage changes. There are not

29. Cardoso (1992).
30. Note, however, that for some samples (not shown here) inflation does have a small independent effect and the coefficient is statistically significant, even after controlling for change in minimum wages.
31. Morley (1992).

enough data to perform separate regressions, but assuming all other coefficients are identical the minimum wage variable can be split into positive and negative growth cases. Table 3-2, equation 2.1, shows raising minimum wages is more effective for reducing poverty during periods of economic growth, but the difference is not statistically significant. The Wald test reported in the lower panel of table 3-2 cannot reject the null hypothesis that the two coefficients are equal.

Dummy variables can also be added to identify differences among regions and sectors. In table 3-2 the real minimum wage change variable is split into observations for Latin America and for Asia plus Africa. Both the extent of poverty and wage policy differ between these two regions. Regression 2.2 compares the effect of minimum wages in the seventeen Latin American observations with those for the Asian and African countries. Again, the Wald test shows the coefficients are statistically indistinguishable.

Although minimum wages can benefit uncovered workers in small open economies, minimum wage policy is clearly associated with urban workers.[32] By constructing a predominately low poverty line sample, including seventeen rural poverty estimates, we compare the impact of minimum wages in rural and urban areas. In every case a national estimate of the minimum wage is used—only a few countries enforce minimum wages by sector or occupation such as agricultural laborer. The results are reported in regression 2.3. The minimum wage coefficient is considerably higher for urban and national poverty. Even though the coefficient on rural minimum wages is not significant at the 10 percent level, the Wald test rejects the null of equal coefficients with about 10 percent confidence.

Lack of data on nominal wages and coverage ratios prevents us from taking these factors into account. Our results, however, indicate a strong correlation between minimum wages and poverty, even without conditioning the relationship on coverage ratios or relative wages. For the cases where minimum wages are not binding and coverage is limited, one would expect to find a much weaker correlation between minimum wages and poverty. Nevertheless, available information shows that minimum

32. The only statistically significant sectoral dummy is that for urban poverty rates. Living in an urban area consistently dampens the rate of change in poverty in any direction. This urban dummy is not consistently significant and has little effect on the other coefficients, so to preserve degrees of freedom, it is not included in the regressions reported here.

wages are usually set at levels higher than a country's poverty lines (see table 3-4), which suggests that to the extent minimum wages reflect unskilled wages (or these move in tandem), a rise in the former can reduce poverty.[33]

Alternative Poverty Indicators

The limitations of the headcount measure of poverty are well known. Our final set of regressions, reported in table 3-3, corroborates the results presented earlier using several other measures of poverty such as the poverty gap and the income gap.[34] Regressions 3.1 and 3.2 use the poverty gap instead of the headcount ratio. Although these samples are small, the results are consistent with the headcount estimates reported in equation 1.5. Again, we find that terms of trade are insignificant for low poverty line groups and that the observed coefficients are larger for the low poverty line sample. The only surprising result is the absence of a per capita growth effect. However, regressing the poverty gap on per capita income alone does yield a significant negative relationship: poverty gaps diminish when per capita income goes up.

Regression 3.3 uses the same time periods and sample dependent but uses the log change in per capita calorie intake as the dependent variable. Evidently, the initial estimates suffer from a heteroskedasticity problem. In equation 3.3a we use per capita growth as a weighting variable, and the weighted least-squares estimates confirm the results of the initial estimate while almost eliminating the heteroskedasticity problem. Again, using the same sample of countries and the same time intervals, our final equation evaluates the effect of minimum wages on unemployment. We find that real minimum wage increases raise unemployment. According to these estimates, a 10 percent rise in minimum wages could increase unemployment by between 0.5 and 1 percent. These estimates must be interpreted with care, since regressing our annual pool of unemployment rates on minimum wage changes yields insignificant results. Also, among those that we evaluate, unemployment is probably the least consistently defined measure of welfare across countries.

33. Table 3-4 presents information for 1985. Minimum wages reached record lows in Latin America during the 1980s (see Cox Edwards, 1996), hence the ratios were probably even higher in earlier periods.

34. Their characteristics and properties can be found in Foster, Greer, and Thorbecke (1986).

Table 3-2. *Poverty and Real Minimum Wages, by Region and Growth Phase*[a]

Poverty line and independent variable	Growth (2.1)			Region (2.2)			Rural or urban (2.3)		
	Common	Negative	Positive	Common	Asia plus Africa	Latin America	Common	Urban-national	Rural
Poverty line[b]	High	…	…	High	…	…	Low	…	…
Per capita income	−0.69	…	…	−0.63	…	…	−1.86	…	…
	(−1.96)	…	…	(−1.84)	…	…	(−2.20)	…	…
Real minimum wage	…	−0.57	−0.70	…	−0.67	−0.63	…	−1.91	−0.63
	…	(−3.47)	(−4.40)	…	(−2.15)	(−4.52)	…	(−3.13)	(−1.54)
Real public spending	…	…	…	…	…	…	…	…	…
Terms of trade	−0.36	…	…	−0.36	…	…	…	…	…
	(−2.64)	…	…	(−2.71)	…	…	…	…	…
Human capital stock[c]	…	…	…	−0.37	…	…	−0.07[d]	…	…
	…	…	…	(−1.34)	…	…	(−1.47)	…	…
Education expenditure[e]	−0.86	…	…	−0.77	…	…	…	…	…
	(−2.31)	…	…	(−2.11)	…	…	…	…	…

Addendum

	(1)		(2)		(3)	
Intercept	0.01	⋯	0.01	⋯	0.04	⋯
	(0.65)	⋯	(0.65)	⋯	(0.95)	⋯
White F test[f]	0.34	⋯	0.48	⋯	1.62	⋯
Probability value	0.96	⋯	0.90	⋯	0.19	⋯
Wald test[g]	0.73	⋯	0.01	⋯	2.81	⋯
Probability value	0.96	⋯	0.91	⋯	0.11	⋯
Adjusted R^2	0.73	⋯	0.73	⋯	0.55	⋯
Number of observations	30	⋯	30	⋯	28	⋯

a. The dependent variable is the log annual change in poverty assessed by the headcount measure; that is, the growth rate of the poor less that of the total population. All variables are expressed as annual log changes, except where noted. t statistics, shown in parentheses, are calculated using a White heteroskedasticity-consistent covariance matrix. Boldface indicates coefficients significant at the 5 percent level.

b. The high and low poverty lines are typically $50–$60 per month and $30 per month in 1985 purchasing power parity dollars, respectively.

c. Human capital growth is proxied by the log change in average years of secondary education per adult.

d. For this low poverty line human capital is proxied by the log of the average years of secondary education per adult.

e. Average education expenditure is expressed as a percent of GDP. This is often important as a state variable.

f. This is the F statistic for White's heteroskedasticity test without cross-terms. A high F or a low probability value suggests that the null hypothesis of homoskedastic errors should be rejected.

g. The null hypothesis for these Wald tests is that the two minimum wage coefficients are equal.

Table 3-3. Poverty and Real Minimum Wages: Alternative Welfare Measures[a]

	Dependent variable						
Poverty line and independent variable	Poverty gap[b]		Per capita calorie intake[c]			Unemployment[c,d]	
	(3.1)[e]	(3.2)[e]	(3.3)	(3.3a)	(3.4)	(3.5)[e]	(3.6)[e]
Poverty line	High	Low					
Per capita income	0.45	0.74	0.17	0.10	...	−0.10	...
	(0.43)	(0.39)	(1.68)	(1.59)		(−1.35)	
Real minimum wage	**−0.79**	**−1.59**	0.06	**0.08**	**0.10**	**0.08**	**0.05**
	(−2.73)	(−2.49)	(1.60)	(3.11)	(3.23)	(2.82)	(2.45)
Real public spending	...	...	...	...	0.04	...	−0.06
					(.61)		(−1.89)
Terms of trade	−0.46	...	...	...	0.08	...	−0.03
	(−2.09)				(1.94)		(−1.08)
Human capital stock[f]	−1.01	−1.35	...	...	...	−0.09	−0.11
	(−2.07)	(−1.77)				(−1.10)	(−1.38)
Addendum							
Intercept	0.03	0.04	0.00	0.00	0.00	0.01	0.01
	(1.19)	(0.80)	(0.2)	(0.98)	(0.37)	(1.36)	(1.47)
White F test[g]	1.58	1.02	3.37	1.90	1.54	0.45	0.91
Probability value	0.28	0.47	0.02	0.14	0.21	0.83	0.54
Adjusted R[a]	0.42	0.56	0.32	0.30	0.37	0.24	0.29
Number of observations	16	16	30	30	30	21	21

a. All variables are annual log changes, except where noted. t statistics are shown in parentheses. Boldface indicates coefficients significant at the 5 percent level.
b. The poverty gap is the headcount ratio times the average income shortfall of the poor.
c. Includes all nonoverlapping observations.
d. The unemployment variable is the change in the unemployment rate divided by the number of years in the interval.
e. t statistics are calculated using a White heteroskedasticity-consistent covariance matrix.
f. Human capital growth is proxied by the log change in average years of secondary education per adult.
g. This is the F statistic for White's heteroskedasticity test without cross-terms. A high F or a low probability value suggests that the null hypothesis of homoskedastic errors should be rejected.

Table 3-4. *Ratios of Nominal Minimum Wages to Poverty Lines, Selected Countries, 1985*

Units as indicated

Country	Minimum wage[a]	High poverty line ratio[b]	Low poverty line ratio[c]
Argentina	79.29	1.32	2.64
Brazil	51.95	0.87	1.73
Colombia	95.34	1.59	3.18
Costa Rica	110.15	1.84	3.67
Mexico	120.99	2.02	4.03
Peru	36.65	0.61	1.22
Philippines	93.19	1.55	3.11
Paraguay	189.06	3.15	6.30
Uruguay	64.25	1.07	2.14

Source: Nominal minimum wages obtained directly from International Labour Organization's data base on "Labor Statistics on Legal Minimum Wages" (LABMINW) and the poverty lines reported in Tabatabai and Fouad (1993).

a. U.S. dollars per month.

b. Ratio of minimum wage to high poverty line ($60 per person per month), expressed as a percentage.

c. Ratio of minimum wage to low poverty line ($30 per person per month), expressed as a percentage.

Concluding Remarks

Our results indicate that minimum wage increases or declines may be associated with declines or increases, respectively, in poverty rates in developing countries. This result is consistent across high and low poverty lines, alternative measures of poverty, and the classification of observations by whether the economy is growing or contracting, by whether the population is urban or rural, and by region (Latin America or Asia plus Africa).[35]

These results, however, are not a flat endorsement of minimum wage increases as a cost effective policy to reduce poverty. Higher minimum wages do seem to raise unemployment. Minimum wage increases may also reduce efficiency and competitiveness. If minimum wage legislation has a negative effect on growth, it could hurt the poor over the long term. Even if raising the minimum wages can be shown to reduce poverty in the short run, in the long run it could reduce employment opportunities.

These caveats in mind, these results suggest reducing minimum wages in developing countries does hurt the poor, at least in the short run.

35. Using a different approach to analyze this question for the United States, Card and Krueger (1995, p. 305) find some evidence that "the effects of the minimum-wage variable on either the overall poverty rate or the poverty rate of workers are negative and marginally significant, suggesting that poverty rates fell faster in states in which the minimum wage had a bigger impact." When the authors control for change in economic conditions across states, the coefficient, although still negative, becomes statistically insignificant.

Appendix 3A: Data Sources and Estimation Issues

This appendix describes the data sources and discusses several estimation issues raised by the income and minimum wage elasticities of poverty estimates presented in this chapter.

In particular, table 3A-1 shows the countries and periods, classified into episodes of growth and recession, used in the regressions. Figures 3A-1 and 3A-2 show the frequency of countries and periods for the "standard" regression, equation 1.7 from table 3-1. Table 3A-2 presents a three-way classification of the full sample for minimum wages, per capita income, and poverty. Finally, table 3A-3 lists all of the poverty measures that serve as dependent variables, along with their published source and any available documentation on the poverty line and the type of survey data used to obtain the poverty estimate (that is, whether the poverty line is defined in terms of income or consumption expenditure, whether the rate refers to households or persons, the region covered by the survey, and so forth). Apart from the wage and unemployment data, most of the data for the dependent variables are from the World Bank's CD-ROM *World Tables 1994*. The primary sources for the minimum wage data are International Labour Organisation (1988) and several unpublished tables of real minimum wages compiled by researchers at the ILO and Comision Economica para la América Latina y el Caribe (CEPAL). Average wages are from ILO (various years), CEPAL (1994); manufacturing wages are from the World Bank's *World Tables 1994*.

The range and average change of the observations included in our standard regression, equation 1.7, are as follows. For the real minimum wage (with the real average wage in parentheses), the change is from −9.6 (−4.3) to 4.7 (10) percent per year; the average for positive observations is 2.5 (3.3) percent per year and the average for negative observations is −3.3 (−1.9) percent per year. For poverty, according to the headcount measure, the range is from −7.7 to 8.4 percent per year, and the averages are 3.5 and −4.5 percent per year for positive and negative observations, respectively. A complete listing of the data in spreadsheet format is available from the authors upon request.

The Magnitude of Poverty Elasticities

The main dependent variable in this study is the headcount measure of poverty. If economic growth raises income uniformly across all persons or households, the rate at which the headcount ratio falls depends both on shape of the Lorenz curve and on the initial level of poverty. This point is illustrated by Cline (1992) in his comment on Morley (1992). The fact that the elasticity varies with the level of the poverty line has potentially important implications for the results reported in table 3-1, where it seems that the minimum wage poverty elasticity is higher for the lower poverty line headcount measure. Is this result due to the fact that increases in the minimum wage mainly benefit lower income groups, or is it simply due to the effect noted above? To gain some insight into this question, we briefly explore the sensitivity of the poverty elasticity to the level of poverty.

Several researchers, including Cline (1972) and Lydall (1968), have found that the Pareto function

$$N = A(ym) - b,$$

where N is the number of persons or households, ym is the lowest observed level of per capita income, and $b > 1$, provides a useful approximation to observed cumulative income distributions. A and B are the parameters that characterize the distribution. Thus for any given poverty line income yp, the number of persons with income above the poverty line is $A(yp) - b$ and the headcount poverty rate, H, is simply given by

$$H = 1 - (yp/ym) - b.$$

Cline then shows the elasticity, E, with respect to a uniform rise in per capita income, y, is given by

$$E = -b / [(yp/ym)b - 1].$$

The Gini coefficient for the Pareto distribution function, $G = 1/[2b - 1]$, can be used to determine a plausible value for b. Given a Gini coefficient of 0.45, b is roughly 1.5. The poverty-income elasticity now depends on the relationship between the poverty line, yp, and the minimum (subsistence) income, ym. Cline argues that a plausible value for the ratio yp/ym is 1.5, yielding a poverty income elasticity of about -1.8, which is very similar to that reported in regression 1.1 of table 3-1.

We now return to the question at hand: how sensitive is the poverty elasticity to change in the poverty line, especially to a lower poverty line? Figure 3A-3 plots the several possible methods of computing the poverty-income elasticity against various poverty lines (more precisely, various ratios of poverty line to minimum income, yp/ym). As is clear from the

Table 3A-1. *Countries and Periods Included in Regressions*[a]

Region and country	Headcount ratio as dependent variable		Poverty gap as dependent variable	
	Recession	*Growth phase*	*Recession*	*Growth phase*
Africa				
Ghana		1987–90[b,c]		
Mauritius		1980–87[b,c]		
Morocco		1970–84[b,c], 1975–80[d,e] 1980–85[d,e], 1984–90[c,f]		1970–84[b,c]
Tunisia		1975–80[c,f], 1975–80[d,e] 1980–85[c,f], 1980–85[d,e] 1985–90[c,f]		
Asia and the Pacific				
India		1977–83[b,c], 1978–83[d,e] 1984–90[c,d], 1984–87[d,e]		1977–83[b,c]
Indonesia		1987–90[b,c], 1990–93[b,c] 1971–85[c,f], 1971–85[d,e]		
Philippines		1985–88[c,f]		
Sri Lanka		1963–82[c,d], 1973–78[d,e] 1985–90[c,f]		1963–82[d,c]
Thailand		1975–81[b,c], 1976–81[d,e] 1981–88[b,c]		1981–86[b,c]

Latin America and the Caribbean

Country				
Argentina	1980–89[f,g]			1986–89[f,g]
Bolivia		1986–89[f,g]	1980–89[b,g]	
Brazil		1980–89[c,f], 1980–89[b,e]		1980–89[c,f]
Colombia	1977–83[b,c], 1977–83[d,c]	1971–78[b,c], 1978–88[b,c]; 1980–89[d,g], 1988–91[c,f]		1971–78[b,c], 1980–89[f,g]
Costa Rica	1981–89[c,f]	1971–77[b,c], 1971–77[d,e]; 1983–86[b,c], 1983–86[d,e]	1977–83[a,c], 1981–89[c,d]	1983–86[b,c]
Guatemala		1986–89[c,f]		1986–89[b,c]
Honduras		1986–89[f,g]		1986–89[f,g]
Mexico	1984–89[c,f]		1979–89[c,f]	
Panama	1979–89[c,d], 1979–89[b,e]			
Paraguay		1983–90[f,g]		
Peru	1979–86[d,g]		1986–90[f,g]	1980–89[f,g]
Uruguay	1981–89[f,g]		1981–89[f,g]	
Venezuela	1981–89[d,e], 1982–89[c,f]			

Source: See tables 3-4 and 3A-3.
a. Minimum wage data are available for each observation included.
b. Dependent variable only available for high poverty line.
c. National.
d. Dependent variable only available for low poverty line.
e. Rural.
f. Dependent variable available for both high and low poverty lines.
g. Urban.

Figure 3A-1. *Frequency of Countries in Standard Regression, (1.7)*

Frequency

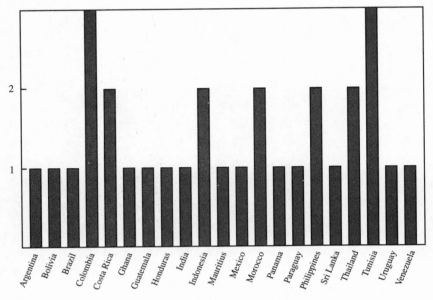

formula for E, this elasticity rises as the poverty line falls. For comparison, we plot the poverty elasticity used here against the same range of change in poverty (that is, log change in H over the log change in income at each poverty line shown on the y-axis of this figure). Both elasticities are sensitive to change in the poverty line, although the elasticity used here is less sensitive. One somewhat arbitrary method that avoids this problem is to use an elasticity based on the change in $\log(1 + H)$ as opposed to $\log(H)$. This is the measure used by Morley (1992). When the high and low poverty line estimates reported in table 3-1 are performed using the change in $\log(1 + H)$ as the dependent variable, similar estimated coefficients are obtained for all variables, except that the difference between the high and low poverty line coefficients is reduced. The elasticity of the lower poverty lines with respect to the minimum wage is still higher, but the difference is insignificant according to the standard F tests. This discussion leads one to conclude that the lower poverty line elasticity appears to be higher than the elasticity for the upper poverty line, but this may be simply an artifact of the method used to gauge change in poverty. All of the elasticities pictured in figure

Figure 3A-2. *Frequency of Periods in Standard Regression (1.7)*

Frequency

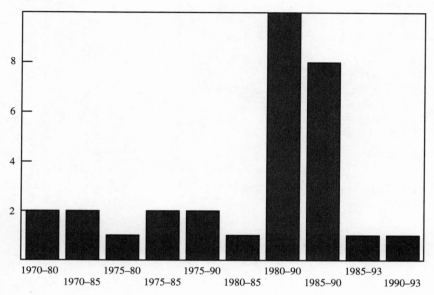

| 1970–80 | 1975–80 | 1975–90 | 1980–90 | 1985–93 |
| 1970–85 | 1975–85 | 1980–85 | 1985–90 | 1990–93 |

3A-3 rise as the poverty line falls relative to the minimum income of the population.

Poverty Data: Sample and Sources

The majority of the poverty measures used as dependent variables in this study come from recent recompilations of survey data undertaken by World Bank researchers and the ILO. The three primary sources are studies by Chen, Datt, and Ravallion (1991), Psacharopoulos (1993), and Tabatabai and Fouad (1993). We also obtain a number of poverty estimates from the World Bank's 1990 *World Development Report* and *World Tables 1994* (on CD-ROM) and from some (unpublished) individual country sources. In total, we provide information on twenty-two countries, nine of which lie outside Latin America. In each case, we use only two observations, based on similar surveys. Of 223 total observations, eighty-nine are based on household data in both years; the remaining are based on individual data. Fifty-five observations use poverty lines based on expenditure, while the rest use poverty lines defined by income. Our

Table 3A-2. *Three-by-Three Plot of Changes in Poverty, Minimum Wages, and per Capita GDP*[a]
Total = 180

Item	Poverty falls		Poverty increases
	Country/period (poverty measure)		Country/period (poverty measure)
	(total = 5)		(total = 37)
Minimum wage and	URY 1981–89 (h)(is)(U)	URY 1981–89 (h)(pg)(U)	ARG 1980–89 (h)(is)(U)	PER 1986–90 (h)(U)
GDP fall	URY 1981–89 (h)(U)	URY 1981–89 (L)(U)	ARG 1980–89 (h)(pg)(U)	PER 1986–90 (L)(is)(U)
	URY 1981–89 (L)(pg)(U)		ARG 1980–89 (h)(U)	PER 1986–90 (L)(pg)(U)
			ARG 1980–89 (L)(U)	PER 1986–90 (L)(U)
			BRA 1980–83 (L)(N)	URY 1981–89 (L)(is)(U)
			MEX 1984–89 (h)(N)	VEN 1981–89 (h)(is)(N)
			MEX 1984–89 (L)(N)	VEN 1981–89 (h)(pg)(N)
			PAN 1979–89 (h)(is)(N)	VEN 1981–89 (h)(R)
			PAN 1979–89 (h)(N)	VEN 1981–89 (L)(is)(N)
			PAN 1979–89 (h)(pg)(N)	VEN 1981–89 (L)(N)
			PAN 1979–89 (h)(R)	VEN 1981–89 (L)(N)
			PAN 1979–89 (L)(is)(N)	VEN 1981–89 (L)(pg)(N)
			PAN 1979–89 (L)(N)	VEN 1982–89 (h)(N)
			PAN 1979–89 (L)(pg)(N)	VEN 1982–89 (L)(N)
			PER 1979–86 (L)(U)	VEN 1987–89 (h)(N)
			PER 1980–90 (L)(U)	VEN 1987–89 (h)(N)
			PER 1980–91(L)(U)	VEN 1987–89 (L)(N)
			PER 1986–90 (h)(is)(U)	VEN 1987–89 (L)(R)
			PER 1986–90 (h)(pg)(U)	

Minimum wage falls but GDP increases (total = 18)

BRA 1983–86 (h)(N)
BRA 1983–87 (h)(N)
COL 1988–91 (h)(N)
COL 1988–91 (L)(N)
CRI 1971–77 (h)(N)
CRI 1971–77 (L)(R)
GTM 1986–89 (h)(N)
GTM 1986–89 (L)(N)
HND 1986–89 (h)(U)
HND 1986–89 (L)(U)
LKA 1985–90 (h)(N)
LKA 1985–90 (L)(N)
PHL 1971–85 (L)(N)
PHL 1971–88 (L)(N)
TUN 1985–90 (h)(N)
TUN 1985–90 (h)(N)
TUN 1985–90 (L)(N)
TUN 1985–90 (L)(N)

(total = 24)

BRA 1979–89 (h)(U)
BRA 1980–87 (h)(N)
BRA 1980–89 (h)(is)(N)
BRA 1980–89 (h)(N)
BRA 1980–89 (h)(pg)(N)
BRA 1980–89 (h)(R)
BRA 1980–89 (L)(N)
BRA 1980–89 (L)(N)
BRA 1980–89 (L)(pg)(N)
BRA 1981–87 (h)(N)
BRA 1985–89 (h)(N)
BRA 1985–89 (L)(N)
GHA 1987–90 (h)(N)
GTM 1986–89 (h)(pg)(N)
GTM 1986–89 (h)(R)
GTM 1986–89 (h)(U)
GTM 1986–89 (L)(R)
HND 1986–89 (h)(U)
HND 1986–89 (h)(U)
HND 1986–89 (L)(pg)(U)
HND 1986–89 (L)(U)
PHL 1971–85 (h)(N)
PHL 1971–85 (L)(R)
PHL 1971–88 (h)(N)

Minimum wage and GDP increase (total = 64)

BRA 1970–80 (L)(N)
COL 1971–78 (h)(is)(N)
COL 1971–78 (h)(N)
COL 1971–78 (h)(pg)(N)
COL 1971–88 (h)(is)(N)
COL 1971–88 (h)(N)
COL 1978–88 (h)(R)
COL 1980–89 (h)(is)(U)
COL 1980–89 (h)(pg)(U)
COL 1980–89 (h)(U)
COL 1980–89 (L)(is)(U)
COL 1980–89 (L)(pg)(U)
COL 1980–89 (L)(U)
CRI 1971–86 (h)(N)
CRI 1971–86 (h)(pg)(N)
CRI 1983–86 (h)(N)
CRI 1983–86 (h)(pg)(N)
LKA 1963–82 (L)(N)
LKA 1963–82 (L)(pg)(N)
LKA 1973–78 (L)(R)
MAR 1970–84 (h)(is)(N)
MAR 1970–84 (h)(N)
MAR 1970–84 (h)(N)
MAR 1980–85 (L)(R)
MAR 1984–90 (h)(N)
MAR 1984–90 (L)(N)
MAR 1984–90 (L)(N)
MAR 1985–91 (h)(N)
MAR 1985–91 (L)(N)
MUS 1980–87 (h)(N)
MUS 1984–90 (h)(N)
PHL 1985–88 (h)(N)
PHL 1985–88 (L)(N)
PRY 1980–89 (h)(pg)(U)

(total = 16)

BOL 1986–89 (h)(is)(U)
BOL 1986–89 (h)(pg)(U)
BOL 1986–89 (h)(U)
BOL 1986–89 (L)(is)(U)
BOL 1986–89 (L)(pg)(U)
BOL 1986–89 (L)(U)
COL 1978–88 (h)(is)(N)
COL 1978–88 (h)(N)
COL 1978–88 (h)(pg)(N)
CRI 1971–86 (h)(is)(N)
CRI 1983–86 (h)(is)(N)
MAR 1975–80 (L)(R)
PRY 1983–90 (L)(is)(U)
THA 1981–86 (h)(is)(N)
THA 1981–86 (h)(N)
THA 1981–86 (h)(pg)(N)

Table 3A-2. (*continued*)

Total = 180

Item	Poverty falls		Poverty increases	
	Country/period (poverty measure)		Country/period (poverty measure)	
	CRI 1983–86 (L)(R)	PRY 1980–89 (L)(pg)(U)		
	IDN 1984–87 (L)(N)	PRY 1983–90 (h)(is)(U)		
	IDN 1984–87 (L)(R)	PRY 1983–90 (h)(U)		
	IDN 1984–90 (h)(N)	PRY 1983–90 (L)(U)		
	IDN 1984–90 (L)(N)	THA 1975–81 (h)(N)		
	IDN 1987–90 (h)(N)	THA 1976–81 (L)(R)		
	IDN 1990–93 (h)(N)	THA 1981–88 (h)(N)		
	IND 1972–83 (h)(is)(N)	TUN 1975–80 (h)(N)		
	IND 1972–83 (h)(N)	TUN 1975–80 (L)(N)		
	IND 1972–83 (h)(pg)(N)	TUN 1975–80 (L)(R)		
	IND 1977–83 (h)(is)(N)	TUN 1975–80 (L)(U)		
	IND 1977–83 (h)(N)	TUN 1980–85 (h)(N)		
	IND 1977–83 (h)(pg)(N)	TUN 1980–85 (L)(N)		
	IND 1978–83 (L)(R)	TUN 1980–85 (L)(R)		
	LKA 1963–82 (L)(is)(N)	TUN 1980–85 (L)(U)		
		(total = 9)		(total = 7)
Minimum wage increases but GDP falls	CRI 1977–83 (h)(is)(N)	CRI 1981–89 (h)(U)	CRI 1977–83 (h)(N)	VEN 1982–87 (h)(N)
	CRI 1981–89 (h)(is)(N)	CRI 1981–89 (L)(is)(N)	CRI 1977–83 (h)(pg)(N)	VEN 1982–87 (h)(pg)(N)
	CRI 1981–89 (h)(N)	CRI 1981–89 (L)(N)	CRI 1977–83 (L)(R)	VEN 1982–87 (L)(R)
	CRI 1981–89 (h)(pg)(N)	CRI 1981–89 (L)(pg)(N)	VEN 1982–87 (h)(is)(N)	
	CRI 1981–89 (h)(R)			

a. Key to entries follows table 3A-3.

Figure 3A-3. *Poverty Elasticities*[a]

Poverty–per capita income elasticity

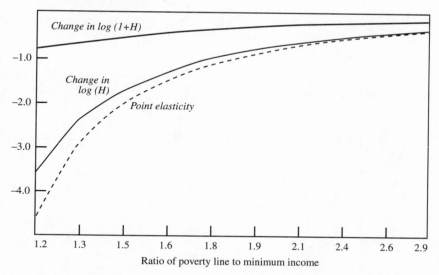

Ratio of poverty line to minimum income

Source: Authors' simulation.
a. Poverty elasticities are sensitive to the poverty line.

total sample includes forty poverty gaps and thirty-nine income gap or shortfall ratios; the remaining 144 measures are headcount ratios. Eighty-three of the observations are based on lower poverty lines (less than $40 per month in 1985 purchasing power parity dollars per person) and the remaining 140 were based on higher poverty lines (above $40). Fifty-three measures came from urban areas, twenty-one from rural areas, and the rest were based on national surveys.

The average interval between observations in a set is almost eight years; the median is seven years. The fact that the majority of the observations are from the 1980s is, in fact, an advantage. In over one-third (eighty-nine) of total observations (including overlapping periods), poverty increases over the interval in question (in 134 cases it decreases). Similarly, real minimum wages rose in about two-thirds of total observations and fell in seventy cases. The implication is that our estimates do not simply represent trends in these two key variables. During normal times, one expects poverty rates to fall and minimum wage rates to rise, but this was not the case during the 1980s. During a period of stable economic growth, real wages are likely to rise while poverty falls, creating

Table 3A-3. *Poverty Data*[a]

Country	Period	Poverty measure	Poverty ratio		Population group	Poverty Line		Source[c]	Unit of ratio	Basis of ratio
			Start of period	End of period		Amount[b]	High or low			
ARG	1980–89	h	3.0	6.4	U	60	H	(1)	H	I
ARG	1980–89	pg	0.6	2.1	U	60	H	(2)	H	I
ARG	1980–89	is	20.0	32.8	U	60	H	(0)	...	...
ARG	1980–89	h	0.2	1.6	U	30	L	(1)	H	I
BGD	1982–89	h	78.8	49.0	N	...	H	(4)	...	...
BGD	1982–89	h	54.1	28.8	N	...	L	(4)	...	...
BGD	1985–88	h	17.0	28.5	N	30.42	L	(5)	P	E
BGD	1985–88	h	74.6	81.6	N	60	H	(5)	P	E
BOL	1986–89	pg	22.8	24.4	U	60	H	(2)	H	I
BOL	1986–89	h	22.5	23.2	U	30	L	(1)	H	I
BOL	1986–89	h	51.1	54.0	U	60	H	(1)	H	I
BOL	1986–89	is	33.8	40.1	U	30	L	(0)		
BOL	1986–89	is	44.6	45.2	U	60	H	(0)		
BOL	1986–89	pg	7.6	9.3	U	30	L	(2)	H	I
BRA	1960–80	pg	23.0	8.6	N	25–60[d]	H	(0)		
BRA	1960–80	is	46.0	41.0	N	25–60[d]	H	(3)	H	I
BRA	1960–80	h	50.0	21.0	N	25–60[d]	H	(3)	H	I
BRA	1970–80	h	47.9	26.2	N	...	L	(4)	...	...
BRA	1979–89	pg	13.7	18.8	N	60	H	(2)	H	I
BRA	1979–89	is	40.2	46.0	N	60	H	(0)		
BRA	1979–89	pg	3.9	7.1	N	30	L	(2)	H	I
BRA	1979–89	h	34.1	40.9	N	60	H	(1)	H	I
BRA	1979–89	is	32.0	38.0	N	30	L	(0)	H	I
BRA	1979–89	h	23.9	33.2	U	60	H	(6)	H	I
BRA	1979–89	h	12.2	18.7	N	30	L	(1)	H	I
BRA	1980–83	h	17.0	30.0	N	...	H	(8)	...	...

BRA	1980–87	h	17.0	24.0	N	…	H	(8)	…	…
BRA	1980–89	h	23.9	33.2	U	60	H	(11)	H	I
BRA	1980–89	h	55.0	63.1	R	60	H	(11)	H	I
BRA	1981–87	h	19.0	24.0	N	25–60[d]	H	(7)	P	I
BRA	1983–86	h	30.0	15.0	N	…	H	(8)	…	…
BRA	1983–87	h	30.0	24.0	N	…	H	(8)	…	…
BRA	1985–89	h	49.6	53.1	N	60	L	(5)	P	I
BRA	1985–89	h	26.7	31.1	N	30,42	H	(5)	P	I
COL	1971–78	is	41.0	24.0	N	25–60[d]	H	(3,7)	P	I
COL	1971–78	pg	41.0	36.0	N	25–60[d]	H	(3,7)	P	I
COL	1971–78	is	16.8	8.6	N	25–60[d]	H	(0)		
COL	1971–88	h	41.0	38.0	N	25–60[d]	H	(3)	P	I
COL	1971–88	pg	41.0	25.0	N	25–60[d]	L	(3)	P	I
COL	1978–88	h	8.6	9.5	R	25–60[d]	H	(0)	P	I
COL	1978–88	h	85.0	68.0	N	…	H	(10)		E
COL	1978–88	is	24.0	25.0	N	25–60[d]	L	(7)	P	I
COL	1978–88	is	36.0	38.0	N	25–60[d]	H	(7)	P	I
COL	1980–89	is	47.7	41.3	U	60	H	(0)		
COL	1980–89	pg	51.7	44.8	U	30	L	(0)	H	I
COL	1980–89	pg	3.1	1.3	U	30	L	(2)	H	I
COL	1980–89	h	6.2	3.3	U	60	H	(2)	H	I
COL	1980–89	h	13.0	8.0	U	60	L	(1)	H	I
COL	1980–89	h	6.0	2.9	N	30	H	(1)	P	I
COL	1988–91	h	23.7	19.7	N	60	L	(5)	P	I
COL	1988–91	h	9.1	6.6	N	30,42	H	(5)	P	I
CRI	1971–77	h	45.0	29.0	R	80	L	(3,7)		E
CRI	1971–77	h	37.0	21.0	N	…	H	(10)		I
CRI	1971–86	pg	18.0	10.6	R	80	L	(0)	P	I
CRI	1971–86	is	40.0	44.0	N	80	H	(3)	P	I
CRI	1971–86	h	45.0	24.0	N	80	H	(3)	P	I
CRI	1977–83	h	21.0	42.0	R	…	L	(10)		E
CRI	1977–83	h	29.0	36.0	N	80	H	(7)	P	I

Table 3A-3. (continued)

Country	Period	Poverty measure	Poverty ratio Start of period	Poverty ratio End of period	Population group	Poverty Line Amount[b]	Poverty Line High or low	Source[c]	Unit of ratio	Basis of ratio
CRI	1977–83	is	44.0	39.0	N	80	H	(7)	P	I
CRI	1977–83	pg	12.8	14.0	N	80	H	(0)	H	I
CRI	1981–89	pg	2.2	0.4	N	30	L	(2)	H	I
CRI	1981–89	h	16.7	3.2	R	60	H	(9)	H	I
CRI	1981–89	pg	5.9	1.3	N	60	H	(2)	H	I
CRI	1981–89	h	13.4	3.4	N	60	H	(1)	H	I
CRI	1981–89	h	9.9	3.5	U	60	H	(1)	P	I
CRI	1981–89	h	61.6	43.0	N	60	H	(5)	H	I
CRI	1981–89	h	5.4	1.1	N	30	L	(1)	P	I
CRI	1981–89	h	33.9	18.8	N	30.42	L	(5)	P	I
CRI	1981–89	is	44.0	38.0	N	60	H	(0)		
CRI	1981–89	is	40.7	36.4	N	30	L	(0)		
CRI	1983–86	is	39.0	44.0	N	80	H	(7)	P	I
CRI	1983–86	h	36.0	24.0	N	80	H	(7)	P	I
CRI	1983–86	h	42.0	25.0	R	..	L	(10)	P	E
CRI	1983–86	pg	14.0	10.6	N	80	H	(0)	H	I
GTM	1986–89	pg	34.6	37.1	N	60	H	(2)	H	I
GTM	1986–89	h	36.6	39.5	N	30	L	(1)	H	I
GTM	1986–89	h	71.8	76.5	R	60	H	(6)	H	I
GTM	1986–89	h	48.7	50.9	U	60	H	(6)	H	I
GTM	1986–89	h	60.0	51.6	N	30.42	L	(5)	P	I
GTM	1986–89	h	82.9	74.9	N	60	H	(5)	P	I
HND	1986–89	h	48.7	54.4	U	60	H	(1)	H	I
HND	1986–89	pg	22.3	24.2	U	60	H	(2)	H	I
HND	1986–89	h	21.6	22.7	U	30	L	(1)	H	I
HND	1986–89	pg	8.3	8.3	U	30	L	(2)	H	I

HND	1986–89	is	38.4	36.6	U	30	L	(0)		
HND	1986–89	is	45.8	44.5	U	60	H	(0)	P	E
IDN	1970–87	h	58.0	17.0	N	25-60ᵈ	H	(3)		
IDN	1970–87	pg	21.5	2.9	N	25-60ᵈ	H	(0)		
IDN	1970–87	is	37.0	17.0	N	25-60ᵈ	H	(3)	P	E
IDN	1980–87	h	44.6	21.6			L	(4)		
IDN	1980–87	h	28.6	17.4			L	(4)		
IDN	1980–90	h	28.6	15.1			L	(4)		
IDN	1984–87	h	14.0	8.3	U		L	(10)	P	E
IDN	1984–87	h	32.6	18.5	R		H	(10)	P	E
IDN	1984–90	h	38.7	21.7	N	30,42	H	(5)	P	E
IDN	1984–90	h	80.9	71.4	N	60	H	(5)		
IDN	1987–90	h	21.6	16.7	N		H	(4)		
IND	1970–89	h	42.5	25.4	N		H	(4)	P	E
IND	1972–83	is	31.0	28.0	N	25-60ᵈ	H	(3)	P	E
IND	1972–83	h	54.0	43.0	N	25-60ᵈ	H	(3)		
IND	1972–83	pg	16.7	12.0	N	25-60ᵈ	H	(7)	P	E
IND	1977–83	h	50.0	43.0	N	25-60ᵈ	H	(7)	P	E
IND	1977–83	is	29.0	28.0	N	25-60ᵈ	L	(0)		
IND	1977–83	pg	14.5	12.0	R		H	(10)	P	E
IND	1978–83	h	52.0	43.0	R	60	L	(5)	P	E
IND	1983–89	h	95.1	94.8	N	30,42	H	(5)	P	E
IND	1983–89	h	73.5	70.9	N		L	(4)		
KOR	1970–80	h	4.8	13.3	N		H	(4)		
KOR	1980–84	h	9.8	4.5	N	25-60ᵈ	L	(0)	P	I
LKA	1963–82	pg	13.0	7.8	N	25-60ᵈ	H	(3)	P	I
LKA	1963–82	h	37.0	27.0	N	25-60ᵈ	H	(3)	P	E
LKA	1963–82	is	35.0	29.0	N		L	(10)		
LKA	1973–78	h	31.6	23.8	R	30,42	L	(5)	P	E
LKA	1985–90	h	30.5	20.5	N	60	H	(5)	P	E
LKA	1985–90	h	77.5	72.5	N		H			
MAR	1970–84	pg	19.8	12.2	N	25-60ᵈ	H	(0)		

Table 3A-3. (continued)

Country	Period	Poverty measure	Poverty ratio Start of period	Poverty ratio End of period	Population group	Poverty Line Amount[b]	Poverty Line High or low	Source[c]	Unit of ratio	Basis of ratio
MAR	1970–84	h	43.0	34.0	N	25-60[d]	H	(3)	P	E
MAR	1970–84	is	46.0	36.0	N	25-60[d]	H	(3)	P	E
MAR	1975–80	h	45.0	45.0	R	…	L	(10)	P	I
MAR	1980–85	h	45.0	32.0	R	…	L	(10)	P	I
MAR	1984–90	h	7.1	1.8	N	30.42	L	(5)	P	E
MAR	1984–90	h	38.3	22.9	N	60	H	(5)	P	E
MAR	1984–90	h	15.9	7.0	N	40	L	(5)	P	E
MAR	1985–91	h	16.5	7.0	N	…	L	(4)	…	…
MAR	1985–91	h	26.0	13.1	N	…	H	(4)	…	…
MEX	1984–89	h	2.5	7.3	N	30	L	(1)	H	I
MEX	1984–89	h	16.6	22.6	N	60	H	(1)	H	I
MUS	1980–87	h	20.3	10.7	N	…	H	(4)	…	…
MUS	1984–90	ph	38.3	22.9	N	…	H	(4)	…	…
MUS	1987–92	h	10.7	5.2	N	…	H	(4)	…	…
MYS	1973–84	h	37.6	19.6	N	…	H	(4)	…	…
MYS	1973–87	is	40.0	24.0	N	118.33	H	(3)	P	I
MYS	1973–87	h	37.0	15.0	N	118.33	H	(3)	P	I
MYS	1973–87	pg	14.8	3.6	N	118.33	H	(0)	…	…
MYS	1973–89	h	13.7	1.7	N	…	L	(4)	…	…
MYS	1984–89	h	19.6	15.5	N	…	H	(4)	…	…
MYS	1984–89	h	34.7	27.5	N	60	H	(5)	P	I
MYS	1984–89	h	12.4	6.4	N	30.42	L	(5)	P	I
PAK	1962–84	pg	21.1	6.0	N	25-60[d]	H	(0)	…	…
PAK	1962–84	h	54.0	23.0	N	25-60[d]	H	(3)	H	I
PAK	1962–84	is	39.0	26.0	N	25-60[d]	H	(3)	H	I
PAK	1979–84	pg	4.0	3.8	N	25-60[d]	H	(0)	…	…

PAK	1979–84	is	19.0	19.0	N	25-60[d]	H	(7)	P	E
PAK	1979–84	h	21.0	20.0	N	25-60[d]	H	(7)	P	E
PAN	1979–89	h	33.0	36.8	R	60	H	(6)	H	I
PAN	1979–89	pg	2.8	6.1	N	30	L	(2)	H	I
PAN	1979–89	pg	10.5	14.3	N	60	H	(2)	H	I
PAN	1979–89	is	33.3	46.2	N	30	L	(0)		
PAN	1979–89	is	37.6	45.0	U	60	H	(0)		
PAN	1979–89	h	26.0	25.9	N	60	H	(6)	H	I
PAN	1979–89	h	27.9	31.8	N	60	L	(1)	H	I
PAN	1979–89	h	8.4	13.2	U	30	L	(1)	H	I
PER	1979–86	h	38.4	52.3	N		L	(10)	P	E
PER	1980–91	h	12.0	17.3	N		L	(4)		
PER	1980–91	h	12.0	22.0	U	30	H	(4)		
PER	1986–90	is	21.2	25.7	N	60	L	(0)	H	E
PER	1986–90	h	31.1	40.5	U	30	L	(1)	H	E
PER	1986–90	h	3.3	10.1	U	30	H	(1)	H	E
PER	1986–90	pg	0.7	2.6	U	60	H	(2)	H	I
PER	1986–90	pg	8.6	13.3	U	60	L	(2)		
PER	1986–90	is	27.7	32.8	R		L	(0)		
PHL	1971–85	h	63.0	63.0	N		H	(10)		
PHL	1971–85	h	35.4	28.1	N		L	(4)		
PHL	1971–85	h	57.0	64.5	N	60	H	(4)	H	E
PHL	1971–88	h	57.0	61.8	N	30.42	L	(4)	H	E
PHL	1971–88	h	35.4	24.1	N	60	H	(4)	H	I
PHL	1985–88	h	72.4	67.1	N	30	H	(5)	H	I
PHL	1985–88	h	34.8	29.7	U	30	L	(5)	P	E
PRY	1983–90	pg	13.1	7.6	U	60	H	(1)	P	E
PRY	1983–90	pg	3.2	0.6	U	30	L	(1)	H	I
PRY	1983–90	h	0.9	0.2	U	30	L	(2)	H	I
PRY	1983–90	pg	3.8	1.8	U	60	H	(2)	H	I
PRY	1983–90	is	28.1	33.3	U	30	L	(0)	H	I

Table 3A-3. (continued)

Country	Period	Poverty measure	Poverty ratio Start of period	Poverty ratio End of period	Population group	Poverty Line Amount[b]	Poverty Line High or low	Source[c]	Unit of ratio	Basis of ratio
PRY	1983–90	is	29.0	23.7	U	60	H	(0)		
SGP	1972–82	pg	11.5	3.3	U	71.7	H	(0)		
SGP	1972–82	is	37.0	33.0	U	71.7	H	(3)	P	E
SGP	1972–82	h	31.0	10.0	U	71.7	H	(3)	P	E
THA	1962–69	h	57.0	39.0	N	...	H	(4)	...	...
THA	1962–86	h	59.0	26.0	N	25-60[d]	H	(3)	H	I
THA	1969–75	h	39.0	30.4	N	...	H	(4)	...	...
THA	1975–81	h	30.4	23.0	N	...	H	(4)	...	...
THA	1976–81	h	32.9	25.8	R	...	L	(10)	P	E
THA	1981–86	pg	5.4	9.1	N	25-60[d]	H	(0)	H	I
THA	1981–86	h	20.0	26.0	N	25-60[d]	H	(7)	H	I
THA	1981–86	is	27.0	35.0	N	25-60[d]	H	(7)	H	I
THA	1981–88	hu	23.0	21.8	N	...	H	(4)	...	...
TUN	1966–75	h	34.0	34.0	U	...	L	(10)	P	E
TUN	1966–75	h	49.0	43.0	R	...	L	(10)	P	E
TUN	1975–80	h	18.0	11.1	N	...	L	(4)	...	...
TUN	1975–80	h	43.0	42.0	R	...	L	(10)	P	E
TUN	1975–80	h	34.0	22.0	U	...	L	(10)	P	E
TUN	1975–80	h	26.5	11.8	N	...	H	(4)	...	...
TUN	1980–85	h	42.0	31.0	R	...	L	(10)	P	E
TUN	1980–85	h	22.0	16.0	U	...	L	(10)	P	E
TUN	1980–85	h	11.1	7.0	N	...	L	(4)	...	...
TUN	1980–85	h	11.8	8.4	N	...	H	(4)	...	...
TUN	1985–90	h	8.4	7.3	N	...	L	(4)	...	...
TUN	1985–90	h	4.6	2.9	N	30.42	L	(5)	P	E
TUN	1985–90	h	7.0	5.7	N	...	L	(4)	...	...

TUN	1985–90	h	25.9	18.8	N	60	H	(5)	P	E
URY	1981–89	pg	0.3	0.2	U	30	L	(2)	H	I
URY	1981–89	is	30.6	26.4	U	60	H	(0)	H	I
URY	1981–89	h	6.2	5.3	U	60	L	(1)	H	I
URY	1981–89	h	1.1	0.7	U	30	L	(1)	H	I
URY	1981–89	is	27.3	28.6	N	30	H	(0)	H	I
URY	1981–89	pg	1.9	1.4	N	60	L	(2)	H	I
VEN	1981–89	h	0.7	3.1	N	30	H	(1)	H	I
VEN	1981–89	h	4.0	12.9	N	60	H	(1)	H	I
VEN	1981–89	is	27.5	32.6	R	60	H	(0)	H	I
VEN	1981–89	h	9.0	23.5	N	60	H	(6)	H	I
VEN	1981–89	pg	0.2	1.1	N	30	L	(2)	H	I
VEN	1981–89	pg	1.1	4.2	N	60	H	(2)	H	I
VEN	1981–89	is	28.6	35.5	N	30	L	(0)	H	I
VEN	1982–87	is	26.0	31.0	N	25–60[d]	H	(7)	H	I
VEN	1982–87	h	12.0	16.0	N	25–60[d]	H	(7)	P	I
VEN	1982–87	pg	3.1	5.0	N	25–60[d]	L	(0)	P	I
VEN	1982–87	h	58.0	71.0	R	…	L	(10)	H	E
VEN	1982–89	h	11.0	22.0	N	…	L	(4)	…	…
VEN	1982–89	h	24.0	31.0	N	…	H	(4)	…	…
VEN	1987–89	h	6.6	20.5	N	30.42	L	(5)	P	I
VEN	1987–89	h	12.3	30.7	N	40	H	(5)	P	I
VEN	1987–89	h	71.0	74.0	R	…	L	(10)	H	E
VEN	1987–89	h	24.9	49.7	N	60	H	(5)	P	I

Sources: (1) Psacharopoulos (1993, table 4.1, p. 58); (2) Psacharopoulos (1993, table 4.2, p. 62); (3) World Bank (1990, table 3.2, p. 41); (4) World Bank's CD-ROM *World Tables 1994*; (5) Chen, Datt, and Ravallion (1992); (6) Psacharopoulos (1993, table 4.5, p. 76); (7) World Bank (1990, table 3.3, p. 43); (8) World Bank (1990, fig. 7.3, p. 110); (9) Psacharopoulos (1993, annex 13); (10) Tabatabai and Fouad (1993); (0) data calculated from other rows according to the following formula: poverty gap equals headcount ratio times income gap.

Note: Not all the data points included in this table could be used because minimum wage data were not available.

a. Key to entries follows this table.

b. U.S. purchasing power parity dollars per month.

c. These studies use different estimation methods to calculate poverty measures; for example, to correct for underreporting. Thus, even though they may be based on the same survey data, their estimates can vary greatly.

d. Specific poverty line is not available, but it falls within the range of U.S. purchasing power parity $25 to $65 per month. For this exercise, we define these as high poverty line observations.

Key to tables 3A-2 and 3A-3:

ARG	Argentina	PR	Puerto Rico
BGD	Bangladesh	PRY	Paraguay
BOL	Bolivia	RWA	Rwanda
BRA	Brazil	SGP	Singapore
CHN	China	TAI	Taiwan
COL	Colombia	THA	Thailand
CRI	Costa Rica	TUN	Tunisia
GHA	Ghana	TZA	Tanzania
GTM	Guatemala	URY	Uruguay
HND	Honduras	VEN	Venezuela
IDN	Indonesia	YUG	Yugoslavia, Federal Republic of
IND	India	E	Welfare measure is expenditure
KOR	Korea, Republic of	H	High poverty line
LKA	Sri Lanka	I	Welfare measure is income
MAR	Morocco	L	Low poverty line
MEX	Mexico	N	National
MUS	Mauritius	P	Individuals
MYS	Malaysia	R	Rural
PAK	Pakistan	U	Urban
PAN	Panama	h	Headcount ratio
PER	Peru	is	Income gap ratio
PHL	Philippines	pg	Poverty gap ratio
POL	Poland		

a potentially spurious correlation over time. But this was certainly not the case during the 1980s—the period from which the majority of our observations are drawn. On the contrary, the 1980s were characterized by high variability in both poverty and real wages. In 89 of our time intervals poverty rose while in 134 cases it fell. Similarly, real minimum wages rose in about two thirds of our observations but fell in 70 cases. This sample of highly variable wage and poverty rates is also useful because minimum wage laws are often considered a "safety-net" policy to protect the poor in periods of economic instability.

The regressions reported in this paper use a number of different samples of poverty changes. The length and country composition of the observations are generally determined by the availability of survey-based poverty measures. We have dropped a few observations because they exhibit unlikely change in poverty, or minimum wages, or both. Some observations have been dropped because large changes in poverty or minimum wages tend to distort the results. The outliers are Venezuela 1987–89 and Peru during the 1980s. Including the outliers increases the effect of minimum wages on poverty but some of the other variables lose significance. Also, because many observations overlap, there are alternative ways to organize the data. The specific sample used for each regression and the complete data set are available from the authors upon request.

References

Bell, Linda. 1995. "The Impact of Minimum Wages in Mexico and Colombia." Policy Research Working Paper 1514. Washington: World Bank.

Card, David, and Alan B. Krueger. 1995. *Myth and Measurement: The Economics of the Minimum Wage.* Princeton University Press.

Cardoso, Eliana. 1992. "Inflation and Poverty." Working Paper 4006. Cambridge, Mass.: National Bureau for Economic Research.

Carruth, Alan A., and Andrew J. Oswald. 1981. "The Determination of Union and Non-Union Wage Rates." *European Economic Review* 16 (2–3): 285–302.

Comisión Económica para América Latina y el Caribe (CEPAL). 1994. *Balance Preliminar de la Economia de America Latina y el Caribe.* Santiago, Chile: United Nations.

Chen, Shaohua, Gaurav Datt, and Martin Ravallion. 1995. "Statistical Addendum to 'Is Poverty Increasing in the Developing World?'" Unpublished paper. Washington: World Bank.

Cicchelli-Velloso, Ricardo. 1990. "Salario Minimo e Taxa de Salarios: O Caso Brasileiro." *Pesquisa e Planejamento Econômico* 20(3): 489–519. Rio de Janeiro.

Cline, William R. 1972. *Potential Effects of Income Redistribution on Economic Growth: Latin America Cases.* Praeger.

———. 1992. "A Note on the Elasticity of Poverty Incidence with Respect to Neutral Growth." Unpublished comment to "Structural Adjustment and the Determinants of Poverty in Latin America," by Samuel Morley. Paper prepared for "Poverty and Inequality in Latin America," Brookings Institution conference, July 1992.

Cole, W. E., and R. D. Sanders. 1985. "Internal Migration and Urban Unemployment in the Third World." *American Economic Review* 75(3): 481–94.

Cox Edwards, Alejandra. 1996. "Labor Market Regulations in Latin America: an Overview." Unpublished paper. Brookings.

de Janvry, Alain, and Elisabeth Sadoulet. 1996. "Growth, Poverty, and Inequality in Latin America: A Causal Analysis, 1970–94." Unpublished paper. University of California, Berkeley.

Fiszbein, Ariel. 1992. "Do Workers in the Informal Sector Benefit from Cuts in the Minimum Wage?" Working Paper 826. Washington: World Bank, Latin America and the Caribbean Regional Office (January).

Foster, James, Joel Greer, and Eric Thorbecke. 1984. "A Class of Decomposable Poverty Measures." *Econometrica* 52 (3):761–66.

Freeman, Richard. 1993. "Labor Market Institutions and Policies: Help or Hindrance to Economic Development?" In *Proceedings of the World Bank*

Annual Conference on Development Economics 1992, 117–44. Washington: International Bank for Reconstruction and Development.

Gramlich, Edward M. 1976. "Impact of Minimum Wages on Other Wages, Employment and Family Incomes." *Brookings Papers on Economic Activity 2:* 409–51.

Hamermesh, Daniel. 1993. *Labor Demand*. Princeton University Press.

International Labour Organization. 1988. "Assessing the Impact of Statutory Minimum Wages in Developing Countries: Four Country Studies." Labour-Management Relations 67. Geneva: International Labour Office.

————. Various years. *Year Book of Labor Statistics*. Geneva: International Labour Office.

Leamer, Edward. 1995. "The Heckscher-Ohlin Model in Theory and Practice." *Princeton Studies in International Finance 77*.

Lipton, Michael. 1995. "Growing Points in Poverty Research: Labor Issues." In *The Poverty Agenda and the ILO Issues for Research and Action*, edited by Gerry Rodgers, 101–68. Geneva: International Labour Office.

Lydall, Harold. 1968. *The Structure of Earnings*. Oxford: Clarendon Press.

Maloney, W. 1996. "The Informal Sector in Mexico." Unpublished paper. University of Illinois, Urbana-Champaign (June).

Márquez, Carlos. 1981. "Nivel del Salario y Dispersión de la Estructura Salarial." *La Economía Mexicana* 3: 45–59. Mexico City.

Mincer, Jacob. 1976. "Unemployment Effects of Minimum Wages." *Journal of Political Economy*. 84(4): S87–104.

Morley, Samuel. 1992. "Structural Adjustment and the Determinants of Poverty in Latin America." Paper prepared for conference on "Poverty and Inequality in Latin America." Brookings, Washington, D.C., July. Revised version to appear in *Coping With Austerity: Poverty and Inequality in Latin America*, edited by Nora C. Lustig. Brookings, 1995.

Psacharopoulos, George. 1993. "Poverty and Income Distribution in Latin America: The Story of the 1980s." Report 27. Washington: World Bank, Latin America and the Caribbean Technical Department Regional Studies Program.

Rama, Martin. 1995. "Do Labor Market Policies and Institutions Matter? The Adjustment Experience in Latin America and the Caribbean." Unpublished paper. Washington: World Bank.

Ravallion, Martin, and M. Huppi. 1989. "Poverty and Undernutrition in Indonesia during the 1980s." Working Paper 286. Washington: World Bank, Agricultural and Rural Development.

Reyes Heroles G. G., Jesús F. 1983. *Política Macroeconómica y Bienestar en México*. Mexico City, Fondo de Cultura Económica.

Rodgers, Gerry, ed. 1995. *New Approaches to Poverty Analysis and Policy*, vol. 1. Geneva: International Labour Office.

Saint-Paul, Gilles. 1994. "Do Labor Market Rigidities Fulfill Distributive Objectives? Searching for the Virtues of the European Model." *IMF Staff Papers* 41(4): 624–42.

Shaheed, Zafar. 1995. "Minimum Wages and Poverty." In *New Approaches to Poverty Analysis and Policy—II: Reducing Poverty through Labour Market*

Policies, edited by José Figueiredo and Zafar Shaheed, 111–32. Geneva: International Institute for Labour Studies.

Tabatabai, Hamid, and Manal Fouad. 1993. *The Incidence of Poverty in Developing Countries: An ILO Compendium of Data.* Geneva: International Labour Office.

Tokman, Victor. 1978. "An Exploration into the Nature of Informal-Formal Sector Relationships." *World Development* 6 (9,10): 1065–75.

Welch, Finis. 1974. "Minimum Wage Legislation in the United States." *Economic Inquiry* 12 (3): 285–318.

Wells, J., and A. Drobny. 1982. "A Distribuição de Renda e o Salário Mínimo no Brasil: Uma Revisao da Literatura Existente." *Pesquisa e Planejamento Econômico,* December. Rio de Janeiro.

Williamson, Jeffrey G. 1989. "Migration and Urbanization." In *The Handbook of Development Economics,* vol. 1, edited by H. Chenery and T. N. Srinivasan. North Holland, Amsterdam.

World Bank. Various years. *World Development Report.* Oxford University Press.

CHAPTER FOUR

Designing an Optimal Unemployment Insurance Program, with Application to Argentina

Hugo A. Hopenhayn
Juan Pablo Nicolini

THE PURPOSE of this chapter is to evaluate the unemployment insurance program introduced in Argentina in 1992. It might seem paradoxical that while the welfare state seems to be in crisis in developed economies, a developing economy should introduce a program that has been widely criticized in recent years. In fact, in several countries, including Spain, Italy, and to some extent the United States, there seems to be agreement that existing programs need rather radical reform. Such criticism is mainly justified by the perverse effects that unemployment insurance has on incentives. For instance, unemployment insurance reduces an unemployed worker's incentive to look for a job. It is also possible that unemployment insurance increases the incentive to participate in the labor force because it increases the private value of being unemployed. In fact, there is clear evidence that the current unemployment insurance programs in the United States and Canada suffer from incentive problems.[1]

1. See Meyer (1990) and Christofides and McKenna (1995).

However, the presence of serious incentive problems does not necessarily mean that the best alternative is to have no insurance at all. Optimal contract theory shows that when there is private information, the optimal contract involves a trade-off between incentives and insurance. In fact, the optimal contract generally provides some insurance and gives up a bit on incentives. In this chapter we illustrate this point by considering one of the most common incentive problems cited in the literature, namely, the pervasive effect that unemployment insurance has on an unemployed worker's incentive to look for a job. We apply modern contract theory to describe the properties of an optimal insurance contract. We also perform a simple numerical exercise to make a preliminary evaluation of Argentina's unemployment insurance program.

In the next section we discuss the evolution of the unemployment rate in Argentina over the past fifteen years and describe the main features of the new unemployment insurance program. We then present our model of an optimal unemployment insurance program and illustrate the intuition behind the general results by solving a simple, two-period version of the model.[2] Finally, we calibrate the model's parameters using Argentinean unemployment data, compute the optimal contract for Argentina, and compare it with the current program.

Unemployment in Argentina

The single most surprising and worrying feature of unemployment in Argentina is the upward trend it has exhibited since the implementation of the stabilization plan in 1991. Figure 4-1 shows the evolution of the unemployment rate together with the rate of growth of GNP for Argentina over the period 1985–94. The unemployment rate exhibits an increasing trend over the whole period, with countercyclical fluctuations during the 1985 and 1989 recessions. It is clear from the figure that the sharp increase in the unemployment rate since 1991 corresponds neither to the overall trend for the period nor to cyclical behavior. Also, the increase is contemporaneous with the highest rates of growth experienced by Argentina for decades.

---

2. This section draws heavily on Hopenhayn and Nicolini (1995), where the complete theoretical model is developed.

Figure 4-1. *GNP Growth and Unemployment, Argentina, 1985–94*

Unemployment   GNP Growth

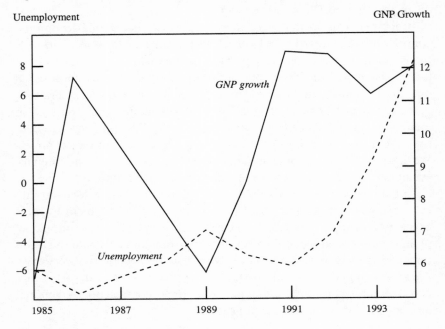

Source: Instituto Nacional de Estadisticas y Censos (various issues).

Figure 4-1 clearly depicts a change in the behavior of the unemployment rate, which could be associated with the structural changes that have accompanied Argentina's move toward a more market-oriented economy. It is far beyond the scope of this paper to discuss the nature of these structural changes and their potential impact on the unemployment rate.[3] However, we would suggest that the implementation of structural reforms leading to a more dynamic economy—in which barriers to entry have been reduced or eliminated and international competition is the rule—has changed the equilibrium natural rate of unemployment. Possibly motivated by these considerations, the Argentinean government recently introduced an unemployment insurance program. In this context, we believe that it is especially important to discuss the properties of an optimal unemployment insurance program.

3. For a very detailed analysis of the recent evolution of unemployment in Argentina, see the chapter by Carola Pessino in this volume.

Unemployment Insurance in Argentina

To qualify for benefits under the unemployment insurance program introduced in 1992, a worker must be legally unemployed (that is, as a result of being fired without fair cause or of the expiration of an employment contract), be registered as unemployed in the Unique System of Labor Registration, and have contributed to the National Fund of Unemployment for at least one year in the three years preceding the termination of employment. An unemployed worker must make sure that all required documentation is kept up to date and is forced to accept any adequate job offered by the Ministry of Labor and Social Security. In the event that any of these requirements are not fulfilled or the unemployed worker takes a temporary job, insurance payments are suspended.

The term of the insurance depends on the prior contribution period. If the worker contributed for more than twelve months but less than twenty-four, the worker will be entitled to four months of insurance. If the worker contributed for more than twenty-four months but less than thirty-six, the worker will be entitled to eight months of insurance. And if the contribution period lasted more than thirty-six months, the worker is entitled to twelve months of insurance.

The monthly benefit depends on the duration of unemployment and on the normal monthly salary during the last six months of employment. For the first four months of unemployment, the benefit is equal to 80 percent of this normal salary. For the next four months it is reduced by 15 percent. And for the last four months it is reduced by an additional 21.5 percent. However, the monthly benefit is subject to maximum and minimum limits.[4] The system is financed by a compulsory 1.5 percent tax on wages and social contributions. By the end of 1994, around 100,000 workers participated, a little less than 10 percent of the pool of unemployed. The system's total budget for 1994 was around 500 million pesos.

The current Argentinean unemployment insurance program has some striking qualitative features. First, the benefit payment decreases with the length of the unemployment, in contrast with most other existing programs, where the benefit is constant for a number of periods and then becomes zero. As we discuss below, this is a qualitative property of the optimal program. In fact, our quantitative analysis shows that the actual

---

4. The maximum monthly benefit was initially set at 400 pesos and the minimum at 150 pesos. These limits were later revised to 350 pesos and 200 pesos, respectively.

program is close to the optimal one along this dimension. Second, the benefits are financed by a tax on income. The optimal program also imposes a reemployment tax. It should be noted, however, that the tax that we consider below *depends* on the duration of unemployment, whereas under the current Argentinean system, the tax is set at a flat rate. In this respect, there is not much difference between the Argentinean program and those of other countries. Our numerical exercise below suggests that it is along this dimension that the existing program could be improved.

The Model

In this section we lay out a simple two-period version of our model and describe the features of an optimal unemployment insurance contract between a risk-averse agent and a risk-neutral principal. As noted above, we develop a more general, infinite-period model with a continuum of possible effort levels elsewhere.[5] The key feature of the environment is that the probability of finding a new job depends on the effort exerted by the agent, which is not observable by the principal. As effort enters negatively in the utility function, a perfectly insured worker has no incentive to put any effort into searching for a job, thus reducing the probability of exiting the state of unemployment. The trade-off between insurance and incentives arises naturally if one assumes that workers are risk averse.

To make these statements precise, assume that the unemployed worker's utility function is

$$(4\text{-}1) \qquad U(b_0) - a + \beta p(a)U(w - \tau) + \beta(1 - p(a))U(b_1),$$

where b_t is the unemployment benefit paid at period t, τ is the tax paid by the worker on reemployment, a is the effort level the worker chooses at period zero, $p(a)$ is the probability of finding a job in the second period as a function of the first period effort level, and β is the discount factor. Since the worker is assumed to be risk averse, the function U is assumed to be concave. Note that we evaluate utility in the unemployed state by using the benefit, which means that we do not allow for a credit market in which agents could borrow or lend. This assumption is standard

5. Hopenhayn and Nicolini (1995).

in the repeated moral hazard literature and makes the analysis much more tractable.[6] Therefore, once the unemployment contract is specified, the only variable for the unemployed worker to choose is the effort level. To further simplify the analysis, we assume that there are only two possible effort levels: zero and one, such that the probability of finding a job is zero if the effort level is zero and is $\rho \in (0, 1)$ if the effort level is one.

Consider now the optimal provision of unemployment insurance, assuming, as is standard in the literature, that the principal is risk neutral. If the effort level is observable, the solution is simple. The risk-neutral party faces all the risk and the risk-averse agent (the unemployed worker) is fully insured.[7] The unemployed worker receives the benefit *conditional* on choosing an effort level equal to one. In this case, there are no incentive problems.

A more interesting case occurs when the effort level cannot be observed by the principal. There are several justifications for this assumption, including arbitrarily high costs of monitoring. Indeed, as we mention above, probably the most common criticism of existing unemployment insurance programs is their negative effect on the incentives of the unemployed to look for jobs. If one could condition the benefit payment to a given effort level, this criticism would lose its substance.

With asymmetric information, the unemployment benefit cannot be made contingent on a specific effort level. Thus for any given sequence of benefits, the effort level is the unemployed worker's choice. The problem facing the unemployed worker in this case is very simple. The effort level will be one if

$$(4\text{-}2) \quad U(b_0) - 1 + \beta \rho U(w - \tau) + \beta(1 - \rho)U(b_1)$$
$$\geq U(b_0) + \beta U(b_1)$$

and zero otherwise. Restriction 4-2 says that the unemployed worker chooses to look for a job only if the utility is higher than that of not looking for a job. This incentive compatibility constraint can be written as

$$(4\text{-}3) \qquad \beta \rho [U(w - \tau) - U(b_1)] \geq 1,$$

which means that the benefit of looking for a job (the present value of the expected increase in utility if a job is found) is larger than the cost (one unit of utility). Obviously, for this constraint to be satisfied, con-

---

6. In Hopenhayn and Nicolini (1995) we do consider a particular form of self-borrowing.
7. In the solution below, we verify that this is indeed the case.

sumption when employed must be larger than consumption when unemployed. In determining the optimal contract, one must take account
of constraint 4-3 and, as we show, full insurance is no longer optimal in
this case.

One can formally consider the optimal unemployment insurance contract as that which maximizes the utility of the unemployed worker subject to two constraints: first, that the expected transfer to the agent is not
higher than the total budget allocated to the program; and second, that
it is in the best interests of the worker to choose an effort level equal to
one—the incentive compatibility constraint. This is to maximize equation
4-1 subject to constraints 4-3 and

$$(4\text{-}4) \qquad\qquad b_0 + \beta(1 - p)b_1 \le \beta\rho\tau + K,$$

where K is the total budget allocated to the unemployment insurance
program, which could be zero if the program is self-financed. As the
objective function is concave and the constraints are linear, this optimum
problem is well defined and a unique solution must satisfy the following
first-order conditions:

$$(4\text{-}5) \qquad\qquad U'(b_0) = \lambda,$$

$$(4\text{-}6) \qquad U'(b_1) = \lambda + \phi\,[p/(1 - p)]\,U'(b_1), \text{ and}$$

$$(4\text{-}7) \qquad U'(w - \tau) = \lambda - \phi\,U'(w - \tau),$$

where λ and ϕ are the Lagrange multipliers of restrictions 4-3 and 4-4.
Incidentally, note that in the perfect information case, constraint 4-3
should not be imposed, which, in the first-order conditions, amounts to
assuming that ϕ is equal to zero. Thus the first-order conditions imply
that the marginal utility of consumption should be the same in all states,
implying that the risk-averse agent is fully insured.

Note that by subtracting equation 4-6 from equation 4-7 one obtains

$$U'(w - \tau) - U'(b_1) = -\phi[U'(w - \tau) + [p/(1 - p)]\,U'(b_1)].$$

But since the incentive compatibility constraint implies that $w - \tau$ has
to be larger than b_1, the left-hand side of this equation is negative. The
term in brackets of the right-hand side is positive, so the multiplier ϕ has
to be positive. But from equations 4-5 and 4-6 one obtains

$$U'(b_1) = U'(b_0) + \phi\,[p/(1 - p)]\,U'(b_1),$$

and therefore

$$U'(b_1) > U'(b_0),$$

which means that the unemployment benefit decreases over time. Hence the optimal contract does not fully insure the worker. The intuition of this result, which extends to infinite-period versions of the model, is that as the effort is not observable, the contract has to ensure that the worker has incentives to choose the right level of effort. The contract provides such incentives by promising a prize—higher consumption—if the worker finds a job and a penalty—lower consumption—if the worker does not find a job. Note that since consumption in the second period does depend on the employment state, the risk-averse worker will be exposed to "some" risk.

In this two-period, two-effort-level case, the solution is simple. The optimal contract has the worker facing the minimum risk necessary to induce the higher effort level. This case highlights the trade-off between incentives and insurance. The principal would prefer to insure the agent fully, because that maximizes utility for a given budget. However, if the worker is "overinsured"—relative to the optimal contract—the worker will choose zero effort. If the worker is "underinsured," it would be possible to increase the worker's insurance marginally and still induce the worker to choose an effort level equal to one. In this case, the presence of incentive problems does not change the optimal effort level. However, when there are several feasible effort levels, the presence of incentive problems may also affect the optimal effort level relative to the optimal contract in the presence of full information.

The solution to this two-period version of the model highlights the features of an optimal unemployment insurance program. Consider a problem similar to that discussed above, but with a continuum of effort levels. On the one hand, if the unemployed is fully insured, there is no private benefit to increasing the effort put into a job search, so the worker will exert no effort. On the other hand, in order to maximize the effort level, one could eliminate unemployment insurance.[8] Thus more insurance means lower incentives and, eventually, higher equilibrium unemployment rates.[9] To sustain that unemployment insurance programs

8. If one allows for negative consumption or assumes that the worker has some other source of income, subjecting the unemployed to a tax on that source would also increase the effort level.

9. Strictly speaking, as this is not a general equilibrium model, one cannot reach any conclusion regarding equilibrium unemployment rates. However, if it is true in a general equilibrium model that all unemployed workers choose lower effort levels, and if there are

should be eliminated, one must show that the optimal solution to the trade-off between incentives and insurance is a corner solution, in which there is no insurance at all.

An obvious way to extend the model considered here is to increase the number of periods. In this way, one could characterize the whole sequence of benefits. In fact, using infinitely repeated versions of the above model, it is possible to show that the whole sequence of benefits should decrease with duration of unemployment. The intuition of the general result is the same as that given above. In order to provide incentives to choose the appropriate level of effort, the utility next period should be higher if the worker finds a job. Applying this argument recursively, one can show that the utility of an unemployed worker has to be lower, the longer the worker has been unemployed. The obvious way to reduce utility over time is to reduce benefit payments over time.

One policy variable that we have not yet discussed is the tax τ. This is an income tax levied on previously unemployed workers who find a job. The two-period version of the model cannot provide insights on the relationship between the magnitude of this tax and the length of a spell of unemployment. However, it is possible to show that in an infinite-period version of the model, the tax should be increased with the length of unemployment.[10] Thus the longer a worker remains unemployed, the higher the tax that the worker should pay on finding a job. The logic behind this result is similar to that behind the result that the sequence of benefits should be decreasing. In order to give appropriate incentives, the utility that the unemployed worker will have tomorrow if the worker finds a job must be higher than the utility to the worker of not finding a job. In the model above, the only way to make this the case is by paying a lower benefit tomorrow, which is the last period. However, in a multi-period environment, there are two ways to reduce utility tomorrow if the worker remains unemployed. One is by providing a lower benefit; the other is by imposing a higher reemployment tax. The optimal contract uses both expedients.

The foregoing analysis suggests that there are two dimensions along which existing unemployment insurance contracts could be improved: first, by decreasing benefit payments over time; and second, by imposing a reemployment tax that is contingent on the duration of unemployment.

no search externalities, it is natural to think that equilibrium unemployment should rise when unemployed workers have more insurance.

10. For details, see Hopenhayn and Nicolini (1995).

In the next section, we quantify each of these effects for the Argentinean case. So far, we have kept the model simple in order to sharpen the discussion of the theoretical results; the generalization to an infinite number of periods and a continuum of effort levels requires a rather too technical language. However, to compute the solution and compare it with the existing unemployment insurance program, one has to use a more realistic environment. Therefore in the following section we use the more general model.

Quantitative Analysis

In this section we solve numerically a parameterized version of the more general model, which allows for a continuum of possible effort levels and for infinite periods. We also provide some rough estimates of the potential advantage of the optimal unemployment insurance contract relative to the current program in Argentina. We first obtain estimates of the hazard rates for Argentina using data from the Encuesta Permanente de Hogares, a twice-yearly survey conducted by the National Institute for Statistics and the Census.[11] We then use these estimates to assign values to the parameters of the hazard function. Finally, we solve the optimal unemployment insurance contract to obtain estimates of the budget reductions that could be achieved for the current programs through the implementation of the optimal contract. This method is very rough, but the results are suggestive about the orders of magnitude of the potential gains.

Specifically, our procedure is as follows:

—We estimate hazard rates, using data on the distribution of unemployed workers by duration of unemployment.

—We solve our model, imposing an unemployment insurance contract similar to the current Argentinean program.

—We assign parameter values, using the theoretical solution of our model and the estimates for hazard rates.

—We use these values to solve for the optimal unemployment insurance contract.

---

11. Argentina, Instituto Nacional de Estadisticas y Censos (various issues). Surveys are conducted each May and October.

—We estimate the reduction in cost to be obtained by adopting the optimal plan without a reemployment tax, and the additional gain that would be obtained by imposing such a tax.

Estimation

In order to obtain a rough approximation to the gains of implementing the optimal contract in Argentina, we use Argentinean data on the duration of unemployment to estimate hazard rates. Ideally, one should use direct data on hazard rates, obtained from the records of the unemployment insurance program itself. However, given that the current program has only been operative for a couple of years and that the amount of unemployed workers receiving benefits is still very low relative to the pool of unemployed (less than 10 percent), such a sample could be severely biased.

The available data comprise the distribution of unemployed workers as a function of the duration of the current spell of unemployment. According to our theory, this distribution (and the corresponding hazard rates) does depend on the existing unemployment insurance. We show elsewhere that under the current U.S. unemployment insurance program, which pays a fixed benefit for a given number of periods, hazard rates should increase with the duration of unemployment.[12] This is a very intuitive result: as the final period of coverage gets closer, the incentives to look for a job increase, and therefore the probability of finding a job also increases.

When estimating the parameters of the hazard function, one must take the existing unemployment insurance into account. However, our sample for Argentina includes observations for periods in which there was no insurance; and for those periods in which there was insurance, the coverage was extremely low. Therefore we believe that it is a better approximation to estimate the hazard rates under the assumption that unemployed workers had no insurance available to them during the sample period. In this case, the solution of the model is stationary. The agent's problem is

$$V^u = \max[U(0) - a + \beta V^u + \beta \, p(a) \, (V^e - V^u)],$$

where V^e is the utility of the worker if the worker finds a job, which, normalizing the wage to 100, is given by

12. Hopenhayn and Nicolini (1995).

Figure 4-2. *Distribution of Unemployed Workers by Length of Unemployment, Argentina, 1991–94: October Survey*

Percent

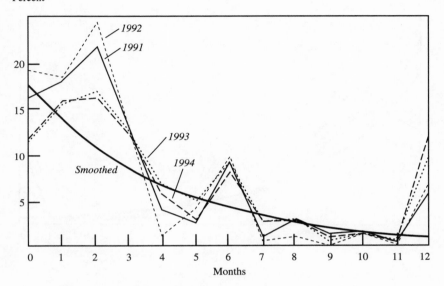

Source: Argentina, Instituto Nacional de Estadisticas y Censos (various issues).

$$V^e = U(100)/(1 - \beta).$$

V^u is the utility if the worker is still unemployed and a is the effort level. The first-order condition for this problem is

(4-8) $$\beta p'(a)(V^e - V^u) = 1,$$

where V^u is defined as

(4-9) $$V^u = [U(0) - a + \beta V^u + \beta p(a)(V^e - V^u)].$$

Equations 4-8 and 4-9 define the *stationary* values for the effort and the utility of being unemployed. Thus if there is no insurance, our model predicts a hazard that is independent of the number of weeks spent unemployed.

Figure 4-2 presents the distribution of unemployed workers by number of months of unemployment, taken from the October surveys of the Encuesta Permanente de Hogares for the period 1991–94. Figure 4-3 presents the corresponding distribution for the May surveys over the

Figure 4-3. *Distribution of Unemployed Workers by Length of Unemployment, Argentina, 1991–95: May Survey*

Percent

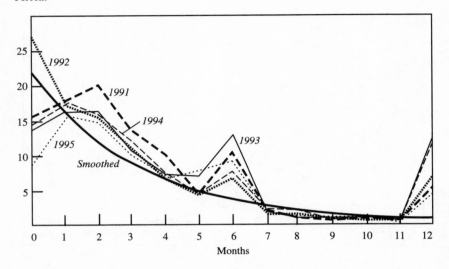

Source: Argentina, Instituto Nacional de Estadisticas y Censos (various issues).

period 1991–95. We would like to interpret these data as a stationary distribution in order to derive the hazard rates. However, the nonmonotonicity of the series indicates a very strong seasonal pattern, inconsistent with constant rates of entry and exit to the unemployed state. As our model does not take seasonal factors into account, it is not able to capture the pattern.[13]

We circumvent this problem in a rather crude way, by adjusting a log-linear function to obtain an ever decreasing sequence of the form

$$h_1 = h_0 e^{-\rho t} \epsilon_1,$$

such that

$$\ln h_1 = \ln h_0 - \rho t + \ln \epsilon_1.$$

13. One could introduce a seasonal movement in the function that relates effort to the probability of finding a job, but it would significantly complicate the analysis.

Note that the log-linear structure *imposes* a constant hazard rate on the curve and allows one to estimate its value.[14] As we show below, the model fits the observations reasonably well, suggesting that the assumption of a constant hazard model is not at odds with the observations.

For the average of the May surveys, a reasonable number for the hazard rate is around 0.3, while a value for ρ close to 0.2 seems consistent with the October surveys.[15] Figures 4-2 and 4-3 plot the adjusted curve and the observed series for the respective surveys to illustrate the quality of the fit. Despite the seasonality, the fitted curves resemble the trends of the series reasonably well.

A lower value for the hazard rate means that being unemployed is a more serious problem, and thus that our calculations are likely to be more important. As our purpose is to illustrate the potential effects of introducing the optimal contract, we prefer to be conservative and use the higher value, that of the May survey. We therefore take 0.3 as the hazard rate in Argentina.

Calibration

We assume that the utility function is of the form[16]

$$U(c) = c^{1-\sigma}/(1 - \sigma).$$

For the hazard function, we use the exponential distribution

$$p(a) = 1 - e^{-ra},$$

with parameter r multiplicative in the search effort.

We need to assign values to three parameters: β, σ, and r. Our time period is one month, which corresponds to the unit time period in the Encuesta Permanente de Hogares. We set β equal to 0.996, which is consistent with a yearly discount factor of 0.95. We set the value of σ to 0.5, giving an intermediate degree of risk aversion. This number may seem small relative to that used in the macroeconomic literature. Note,

14. A more sophisticated and, econometrically, more satisfactory procedure would be to estimate the hazard rates using available data and test the hypothesis of constant hazard rates. Given that our main objective is to illustrate the potential gains of explicitly addressing the problem of incentives and the quality of the data, we choose this simpler route.

15. Seasonality might also explain why the numbers for October and May are different. There is no reason to believe that either May or October presents decent approximations to the yearly value, but there is no other source of information with which to check this.

16. This utility function is widely used in the literature.

Table 4-1. *Simulation of an Optimal Unemployment Insurance Contract for Argentina*

Month	Benefit with tax[a]	Reemployment tax[b]	Benefit without tax[a]
1	99.77	−0.87	111.6
2	99.34	−0.48	92.3
3	98.98	−0.08	77.6
4	98.59	0.30	66.3
5	98.21	0.69	57.3
6	97.81	1.08	50.2
8	97.03	1.86	39.6
10	96.25	2.65	32.5
12	95.46	3.43	27.2
14	94.68	4.21	23.1
16	93.89	4.99	19.8
18	93.11	5.78	17.1

Source: Authors' model, as described in text.
a. Relative to prior wage, $w = 100$.
b. Percent.

however, that we are using monthly data and the elasticity of substitution between weekly consumption is most probably larger than that between quarterly consumption. The rationale for using a smaller number hinges on this assumption. A higher value of σ implies a greater degree of risk aversion, increasing the pertinence of the insurance mechanism, so to use a lower value is once again the conservative route.[17] Finally, to assign a value for r we solve the model using the upper bound (0.3) obtained in the estimation discussed above. The wage, w, is normalized to 100.

Simulation

We use the parameter values obtained above to solve the model numerically. Table 4-1 reports the evolution of the optimal unemployment insurance contract for a worker who starts with a utility level equal to that attained by an employed worker. We present the results for the general case, in which the principal can impose a reemployment tax, and the restricted case in which such a tax cannot be used as a policy instrument (that is, it is always set equal to zero).

The first column gives the number of months since the contract has started. The second column gives the replacement ratio, or the benefit paid. As the wage is normalized to 100, this could be interpreted as the

17. We explore the sensitivity of the results to higher values of σ for the U.S. economy in Hopenhayn and Nicolini (1995).

percentage of the preunemployment wage. Note that the optimal benefit payment decreases with the duration of unemployment. The numbers may seem very large, especially relative to the current insurance program, which starts at benefits at 85 percent of the prior wage. This is because we are solving for the optimal contract that promises the unemployed the same utility as the employed worker. As the model solves for the whole Pareto frontier, one can obtain the optimal contract for any utility; it might be of particular interest to solve for the utility level at which the program budget is zero. In any case, the purpose of the exercise is to illustrate the behavior of the variables over time.

The third column presents the tax on wages after the unemployed worker finds a job, as a function of the number of periods that the prior unemployment lasted. Note that the tax is used in the optimal contract and that it decreases with the length of unemployment. Also, since the tax can be negative, for some utility levels it makes sense to *subsidize* unemployed workers who find a job quickly.[18] Finally, the fourth column reports the optimal sequence of payments when the government does not use the reemployment tax. Note that this sequence also decreases, although more dramatically. After a year and a half of unemployment, under the optimal contract with the tax the unemployed worker still receives more than 90 percent of the prior wage, whereas under the optimal contract without the tax, the unemployed worker receives 17 percent. The intuition of this result is clear. As the government cannot penalize unemployed workers by increasing future taxes in the event that they find a job, all the incentives to look for a job must derive from reductions in the benefit over time. Consequently, the insurance vanishes much more quickly.

One can use the calibrated model to compute the utility attained by the agent under the current contract. Plugging this number into the value function for the principal, one obtains the minimum cost of providing that same utility level under the optimal contract with the reemployment tax and under the optimal contract without the tax. Relative to the cost of the current program in Argentina, normalized to 100, the program budget under the optimal contract without the tax is 96.2, and that under the optimal contract with the tax is 83.6. This represents savings of almost 17 percent under the optimal contract described in this chapter, and

18. Subsidizing workers who leave the unemployment pool is a policy that has recently received attention in the United States.

Figure 4-4. *Hazard Rates under Optimal Unemployment Insurance Contract and Current Argentinean Program*

Hazard rates

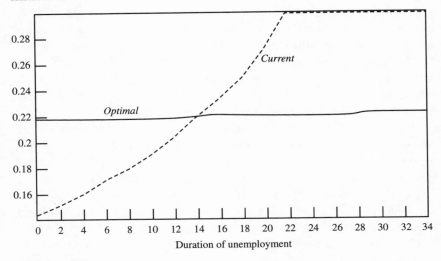

Source: Authors' model, as described in text.

moderate savings (slightly less than 4 percent) under the optimal contract without the tax. These results suggest that the step-wise decreasing sequence of benefits in Argentina's current unemployment insurance program approximates the optimal contract very well. However, they also suggest that adopting a reemployment tax that is contingent on the duration of unemployment could yield important budget savings.

The optimal contract might be cheaper than the current program for one of two reasons. On one hand, the optimal contract might provide better incentives and thus increase the probability of exiting unemployment. On the other hand, the optimal contract might provide better insurance and thus reduce the expected transfer to the unemployed. The contract optimizes the trade-off between incentives and insurance, whereas the current contract could either be providing too much insurance (and therefore giving very little incentive) or providing too little insurance (and therefore giving too much incentive).

A partial answer to the question can be found in figure 4-4, which plots the hazard rate as a function of the duration of unemployment under the optimal contract with the tax and under the current contract.

Figure 4-5. *Probability of Unemployment over Time under Optimal Unemployment Insurance Contract and Current Argentinean Program*

Probability

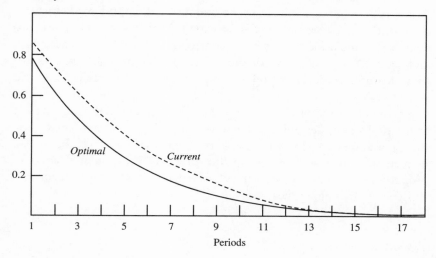

Periods

Source: Authors' model, as described in text.

The optimal contract provides better incentives to look for a job in the early stages of unemployment, but the current contract provides better incentives in later stages. This is because the current contract provides too much insurance at the beginning, but no insurance after a number of periods. Which effect dominates? The answer can be found in figure 4-5, which plots the probability of being unemployed after a given number of periods under the current and under the optimal contracts. In fact, the first effect dominates and the probability of finding a job is higher under the optimal contract for the most relevant range. Therefore in this case substituting the optimal contract for the current contract improves welfare, and it also reduces the unemployment rate.

However, this need not be so in general. The implementation of the optimal contract does not have clear implications for the duration of unemployment, and therefore the potential effects on the equilibrium unemployment rate are not clear. The reason is that the optimal contract maximizes the utility of risk-averse workers; it does not minimize the unemployment rate.

Finally, it is worth pointing out the limitations of our analysis. First, the theoretical model ignores other incentive problems that undoubtedly arise in this context. In particular, adverse selection problems are bound to be important, given the heterogeneity of the labor force. Second, the workers in the model are infinitely long-lived, yet it is clear that a mandatory retirement age will affect the optimal contract of a worker who is close to that age in a way that is not captured by the model. Third, we assume that the principal has direct control over the agent's consumption and hence we do not allow for the presence of credit markets. Most of these features could be introduced into the model to obtain numerical solutions.

The numbers in this chapter should not be considered the final answer to the problem of designing unemployment policy in Argentina. Rather, they should be viewed as an example of how modern contract theory can help in this endeavor, and as an illustration of the potential gains to properly addressing the problem of incentives. We strongly encourage further research along these lines.

Conclusions

In this paper we apply optimal dynamic contract theory with moral hazard to characterize an optimal unemployment insurance policy for Argentina. The theory is designed to address some of the adverse incentive effects for which current unemployment insurance programs in several countries have been criticized. Our study is motivated, on the one hand, by the significant change in the behavior of the unemployment rate in Argentina over the past four years, and by the government's recent decision to launch an unemployment insurance program, on the other. We show that modern contract theory can be of great use in policy design by offering clear answers to questions in a coherent framework. We calibrate the model with Argentinean data and solve the model numerically. We then use the numerical solution to characterize the optimal contract and to approximate the reduction in the budget implied by the adoption of this contract. Our estimates indicate that around 17 percent of the budget of the current program in Argentina could be saved under the optimal policy.

References

Christofides, L., and C. McKenna. 1995. "Unemployment Insurance and Moral Hazard in Employment." *Economics Letters* 49(2): 205–10.

Hopenhayn, Hugo A., and Juan Pablo Nicolini. 1995. "Optimal Unemployment Insurance and Employment History." Unpublished paper. Universitat Pompeu Fabra.

Meyer, B. 1990. "Unemployment Insurance and Unemployment Spells." *Econometrica* 58 (2): 757–82.

Instituto Nacional de Estadisticas y Censos. Various years. "Encuesta Permanente de Hogares." Argentina.

Part Two

INSTITUTIONS, REGULATIONS, AND LABOR MARKET REFORM IN LATIN AMERICA

CHAPTER FIVE

Labor Market Regulation in Latin America: An Overview

Alejandra Cox Edwards

AFTER MORE THAN three decades of inward-oriented policies and heavy state intervention, in the 1980s many Latin American countries initiated a series of market-oriented reforms to stabilize their economies and reestablish economic growth. These reforms are redefining the role of the state, as it pulls back from the production of goods and delivery of services and from intervention in the setting of prices and the allocation of investment to focus on budgetary constraints, monetary stability, and additional policy instruments to improve the functioning of markets. This chapter examines the implications of these reforms for labor policy.

As early as the 1920s, many Latin American governments introduced legislation that guaranteed workers' rights and at the same time established public controls directed toward the resolution of labor conflicts. The direct involvement of the government in collective bargaining encouraged labor organizations to line up with political parties and, through legislative changes, formal sector employees obtained a number of guarantees, the most important being job security. These conditions underwent major transformation in the 1970s, when a number of countries were faced with military dictatorships. In this context, the traditional cooperation between political leaders and the union movement was not only cut; in many cases, unions were banned. With the turn to democracy in the 1980s, unions were reestablished as political organizations, but this time in a rapidly changing economic environment marked by trade liberalization.

Economic reforms and increased domestic and international market competition for goods and services have challenged the traditional corporatist pattern of relations between labor and the state. This is evident in Mexico, for example, where the Federation of Unions of Goods and Services broke with the Mexican Confederation of Workers in April 1996. This process, although incipient in the region, is highly influenced by legislation that imposes standard contracts. The acceptance of market discipline in industrial relations requires the development of a new type of unionism, that is independent of state controls, is sustained by the voluntary support of individual workers, and can offer gains from collective bargaining in a competitive environment.

While most governments in the region have reconsidered their regulatory role in the labor market, only a few have introduced broad changes. Chile, Colombia, and Peru have lowered labor taxes (as they reformed their social security systems), reduced the costs (or procedure-related uncertainties) of dismissals, made union representation contestable, extended the freedom to organize unions, and reformed labor codes to internalize the costs of labor disputes, confining such costs to the parties directly involved. Peru has replaced its traditional tripartite negotiation procedure with "final offer" arbitration. Although it is difficult to isolate the labor market impact of these reforms from those of trade liberalization or stabilization, labor reforms have been followed by improved labor market performance. Peru has seen significant growth in labor demand in the 1990s, of the order of 3.6 percent annually.[1] Chile experienced an average rate of growth in employment of 4.5 percent between 1983 and 1994.[2] In Colombia, while unemployment reached a historical low of 8 percent in 1994, there has not been such fast growth in labor demand. But further analysis reveals a significant labor demand effect associated with Colombia's labor reforms. Eduardo Lora and Marta Henao report evidence of structural change in the output-employment elasticity after the labor reforms. They argue that this effect helped labor market performance, in spite of a sharp increase in the capital-to-output ratio, associated with declining user costs of capital, between 1992 and 1994:

1. Yamada (1995).
2. Cortazar (1995).

"had the coefficients remained at their previous levels, labor demand would have been up to 28 percent smaller than it actually was."[3]

To redirect labor policy toward the enhancement of employment opportunities, payroll taxes have to be reduced and market forces must work their way into negotiations over compensation and working conditions. Yet neither of these policy reforms is sufficient. Their ultimate impact on employment and workers' well-being also depends on other factors that affect the level of economic activity, such as trade orientation and macroeconomic stability.

This chapter gives special attention to four areas of direct intervention by government in the labor market: wage determination, including collective bargaining and dispute resolution; job security legislation; mandatory contributions to social security and other social programs; and subsidies for workers' training. The chapter also discusses alternative policy instruments with which to address the alleviation of poverty. This is an important complement to the analysis of labor policies, because in the period 1960–80, labor market intervention was promoted as a means of reducing poverty and inequality. Therefore, in policy discussions, attempts to redirect labor policy toward the enhancement of employment opportunities have typically been challenged with an important question: what policy instruments are available to reduce poverty and improve income distribution?

Current Labor Market Interventions and the Road to Reform

Basic labor standards, broadly defined, typically include the freedom to organize, the prohibition of child labor, and safety provisions. Additional regulations of general application include a minimum wage, a normal work schedule with an overtime premium, and days of rest, including maternity-related leave. Labor policy includes all of the above, along with government mandates on contributions to social security programs, support for the collection and dissemination of labor-related information, special programs for employment creation, and subsidies toward workers' training.

In most countries of the Latin American and Caribbean region, basic working standards include a minimum working age, safety standards, a

3. Lora and Henao (1995, p. 15).

minimum wage, a normal work schedule, and an overtime premium. But current labor legislation goes much further, establishing detailed conditions for labor contracts for all workers in the economy; for example, limits to temporary contracts, legal barriers to employer-initiated dismissal, employer liability in the case of dismissal, vacation days, maternity leave, and employer obligation to provide meals, transportation, and accommodation. While it is true that statutory provisions can improve an employed worker's well-being, in reality they apply only to those who hold formal jobs—and the creation of a formal job is a voluntary decision that takes into account costs and benefits.

In essence, legal provisions alone cannot improve the options that the majority of workers face. Labor policy can, however, improve the functioning of labor markets, by assigning property rights to representation in collective bargaining, assigning limited liabilities to internalize potential externalities (for example, those associated with accidents on the job), providing information, and so forth. But legal provisions have been used to impose specific practices, often in response to international pressure to address social problems, rather than in an effort to improve the working of the domestic labor market.

Unfortunately, the good intentions of the international community have often been hijacked by anticompetitive interests. It is clear that when higher labor standards are proposed, the interests of workers who already enjoy high standards are protected. Therefore, recognizing that access to paid employment is an important vehicle for escaping poverty, and in the name of enhancing the role and scope of the labor market, Latin American governments should act as watchdogs and resist the pressure to raise labor standards before market realities allow. This strategy calls for the revision of current labor statutes wherever they grant privileges to a few and ignore the poor conditions of the many.

Government and Wage-Setting Mechanisms

Government policy can affect the setting of wages directly, through the indexation system—which applies to countries with a tradition of inflation—and minimum wages; and indirectly, through intervention in the resolution of labor conflicts. With a few exceptions, minimum wages declined throughout the region during the 1980s and have largely become nonbinding.[4] The emphasis on fiscal discipline and inflation control in

4. See Cox Edwards (1991). This does not mean that (potential) hikes in minimum

the 1990s has reduced the role of indexation. In this environment of price stability, the setting of real wages and the response of these wages to labor market conditions takes on greater importance.

However, governments continue to influence the wage-setting mechanism through the rules that govern conflict resolution systems. Table 5-1 highlights the most important features of dispute resolution mechanisms in ten Latin American countries as of May 1992. In Argentina, for example, only those organizations with union representation (*personalidad gremial*) can speak for workers in collective negotiations; representation is the task of the largest organization in a particular region, or profession, or both.[5] The agreements (*convenios*) that these organizations reach affect all represented workers and extend to the corresponding region, profession, or both. Eight unions have the power to sign such *convenios*, including those in banking, commerce, construction, agriculture, and the stock market. The law states that union contributions determined by a *convenio* are required from all workers covered by the agreement and that they must be deducted by employers. This means that while union affiliation is optional, contributions to the union movement can be obligatory for nonunion workers. Moreover, the agreements apply to workers independent of their participation or representation in the negotiation process, or in the election of leaders (the principle of *erga omnes*).

In many developing countries the state has promoted a bureaucratic union structure and, as a result, labor conflicts have become confrontations with the public authorities. Nowhere is this situation more evident than in Brazil during the period of military control (1964–85). Salvador Sandoval uses a variety of sources, including his own compilation of newspaper reports, to document strike activity in Brazil from 1945 to 1989.[6] He finds a recurring pattern of a heightening of labor strikes (for example, 1945–46, 1961–63, and 1978–79) followed by government repression, as evidenced by a substantial increase in the number of min-

---

wages will have no effects in the future, nor does it mean that minimum wages have no distortionary impact today. Even low minimum wages can have an impact on efficiency, especially if they are complemented by other required compensation. In Ecuador, for example, basic wages are set for more than one hundred occupations and a number of components are added to the basic salary. As a result of these additions, which include four extra salaries per year, basic wages are set at just a small proportion of the minimum monthly pay established by law. This policy creates unnecessary administrative costs and impedes direct negotiations over working conditions.

5. See Cox Edwards (1996).
6. Sandoval (1993).

Table 5-1. *Dispute Resolution Systems, Ten Latin American Countries, Mid-1990s*[a]

| Country | Judicial body | Right of employees | | | Right of employers | | Maximum duration of strike |
		To strike	To wage replacement while on strike	To renounce union membership and go back to work	To lock out	To temporarily replace workers	
Argentina	Civil courts.	Must be called by union. After conciliation channels are exhausted, Ministry of Labor legalizes.	No, if workers fail to accept arbitration; yes, if employer locks out workers.	No	No, unless strike is illegal.	No	None
Bolivia	Labor courts.	After arbitration has failed: at least 24 days after presentation of petition to labor inspector. Majority of union or 2/3 of workers must agree.	No. Strike suspends labor contracts.	Yes	Yes	No	None. And in spite of the law, many strikes start before the tribunal's decision.
Brazil	Labor courts.	Yes, in the context of collective contracts negotiation. Quorum to be decided by union, on basis of head count vote.	No	Yes Strike does not suspend contracts.	Requires prior authorization.	No, unless strike is declared "abusive" by the court.	None

Colombia	Labor court. Within 2 days of declaration, Ministry of Labor may call for arbitration.	After direct negotiations. Must be agreed in a secret ballot by absolute majority of workers.	No. Strike suspends labor contracts.	No	Requires prior authorization from Ministry of Labor.	No, unless risk of serious damage to facilities.	60 days
Chile	Labor courts, over questions arising from application of law.	Yes, in the context of collective contracts negotiations.	No	Yes	Yes, if strike affects more than 50% of workers, or if strike stops "essential" work.	Yes. From the first day of the strike if the last offer is equivalent to the previous contract adjusted by CPI. Only after 15 days, otherwise.	Until more than half of the workers have returned to work.
Ecuador	Labor inspectorate.	Yes, if direct negotiations fail, as long as an absolute majority of workers agrees. "Solidarity" strikes permitted.	Yes	No	No	No	Until tribunal resolves the strike.
Mexico	Labor courts.	Tripartite board must declare "existent" or legal.	No, unless the board decides strike is "imputable" to employer.	No	No	Only if tripartite board has determined that activities are "essential" for the public good and regular workers refuse to go back to work.	None

Table 5-1. *(continued)*

Country	Judicial body	Right of employees			Right of employers		Maximum duration of strike
		To strike	To wage replacement while on strike	To renounce union membership and go back to work	To lock out	To temporarily replace workers	
Nicaragua	Civil courts.	Yes, if agreed by majority in head count vote. Does not have to occur in the context of collective bargaining.	Yes	Yes, but wages are paid in any case.	Yes, after conciliation, if authorized by labor inspector.	No	None
Peru	Ministry of Labor.	Yes, with majority agreement. Very few limitations.	No. Strike suspends labor contracts.	Not regulated.	No	Not regulated.	None
Venezuela	Labor inspectorate.	Yes, if direct negotiations fail, as long as an absolute majority of workers agrees. "Solidarity" strikes permitted.	No. Strike suspends labor contracts.	No	Not regulated.	Not regulated.	None

Source: Cox Edwards (1993) and labor laws of specified countries.
a. In several countries, system was in process of implementation.

isterial interventions. "By restricting legal strike actions and by withdrawing the issue of wage increases (through official indexation) and working conditions (through detailed labor regulations), the military government sought to perfect the autocratic labor structure and eliminate class conflict, while the unions retained the tasks of administering their welfare activities."[7] Sandoval also explains that underlying the official union movement and the increasingly politicized industrial action, new forms of workplace representation gained importance after 1964. In many factories, for example, informal groups known as factory commissions were formed to deal with management.

The process of democratization in the 1980s coincided with a continuous growth in strike strength. By this time, service workers had gained importance over industrial workers in terms of employment share, and industrial action came to be dominated by civil servants, public sector teachers and health workers, bank workers, and city transport workers. All of these employment categories are characterized by a monopolistic or oligopolistic employer structure, which facilitates the organization and mobilization of workers. The resurgence of general strikes in the 1980s is explained by two complementary forces. First, worker stoppages in concentrated sectors were able to paralyze the economy. Second, as the size of protests grew, workers increasingly saw general strikes as an opportunity to air frustrations, to protest inflation and "the system" in general, without immediately threatening their own employment.

Brazil's 1988 constitution helped to democratize the labor movement, because it ended the Labor Ministry's power to intervene in the internal affairs of labor unions and guaranteed the unrestricted right to strike (except in "essential" activities). These are two important ingredients for the modernization of the labor movement. Increased exposure to international competition and the breakup of domestic monopolies in the delivery of services will further encourage the evolution of labor organizations that, on the one hand, represent the interests of workers on the shop floor, and on the other, absorb the costs associated with their negotiating positions in collective bargaining.

In order to add economic rationality to the resolution of labor disputes, collective negotiations have to be opened to market forces. This is contingent on a number of factors: goods and services markets have to be opened to competition; individuals must reserve the right to choose

7. Sandoval (1993, p. 18).

whether to join a union; and strikes and lockouts have to be permitted. If the rights to strike and to lock out workers were recognized, the potential occurrence of these actions would be incorporated by workers and employers into their negotiation plans. In general, whether a strike or the threat of a strike will enable a union to win concessions from management depends on the following four factors: (1) the profitability of the firm and its ability to raise prices without losing market share— clearly, unions in concentrated industries will be in a stronger position than those in competitive industries; (2) the ability of the union to impose costs on the firm, which, in turn, depends on whether the firm can stockpile its product in anticipation of a strike and use nonunion workers to operate a plant during a strike; (3) the ability of the firm to withstand the financial losses that it would incur during a strike; and (4) the ability of the union to withstand any loss of income by its members during the strike. However, the degree to which market realities permeate collective bargaining can be altered by law. For example, in many Latin American and Caribbean countries the replacement of striking workers is prohibited. This type of guarantee strengthens the credibility of a threat to strike and gives workers bargaining power beyond market realities, thus allowing unions to obtain a wage premium.

In Latin America, government discretion in conflict resolution has also been influenced by other factors, such as price fixing and trade restrictions, which provide additional avenues for matching demands on compensation with cost considerations. As price controls and international trade barriers are removed, competition in the product markets intensifies and the preservation of jobs becomes the overriding concern. For workers, what really matters is their economic power, which comes with opportunities for alternative jobs.

In the area of dispute resolution, a key principle is to ensure that the parties engaged in bargaining absorb the costs of their actions, rather than passing them on to third parties. One factor that is essential for the costs of a dispute to be internalized is the existence of competition in the market for the good in question as well as in the labor market. Competition will establish limits to the potential gains and losses of delaying a settlement, allowing each party to negotiate within common boundaries and rewarding efforts to increase total factor productivity. Negotiations between unions and public enterprises show starkly how unions are able to achieve distorted outcomes when third parties—that is, taxpayers— bear the cost of negotiated agreements. If a public enterprise can turn to the government for subsidies or easy credit when it is in financial difficulty, the burden of high settlements falls on those who pay higher prices or higher taxes to cover the enterprise's increased costs, not on the workers or the enterprise managers who negotiate the increase.[8]

In short, government intervention and the strict application of principles of seniority in wage determination have to give way to a system that rewards effort, high productivity, and good management within a framework that relies on the voluntary negotiation of working conditions between workers and firms (individually or collectively), rather than on the reinforcement of conditions imposed by law. This requires the removal of a number of statutory provisions—such as those restricting firm-level bargaining, narrowing the scope of negotiation items, and preventing employers from replacing striking workers—that isolate collective bargaining from market realities.

Hiring and Firing Practices

Latin American labor legislation has a long tradition of protecting job security. Typical measures include severe limitations on temporary hiring and the imposition of substantial costs—in the form of severance payments—on dismissals. Recent studies of developed and developing countries have called attention to the relative magnitude of the flow of workers across jobs relative to the overall number of jobs.[9] *On average, for each additional job added to the stock of employment in an economy, nine workers move across firms.* Since flows are so important, labor policy addressing due process in dismissals must be reconciled with the goal of preserving the effective operation of the labor market.

The labor market impact of employment protection laws largely depends on how firms and workers perceive these laws. If severance is seen as a delayed payment mechanism, its effect on hiring and other decisions will be minimal. However, in most countries in the region the legislation that determines employer liability in the case of dismissals makes sever-

---

8. The principal problem of public sector unionism is that disputes tend to be more costly because the markets of the services produced tend to be monopolistic. For this reason, it is natural to seek alternatives to strikes and lockouts. Arbitration by third parties is the obvious alternative, in particular, final offer arbitration. Under this procedure, the arbitrator is constrained to choose either management's final offer or the union's final offer, which encourages moderation rather than excess in each party's proposal.

9. See Hamermesh (1993).

ance payments equivalent to a tax on dismissals, discourages voluntary quits, and has detrimental effects on labor-management relations.

Table 5-2 summarizes the main characteristics of employment protection legislation in ten Latin American countries as of May 1992. In almost every case there are severe restrictions on temporary contracts and differences between the severance payments mandated for "justified" and "unjustified" dismissals. Just cause dismissal is predicated on serious misconduct and, for the most part, excludes an employer's economic considerations, such as financial distress or increased foreign competition. In other words, firms that are restructuring are penalized. Mass dismissals are often contended in court. Another salient aspect of employment protection legislation is that severance payments are directly related to a worker's tenure in the firm, typically by the formula, "x monthly salaries per year of service."

In many Latin American countries, job protection legislation attempts to use a single instrument to address two policy objectives: penalizing wrongful dismissals and providing unemployment insurance. The problem is that neither objective is well served. Firms devise ways to reduce the costs associated with mandated severance payments, and employees attempt to transform voluntary quits into dismissals in order to qualify for severance payment. The law has the effect of transforming labor into a fixed factor. As a result, formal hiring and firing decisions are subject to delay and temporary contracts are informal.

Hiring and firing decisions have three salient characteristics: they entail sunk costs, they take place in an uncertain environment, and they must allow for some freedom of timing.[10] Onerous job security regulations that render hiring decisions practically irreversible and worker representation and dispute resolution mechanisms that are subject to government discretion add uncertainty to the estimation of labor costs. This has a direct negative impact on the level of employment as well as on the speed of labor market adjustment.[11]

Reducing the payoffs associated with litigation and transforming severance payments into a deferred compensation scheme would greatly increase the efficiency of Latin American labor markets. Reducing litigation payoffs requires also defining employer liability in cases of dismissal for economic cause. Argentina and Chile have amended their

10. See Hamermesh (1993).
11. For evidence on the links between uncertain labor costs and employment creation in the United States, see Dertouzos and Karoly (1994).

Table 5-2. Job Protection Legislation, Ten Latin American Countries, May 1992

Country	Restrictions on temporary contracts	Probation period (months)	Advance notice of dismissal (months)	Severance payment[a] With just cause[b]	Without just cause	With economic cause
Argentina	2 years, nonrenewable	3	1 to 2	None	W*T[c]	0.5*[W*T][c]
Bolivia	1 renewal	3	3	None	W*T	W*T
Brazil	2 years, nonrenewable	12	1	Fund	1.4* [Fund]	1.4* [Fund]
Colombia	3 years, nonrenewable	2	0.5[d]	Fund	Fund + [15 to 40 days' wages]*T	Fund + [15 to 40 days' wages]*T
Chile	1 year, nonrenewable	12	1	None	1.2[W*T][e,f]	W*T[c]
Ecuador	2 years, nonrenewable	3	1	0.25*[W*T] + Fund	0.25* [W*T] + 3*W if T < 3, or T*W if 3 < T < 25, or pension if T > 25	0.25* [W*T] + 3*W if T < 3, or T*W if 3 < T < 25, or pension if T > 25
Mexico	None	12	1	W*3	[20 days' wages]* T	[20 days' wages]* T
Nicaragua	2 years, nonrenewable	12	1 to 2	W*T	2* [W*T]	2* [W*T]
Peru	2 years, nonrenewable	3	6 days	Fund	Fund + W*T[c]	Fund + W*T[c]
Venezuela	1 renewal	3	1 to 3	[10 to 30 days' wages] *T	2* [10 to 30 days' wages]*T	2* [10 to 30 days' wages]*T

Source: Cox Edwards (1993) and labor laws of specified countries.
a. W represents the monthly wage; T represents years of tenure; see text for explanation of "funds."
b. Legislation generally specifies "just causes" for dismissal. These include serious misconduct (absenteeism, drunkenness) but not technical requirements or economic factors.
c. Law establishes a maximum W, thus capping severance payment.
d. Minimum severance payment, equivalent to 45 days' wages, is payable in event of dismissal except in case of just cause.
e. Law establishes a maximum T, thus capping severance payment.
f. Burden of proof on employer. Failure to prove allegations of just cause may incur a penalty of up to 50 percent over the normal severance payment (W*T).

legislation to allow this distinction. Some countries have begun to transform severance payments into deferred compensation plans. In Bolivia, for example, all workers have access to the same severance payment, whether they quit or are laid off, after five years on the job. Other countries, including Brazil and, more recently, Peru and Colombia, have replaced severance pay arrangements (based on the formula of one month's pay times the number of years of service) with a time-of-service fund. In Brazil and Peru, a fraction of the employee's salary (8 percent in Brazil and 8.33 percent in Peru) is paid into the fund (in Brazil, the Fondo de Garantia do Tempo de Servicio, and in Peru, the Compensacion por Tiempo de Servicio) in case of separation, either as a "justified" layoff or a quit. Chilean law allows workers to choose this type of arrangement instead of the traditional severance payment after seven years on the job. In this case, employers are required to deposit the equivalent of one month's salary in a savings account in the employee's name. Reducing the payoff associated with litigation would put benefits in the hands of workers quickly, when they are most needed, and induce employers to make hiring and firing decisions without delay.

If severance payments systems in Latin American and Caribbean countries are reformed to become contribution-defined funds, benefits would be accessible in the event of quits or layoffs. Each worker would make contributions to an individual account and could access the account when unemployed. A national unemployment insurance scheme would therefore be unnecessary. In fact, if such a scheme were strictly financed by beneficiaries, it would accomplish exactly the same objective as funded unemployment benefits. This is better than the typical systems of unemployment insurance because in practice it is difficult to find an adequate form of funding for these unemployment insurance programs. The use of payroll taxes generates an incentives problem, because all workers are subject to the same tax, irrespective of their unemployment history. In the United States, the unemployment insurance tax is directly linked to the incidence of unemployment by means of "experience ratings" of the tax rate. Thus the unemployment insurance tax rate is set at a minimum level (by each state), but is raised for specific employers if their former employees have used up their corresponding unemployment insurance reserve. The limited state unemployment insurance system reduces the extent of cross-subsidies across firms, but does not avoid cross-subsidies across workers. Therefore it is inferior to a severance payments program financed by individual accounts.

In short, it makes sense to distinguish between a mechanism that establishes employer liability in cases of wrongful or arbitrary dismissal and a system that prepares workers for justified dismissals and voluntary changes in employment. The latter must be funded by its beneficiaries and should represent the major part of severance benefits. Transforming the system of mandatory severance payments into a requirement to build a fund that can be withdrawn on separation (dismissal or resignation) would accomplish this goal. A number of countries in the region have either moved in this direction or are considering changes along these lines. An important objective of such changes is to reduce the payoff associated with litigation, thus encouraging the dynamism of the economy.

Social Security and Other Mandatory Contributions

Social security systems in the region generally entitle workers to pensions, health care services, and accident insurance. These systems were initially intended to be funded by both employee and employer contributions, but they eventually incurred very large deficits. In the early years the benefits were very attractive, but as programs have aged, access to benefits has sometimes been rationed, contribution rates have been raised, and benefits have been reduced at the stroke of a pen.

In terms of the incidence of economic costs and equity, social security systems are in trouble in most countries in the region. First, most pension funds encourage early retirement, generating a serious burden for the country even though the retiree is in the prime of his or her productive life. Second, pensions are often unrelated to an individual's contributions to the system. Third, as health care providers, social security systems have not introduced internal mechanisms to make socially efficient choices between expensive high-technology treatments and cheaper preventive care. In most cases, contributions to the health care component of a social security system are independent of marital status, family size, and age. Benefits, however, automatically extend to dependents. As the population ages, this feature has reduced the willingness of the economically active population to support the systems; for example, in Peru. Fourth, programs that were originally designed solely for contributing workers have often been extended to the population at large, creating enormous cross-subsidies and conflicts of interest. Over time, contributions have become purely a tax and benefits have come to be seen as entitlements. Finally, in many countries pension programs have become

Figure 5-1. *Payroll Taxes as Percent of Gross Wages, Selected Countries, Early 1990s*

Percent

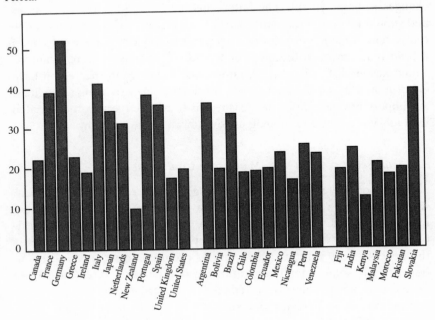

Source: Cox Edwards (1993) and World Bank, unpublished data.

financially insolvent and money has increasingly been diverted to pension benefits from health care, with the unfunded health care liability being imposed on the rest of the economy.

Payroll taxes are of concern to workers because they are generally earmarked to finance a number of programs that benefit workers. The primary use of payroll taxes is to fund pensions, and next, health care programs (which are generally limited to workers or targeted to the poor, but in some cases extend to the entire population). Third in importance is the funding of workers' compensation for work-related accidents. In some countries, payroll taxes also fund unemployment insurance and housing programs. In a number of countries in Latin America and the Caribbean payroll taxes fund training institutes.

Figure 5-1 presents payroll taxes as a percentage of gross wages in selected countries throughout the world. Payroll taxes typically are high in developed countries—in European countries, in particular—ranging from 20 to 50 percent of gross wages. But they are also high in some developing countries, notably in Latin America, ranging from 20 to 40 percent of gross wages. Yet the magnitude of the actual tax burden in a given country requires more careful examination, including attention to the role of nontaxable wages and tax compliance. The labor market is not distorted simply by the presence of a payroll tax, but by weak links between contributions and benefits.

In the Latin American region, social security systems not only impose burdens on the labor market, but they have run into serious financial problems. An important process of reform has been underway since the early 1980s. Public intervention to make such programs mandatory is often justified on the grounds that workers would not otherwise save for retirement or health insurance, and that employers would not insure against the risk of accidents on the job or provide training programs. In the best case scenario, workers value the benefits and bear the burden of mandated contributions, with no effect on economic efficiency. In the worst case scenario, workers do not value the benefits; they see their take-home pay fall and their employment opportunities shrink as the cost of labor rises. The latter is particularly true in economies where the formal (tax-paying) sector competes with an informal (tax-free) sector, and also in open economies where higher costs of production cannot be translated into higher output prices.

A number of countries in the region are trying to replace pay-as-you-go pension regimes with a combination of individual capitalization accounts and minimum services insured by the government. This type of system has been in operation in Chile since the early 1980s and is currently in the process of being implemented in Argentina, Colombia, Mexico, and Peru. Health care reforms have taken longer to define but are also under consideration. Both types of reform will have very important effects on the efficiency of the labor market if they reduce payroll taxes and their distortionary impact.

The 1994 World Bank study *Averting the Old Age Crisis* lays out the general principles of a social security system that would address the twin objectives of old-age security and economic growth.[12] The study proposes a model with three pillars. First, a mandatory public system, financed by taxes, providing a minimum, uniform, guaranteed benefit to address

12. World Bank (1994). The study also describes individual Latin American countries' experiences of reform.

distributional and insurance objectives. Second, another mandatory pillar, administered by the private sector and regulated by the state, based on individual accounts with the objective of saving and insurance coverage. And third, a voluntary pillar, similar in form and objective to the second pillar. The fundamental reform accomplished by the second pillar is essential for economic growth, especially in those countries where the distortionary effects of payroll taxes are significant, where public resources are subject to misallocation, and where national saving has been low. Fundamental reform is also critical for distributional objectives in countries where political pressure for attractive early retirement benefits goes unchecked and where there is evidence of regressivity in the present social security system.

As of December 1995, seven Latin American countries had introduced pension reforms: Argentina, Chile, Colombia, Costa Rica, Mexico, Peru, and Uruguay. There is important variation across countries in the elements of reform introduced. Reform measures include strengthening the financial health of the public system (Chile, Costa Rica, and Uruguay); introducing an obligatory complementary saving program (Mexico); phasing out the public defined benefit program (Chile); introducing a mandatory defined contribution program (Chile); introducing an optional defined contribution program in addition to a reformed public defined benefit program (Argentina and Uruguay); and introducing choice between a defined benefit program and a privately managed defined contribution program (Colombia and Peru).

In regard to work-related accidents and workers' compensation, addressing the diverse safety and health hazards that emanate from industrial activity involves many actors. Employers are interested in avoiding interruption to their operations and minimizing production costs. If unsafe practices lead to costly operations or delays, they will pursue safer methods. Workers are interested in preserving their health and safety. Therefore if they can be persuaded that a safer practice will free them from risk, they will likely adopt that practice. There is room for policymaking in terms of encouraging the adoption of safe methods as well as assigning liability for identifiable unsafe practices.

The available evidence is inconclusive on the role of safety and health standards in the promotion of safe work habits. This is a very complex area of policymaking, in which the costs of monitoring and implementation are very steep. The promotion of workers' safety cannot be assured simply by increasing the number of inspectors with the Ministry of Labor.

Programs that provide compensation for work-related injuries and occupational illnesses have a long tradition throughout the world, including in Latin America. There are two basic types of system: social insurance systems that make use of a central public fund, and private arrangements required by law. About two-thirds of workers' compensation programs operate through a central public fund. Among the countries that rely primarily on private arrangements, about twenty (including the United States) require that employers insure their employees against the risk of employment injury. In about half of these, only private insurance is available. In the remainder, a public fund does exist, but employers are allowed to opt out of the public system. Publicly managed systems are funded by equal contributions (at a single rate) as in Norway and Sweden. Private or mutual insurance companies base premiums on past experience of work accidents by industry and even by firm. Thus the cost of protection varies widely.

In most countries in the Latin American region, safety standards are the responsibility of the Ministry of Labor and the consequences of accidents on the job are the responsibility of the social security system; that is, the social security system covers compensation (established by law) and medical expenses associated with work-related accidents. Risk premiums are set by industry, meaning that, for example, all construction companies pay the same contribution to cover their workers' risks of accident. This state of affairs is quite unsatisfactory. There are no checks and balances to encourage employers and workers to internalize the costs associated with unsafe practices.

Attention to the relationship between income and expenditure would arise naturally in a competitive market for insurers. Sector-specific and company-specific safe practices would be encouraged if those employers who invested in safety saved on insurance premiums. The Ministry of Labor's role could also be enhanced. For example, analysis of data on work-related accidents, change over time, and the links between these trends and the ministry's activities could be used to influence priorities and induce greater effectiveness.

Workers' Training Programs

Workers' training is one of the most underreported and misunderstood activities carried out by enterprises. Governments do not have to encourage training because private firms and workers want to invest in it anyway.[13] It is often argued that firms underinvest in training and that it is in the interest of society to encourage more training. In fact, firms have no alternative but to invest in firm-specific training, because workers cannot perform without it. Employers often complain that their trained workers are "poached" by other firms. The fact is that firms are willing to pay for "general capital," and thus this type of human capital is of value to individual workers. For this reason, workers are often willing to incur fees or accept lower wages while engaged in on-the-job training, in anticipation of higher wages in the future. In sum, whenever there are gains to be made from training, and as long as it is possible to negotiate working conditions, firms and workers are able to find a solution whereby workers contribute in part to the costs of training.

The amount of training undertaken by a firm varies across countries and sectors, and even across firms within sectors, depending on size and ownership. In 1991, 24 percent of Mexican workers reported receiving some form of training on the job; the corresponding figure for Japan was 37 percent. Firms in high-technology industries and export-oriented enterprises are the most likely to provide training.[14]

Government intervention in the market for training is only justified in the case of market failure or in order to pursue goals other than market efficiency. Most countries in Latin America and the Caribbean, with the exception of Mexico and Argentina, have created public training institutions modeled on Brazil's SENAI (National Service for Industrial Apprenticeship, which dates back to the 1930s). In each country, an autonomous public agency promotes industrial training, financed by payroll contributions (usually set between 1 and 2 percent) and managed jointly by government, workers, and employers. These agencies offer subsidized training to some industries, often to public sector enterprises, with little accountability to those who are funding their activities. Over time, funding for the system has essentially turned into a tax on modern sector labor. There is no justification for this policy. A more effective approach for the public sector would be to spread opportunities for secondary

13. It is often argued that the importance of government involvement in training is highlighted by Germany's success on this front. The German "dual' system of vocational education relies on a general education system financed at the state and local government level and an employer-based training on job-specific skills funded by enterprises. See Gill and Dar (1996) for an account of the centrality of entrepreneurs' associations to the "dual system" in Germany.

14. World Bank (1995).

Figure 5-2. *Secondary School Coverage, Latin America and the Caribbean, 1970–90*

Percent

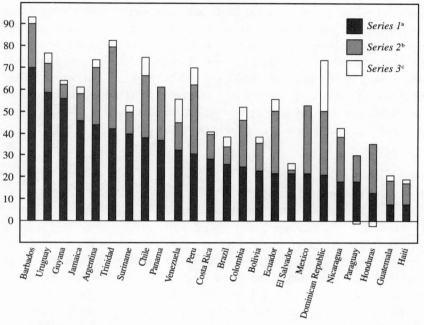

Source: World Bank (1993).
a. Secondary school coverage, 1970.
b. Progress in secondary school coverage, 1985 relative to 1970.
c. Progress in secondary school coverage, 1990 relative to 1985.

education. There is evidence from a number of countries that secondary education is a prerequisite for access to training on the job. Yet as figure 5-2 shows, the coverage of secondary education in Latin America and the Caribbean has grown over the past decade but remains low in a number of countries.

It is clear that training institutions must adapt in order to be effective in an environment of economic dynamism and change, and indeed, there has already been some change. In some cases, pressure has come from legal reforms that have deprived training institutions of traditional funding (Bolivia, Colombia, and Costa Rica), or they have faced greater exposure to competition for public funding (Chile). Entrepreneurs have sometimes been asked to participate more closely in program development (Brazil) or to take over the management of a system (Peru).[15]

Bolivia eliminated a tax earmarked to funded public training institutes in the late 1980s. Chile has eliminated an equivalent tax but still provides public subsidies toward training, although it has significantly changed the incentives structure. In the formal sector, firms can get a tax credit (of up to 1 percent of payroll) if they spend at least the equivalent of 1 percent of payroll on workers' training. This training can be given on the job or may be provided by public and private training institutions. The government also distributes training scholarships to targeted groups and auctions the provision of courses to a competitive market. The intent is to use these subsidies as a distributional instrument.

Conclusions

Many Latin American countries have initiated a process of reform process that could potentially yield important gains for workers in years to come. Their chance of success is a function of domestic policies and also of international conditions. The capacity of a country's economy to modernize, reorient toward the exports market, adapt new technologies, improve services delivery, and so forth rests on an improved use of resources and a more efficient productive sector. Labor policy plays an important role, which has been generally overlooked. This is a mistake. Labor policy must be redefined in order to expand employment opportunities in all sectors; that is, in order to "open the formal labor market."

To open the formal labor market, a number of changes in labor market law and institutions are required. The most important include:

—Establishing the freedom to choose labor representation and dispute resolution mechanisms that enhance the participation of workers and employers at the plant level.

—Replacing job security legislation with a system that prepares workers for change. This does not necessarily require the establishment of new unemployment insurance programs; it can be accomplished by improving current severance payment systems.

15. See de Moura Castro (1994).

—Revising social security contracts and lowering payroll taxes. Making pensions a function of individual saving will enhance efficiency in the labor market and encourage saving. This does not mean that the state need repudiate promises made to those who have already contributed to the system or who depend on pensions, nor does it eliminate the distributional objective. Reform is not inconsistent with the establishment of transfer programs toward the elderly who qualify as poor. But reform can reduce labor market distortions and encourage active employees to save toward retirement.

—Transferring training subsidies to the demand side. This is necessary in order to make training institutes more responsive to rapidly changing labor requirements, particularly in countries that are integrating into the world economy. Evidence from a number of countries shows that investment in industrial training is concentrated on individuals who have completed secondary schooling. This means that public support toward training does not generally favor the poor. Subsidies to the demand side have two advantages over the current system, which funds public institutes directly. First, they encourage competition and innovation. Second, they can be targeted to specific groups, addressing equity objectives while enlarging, rather than replacing, the existing private market for training.

Although labor regulations may, in some instances, improve the lot of the poor, poverty cannot be eliminated by decree. One of the main survival strategies of poor families is to increase the number of working individuals, including children. Child labor continues to be prevalent in Latin America, despite legal restrictions. For example, it is estimated that in Brazil around 18 percent of children between the ages of ten and fourteen work. This percentage remained relatively constant between 1981 and 1990. The incidence of child labor is significantly higher among low-income families and, in particular, poor female-headed households. But there are also local increases in incidence, where the demand for child labor is high and where the quality and availability of schooling are relatively low. Reaching out to the poor in order to increase their opportunities to participate in the market economy requires a comprehensive approach that takes into consideration the interrelation of labor market conditions, schooling, child labor, and poverty. The enforcement of labor regulations alone may reduce child labor, but may worsen the overall condition of some poor families.

References

Cortázar, René. 1995. "The Evolution and Reform of Labor Markets in Chile." Paper prepared for conference on "Labor Markets in Latin America." Brookings and World Bank, Buenos Aires, Argentina, July 6–7.

Cox Edwards, Alejandra. 1991. "Wage Trends in Latin America: A view from LATHR #18." Latin America and the Caribbean Technical Department. Washington: World Bank.

———. 1993. "Labor Market Legislation in Latin America and the Caribbean." Report 31. Washington: World Bank, Latin America and the Caribbean Technical Department Regional Studies Program.

———. 1996. "The Unemployment Effect of Labor Market Interventions." In *Estimating the Benefits of Labor Reform in Argentina.* Annex 3. Washington: World Bank.

de Moura Castro, Claudio. 1994. "La Formacion Profesional en America Latina: Nuevos Remedios para un Nuevo Paciente." *Planeacion y Desarrollo* 25, special edition (May): 237–56. Bogota, Colombia.

Dertouzos, James N., and Lynn A. Karoly. 1994. *Labor-Market Responses to Employer Liability.* Santa Monica, Calif.: Rand, Institute for Civil Justice.

Gill, Indermit, and Amit Dar. 1996. "Germany's Dual System: Lessons for Low and Middle Income Countries." Mimeo. Washington: World Bank, Poverty and Social Policy Department.

Hamermesh, Daniel. 1993. *Labor Demand.* Princeton University Press.

Lora, Eduardo, and Marta L. Henao. 1995. "The Evolution and Reform of Labor Markets in Colombia." Paper prepared for conference on "Labor Markets in Latin America." Brookings and World Bank, Buenos Aires, Argentina, July 6–7.

Sandoval, Salvador. 1993. *Social Change and Labor Unrest in Brazil since 1945.* Westview.

World Bank. 1993. *Human Resources in Latin America and the Caribbean: Priorities in Action.* Oxford University Press.

———. 1994. *Averting the Old Age Crisis: Policies to Protect the Old and Promote Growth.* Oxford University Press.

———. 1995. *World Development Report, 1995.* Oxford University Press.

Yamada Fukusaki, Gustavo. 1995. "Apuntes sobre las reformas laborales en el Peru 1980–1995." Centro de Investigación de la Universidad del Pacífico. Lima, Peru.

CHAPTER SIX

Argentina: The Labor Market during the Economic Transition

Carola Pessino

IN ARGENTINA the process of economic reform has involved moving large numbers of workers from old production activities in the protected sectors to new production activities in the emerging competitive sectors. In the transition, some firms cease to exist, displacing workers and increasing unemployment. The creation of new firms and the restructuring of old firms should lead to a subsequent increase in recruitment that will tend to increase employment and absorb displaced workers. However, transition is turbulent for many workers, for two reasons. First, those who leave the protected sector also abandon specific skills. They must try to find a new job with new skills, a process that takes time, involves uncertainty, and usually requires accepting a lower wage in the new job. Moreover, some workers are older than is optimal for retraining and learning new skills, so they may either remain unemployed for a long period or find work in the informal sector of the economy. Second, current labor legislation and Argentina's present macroeconomic situation are not helping to smooth the transition. To the contrary, they are,

I acknowledge the helpful comments of Edgardo Favaro and Silvia Montoya and the excellent research assistance of Luis Andrés.

for the most part, increasing the amount of unemployment beyond that expected as a by-product of economic liberalization.

With respect to labor regulations in Argentina, the mobility of workers is hampered as a result of mandatory severance payments, high fixed costs of hiring, and impediments to moving workers functionally within a firm. High payroll taxes—which are of no obvious benefit to workers, since the state has been very inefficient at providing social security— reduce labor demand, and the presence of unions and restrictive collective bargaining agreements not only deters labor mobility but may be an impediment to needed wage reductions. The macroeconomic situation is disadvantageous because relative prices favor capital goods against unskilled labor and push dollar wages up very high, while the domestic purchasing power of wages is, on average, very low. The reduction in real wages necessary to bring down unemployment is clearly not facilitated by the low purchasing power of the wages of less skilled workers. Not only collective bargaining agreements, but also efficiency wage considerations can impede the process.

This chapter describes data on unemployment, employment, the labor force, and wages and their determinants before and during the transition. My aim is to show which sectors and activities are losing employment and which are gaining, which workers are hit by unemployment, and which skills are rewarded more and which less in the emerging economy. In the light of this evidence, standard theory can be applied to analyze the likely impact of the macroeconomic situation and current labor market legislation on this transition. Labor market legislation might delay or prevent restructuring. Active labor market policies might even harm the transition, since it is not clear that they can reduce social costs to the more damaged workers. There is an obvious trade-off between efficiency and the social protection of labor. While some regulations or policies can affect both in the same direction, others might achieve efficiency and competitiveness with higher levels of inequality and poverty in the short to medium run.

The plan of the chapter is as follows. First, I describe the impact of the transition on employment and unemployment, analyzing the reasons for the increase in unemployment and its sociodemographic composition. Next, I analyze its impact on the structure and inequality of wages. Finally, I describe the main legal and institutional regulations in the labor market and analyze their likely impact on the transition.

Major Labor Market Trends

After the end of hyperinflation in 1990 and the introduction of the exchange rate-based stabilization program known as the Convertibility Plan in 1991, the rate of unemployment tripled and average real wages began to rise, continuing at least until 1994. Given stagnation in the wages of the unskilled, increases in wages of skilled workers have made wage differentials larger. Also, employment has been growing more slowly than GDP, resulting in higher average labor productivity; but productivity has not increased fast enough to compensate for the rise in real wages or in dollar-denominated wages. Meanwhile, needed reforms in labor market regulations and institutions have been introduced too slowly, and some—such as the reduction of payroll taxes—have even been reversed in order to finance the government deficit. Others are still under endless discussion in congress and the administration.

The current administration has inherited an inward-looking protected country undergoing structural reform, in terms of trade liberalization and extensive privatization of state-owned companies. Such structural changes in both the public and private sectors are no doubt affecting employment and unemployment, since reform produces sectoral changes as well as changes in the composition of skills within sectors. It is expected that negative effects will be reversed if and when thriving sectors begin to absorb the excess labor of shrinking sectors and workers either acquire new skills or demand, accept, or can be offered lower wages.

One side effect of the Convertibility Plan, however, has been a real appreciation of the exchange rate, or equivalently, an increase in dollar-denominated wages in Argentina. The plan also eliminated tariffs on imported capital goods, resulting in a 40 percent decline in the relative price of capital, according to government estimates. Thus the effect of trade liberalization on the price of capital has been compounded by the appreciation of the peso, hurting the employment of unskilled labor, in particular. Note also that the opening of the Argentinean economy after several years of stagnation has meant low levels of investment, resulting in the high marginal productivity of physical capital. Furthermore, the transition occurred at a time when most of the developed world was undergoing technological change that favored skilled labor.

In conclusion, as a result of the Convertibility Plan, there have been several changes in the variables that affect labor market outcomes, including increased labor mobility across jobs and sectors; a higher relative price of labor with respect to capital in the aggregate; and a large increase in GDP growth until 1994, followed by a decrease in 1995. Yet there has been almost no change in the ways in which labor market institutions operate.

This chapter highlights four major trends in the labor market since the implementation of the Convertibility Plan that are direct or indirect consequences of the changes listed above: (1) absence of employment growth; (2) increase in labor force participation; (3) increase in unemployment, and (4) rising wage differentials. While I do not claim that these are consequences of implementing other structural reforms without corresponding reform in the labor market, the lack of labor market reform cannot be dismissed as a causal factor. In a labor demand and supply framework, lower labor demand together with increased labor supply will produce higher unemployment, given the intrinsic time needed to match workers to new jobs. However, matching will take even longer if there are restrictions in the labor market. This is supported by evidence from a number of studies.

Using data from the greater Buenos Aires area for the period 1974–94, Indermit Gill and I show that labor demand is quite inelastic with respect to output and more elastic with respect to wages.[1] We also show that labor-saving technological change took place during this period, induced in part by the high relative price of capital with respect to output since 1990. Hence the huge increase (around 30 percent) in GDP between 1990 and 1994 was countered by a disproportionate increase in labor costs, with the result that labor demand remained unchanged. In 1995, when Argentina experienced a sharp recession as a side effect of the Mexican crisis, labor demand actually fell in absolute terms, while labor costs decreased only slightly. With respect to labor supply, I show elsewhere, with Leonardo Giacchino and also with Gill, that apart from the secular increase in labor force participation in Argentina since the beginning of the 1980s, there has been a cyclical effect, operating through the increased unemployment of prime-aged males (an income effect) and through higher real wages (a substitution effect).[2] While I do not here

1. Pessino and Gill (1996a). We estimate several econometric models of conditional (on output) labor demand. The results are quite robust with respect to the different functional forms. The mean estimates are about 0.25 for the output elasticity of labor demand and −0.40 for the wage elasticity.

2. Pessino and Giacchino (1994); Pessino and Gill (1996b).

provide a full econometric analysis linking developments in labor demand and supply with the increase in unemployment in the 1990s, my analysis of the structural evolution of unemployment during this period at least confirms that the hardest hit were those for whom labor demand declined the most and labor supply increased the most.

In the rest of this section I describe the main trends in unemployment, linking them with both the demand side (employment and underemployment) and the supply side (labor force participation). In the following section, I examine whether these developments have resulted or are expected to result in productivity growth, emphasizing sectoral differences. My aim is to discover which forces of supply and demand have affected these variables and whether there is any indication that some sectors have begun to grow and absorb excess labor, hence increasing aggregate employment and reducing unemployment.

Major Trends in Employment

Employment growth has not been steady since 1974. According to household data for greater Buenos Aires, employment grew at an annual rate of 1 percent between May 1974 and May 1995. Figure 6-1 compares employment growth in greater Burenos Aires, North America, Oceania, Japan, the European Free Trade Association (EFTA), and the European Community (EC) over this period. Employment growth has been strongest in North America (1.7 percent per year) and weakest in the EC (0.2 percent) and EFTA (0.2 percent). Employment growth in Japan (1.1 percent) and Oceania (1.2 percent) lie between that in Argentina and in North America.

Table 6-1 presents growth in employment, labor force, and population for the same regions over the period 1974–94. As employment growth shows wide variation between regions, so do population and labor force growth. Part of the variation in employment performance between the countries of the Organization for Economic Cooperation and Development (OECD) and Argentina can be ascribed to differences in population growth.

According to the first column of table 6-1, Argentina has an intermediate position in employment growth. However, taking into account population growth, Argentina fares worst: with a yearly population growth rate of 1.3 percent (in greater Buenos Aires), employment growth less population growth gives an average decrease of 0.29 percent per year in

Figure 6-1. *Employment Growth, Selected Regions and Countries, 1974–95*

Index, 1974 = 100

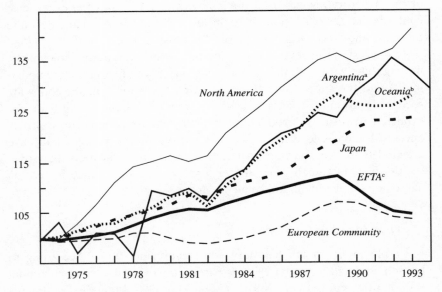

Source: For Argentina, author's calculations using data from OECD, *Employment Outlook*, various issues, and the Permanent Household Survey.
a. Greater Buenos Aires.
b. Australia and New Zealand.
c. European Free Trade Association.

employment. In this context, Argentina is much closer to the EFTA and EC countries than when considering absolute changes in employment. Note that North America and Japan fared best on this index, generating the highest employment growth compared to population growth. As noted above, in Argentina the overall labor force participation rate grew during this period, implying that growth in labor force participation should be higher than population growth. In fact, labor force participation grew at an annual rate of 1.8 percent, while the population grew at only 1.3 percent per year.

This growth was mainly due to the increase in female labor force participation. However, comparison of the second and fourth columns of table 6-1 highlights the fact that female labor force participation (and hence overall labor force participation) in Argentina during this period

Table 6-1. *Growth in Employment, Population, and Labor Force, Selected Regions and Countries*[a]

	Employment[b] (1)	Population[c] (2)	Average annual employment decrease (1)–(2)	Labor Force[d] (3)	Difference between employment growth and labor force growth (1)–(3)
Argentina[e]	1.01	1.30	-0.29	1.80	-0.79
North America	1.73	1.05	0.68	1.80	-0.07
Oceania	1.25	1.20	0.04	1.75	-0.50
Japan	1.06	0.70	0.36	1.10	-0.04
EFTA	0.23	0.35	-0.12	0.70	-0.47
European Community	0.17	0.35	-0.18	0.55	-0.38

Source: Author's calculations. Data for the Organization for Economic Cooperation and Development (OECD) are from OECD, *Employment Outlook*, various issues. For Argentina, employment and labor force data are from the Permanent Household Survey, and population growth is estimated from census data over the period May 1974 to May 1995.

a. Employment and labor force data are for the working-age population (ages fifteen to sixty-four). Population data are for the total population. Therefore the population growth numbers in this table may not reflect the potential labor force growth of the working-age population. In greater Buenos Aires, according to the Permanent Household Survey the working-age population grew at an annualized rate of 1.2 percent over the period 1974–94.

b. 1974–94.

c. 1975–92, except for Argentina, which covers 1970–91.

d. 1974–94.

Figure 6-2. *Job Creation by Sector, October 1991–May 1995*

Thousands of jobs

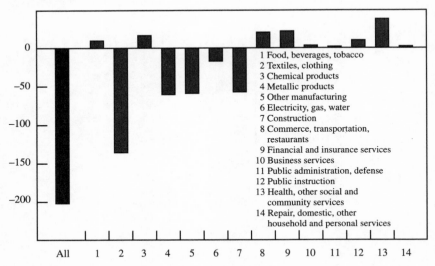

1 Food, beverages, tobacco
2 Textiles, clothing
3 Chemical products
4 Metallic products
5 Other manufacturing
6 Electricity, gas, water
7 Construction
8 Commerce, transportation, restaurants
9 Financial and insurance services
10 Business services
11 Public administration, defense
12 Public instruction
13 Health, other social and community services
14 Repair, domestic, other household and personal services

Source: Author's calculations using data from the Permanent Household Survey.

was much smaller than in the rest of the countries in the OECD.[3] The last column of the table shows the difference between employment growth and labor force growth. This number is negative for all the countries because unemployment rates grew throughout. Once again, the countries that fare best (in the sense that unemployment grows less) are the United States and Japan. Argentina fares worst, with a 0.8 percent decrease per year. In sum, although Argentina did generate a relatively large amount of jobs (at least until 1993), there were not enough to support the increase in population since 1974.

Figure 6-2 summarizes total change in employment, by sector, between the introduction of the Convertibility Plan in October 1991 and May 1995. The 220,000 decrease in the number of the employed was concentrated in import-competing sectors in manufacturing: the textile and clothing

3. In fact, one of the major consequences of development during this century has been the incorporation of more women into the labor force. As Argentina has lagged in development with respect to OECD countries, it is not surprising to find that female labor force participation is still much lower in Argentina than in OECD countries and has been growing at a slower pace.

industries lost approximately 150,000 jobs and metallic products together with other manufacturing lost another 100,000.[4] As a consequence of this sectoral shift, the share of the service sector in total employment has been on the rise since 1991, at the expense of that of manufacturing.[5]

Major Trends in Unemployment and Underemployment

Argentina has traditionally had relatively low unemployment rates. However, as in most European countries and countries undergoing an economic transition, the unemployment rate has risen steadily during the period: from an average of less than 5 percent before 1985, it had risen to an average of 7 percent by 1992 and accelerated thereafter, surpassing 10 percent in 1993 to reach almost 13 percent by the end of 1994. Most recently, unemployment rates of 20.2 percent and 17.4 percent for May and October 1995, respectively, in greater Buenos Aires have coincided with the peak of a recession. During the first half of 1995, Argentina suffered from the so-called Tequila effect (that is, international shock-waves from the Mexican crisis), which created a run on the banks, almost completely halted private credit, and lowered industrial production. Hence the structural unemployment that is the subject of this chapter has been compounded by the usual story of unemployment caused by recession. However, analysis of the latest data shows that the process described here has merely been magnified, without any change in the structure of unemployment.

Figure 6-3 presents the evolution of the unemployment rate over the period 1974–95 in all twenty-five urban conglomerates in Argentina and in the greater Buenos Aires area alone. In both, the trend is rising with numerous peaks. The first peak, at an unemployment rate of 4 percent in 1976, coincided with a recession (see figure 6-4). At the second peak, in 1981, unemployment increased to more than 5 percent, coinciding with

4. Note that even protected sectors like metallic products and paper generated negative employment. This contradicts the conventional argument for tariff protection as a means of employment protection.

5. The sectoral composition of employment is drawn from data for greater Buenos Aires, an urban area. Census data from 1980 show that, countrywide, 13 percent of total employment was in the primary sector, 21 percent in manufacturing, 13 percent in the secondary sector (including construction), and 53 percent in services. According to these numbers, Argentina has a very high employment share in services—similar to that of the United States and higher than in other Latin American and European countries—and a relatively low (and shrinking) share in manufacturing, as compared with Europe and the United States, although it is higher than in most other Latin American countries.

Figure 6-3. *Urban Unemployment Rates, 1974–95*

Percent

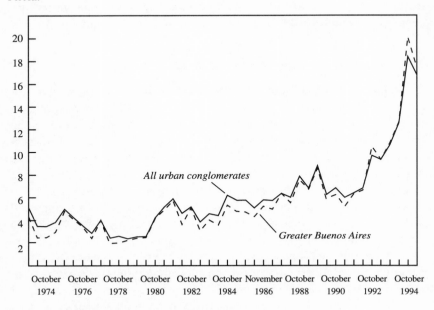

Source: Author's calculations using data from the Permanent Household Survey.

a recession that began in 1980 and continued until 1982. The third peak, in 1985, when unemployment again reached 5 percent, coincided with another drop in GDP per capita, as did the fourth peak, in 1989, when unemployment surpassed 7 percent. The 1994 peak, however, when unemployment reached 13 percent, is the first in this period not to have been accompanied by a recession. To the contrary, per capita GDP growth was at its highest for the period. In 1995 GDP fell by 4.4 percent and unemployment reached its highest level.

For the rest of this study, analysis of Argentinean labor market data will concentrate on the greater Buenos Aires area, because this is the only urban conglomerate for which microdata are available for the period 1986–94. Moreover, as can be seen from figure 6-3, both trend and cyclical unemployment are similar in greater Buenos Aires alone and in all the urban conglomerates taken together. The greater Buenos Aires area accounts for almost 40 percent of the country's population and more than 50 percent of GDP.

Figure 6-4. *GNP per Capita. 1974–95*

1970 Australes

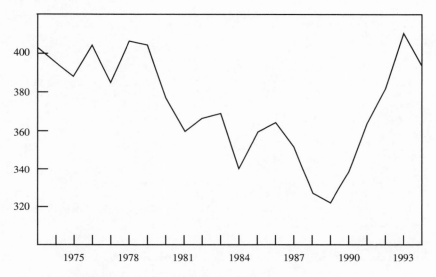

Source: Author's calculations using data from the Permanent Household Survey.

In Argentina, as in most countries, unemployment rates differ by gender, age, occupation, education, family status, and the previous industry of employment. Identifying the unemployed is of the utmost importance to understanding the effects of government policies. Table 6-2 presents unemployment rates by age and gender for October 1987 and from October 1991 to May 1995. For May 1993, the table shows that young people are much more likely to be unemployed than older people.[6] In particular, teenage unemployment rates are between three and four times higher than those for both prime-aged (that is, thirty-five to forty-nine years old) males and females. The teenage unemployment data are comparable to those for the United States; but the large differential between teenage and prime-aged unemployment is shared mainly with other countries with similarly regulated labor markets, such as Italy and

6. I choose May 1993 simply because there is more information available with which to analyze the characteristics and causes of unemployment during this period. For a comparable analysis for 1987 of unemployment in Argentina relative to other countries that have been widely studied, such as the United States and Great Britain, see Pessino and Giacchino (1994).

Table 6-2. *Unemployment Rate, by Age and Gender, Greater Buenos Aires, October 1987–May 1995*

Percent

Gender and age	October 1987	October 1991	May 1992	October 1992	May 1993	October 1993	May 1994	October 1994	May 1995
Males									
15–19	14.3	16.9	12.9	17.3	19.4	21.8	28.9	31.4	46.8
20–34	4.2	4.7	7.6	6.4	8.3	8.1	8.9	10.4	15.3
35–49	2.9	3.5	4.0	4.4	7.1	6.1	6.6	6.8	11.9
50–64	3.8	3.3	4.0	7.1	9.1	6.2	8.2	12.7	16.3
15–64	4.4	4.9	6.0	6.8	8.9	8.0	9.6	11.4	17.1
Females									
15–19	17.3	17.5	21.9	14.3	33.0	40.3	33.0	38.9	58.9
20–34	7.3	6.7	9.0	7.2	13.7	12.6	12.4	15.1	25.2
35–49	4.2	3.9	5.8	4.2	7.9	10.5	10.4	13.2	19.0
50–64	3.0	2.8	2.2	5.7	14.2	5.4	11.9	10.2	17.4
15–64	6.3	5.9	7.9	6.4	13.2	12.6	13.3	15.4	24.8
Total	5.1	5.3	6.7	6.6	10.6	9.8	11.0	12.9	20.2

Source: Author's calculations using data from the Permanent Household Survey.

Table 6-3. *Unemployment Rate, by Sector, Greater Buenos Aires, October 1987–May 1995*

Percent

Sector	October 1987	October 1991	May 1992	October 1992	May 1993	October 1993	May 1994	October 1994	May 1995
Manufacturing	5.5	5.3	6.6	6.7	9.8	9.0	10.3	12.9	19.0
Services	4.5	4.3	4.6	5.1	8.9	8.6	8.6	10.9	16.7
Construction	11.0	6.0	13.0	15.3	18.8	16.7	20.5	21.9	36.2
Public sector	1.1	2.0	1.4	3.4	2.7	2.1	6.8	4.0	9.6

Source: Author's calculations using data from the Permanent Household Survey.

Spain.[7] With respect to gender, female unemployment rates were 50 percent higher than corresponding male unemployment rates in May 1993. As with the distribution of unemployment by age, the distribution by gender in Argentina is much more similar to that in the European Community than that in the United States and other developed countries.

Table 6-3 presents unemployment in Argentina by industrial sector, over the same periods. These data exhibit a familiar pattern, with the highest rates in construction—mainly because of high turnover—and somewhat higher rates in manufacturing than in services. Note that in May 1993 the public sector had the lowest proportion of unemployment

7. See Layard, Nickell, and Jackman (1991, table 2).

Table 6-4. *Unemployment Rate, by Occupation and Education Levels, October 1987–May 1995*

Percent

Occupation and education levels	October 1987	October 1991	May 1992	October 1992	May 1993	October 1993	May 1994	October 1994	May 1995
Occupation									
Professional	0.8	2.4	2.6	2.1	3.8	1.1	3.6	3.1	4.4
White collar	3.8	4.3	4.7	5.5	8.5	8.0	8.8	11.1	16.8
Blue collar	7.1	5.1	6.9	8.4	12.9	12.1	13.9	15.0	24.3
Education									
Primary									
Incomplete	7.6	3.5	7.5	9.8	12.0	9.3	10.7	14.6	23.4
Complete	6.4	5.5	7.8	11.7	11.7	11.6	12.4	13.8	22.0
Secondary									
Incomplete	6.3	6.3	8.2	7.7	10.4	12.2	13.6	17.0	25.5
Complete	4.0	6.1	5.9	5.5	10.5	8.2	8.1	12.4	19.3
University									
Incomplete	3.4	3.5	4.7	5.3	11.7	9.4	12.6	12.6	19.0
Complete	2.2	3.9	3.4	3.1	5.7	3.6	5.4	3.6	6.7

Source: Author's calculations using data from the Permanent Household Survey.

(2.7 percent), contradicting the view that public sector layoffs have been a major cause of the rise in unemployment. However, differences in unemployment rates by industrial sector are less meaningful than other measures, since the unemployed are attributed to the industry in which they were last made unemployed, but may eventually find work elsewhere. For example, a large shift in employment from manufacturing to services may provoke crowding in sevices; the resulting higher unemployment in the service sector in fact originated in manufacturing. Hence it is more meaningful to compare unemployment rates by skill level.

Table 6-4 shows that occupational rates of unemployment for May 1993 again exhibit a customary pattern. That is, unemployment rates are highest for less skilled workers, since they have a higher incidence of unemployment than other groups. The unemployment rate of blue collar workers is nearly four times higher than that of professionals, as is the case in the United States and Great Britain. The lower panel of the table shows unemployment rates by educational attainment. Since education, unlike occupational level, is a relatively stable personal characteristic, these rates can be even more meaningful. The data confirm that education—especially as measured by completed degrees—is inversely related to the probability of unemployment. In May 1993 the unemployment rate for those who had completed university studies was half that for individuals who had only completed primary schooling.

To understand whether quits and layoffs contribute more to unemployment than entry into the labor force, I look at the causes of unemployment reported by respondents during the period 1985–94. Unfortunately, the data are not broken down into the standard categories of causes of unemployment. Essentially, one can distinguish unemployment for new entrants to the labor force from the rest (quits, layoffs, and reentrants). In October 1994, when the total unemployment rate was 12.9 percent, unemployment for new entrants amounted to 1.7 percent and for those with previous occupations, to 11.2 percent. For May 1993 one can further decompose the causes of unemployment for those with previous occupations. In this group, the majority of the unemployed fall in the layoff category, which includes layoffs and completion of temporary jobs. Although the exact proportion cannot be calculated, it ranges between 56 and 96 percent.[8]

Was there any change in the structure of unemployment between October 1987 and 1994? Which groups experienced the greatest growth in unemployment?[9] In terms of gender, male and female unemployment rates increased in the same proportions: from 1987 to 1995 females contributed 7.9 percentage points and males 7.7 percentage points to the 15.6 percentage point increase in the total unemployment rate, as shown in figure 6-5. Note, however, that male unemployment increases at a higher rate between October 1987 and 1992, whereas female unemployment takes the lead thereafter. Considering contributions by age group, those between twenty and forty-nine years of age contributed 9.6 percentage points (4.4 percentage points by males and 5.2 percentage points by females) to the total increase, showing that the unemployment increase is not caused by higher female or teenage unemployment. Rather, it has hit the more stable portion of the labor force.[10]

8. It is likely that the data overrepresent the quit category and hence the number of layoffs will be closer to the lower bound.

9. Although I chose 1987 as the base year, the results would have been similar if I had chosen 1991. As figure 6-3 shows, 1987 is the trough of a cycle of unemployment that ended in 1991. Likewise, I could have chosen 1985 as the base year for the comparison. This year, which appears as a peak in figure 6-3, shares some characteristics with the high unemployment years, although unemployment rates were lower than in 1991.

10. Decomposition of the increase in the unemployment rate ($U = \Sigma\, s_i U_i$, where s_i is the share of the group in the labor force and U_i is the group-specific unemployment rate)

Figure 6-5. *Unemployment Rate, by Gender, October 1987–May 1995*[a]

Percent

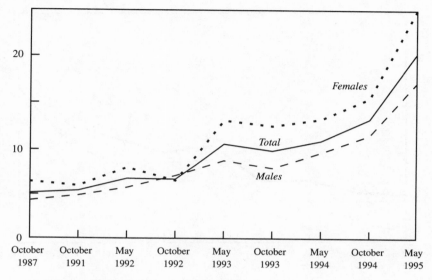

Source: Author's calculations using data from the Permanent Household Survey.
a. For population ages fifteen to sixty-four.

Figure 6-6 shows change in unemployment rates by industrial sector, excluding construction, which has the highest unemployment rates but the lowest share (7 percent) in the labor force. Over the period 1987–95, unemployment tended to increase in similar proportions in services and manufacturing, but was higher in the latter.[11]

into its three components between October 1987 and May 1995 reveals that the 15.6 percentage point increase is predominately due to the increase in U_i (14.8 percentage points), leaving the shares constant, while the other two components contribute 0.8 percentage points. Furthermore, in this 14.8 percentage point rise due to the pure increase in unemployment rates, the contributions of men and women between ages twenty and forty-nine are virtually identical: 4.8 percentage points and 4.6 percentage points, respectively. The differential, noted above, between a 5.2 percentage point increase for females and 4.4 percentage points for males in this age group is due to the increase in the share of females in the labor force from 0.36 to 0.40.

11. The October 1994 data show unemployment in the service sector beginning to catch up with unemployment in manufacturing in Argentina. This coincides with the beginning of a recession, when the service sector will be hardest hit because of lower internal demand.

Figure 6-6. *Unemployment Rate, Selected Sectors, October 1987–May 1995*

Percent

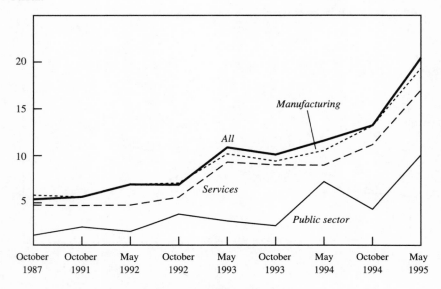

Source: Author's calculations using data from the Permanent Household Survey.

In terms of occupation, figure 6-7 shows that white collar and blue collar workers have had similar experiences of unemployment since October 1987, while professionals have suffered the least. Note how wide the gap in unemployment rates among occupations had become by May 1994. Also, the last two data points for 1994 seem to indicate a trend toward a steeper increase in white collar unemployment.

The change in unemployment by educational attainment shows a different pattern (see table 6-4). First, the data for 1993 do not show uniformly lower rates of unemployment for successively higher educational groups. The unemployment rates of those who did not complete a secondary or tertiary degree increased proportionately more than the rates for those who did complete these degrees. For workers with completed degrees, there is an inverse relationship between education and unemployment, but (unexpectedly) with the exception of holders of tertiary degrees, the increase in unemployment is *directly* related to education: unemployment increases by 92 percent for those with lower education (incomplete primary schooling), but rises more quickly for those with more education: it increases by 115 percent, 170 percent, 210 percent,

Figure 6-7. *Unemployment Rate, by Occupational Level,*
October 1987–May 1995

Percent

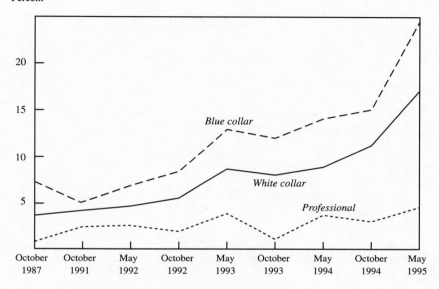

| October 1987 | October 1991 | May 1992 | October 1992 | May 1993 | October 1993 | May 1994 | October 1994 | May 1995 |

Source: Author's calculations using data from the Permanent Household Survey.

and 270 percent for those with complete primary, incomplete secondary, complete secondary, and incomplete tertiary schooling, respectively.

Furthermore, figure 6-8 shows that while the unemployment rate for those with only primary schooling peaked at 13.8 percent in October 1992 (having more than doubled since 1987), the unemployment rates for those with secondary and tertiary degrees did not grow significantly before October 1992. In fact, the increase in unemployment since October 1992 is mostly due to the doubling of unemployment rates for those with secondary education. Note that this is consistent with layoffs being the main reason for the increase in unemployment since 1992. In the process of downsizing, workers with lower educational attainment tend to be laid off first. As the process continues, more educated individuals are laid off, including those with more human capital, albeit obsolete.

The unemployment rate is determined by inflow into unemployment and the average duration of unemployment spells. The same level of unemployment may be associated with high inflow rates and relatively short spells in one period or country, but with low inflow rates and long

Figure 6-8. *Unemployment Rate, by Educational Attainment,*
October 1987–May 1995

Percent

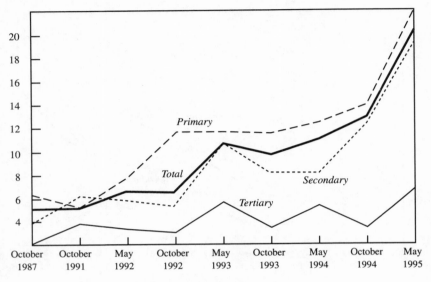

Source: Author's calculations using data from the Permanent Household Survey.

spells of unemployment in another. Long spells of unemployment entail
high social costs, since skills and motivation may depreciate during long
periods without work and employers might be unwilling to hire the long-
term unemployed ("stigma effect"). High inflows into unemployment
might entail high economic efficiency, in that the best match between
workers' skills and needs of firms are maximized through screening and
labor turnover; however, they can also have high social costs if excessive
turnover entails the loss of job-specific skills and imposes transaction
costs on workers and employers. When unemployment is due to the
increased use of fixed-term contracts, so that workers in permanent jobs
remain relatively immobile, a few groups, such as younger and female
workers, may bear an excessive proportion of the burden. In sum, the
best scenario would be short spells of unemployment and moderate rates
of turnover.

I show elsewhere that higher duration of unemployment and higher
inflow into the pool of the unemployed are both responsible for the

increase in the total unemployment rate in Argentina.[12] Moreover, compared with more developed countries, by 1994 Argentina had the highest inflow rate and shortest average duration of unemployment (although this grew substantially during the transition period). The inflow rate increased from 1.5 percent a month in October 1991 to 2.8 percent in October 1994. The average duration of all unemployment spells increased from 3.6 months to 4.6 months in the same period, while the average duration of more recent spells rose from 6.6 months to 8.6 months.[13] Giacchino and I find that at least part of the increased duration of unemployment is associated with the introduction of unemployment insurance in 1992. This issue is analyzed below.[14]

In conclusion, the increase in unemployment rates observed in Argentina since 1991 is due to proportional increases in the unemployment rates for males and females in all age categories, especially prime age. Although not biased against the less skilled or less educated, rising unemployment has hit those with incomplete degrees hardest. An important feature revealed by the data is that unemployment does not increase in proportion to lack of skills or education. Although the less educated or those with unfinished degrees suffered most at first, at a later stage unemployment begins to hit the more educated portion of the labor force harder.

During the period of structural reform, when job creation was sluggish and labor force participation was growing, there was an increase in involuntary part-time work—or underemployment.[15] While it is true that from the point of view of firms, growth in part-time work may reflect

12. Pessino (1996).
13. Since the latter variable measures the average length of time a currently unemployed person will remain unemployed, it is larger than the first measure, which accounts for the duration of all the unemployment spells that begin in a given year. Moreover, since inflow almost doubled between 1991 and 1994, the "more recent" duration measure also shows a larger increase.
14. Pessino and Giacchino (1994).
15. The definition of part-time work varies considerably across countries. Essentially, there are two possible approaches with the Argentinean database: (1) to classify workers who worked less than thirty-five hours a week on the basis of their own perceptions of their employment situations; or (2) to apply a cut-off (generally at thirty or thirty-five hours) based on actual hours worked during the reference week. In the Argentinean data, in accordance with international standards, involuntary part-time work is defined as "underemployment"; that is, working less than thirty-five hours but being willing to work more. Since willingness to work more hours is not a clearly defined concept, I use "underemployed" as defined by INDEC.

Figure 6-9. *Underemployment as a Share of Total Employment, 1974–95*

Percent

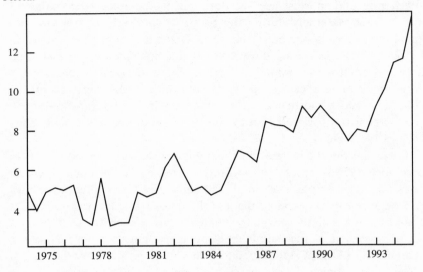

Source: Author's calculations using data from the Permanent Household Survey.

greater labor market flexibility, it may not always correspond to the needs and wishes of employees. In the period 1986–94, between 40 and 50 percent of all workers working thirty hours or less a week said that they were working part-time involuntarily.[16] Figure 6-9 shows the growing importance of underemployment as a share of total employment in greater Buenos Aires. Between 1974 and 1984 this share fluctuated around 5 percent, between 1984 and 1991 it increased by roughly 3 percentage points to 8 percent, and from 1991 to 1994 it increased by a further 3 percentage points to reach more than 11 percent of total employment.

16. Lamentably, the database does not allow one to identify those underemployed who not only declare themselves willing to work more hours but are actively looking for more work. According to government officials, the percentage of underemployed looking for another occupation is quite low. However, from the May 1993 unemployment module it appears that 44 percent of the underemployed and 27 percent of the part-timers (those working less than thirty hours a week) were looking for work. In October 1994, INDEC formally began to distinguish between the "demanding underemployed" (that is, those actively looking for work) and the "nondemanding underemployed" in official statistics. During this period, 53 percent of the underemployed fell in the first category. Note that as the concept of underemployment is itself a bit loose, so is the difference between those who are searching for a job and those who are too discouraged to search for a job.

The impact of changes in the sectoral distribution of employment, as well as the rise in underemployment, has given rise to contradictory concerns about the types of jobs that are being generated. On the one hand, the reduction in manufacturing jobs and the emergence of low-quality work in the service sector may imply a less skilled workforce. On the other hand, increases in earnings of skilled workers relative to those of the unskilled since 1990 (see below) might be explained as a result of trade liberalization and technological change biased in favor of skilled workers. This combination has probably created an underclass of low-skilled workers and more skilled but "obsolete" workers who are poorly paid, underemployed, or unemployed. Rapid changes in skill requirements have been evoked as a possible cause of higher unemployment due to the mismatch between jobs and job-seekers.

One problem facing any skill-based analysis of the labor force is the lack of an objective or direct measure of the skills required for a job or embodied by a worker. Common proxies are occupation, education, or, directly, earnings. This section concentrates on changes in the composition of employment by level of education. Figure 6-10 shows the composition of the Argentinean labor force in terms of fully employed, underemployed, and unemployed workers, by highest educational attainment, for 1987, 1991, and 1995. Over the period 1987–95 there was an extraordinary increase in the educational attainment of the labor force: whereas in 1987, 17 percent of the labor force had a tertiary degree (complete or incomplete), by 1995, this fraction had increased to 23 percent. Conversely, the proportion of the labor force with no more than primary schooling fell from 53 percent in 1987 to 37 percent in 1995.

If one looks at the composition of the labor force across periods, one can see that 1987 and 1991 were similar in terms of the overall unemployment rate: 4.7 percent and 5.3 percent, respectively. However, there was a higher proportion of underemployment in 1987. The greatest change occurred between 1991 and 1995, when the shares of unemployment and underemployment increased in all categories of education. Evidently there has been an upgrade in education of the labor force, and it continues to be true that the less educated are hardest hit by unemployment and underemployment. Yet between 1991 and 1995 most of the increase in the labor force was accommodated by underemployment and unemployment. By 1995, fewer workers with only primary schooling had full-time jobs, for those with only secondary schooling the number stayed constant, and for those with a university education it had risen slightly.

Figure 6-10. *Degree of Employment and Educational Attainment,*
Greater Buenos Aires

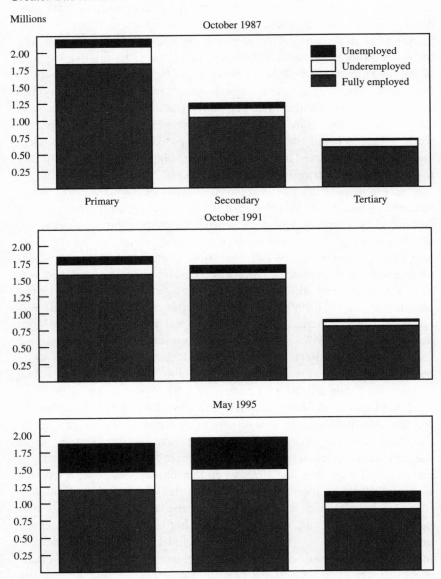

Source: Author's calculations using data from the Permanent Household Survey.

Finally, the finding that the most educated individuals experienced the highest employment growth as well as increased underemployment and unemployment suggests that between 1991 and 1994, demand for highly educated individuals increased not only at the expense of less educated individuals but also of those who were highly educated but had bad credentials or obsolete skills. This could develop into a serious problem of persistent mismatch, especially if the skills required for new jobs are substantially different from those of the jobs being lost.

Major Trends in Labor Force Participation

In an accounting sense, unemployment increases if the growth rate of labor force participation surpasses the growth rate of employment. While it is evident that most of the increase in unemployment in a given period corresponds to those who have previously been employed, it is possible that women might contribute to the increase by reentering the labor force. In Argentina, as in other Latin American countries, there has been an increase in the labor force participation of women.

The slight increase in the participation of males matched their population growth during the period 1987–95, resulting in a constant male labor force participation rate of 84 percent. However, the labor force participation rate of women between the ages of fifteen and sixty-four increased from 43 percent in 1987 to 52 percent in May 1995. Figure 6-11 shows that the female labor force participation rate increased very rapidly from October 1991 to a peak of 51 percent in May 1993, decreased by 2 percentage points in 1994, and increased again during 1995. As Giacchino and I predict, it was not the mere increase in female participation that drove up overall unemployment rates.[17] It is shown that the unemployment rate with constant female labor force participation is almost identical to the actual unemployment rate with compositional changes netted out. In the same vein, the higher teenage labor force participation rate did not contribute significantly to changes in the unemployment rate.

Another important issue arising from the data on participation is that in greater Buenos Aires the participation rates of teenagers and the old increased (or did not decrease) over the period 1987–95. This contradicts worldwide trends, since higher income is usually associated with a shorter

17. Pessino and Giacchino (1994).

Figure 6-11. *Female Labor Force Participation Rates, by Age,*
October 1987–May 1995

Percent

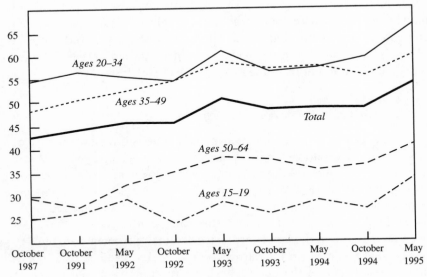

Source: Author's calculations using data from the Permanent Household Survey.

lifetime career, as a result both of delayed entry into the labor force due
to further schooling and of earlier retirement. In this case, it appears
that either lower wealth or higher real wage rates drove more of the old,
the young, and the female populations into the labor force.

My work with Giacchino, later corroborated with Gill, presents evidence that many females respond to lower income or higher unemployment in their family unit by joining the labor force.[18] This is known in
the literature as the added worker effect. In this case, the increase in real
wages from 1991 to 1993 (discussed further below) also gave rise to a
reverse "discouraged worker effect"; that is, the substitution effect further increased female labor force participation.[19] However, the slowdown

18. Pessino and Giacchino (1994); Pessino and Gill (1996b).
19. Usually the discouraged and added worker effects work in opposite directions
during a recession that causes prime-age male unemployment rates to increase (and hence
expected household income to decrease) and real wages to decrease, since the lower household income tends to increase the labor force participation of secondary workers and the
lower real wage rate tends to decrease it. Hence it is relatively easy to predict whether the

and slight fall in female labor force participation since 1993 might indicate
that the decline in real wage growth together with higher female unemployment rates has resulted in lower expected real wages for some
women. By October 1994, overall labor force participation continued at
the same level as in May 1994. Most recently, the May 1995 employment
survey again shows a high increase in female labor force participation
coupled with a huge increase in unemployment for male heads of household, confirming that an added worker effect is in operation.

Coverage of Social Security and Other Mandatory Benefits

In general, the self-employed are not covered by labor benefits. The
share of the self-employed in total employment in Argentina was around
25 percent in October 1994. The premium to self-employment had increased with hyperinflation, since to the extent that the self-employed
have contracts these are loose and hence can deal better with inflation.[20]
In fact, the number of self-employed grew from approximately 870,000
in October 1985 to 1,040,000 in October 1989, a 19 percent increase,
while the number of wage-earners increased only by 7.5 percent, resulting
in an increase of 11 percent in total employment. After 1989 the number
of self-employed decreased by approximately 4 percent and began to rise
again after the introduction of the Convertibility Plan in 1991. However,
this increase was moderate: between October 1991 and May 1994, self-
employment increased by 1.5 per cent while total employment increased
by 2.3 percent.

Part of the rise in self-employment reflects a tendency of firms to
contract out work and so does not represent a net addition to the number
of jobs available. This is usually the case in countries where restrictive
job security legislation or high employer contributions to social security
provide strong incentives to contract work out. In Argentina before 1990,
there were strong incentives to contract out and the self-employed were
not monitored closely on their contributions to social security. However,
the Menem administration introduced new procedures for monitoring
the self-employed—in particular, by the DGI ("tax secretary")—taking
away some of the benefit of being self-employed. Moreover, the new

discouraged or added worker effect is operating. In the Argentinean case, with higher real
wages but lower expected income (at least for some groups), both effects will tend to
increase the labor force participation of secondary workers.

20. See Pessino (1993).

social security legislation enacted in 1993 established that a person working for the same firm on a regular basis, more than three times a week
and for more than five hours, cannot be defined as self-employed. Hence,
whereas before 1991 the self-employed tended to be outside the social
security system, the current self-employed are more likely to be
contributors.

The self-employment category might include individuals who do contribute toward social security and other benefits and those who do not.
At the same time, some of the workers categorized as wage-earners might
violate the law and not contribute to the social security system.[21] The
employment survey identifies whether wage-earners receive some benefits, with or without severance payments, all available benefits, or no
benefits. These benefits include mandated paid vacation, a thirteenth
month of pay, pension benefits, health insurance, and so on. Table 6-5
shows the percentage of wage-earners in each category for October 1987,
October 1991, May 1994, and May 1995. Since women in Argentina are
more expensive in terms of the social benefits, as a result both of mandated paid maternity leave and also shorter tenure, it is not surprising that they represent a higher share of wage-earners without benefits
than men.

The data presented in table 6-5 show a clear increasing trend in the
proportion of wage-earners without any benefits. Their share grew from
20 percent in October 1987 to 27 percent in May 1995. The main increase
occurred during the hyperinflationary period 1988–90 and corresponded
with a decline in the proportion of wage-earners with some benefits.
Since 1991, their share has remained roughly constant. The underemployed are much more likely to receive no benefits, and part of the
increase in the category without any benefits can be attributed to the
increase in underemployment since 1987.[22] The share of those with all
available benefits oscillated between 56 and 62 percent over the period.

21. According to official social security data, approximately 6.6 million people (both
wage-earners and self-employed) were affiliated with the program by the end of 1995.
However, the number of people actually contributing was only around 4.6 million. Thus,
of an estimated 12 million employed, only 40 percent are contributing to social security.

22. In May 1994, 26 percent of fully employed wage-earners received no benefits, while
60 percent of the underemployed reported receiving no benefits.

Table 6-5. *Benefit Levels of Wage Earners, by Gender, Greater Buenos Aires*
Percent

Benefit level	October 1987			October 1991			May 1994			May 1995		
	Total	Male	Female	Total	Male	Female	Total	Male	Female	Total	Male	Female
All benefits[a]	59.5	65.3	50.3	60.6	63.2	56.0	56.1	58.2	52.8	62.2	65.7	56.8
Some benefits, total	20.5	17.1	25.9	11.4	9.3	14.7	15.3	14.0	17.7	10.6	8.7	13.5
One benefit and 13th month of pay[b]	4.7	2.5	8.4	2.9	1.6	5.2	3.4	1.9	5.8	3.5	2.7	4.8
Some benefits and severance pay	5.7	5.0	6.5	3.4	3.0	4.0	5.4	5.3	5.7	3.4	2.9	4.0
Some benefits, no severance pay	10.1	9.6	11.0	5.1	4.7	5.5	6.5	6.8	6.2	3.7	3.1	4.7
No benefits	20.0	17.6	23.8	28.0	27.5	29.3	28.6	27.8	29.5	27.2	25.6	29.7
Total	100.0	100.0	100.0	100.0	100.0	100.0	100.0	100.0	100.0	100.0	100.0	100.0

Note: The category "all benefits" includes vacations, thirteenth-month severance payment, unemployment insurance, and social security contributions. The category "some benefits" includes first, one of the above benefits (except severance payment) plus thirteenth month, the second some of the benefits (but not all) plus severance payment, and the third some of the benefits but without severance payment. The category "without benefits" does not include any of the aforementioned benefits.
Source: Author's calculations using data from Permanent Household Survey.
a. Includes vacations, a thirteenth month of pay, severance pay, work insurance, and social security contributions.
b. Does not include severance pay.

Determinants of Unemployment

For policy purposes, it is important to understand the course of unemployment in Argentina, in particular, since the change in macroeconomic regime and the structural reforms introduced in 1990–91. To this
end, one should test whether the probability of unemployment decreases
with education, leaving other factors constant, and the extent to which
each additional year of education helps in avoiding unemployment. Likewise, one should analyze how unemployment varies with experience and
examine the empirical support for the stylized fact that those with obsolete skills have a higher incidence of unemployment. Finally, one should
examine whether the trade liberalization process combined with higher
dollar wages implies a higher concentration of unemployment in import-
competing sectors. To address these questions, I estimate a probit model
for two points in time: October 1991, the beginning of the reform process,
and October 1994. These results are then compared to determine whether
there are structural differences between the two periods and to test and
quantify the importance of the variables, such as education and experience, on the likelihood of unemployment. (The model and its results are
presented in detail in appendix 6A.)

The results show that, in both years, the probability of unemployment
first increases and then decreases with employment experience, but that
the effect is much more pronounced in 1994 (see figure 6-12 and table
6A-1). For a worker over forty-two years old and with ten years of schooling (the average for this group) the probability of unemployment begins
to rise in 1994, although in 1991 it remains almost flat. With respect to
education, the probability of unemployment decreases with years of
schooling, and the effect is higher in 1994. For a worker with an average
level of experience (in terms of the sample), one more year of schooling
reduces the probability of unemployment by 0.7 percentage point in 1994,
but by only 0.2 percentage point in 1991. Finally, the results seem to
confirm that skill obsolescence was a cause of unemployment in 1994, as
figure 6-13 shows.

The empirical analysis does not find evidence for the contention that
the import-competing sectors (that is, manufacturing) laid off a higher
proportion of workers. However, to test this hypothesis properly one
would need more disaggregated data than is currently available.

While some highly educated workers faced a higher likelihood of unemployment, others found that their skills earned them a higher reward.

Figure 6-12. *Estimated Probability of Unemployment as a Function of Experience*

Probability

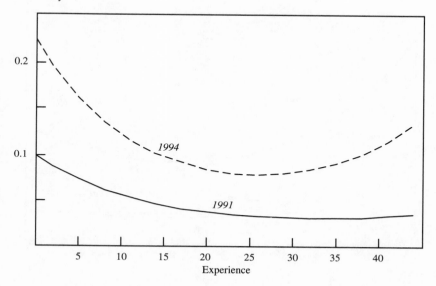

Source: Author's model, as described in appendix 6A, using data from the Permanent Household Survey.

Figure 6-14 shows a significant increase in the rate of return to education, as measured by earnings, for workers who had completed tertiary education, starting at 15 percent in 1990 and peaking at 25 percent in May 1994. Note that although returns to primary education remain fairly close to 5 percent from the introduction of the Convertibility Plan, and are essentially without trend, returns to the three next educational levels fluctuate considerably around 10 percent, also without clear trend. The higher increase in returns for individuals who have completed tertiary studies reveals the increase in their relative demand and, presumably, low elasticity of substitution. This increment in the rate of return to higher education occurred in spite of the growth in supply of highly educated individuals during the period; the stagnation of the 1980s drove more people to school. As a consequence of these factors, income distribution in the greater Buenos Aires area worsened after the introduction of the Convertibility Plan: if rates of return to education increase, so will (other things constant) the variance of log wages. This phenomenon is illustrated in figure 6-15, which plots average earnings of the

Figure 6-13. *Estimated Probability of Unemployment as a Function of Experience and Education*

Probability

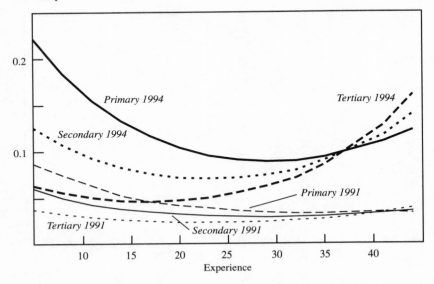

Source: Author's model, as described in appendix 6A, using data from the Permanent Household Survey.

highest income decile divided by the lowest decile over the period 1980–95.

Wages, Productivity, and Competitiveness

One of the main mechanisms matching people and jobs is wage adjustment. Wages have significant consequences for employment and unemployment. The process of wage determination is strongly influenced by macroeconomic events, labor market pressures, legislation, and industrial relations systems, all of which affect the evolution of real wages and wage differentials.

The more promptly wage adjustments occur, the lower is the risk of mismatch unemployment. Institutional factors, such as the presence of unions and rigid labor legislation, can delay the process of adjustment. Both aggregate real wages and relative wages matter in the process of

Figure 6-14. *Marginal Returns to Education, Males Ages Twenty-five to Sixty-four, Greater Buenos Aires, 1986–May 1995*

Percent

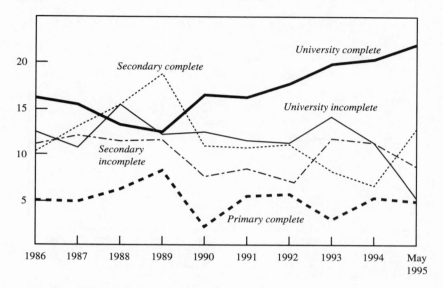

Source: Author's calculations using data from the Permanent Household Survey.

adjustment. Aggregate real wages are important for determining the overall demand for labor as against physical capital. Changes in relative wages between skilled and unskilled labor or across industries are important since they allow the different types of labor to adjust to changes in demand or supply.

There are several forces that influence aggregate demand for labor. Among the most important is the relative price of labor vis-à-vis capital, which includes both variable and fixed costs of contracting. In Argentina fixed costs are substantial, due to high costs imposed by work-related accident laws, large mandated severance payments, and high payroll taxes. The relative price of labor is influenced not only by changes in aggregate demand or supply, but also by international shocks. In particular, since most intermediate capital goods are imported in Argentina, lower tariffs or a peso appreciation will tend to lower their domestic prices. At the same time, an appreciated peso translates into high real wages denominated in dollars. Hence trade liberalization and the Convertibility Plan have made capital goods cheaper and labor more expen-

Figure 6-15. *Income Distribution, Greater Buenos Aires, 1980–95*[a]

Percent

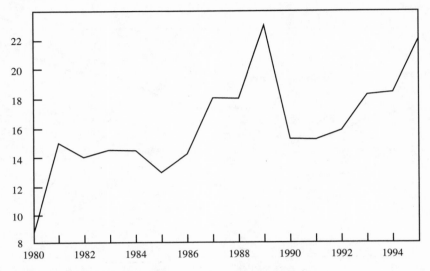

Source: Author's calculations using househhold-level data from the Permanent Household Survey.
a. Income distribution is measured as highest income decile divided by lowest income decile.

sive in dollar terms (affecting, in particular, the sector that trades goods in international markets). According to official figures, the relative price of capital vis-à-vis labor has fallen considerably since the Convertibility Plan.[23] Using 1990 as the base, this index averaged 97.6 during the period 1980–89 and then fell steadily to 85.9 in 1991, 72.3 in 1992, and 60.9 in 1993.[24]

Figure 6-16 shows aggregate real monthly earnings for males aged twenty-five to fifty-four—both wage-earners and the self-employed—over the period 1986–95, using microeconomic data from the household surveys in greater Buenos Aires.[25] The data show that aggregate real

23. The price of capital is calculated from Divisia indexes, using implicit prices of gross investment from the national accounts. The source for the wages is not cited; however this branch of government tends to use data from the EPH, so I suspect that they are correct. The Divisia indexes suffer from the problems usually cited in the literature on price indexes but, given the level of change occurring in Argentina, these are second-order problems.

24. Figures given by the undersecretary of labor and social economics.

25. Nominal wages are extracted from the household surveys for October of each year. There are other, mainly sectoral, surveys that calculate much lower rates of change in real wages for the period after 1990; see FIEL (various issues) and Estudio M. A. M. Broda y

Figure 6-16. *Real Monthly Earnings, Males Ages Twenty-five to Fifty-four, Greater Buenos Aires, October 1986–May 1995*[a]

Index, September 1989 = 100

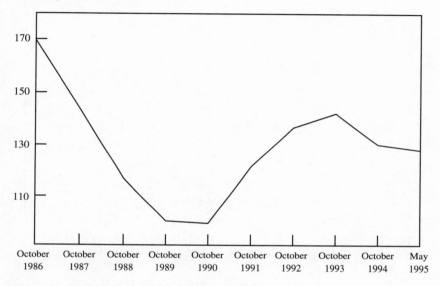

Source: Author's calculations using data from the Permanent Household Survey.
a. Sample includes wage-earners and the self-employed.

earnings increased from the introduction of the stabilization plan until October 1993, when they began to decline.[26]

However, figure 6-17, which considers earnings differentiated by occupational level, shows that professional earnings have risen more than those of white collar workers and the real earnings of blue collar workers have remained constant.[27] Note that in the period in the figure, the recorded real earnings of professionals and white collar workers seem to

---

Asoc. (various issues). However, in those surveys the less skilled workers, whose wages have increased the least or not at all, tend to be weighted more.

Note, also, that there are other determinants of real wages besides relative prices. In particular, the increase in GDP and capital per worker in the Argentinean economy is consistent with higher average real wages.

26. A similar picture emerges when considering wage rates, that is, earnings divided by hours of work.

27. Data from the Help Wanted Index (FIEL, 1994) also show that relative demand for professionals and more skilled workers rose, while that for less skilled workers stagnated or declined.

Figure 6-17. *Real Earnings, by Occupational Level, Males Ages Twenty-five to Fifty-four, Greater Buenos Aires, 1986–May 1995*

Thousands

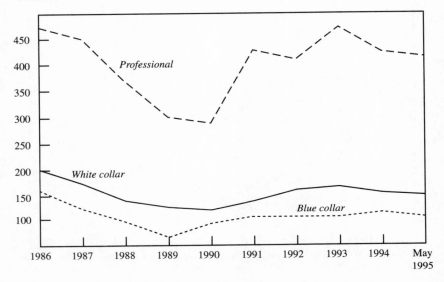

Source: Author's calculations using data from the Permanent Household Survey.

decline slightly. Higher unemployment rates, stemming from lower employment levels, sooner or later had to result in lower real earnings.

The picture that emerges of Argentina is that structural reform—which was expected to reduce employment in declining sectors and increase it in booming sectors—has only progressed halfway, and so far the contractionary effect has been predominant. The record high real appreciation of the peso must prevent the tradeable sector from flourishing unless it is accompanied by unprecedented growth in productivity, or a fall in real wages, or both, which would lower unit labor costs and increase competitiveness.

Since Argentina's GDP growth rate has been higher than the meager or zero growth in employment, the average productivity of labor likely has risen. Moreover, the increased rate of return to education, higher wages for skilled workers, higher unemployment (due both to sectoral shifts and the incorporation of capital intensive techniques), and the discharge of workers with obsolete human capital should result in an increase in labor productivity. This increase should be higher in the sectors in which these changes have been most prevalent.

Data on nationwide employment by sector are not readily available. Hence the information on productivity trends presented here comes from several sources. Table 6-6 shows average productivity for different sectors of the economy over the period 1980–93, calculated from national accounts data on total production and estimated data on total employment from the Latin American Economic Research Foundation (FIEL). Between 1990 and 1993, average labor productivity increased by approximately 5.5 percent per year, or 17 percent over the period. Taking 1994 into account also, the annual increase is 6.5 percent, giving 22 percent over the period. By contrast, before 1989 average labor productivity decreased by 1.9 percent a year. There are clear differences in productivity growth by sector. Between 1990 and 1993, average labor productivity in agriculture increased by around 3 percent a year, in mining by 2.6 percent, in manufacturing by 11.7 percent, in construction by 12.7 percent (although it had been close to this higher level in 1987 and 1988), in electricity by 3.9 percent, in trade by 3.9 percent, in transportation by 1.6 percent, in the financial sector by 8.3 percent, and in personal services it decreased by 0.7 percent a year. The largest increases in productivity have been obtained in manufacturing and construction, the former mostly composed of import substitutes and the latter of nontradeables. The exportable goods sectors, such as mining and agriculture, have experienced the lowest increases in productivity.

Although the trend toward higher labor productivity is positive, unit costs of production (as proxied by dollar wages divided by average labor productivity) are still much higher than at the beginning of the Convertibility Plan.[28] Table 6-7 compares dollar wages, average productivity, and their ratio—that is, unit costs—for 1989, 1991 (the beginning of the Convertibility Plan), and 1993. It shows that because of the rise in productivity, unit costs increased by less than dollar wages.

Did the increase in productivity help to alleviate the lack of competitiveness created by the historically high appreciation of the peso? It is

28. It would be more accurate to measure unit labor costs in terms of wages received by employees plus all the payroll taxes of employees and employers and all forms of wage compensation. The major change during the period was a 30 percent reduction in employer payroll taxes. However, this reform was enacted in 1994 and reversed in the first half of 1995.

Table 6-6. *Average Labor Productivity, 1980–93*[a]

							Sector			
Year	*Total GDP*	*Agriculture*	*Mining*	*Manufacturing*	*Construction*	*Electricity and water*	*Trade*	*Transportation and communications*	*Financial*	*Personal services*
1980	1.02	0.58	3.86	1.42	0.77	1.49	1.05	0.78	3.23	0.59
1981	0.96	0.63	4.06	1.32	0.71	1.50	0.87	0.73	3.34	0.60
1982	0.92	0.63	3.57	1.28	0.76	1.52	0.78	0.75	2.96	0.58
1983	0.96	0.65	4.20	1.39	0.80	1.62	0.83	0.76	2.80	0.60
1984	0.95	0.64	4.45	1.37	0.72	1.69	0.82	0.85	2.85	0.58
1985	0.89	0.64	4.58	1.25	0.65	1.59	0.73	0.79	2.66	0.56
1986	0.92	0.66	4.53	1.40	0.83	1.68	0.71	0.81	2.87	0.54
1987	0.95	0.64	4.24	1.42	0.90	1.73	0.76	0.85	2.77	0.55
1988	0.92	0.72	4.51	1.31	0.87	1.62	0.74	0.85	2.81	0.54
1989	0.86	0.66	4.67	1.30	0.68	1.39	0.65	0.86	2.64	0.52
1990	0.86	0.75	4.93	1.39	0.60	1.38	0.65	0.81	2.51	0.50
1991	0.90	0.79	4.65	1.69	0.64	1.22	0.69	0.84	2.58	0.48
1992	0.97	0.81	5.03	1.83	0.81	1.45	0.73	0.83	3.02	0.48
1993	1.01	0.82	5.32	1.93	0.86	1.55	0.73	0.85	3.19	0.49

Source: Author's calculations based on sectoral GDP data from the national accounts published by Argentina's Economic Ministry and employment figures estimated by the Latin-American Economic Research Foundation.

a. Average labor productivity is calculated as GDP (in 1986 prices) divided by total employment.

Table 6-7. *Dollar Wages, Average Labor Productivity, and Unit Costs*[a]

Item	1989	1991	1993	1991–89	1993–91
Average labor productivity	0.86	0.90	1.01	4.7	12.2
Dollar wages	203.1	659.6	986.1	224.8	49.5
Unit costs	236.2	732.9	976.4	210.3	33.2

Source: Author's calculations using data from the Permanent Household Survey.
a. Average labor productivity is calculated as GDP (in 1986 prices) divided by total employment. Nominal dollar wages and unit costs are nominal dollar wages divided by average labor productivity.

difficult to establish a benchmark period with a "normal" real exchange rate. However, it is clear that relative prices are not favoring the tradeable sector of the economy today and that one way to deal with the problem would be to reduce unit costs by raising productivity growth rates and reforming labor market regulations.[29]

Reform of Labor Market Regulations in Perspective

I show above that the Convertibility Plan had important consequences for labor market outcomes. First, the increase in GDP during the period was accompanied by a rise in open unemployment and slow growth in employment in the first two years of the Plan, and an absolute decline in the latter part of 1993. Second, during the second half of the 1991–94 period, an increase in total employment was accomplished through an increase in underemployment. Third, employment shifted from the manufacturing sector to the service sector. The sectors losing the most employment are the more vulnerable (in terms of their lack of efficiency) tradeable sectors, such as textiles and clothing. Hence the structural reforms intended to eliminate jobs in "inefficient" sectors and create jobs in more efficient competitive sectors have achieved only half of their goal.

Although there has been a significant increase in the labor force due to the incorporation of more women, the rise in the unemployment rate has been caused mainly by lower demand for labor, rather than higher labor supply. The entry of women into the labor force is not causing the problem, but it is making it worse. In addition, there is some evidence

29. My analysis of change in unit cost for more disaggregated sectors of the economy finds evidence that since 1990, among the manufacturing sectors, metallic products and food have had the lowest increases in unit production costs, averaging between 12 and 18 percent. The highest increase, 95 percent, is found in chemical products. In addition, the data available in 1994 seem to indicate a trend toward declining unit costs in food, textiles, and chemical products. In the latter case, the main reason is a decrease in total employment.

of mismatch unemployment, and the higher duration of unemployment observed during this period can be attributed, in part, to workers' lack of the training or skills required for the new sectors. Another important cause is lack of expansion in sectors that are supposed to have a comparative advantage in international markets.

The real wages of individuals with higher education rose during this period, notwithstanding their increased supply, and, as a consequence, wage inequality increased.[30] The forces that produced higher rates of return for individuals with tertiary education also implied lower demand for less skilled workers. Furthermore, economic restructuring led to lower demand and higher unemployment for workers whose skills were obsolete.

Given the need to improve productivity, it is unlikely that employers will try to reduce wages significantly in the face of higher unemployment, at least in the short run, since they must maintain or even increase wages in order to motivate the current labor force. If this is indeed the case, there is no short-run cure for unemployment.[31] However, the most recent data, from October 1994, show the beginnings of a decrease in real wages. And casual observation indicates that the nominal wages of permanent employees have been reduced in some firms. The appreciated peso has not translated into a proportional increase in unit costs of production, because labor productivity increased after 1990. Nevertheless, these costs are still higher than previous levels and further increases in productivity are needed.

The introduction of the Convertibility Plan and economic reform (notably, trade liberalization) was accompanied by very timid, almost nonexistent, labor market reform.[32] The following are positive changes that have been fully or partially implemented and areas that still need to be addressed:

PAYROLL TAXES. At the time of writing, payroll taxes represent a wedge between gross and net wages of approximately 55 percent, gen-

30. In a study of the experience of trade liberalization in Chile after 1975, Robbins (1994) also finds that the spread of relative wages widened in favor of skilled workers. During the early 1980s, Chile also experienced very high unemployment rates and low real exchange rates.

31. However, from efficiency wage theory one would expect that higher unemployment, in itself, will come to act as an incentive for workers, so that it might no longer be necessary to motivate them through wage increments; see Bulow and Summers (1986).

32. For an excellent description of the main features of the current labor legislation, see FIEL (1992).

erated by employee contributions of 22 percent (16 percent for social security and 6 percent for health insurance) and employer contributions of 33 percent (16 percent for social security, 8 percent for health insurance, 7.5 percent for family assignments, and 1.5 percent for unemployment insurance).[33] If one includes a thirteenth month of pay and provisions for work-related accidents and severance payments, the differential between gross and net wages becomes more than 80 percent.

CONTRIBUTIONS. In general, workers regard most contributions as taxes. Although in 1994 the social security system was transformed from a pay-as-you-go state-run system into a mixed system that allows workers to choose between the public system and a private fully funded system based on individual accounts, the low pensions received by current retirees and the normal uncertainty surrounding the introduction of a new system encourage workers to perceive a large part of this contribution as a tax. Moreover, employer contributions finance only the state-run system (from which each worker enrolled in the private system will receive a considerably lower benefit than if the amount were capitalized). Health insurance, by contrast, is administered by the union representing a firm. Unions keep approximately 14 percent of payroll taxes and the services that they provide with these funds are, on average, very poor. This implies that some of the poorer workers in the system have to use public hospitals and less poor workers have to contract private health insurance (in some cases, the firm elects to provide this contribution). The most recent modification to this law, passed in June 1995, allows a worker to choose a health insurer, although within the union system.

LABOR COSTS. In the case of layoffs "without cause," severance payments are mandatory and advance notice of one or two months, depending on seniority, has to be given to the worker. The Employment Law passed in 1991 established that compensation should equal one month's salary per year of service, with a maximum yearly payment of three times the average wage produced by collective bargaining agreements relevant

---

33. In 1994, the government imposed a maximum limit to the wage against which these contributions can be charged. Moreover, during that year employer contributions were reduced by 30 to 80 percent, depending on location. They were raised again in response to the Tequila effect, but recently, because of increasing unemployment, the government announced that the reduction would gradually be reintroduced.

to the worker and a minimum yearly payment of two months' wages.[34] This scheme imposes a high cost on layoffs. Mandatory compensation for work-related injuries represents another high fixed cost of labor.

The high costs of severance payments and other mandated benefits led the government to introduce a few regulatory changes in a law passed in 1991. For example, the law sets a maximum of 55,000 dollars for compensation for a work-related injury. However, the worker can sue the employer under the Civil Code, which does not impose a limit. Hence it offers the possibility of much higher compensation, but also the uncertainty associated with the determination of the settlement. A new law that would create an insurance system for work-related injuries is under discussion in congress.

To bypass the high costs implied by existing labor laws, the employment law of 1991 and subsequent initiatives have introduced new forms of contracts for specific groups in the labor force, some of which include lower payroll taxes and lower severance payments. The Encouragement to Employment contract, for instance, is exclusively for registered unemployed workers. It allows a 50 percent exemption of the employer's contributions and a 50 percent reduction in severance payments, and its term must be between six and eighteen months. Among these new contractual arrangements, the most frequently used is the Contract for Opening a New Activity, which allows the same exemptions as that previously described, with a term ranging from six to twenty-four months. The rest of the agreements apply to the young (up to twenty-four years of age) and are mainly for apprenticeships. These exempt employers from all contributions and severance payments. In addition, in 1995 a new law directed to small and medium-sized firms (known as the PYMES) established reductions in payroll taxes and severance payments for firms with less than forty workers.

UNEMPLOYMENT COMPENSATION. Until 1992 there was no unemployment compensation in Argentina. However, there were stringent rules for layoffs; almost all layoffs resulted in quite substantial severance payments. The 1991 Employment Law created an unemployment insurance system, which was implemented in March 1992. In broad outline, the unemployment compensation system is as follows. Virtually all workers

---

34. Before 1991 the maximum payment per year of service was calculated on the basis of the minimum wage.

are covered, except those who lose jobs in construction, agriculture, or domestic services. When potentially eligible workers become unemployed, their eligibility and level of compensation are determined on the basis of previous employment experience and the reason for present unemployment. To be eligible for benefits, the individual must have become unemployed as of 1992. Only workers who are laid off "without cause" and can demonstrate that they received a salary during the last six months are covered. Those who participate in voluntary retirement programs are not eligible. The minimum labor market experience required is one year on the last job. Benefits are related to the individual's previous earning level. They cover 80 percent of previous earnings that fall between a minimum of 120 pesos and a maximum of 400 pesos. Compensation is reduced over time. Payment extends for four months for those with between twelve and twenty-four months of tenure at the last job; eight months for those with between twenty-four and thirty-six months of tenure; and one year for those with more than thirty-six months of tenure. Unemployed workers are also given allowances for dependents. The benefits paid out by the unemployment insurance system are financed by a 1.5 percent payroll tax on employers.

Given that the average wage rate for October 1993 was 840 pesos (for individuals working more than thirty hours a week), with at least 30 percent of the sample earning less than 400 pesos, it is not surprising to find that the system's coverage has been rising over time. Indeed, the number of people receiving unemployment benefits increased from 3,495 in April 1992 to 18,298 in September 1992 to 20,988 in January 1993 and to 99,301 in September 1993. Nationwide, the system covered slightly less than 10 percent of the unemployed. Of the 99,301 unemployed receiving benefits in September 1993, 47.6 percent lived in the greater Buenos Aires area. (Since there are close to 500,000 unemployed people in greater Buenos Aires, the same proportion of the unemployed is covered here as nationwide.) While coverage of the unemployed population remains low in Argentina, perhaps due to lack of information and restrictions applying to some groups, part of the increase in unemployment rates during 1993 may have been caused by the higher duration of unemployment among this covered 10 percent.[35]

35. In August 1994, the unemployment compensation system was amended to establish a maximum benefit of 250 pesos. Evidently, the system could not be financed as it existed before.

In light of the failure and near bankruptcy of the unemployment insurance system, the government decided that instead of subsidizing unemployment, it should subsidize employment, especially employment that provides some kind of training. Since 1993, a number of such programs have been introduced, including the Intensive Employment Program, the Private Employment Program, and the Youth Program.

DOWNWARD WAGE FLEXIBILITY. The downward wage flexibility required to absorb unemployment is severely restricted both by labor legislation (*Ley de Contrato de Trabajo*) and by collective bargaining agreements. Workers are considered laid off (and therefore eligible for severance payments) if either their wages are reduced or they are moved to a different activity within the firm. In fact, new collective bargaining agreements cannot reduce benefits granted to workers in previous agreements. Only if a firm declares a "crisis" can it engage the union in negotiations for a contract with lower wages or the horizontal movement of workers within the firm. This new type of agreement has to be approved by the Ministry of Labor. Several firms have resorted to this option since 1994.

Moreover, before 1991 virtually all new contracts and collective bargaining agreements indexed salaries to cost of living increases. A series of decrees issued in 1991 and 1993 restricted indexation and only allowed increases in wages in the context of productivity increments. However, in a study of agreements drawn up between 1975 and 1993, Carlos Aldao-Zapiola, Hugo Hulsberg, and Claudio Jaureguiberry find that most of the new agreements use very imprecise measures of productivity increase and ultimately adjust wages, on average, at the same rate as the consumer price index.[36] Note that most agreements are signed by activity; very few are signed at the firm level, although this is permitted by law.

To ease the costs of economic restructuring, the government should lift restrictions on mobility in the labor market and thus prevent an increase in unemployment beyond that necessary for reform. It should also lower payroll taxes, both by reducing employer and employee contributions and by modifying legislation on mandatory severance payments and compensation for work-related accidents.

36. Aldao-Zapiola, Hulsberg, and Jaureguiberry (1995).

Appendix 6A: Probit Model

THIS APPENDIX describes the probit model that underlies the discussion of the determinants of unemployment in the text. Ideally, to analyze the determinants of unemployment one would use data that allowed the transition from employment to unemployment to be modeled as a function of the relevant explanatory variables. However, the data available are from repeated cross-sections and only allow estimation of a binary choice, or probit, model. I estimate such a model for October 1991 (the beginning of the transition period) and October 1994.

The economic interpretation is not straightforward, but previous empirical results suggest that the outcome of the dependent (dummy) variable represents unemployment as the combination of two events: first, the firm's decision to lay off workers, depending on their characteristics; and second, the individual's decision to remain unemployed for some period of time, owing to frictions in the labor market and the possession of assets that keep the reservation wage high. In regard to quits and layoffs, since the data do not distinguish between the two, and since the hypothesis incorporates the individual decision to remain unemployed after being laid off from or quitting a job, the distinction is not significant. Moreover, in the later period, most of the unemployment is due to layoffs.

I first model the decision of firms to lay off a worker (or to induce a quit). The dummy variable L_i represents this decision, such that it is equal to one if the firm decides to lay off a given worker and is equal to zero otherwise.

In a stationary economy, without large changes in relative prices to cause wide sectoral shifts, an idiosyncratic negative shock to a firm might prompt it to lay off some workers. Available theory specifies that the first to be laid off are those with no skills, rather than those with specific training or tenure in a firm. In a transition economy such as Argentina, the usual reasons for layoffs are augmented by (1) a large change in relative prices, to the disadvantage of import-competing sectors; (2) an increase in the price of capital relative to labor, which lowers demand for low-skilled workers and raises demand for high-skilled workers; and (3) the obsolescence of specific human capital from the old regime.

Hence the probability of deciding to lay off a worker will usually decrease with increased education (as a proxy for skills) and will tend to be of a higher order during the economic transition. However, in a stationary economy this probability will tend not to vary with general experience: more general training will not decrease the probability of layoff, *other things constant*. But other things are not constant. In fact, general and specific human capital tend to be correlated (see Marshall and Zarkin, 1987), and if there are no controls for tenure or specific human capital, general experience captures the effect of both. The data used here do not have measures of specific human capital for the unemployed, and hence this variable is expected to be proxying the effect of tenure; that is, if the probability of unemployment does vary with general experience, this is due to the effect of specific human capital or tenure. Under this interpretation, in a stationary economy the probability of unemployment should decrease with general experience. This is not true of a transition economy, where there is obsolescence of specific human capital. In this case, one would expect that as years of education increase, more experienced workers will face a higher probability of unemployment. Hence the probability of unemployment will first decrease and then increase, and it will tend to increase more for better educated workers.

Thus the probability that L_i is equal to one can be written as

$$P(L_i = 1) = F(\alpha + \beta_1 X_i + \beta_2 X_i^2 + \beta_3 s_i$$
$$+ \beta_4 X_i s_i + \Sigma \beta_5 I_i + \Sigma \beta_6 T_i),$$

where P is probability, F is normal cdf, X is experience, s is years of education, I is a dummy for the sector, and T is a dummy for the size of the firm. It is expected that $\beta_1 < 0$, $\beta_2 > 0$ and is larger during the transition period, $\beta_3 < 0$ and is larger during the transition, $\beta_4 > 0$ and larger for the transition period, and β_5 measures the dummies for sector. It is also postulated that the probability of layoff decreases if the worker is covered by mandatory severance payments. The only variable available to proxy that restriction is the size of the firm, T_i; the larger the firm, the lower the probability of unemployment.[37]

The probability of unemployment is the probability of the intersection of the event of the firm laying off a worker and the event of a worker deciding to remain unemployed. The dummy variable R_i represents the latter decision, such that it is equal to one if the worker decides to remain unemployed and equal to zero otherwise.

37. The coverage of severance payments among employed workers is available in the data and is highly positively correlated with the size of the firm.

The worker's decision is influenced by the worker's reservation wage in comparison to the expected market wage. The reservation wage will be higher, the higher is the worker's level of wealth, W_i, among other factors.[38] Hence the probability of unemployment for a worker who has previously been employed, U_i, can be written as[39]

$$P(U_i = 1) = P(L_i = 1, R_i = 1)$$
$$= F(\alpha + \beta_1 X_i + \beta_2 X_i^2 + \beta_3 s_i + \beta_4 X_i s_i + \Sigma \beta_5 I_i + \Sigma \beta_6 T_i + \beta_7 W_i),$$

where W is a measure of wealth and it is expected that $\beta_7 > 0$. There is no good measure of wealth in the data. Therefore a dummy variable measuring whether the worker or the worker's family owns or rents a residence is used as a proxy, since ownership usually represents a higher level of wealth.

The results of the estimation for both 1991 and 1994 are shown in table 6A-1. Note, first, that in both years the probability of unemployment first decreases and then increases with employment experience. As expected, the effect is more pronounced for 1994. The level of experience at which the probability of unemployment reverses and begins to increase is 32.5 for 1991 and 26 for 1994 (calculated at the average number of years of education). That is, for 1994 the probability of unemployment begins to increase for a worker over forty-two years of age and with ten years of schooling. However, as seen in figure 6-12, for 1991 the probability of unemployment as a function of experience is practically constant beyond that experience level (it increases very slightly).

With respect to education, this probability of unemployment decreases, the higher is the level of education, and, as expected, both the size and the significance of this coefficient are higher for 1994. Note that, given the presence of the interaction term, the effect of education on the probability of employment depends on the level of experience. Using the average level of experience for this sample of workers, one more year of education decreases the probability of unemployment by 0.7 percentage point in 1994, but by only 0.2 percentage point in 1991. For an individual without experience in the labor market, one more year of education

38. Furthermore, some of the variables modeled in the decision of firms to lay off will also influence the worker's decision. An example is education, which could help the worker to avoid frictions in the labor market and to find a new job more quickly.

39. New entrants into the labor force are excluded from U_i because their contribution is not the main reason for the increase in unemployment, and besides, they could not have been laid off by a firm.

Table 6A-1. Probability of Unemployment: Linear and Probit Estimates[a]

| | October 1991 | | | | | | October 1994 | | | | | |
| | Model A | | | Model B | | | Model A | | | Model B | | |
Variable	Linear (1)	Probit (2)	Slope (3)	Linear (4)	Probit (5)	Slope (6)	Linear (7)	Probit (8)	Slope (9)	Linear (10)	Probit (11)	Slope (12)
Constant	0.129	−1.081		0.145	−0.899		0.347	−0.267		0.359	−0.204	
	(4.588)	(−3.707)		(5.061)	(−2.995)		(8.360)	(1.175)		(8.383)	(−0.874)	
X	−0.0055	−0.048	−0.0011	−0.0056	−0.049	−0.0012	−0.0154	−0.075	−0.0018	−0.0157	−0.076	−0.0019
	(−3.928)	(−3.346)		(−3.944)	(−3.384)		(−7.395)	(−7.039)		(−7.469)	(−7.096)	
X^2	0.00062	0.00055		0.00062	0.00055		0.000194	0.00096		0.000197	0.00098	
	(3.082)	(2.587)		(3.064)	(2.568)		(6.492)	(6.277)		(6.558)	(6.332)	
s	−0.0058	−0.0509	−0.0022	−0.0057	−0.0504	−0.0020	−0.0179	−0.0893	−0.0069	−0.0181	−0.0904	−0.0068
	(−3.251)	(−2.765)		(−3.151)	(−2.702)		(−6.786)	(−6.307)		(−6.830)	(−6.326)	
Xs	0.00016	0.00124		0.00016	0.00129		0.00052	0.00244		0.00053	0.00250	
	(2.218)	(1.598)		(2.238)	(1.636)		(4.914)	(4.353)		(4.996)	(4.433)	
CONSTR	0.032	0.389	0.035	0.024	0.309	0.027	0.171	0.966	0.172	0.170	0.956	0.170
	(2.003)	(2.174)		(1.488)	(1.691)		(7.429)	(7.121)		(7.178)	(6.921)	
MANUF	0.023	0.291	0.026	0.022	0.287	0.025	0.080	0.581	0.104	0.081	0.584	0.104
	(1.886)	(3.981)		(1.780)	(1.940)		(4.488)	(4.879)		(4.499)	(4.891)	
SER1	0.016	0.222	0.020	0.012	0.193	0.017	0.054	0.437	0.078	0.054	0.439	0.078
	(1.419)	(1.603)		(1.088)	(1.364)		(3.345)	(3.881)		(3.305)	(3.856)	
SER2	0.014	0.204	0.018	0.006	0.118	0.010	0.067	0.502	0.090	0.065	0.485	0.086
	(1.123)	(1.328)		(0.458)	(0.557)		(3.609)	(4.135)		(3.344)	(3.892)	

	(1)	(2)	(3)	(4)	(5)	(6)	(7)	(8)	(9)	(10)	(11)	(12)
SIZE1				−0.019 (−2.477)	−0.197 (−2.491)	−0.017				−0.014 (−1.195)	−0.073 (−1.174)	−0.013
SIZE2				−0.031 (−3.198)	−0.385 (−3.281)	−0.033				−0.004 (−0.271)	−0.023 (−0.301)	−0.004
SIZE3				−0.015 (−1.017)	−0.139 (−0.821)	−0.012				−0.015 (−0.705)	−0.111 (−0.873)	−0.020
MEN	−0.012 (−1.747)	−0.129 (−1.713)	−0.011	−0.011 (−1.542)	−0.117 (−1.535)	−0.010	−0.056 (−5.486)	−0.306 (−5.567)	−0.055	−0.055 (−5.355)	−0.302 (−5.440)	−0.054
PROP	0.014 (1.724)	0.163 (1.690)	0.014	0.014 (1.673)	0.154 (1.592)	0.013	0.024 (1.912)	0.130 (1.877)	0.023	0.023 (1.897)	0.130 (1.877)	0.023
Summary statistics												
$\bar{R}^2$	0.009			0.011			0.037			0.037		
Mean standard error	0.043			0.043			0.098			0.098		
F statistic	4.626			4.485			18.755			14.558		
Degree of freedom	10,4174			13,4171			10,4560			13,4557		
Log likelihood	−748.66			−741.88			−1541.16			−1540.23		

Source: Author's model, as described in appendix 6A.

a. See appendix 6A for all variabes. Asymptotic t statistics are shown in parentheses.

decreases this probability by 1.8 percentage points in 1994, but by only 0.7 percentage point in 1991.

In both years, the coefficient of the interaction is positive and significant. Once again, however, it is substantially larger in 1994, confirming the hypothesis that skill obsolescence has played a role in the creation of unemployment. As seen from figure 6-13, which plots the probit estimate of unemployment as a function of experience for workers with complete primary, secondary, and tertiary education, the lower the experience, the higher the differences in the likelihood of unemployment for different educational groups. As experience increases, unemployment probabilities tend to converge for different levels of education. This trend is more pronounced for 1994, when unemployment probabilities tend to be higher for more educated groups with very high levels of experience.

All of the coefficients that control for sector of employment are significant; the omitted sector is the public sector and other nonspecified sectors. *CONSTR* refers to the construction sector, *MANUF* to the manufacturing sector, *SER1* to the more human-capital-intensive portion of the service sector, and *SER2* to the rest of the service sector. Note that differences in probabilities of layoff by sector widen in 1994 but, except for construction, tend to increase almost proportionately. Also, in 1994 the probability of unemployment is higher in the less formal service sector, although there is no significant difference in 1991. Women are much more likely to be unemployed than men in 1994 than in 1991, possibly due to higher costs of employment (such as paid maternity leave), which become more relevant during a transition. Finally, *PROP*, the variable proxying wealth, has the expected sign, although it is significant only in 1994.

Model B includes controls for size of firm: *SIZE1* represents firms with two to twenty-five workers, *SIZE2* represents firms with twenty-six to five hundred workers, and *SIZE3* represents firms with more than five hundred workers; the omitted variable is firms with only one worker. Note that the larger the firm, the lower the probability of unemployment, although this monotonicity is not preserved in *SIZE3*.

In conclusion, during the transition, unemployment rates were high not only for those with few years of experience but also those with much experience and better educated workers, supporting the hypothesis of the obsolescence of human capital. With respect to sector, at this level of aggregation there is not much evidence that manufacturing (competitive with imports) dropped a higher proportion of workers. In fact, the widest variations in employment occur in construction and in the less formal service sector.[40] However, as discussed in the text, this might be due to the crowding out of low-skilled workers and those with obsolete skills in the less formal sectors of the economy.

40. Incorporation of more disaggregated sectoral dummies confirms that the construction sector has the largest increase in unemployment, followed next by repair services, and then by import-competitive chemical and textile manufacturing.

References

Aldao-Zapiola, Carlos, Hugo Hulsberg, and Claudio Jaureguiberry. 1994. *Productividad y Negociacion Colectiva: La Discusion Salarial en la Argentina en el Marco de los Convenios Colectivos de Trabajo*. Ed. Macchi.

Bulow, Jeremy I., and Lawrence H. Summers. 1986. "A Theory of Dual Labor Markets with Application to Industrial Policy, Discrimination, and Keynesian Unemployment." *Journal of Labor Economics* 4(3): 376–414.

Estudio M. A. M. Broda y Asoc. Various years. *Carta Económica*. Buenos Aires, Argentina.

FIEL (Latin American Economic Research Foundation). 1992. "Costos Laborales Comparados en el Mercosur." DT 35. Buenos Aires, Argentina: FIEL.

———. 1994. "Educación y Mercado de Trabajo en Argentina." Unpublished paper. Buenos Aires, Argentina: FIEL.

———. Various years. "Indicadores de Coyuntura." Buenos Aires, Argentina: FIEL.

Layard, Richard, Stephen Nickell, and Richard Jackman. 1991. *Unemployment: Macroeconomic Performance and the Labour Market*. Oxford University Press.

Marshall, Robert C., and Gary A. Zarkin. 1987. "The Effect of Job Tenure on Wage Offers." *Journal of Labor Economics* 5(3): 301–24.

Pessino, Carola. 1993. "From Aggregate Shocks to Labor Market Adjustments: Shifting of Wage Profiles under Hyperinflation in Argentina." Serie Documentos de Trabajo 95. Buenos Aires, Argentina: CEMA.

———. 1995. "Returns to Education in Greater Buenos Aires 1986–1993: From Hyperinflation to Stabilization." Serie Documentos de Trabajo 104. Buenos Aires, Argentina: CEMA.

———. 1996. "La Anatomía del Desempleo." *Desarrollo Económico* 36 (special issue): 223–62.

Pessino, Carola, and Leonardo Giacchino. 1994. "Rising Unemployment in Argentina: 1974–1993." Paper prepared for the Thirteenth Latin American Meeting of the Econometric Society. Caracas, Venezuela.

Pessino, Carola, and Indermit Gill. 1996a. "Determinants of Labor Demand in Argentina: Estimating the Benefits of Labor Policy Reform." Unpublished paper. Washington: World Bank.

————. 1996b. "Determinants of Labor Supply in Argentina: The Importance of Cyclical Fluctuations in Labor Force Participation." Unpublished paper. Washington: World Bank.

Robbins, Donald J. 1994. "Earnings Dispersion in Chile after Trade Liberalization." Unpublished paper. Harvard University (July).

CHAPTER SEVEN

Brazil: Regulation and Flexibility in the Labor Market

Edward J. Amadeo
José Márcio Camargo

THIS CHAPTER addresses two basic questions. First, to what extent is the Brazilian labor market flexible? Second, to what extent are labor market regulations (such as the minimum wage and mandated benefits and costs for dismissals) an impediment to employment creation, the formalization of labor contracts, and the flexibility of the labor market? To answer the first question, one simply has to attempt to measure labor market flexibility. To answer the second question is much more complex, since one must associate such measures with the regulatory apparatus.

These two questions can be broken down into four specific questions:

—How rigid is the real wage in Brazil, and hence, to what extent does it impede job creation or increase unemployment and informality in the economy?

—To what extent are payroll taxes and mandated benefits too large; that is, hourly compensation is so high that it hinders the competitiveness of Brazilian industry?

—To what extent do the levels of the minimum wage and mandated benefits determine or affect the degree of informality in the economy?

—To what extent do costs (that is, severance payments) and other impediments to the dismissal of workers in Brazil affect employment flexibility?

The answers to these questions are not clear-cut and each is shaped by the available data and previous theoretical and empirical work on the subject. In cases where other research provides reliable information, this is used. In cases where it does not, we attempt to collect the relevant data ourselves. The theoretical discussion concerning the minimum wage and mandated benefits is the most elaborate, since this theme seems central to examining the causes of the magnitude of the informal sector in Brazil.

Real Wage Flexibility

Real wage flexibility is widely interpreted as the best measure of labor market flexibility. In face of a macroeconomic shock, the extent to which real wages adjust will determine the cost of adjustment as measured by unemployment and output losses.[1]

The "wage curve" developed by David Blanchflower and Andrew Oswald is perhaps the most sophisticated measure of real wage flexibility.[2] In theoretical terms, it answers the following question: given a shock, what is the reduction in real wages necessary to maintain a stable rate of unemployment? The assumption is that there exists a level of wage flexibility that eliminates losses in employment and output. If there is some rigidity, wages will fall less than is required and unemployment will increase.

Blanchflower and Oswald try to estimate the slope of their wage curve empirically by asking the following question: what is the reduction in real wages associated with a 1 percentage point increase in a rate of unemployment around 5 percent? The greater the reduction in wages, the greater the level of flexibility, since the adjustment in wages reduces the effect on employment. In the limit, wages would adjust fully, the rate of unemployment would remain constant, and the wage curve would be flat. In fact, estimates for the wage curve in various countries show remarkable

1. The shock can be either exogenous to the economy (for example, a change in terms of trade or international interest rates) or a policy shock (an induced recession, for example, to curb inflation).
2. Blanchflower and Oswald (1990).

uniformity: the slope is around −2, implying that a 1 percent increase in unemployment is associated with a 2 percent reduction in the real wage.

To consider the case of Brazil, it is important to start by providing a brief account of the nature and magnitude of macroeconomic shocks from the early 1980s to the mid-1990s. During this period there were two major negative shocks and one positive shock. The first negative shock, 1981–83, was a response to the oil and interest rate shocks and the Mexican moratorium. A policy-induced recession and a currency devaluation followed, with the objective of reducing the current account deficit.

The positive shock was induced by the Cruzado stabilization plan in 1986. The plan can be seen as a shock in the sense that it changed the way in which goods and labor markets functioned—essentially, by means of a price freeze and an accommodative aggregate demand policy—and triggered important behavioral changes. It caused a significant increase in propensities to consume and invest, provoking a situation of excess demand and the expected effects on the labor market.

The second negative shock came in 1990, with the Collor stabilization plan. In this case the price freeze was followed by a major recession. The short-run effects of the recessionary measures were coupled with change in the trade regime, as the economy became open, leading to a major microeconomic restructuring effort that resulted in a 20 to 25 percent reduction in industrial employment between 1989 and 1992.

How did the labor market respond to these shocks? The work of R. Barros and R. Mendonça replicates the methodology of Blanchflower and Oswald to estimate wage curves for the urban labor market in Brazil.[3] The slope of this wage curve varies over time. In the period 1982–84, during the first negative shock, the slope of the wage curve is −6. Between 1985 and 1987, the period that encompasses the Cruzado plan, the slope of the curve is −8. The slope then falls to −3 between 1988 and 1990 and increases to −5 in 1989–91 and 1990–93, when the second negative shock took place. The average slope over the period 1982–94 is −5, showing that the Brazilian labor market has significantly greater wage flexibility than the average in the economies studied by Blanchflower and Oswald.

There are other ways to examine the degree of wage flexibility. Figure 7-1 presents the behavior of real wages in the urban formal and informal

<hr>

3. Barros and Mendonça (1994). It is important to note that Barros and Mendonça include informal sector unemployment in their calculations. Therefore their results refer to the whole labor force, not only to workers in the formal sector.

Figure 7-1. *Real Wages in the Urban Formal and Informal Sectors and in Industry, Brazil, 1983–94*

May 1983 = 100

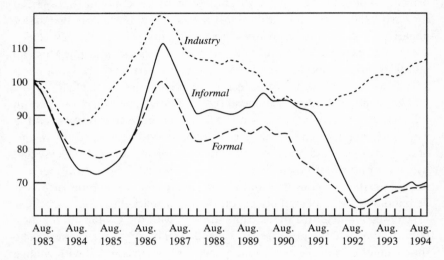

Source: IBGE, *Pesquisa Mensal de Emprego* (*PME*) (various years) and *Pesquisa Industrial Mensal* (*PIM*) (various years).
a. Wages are twelve-month moving averages.

sectors and in industry for Brazil. Coming out of the 1981–83 recession, industrial sector wages increased by around 35 percent, formal sector wages by 25 percent, and informal sector wages by 45 percent. In the 1990–92 recession, wages in industry fell by around 15 percent and then recovered, while in the formal and informal sectors wages fell by around 25 percent and 30 percent, respectively.

These figures show that wages are very flexible. When these three sectors are compared, it is notable that wages in the industrial sector exhibited the least flexibility during the recent recession. This results, first of all, from a statistical bias (the wage of core workers, who remained employed, is higher than average) and also from a very significant increase in labor productivity, which compensates for the effect of the increase in wages on the unit labor cost. Wages in the informal sector are more flexible than in the formal sector, but only very mildly so. Indeed, in the recent recession, formal sector wages fell by almost as much as those in the informal sector.

Figure 7-2. *Average Income and Share of Unemployed and Informal Workers, Urban Labor Force, Brazil, 1983–94*

Index, June 2, 1982 = 1   Percent[a]

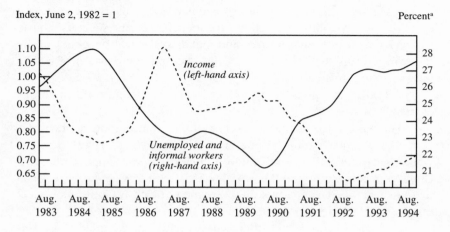

Source: IBGE, *PME* (various years) and *PIM* (various years).
a. Share of unemployed and informally employed workers.

The rate of open unemployment increased from around 4 percent in 1989 to around 6.5 percent in 1992–93. Together with the figures on wages, the behavior of the unemployment rate could, in principle, be seen as an indication of impressive flexibility. Indeed, mimicking the calculation of the wage curve using aggregate data (rather than micro-level data, as do Blanchflower and Oswald) for the recent recession would lead to a slope of -10 (that is, the ratio of the percent growth in real wages to the percentage point growth in unemployment: $-25/2.5$).

However, the growth of the informal sector is hiding an increase in the rate of unemployment. As shown in figure 7-2, the share of unemployed and informally employed workers grew from 21.5 percent in 1989 to 27.5 percent in 1994, an increase of 6 percentage points. Meanwhile, the average urban income fell roughly 27 percent. In this case, the mimic of the wage curve would imply a slope of -4.5 ($-27/6$).

Social Benefits, Payroll Taxes, and the Cost of Labor

High payroll taxes are usually seen as a hindrance to employment creation, at least in the formal sector. For given levels of technology and protection against foreign competition, there exists a certain unit labor cost that makes a sector or firm noncompetitive. This unit labor cost depends on the exchange rate, hourly compensation, and the productivity of labor. Hourly compensation, in turn, depends on the workers' hourly pay and the size of payroll taxes and mandatory social benefits paid by the firm. In this section we discuss the size and composition of hourly compensation in Brazil.

The hourly compensation in Brazil can be decomposed into four elements:

—The basic wage (including overtime) plus some supplementary pay, such as an annual bonus of one month's salary, a contribution to the worker's capitalization fund Fundo de Garantia por Tempo de Serviço (FGTS), a contribution to the worker's assistance service, Serviço Social da Industria (SESI), and other direct payments (such as family allowance, pregnancy leave, transport subsidies);

—Payment for hours not effectively worked, for example, vacations and holidays;

—Contributions to social security and to fund educational services (*salário educação*), and work-related accident insurance that is mandatory for all firms and proportional to the payroll; and

—Contributions to the official training system, Serviço Nacional de Aprendizagem Industrial and Serviço Nacional de Aprendizagem Comērciol (SENAI and SENAC) and to assistance for small enterprises through Serviço de Apoioàs Pequenas Empresas (SEBRAE). These monies and institutions are managed by employers' federations and confederations.

The first component of hourly compensation is, in principle, appropriated by the workers, directly, through a capitalization fund, or indirectly, through use of the services of SESI. Workers only have access to the capitalization fund in limited situations, such as financing the purchase of a home, when fired without just cause, or at retirement. Workers do not have equal access to the social services provided by SESI, since this depends on certain idiosyncrasies of the federations of trade and industry that manage the facilities in each state.

The second component, paid vacations and holidays, directly benfits the individual worker.

The third component of hourly compensation goes to the federal government, to finance the social security, work-related accident insurance, and education systems. Although, in principle, workers are the final

Table 7-1. *Hourly Compensation and Labor Costs, Brazil*

Component	Share[a]	Total
Basic wage (plus overtime)	. . .	100
Annual bonus	0.083	. . .
FGTS	0.080	. . .
SESI	0.015	. . .
Other benefits[b]	0.10 to 0.20	. . .
Total pay[c]	. . .	131 to 142
Paid leisure	0.12	. . .
Total pay plus leisure	. . .	147 to 160
SENAI and SEBRAE	0.016	. . .
Social Security, accident insurance, and education	0.245	. . .
Total labor cost	. . .	185 to 202

Source: Brazilian Labor Code and Brazilian Constitution.
a. Percent.
b. These include benefits that do not apply to all workers, such as family allowances, pregnancy leave, transport subsidies, and so forth.
c. Monthly, based on a forty-four-hour week.

beneficiaries of these contributions, the quality of the services is so low that they are perceived as not worth financing.

The contribution to the official training system, SENAI and SENAC, is difficult to allocate. On the one hand, it benefits workers because they can increase their qualifications through these systems and thus obtain occupational and wage improvements. On the other hand, the fact that the contributions and the training institutions are managed by employers' federations and confederations suggests that employers receive greater direct benefit. In fact, part of these contributions is used to finance other activities of the employers' federations and confederations.

Table 7-1 decomposes the hourly compensation and labor costs in Brazil, and table 7-2 presents estimates of the absolute value of hourly compensation as well as its composition in Brazil and a few countries of the Organization for Economic Cooperation and Development (OECD). From table 7-2 it can be seen that in Brazil, workers appropriate approximately 77 percent of hourly compensation. The other countries in the table show roughly the same share, except for Italy, where the share is around 70 percent. The share of social security contributions and other payroll taxes in Brazil is also close to the levels in the other countries, with the exception of Japan and Korea. As for the division of the worker's share of total hourly compensation between pay for time worked and other forms of direct pay, this is roughly the same in Brazil as in Germany and Japan. The share of other forms of direct pay is smallest in the United

Table 7-2. *Hourly Compensation, Manufacturing Production Workers, Selected Countries, 1992*

Percent, except where indicated

Value and composition	Brazil	United States	Germany	Japan	Italy	Mexico	Korea
Hourly compensation[a]	Total 2.52 São Paulo: 3.4	16.17	25.94	16.16	19.41	2.35	4.93
Share of:							
Pay for time worked	50	70.8	55.8	58.4	51.4	. . .	. . .
Other direct pay	27	6.6	21.4	28.1	18	. . .	. . .
Social insurance and other labor taxes	23[b]	22.6	22.8	13.1	30.6	. . .	11.1

Source: For Brazil, authors' calculations based on IBGE, *PIM,* and, for São Paulo, DIEESE. For all other countries, U.S. Bureau of Labor Statistics (1992).
a. U.S. dollars.
b. Including contributions for social security, accident insurance, education, and industrial training.

States. In sum, the decomposition of total hourly compensation in Brazil is not very different from the OECD average.

There is, however, a remarkable difference between Brazil and the OECD countries in the absolute value of hourly compensation. Table 7-2 presents two estimates for hourly compensation in Brazilian industry. The first comes from the Pesquisa Industrial Mensal (monthly industrial survey) (PIM), conducted by Instituto Brasileiro de Geografia e Estatística (IBGE) for a national sample of industries.[4] The second comes from a household survey conducted by Departamento Intersindical de Estatística e Estudos Sócio-Económicos (DIEESE) in greater São Paulo.[5] From the PIM, the average annual hourly compensation in 1992 was U.S.$2.52. In greater São Paulo, where the core of Brazilian industry is concentrated, the hourly compensation was around U.S.$3.40 in the same year. Figure 7-3 shows that hourly compensation in greater São Paulo increased from approximately U.S.$2 in 1985 to U.S.$4.30 in 1994.

In 1992, hourly compensation in Brazil was roughly the same as that in Mexico, half of that in Korea, 15 percent of that in Japan and the United States, and 10 percent of that in Germany. In sum, the evidence suggests that, by international standards, neither the absolute value of hourly compensation nor the shares of other forms of pay (including social benefits and hours paid but not worked) or contributions to social security and other payroll taxes is high in Brazil.

4. This data set provides the total wage bill (except for the contributions to FGTS, social security and other programs, SENAI, SESI, and SEBRAE), the number of hours paid, and the share of additional hours in the wage bill. In our calculations, we assume that 90 percent of hours paid are effectively worked. This is approximately equal to the ratio of the number of vacation (plus a mandated bonus of ten days' pay) and holiday hours to the total number of hours worked.

5. The DIEESE data, since they are furnished by the worker, do not provide any information on the number of hours worked or contributions—the worker simply reports a given month's wages. Therefore, we make the following assumptions: (1) that the workweek is forty-five hours, which is calculated on the basis of the maximum regular working day according to the Brazilian labor code, plus an extra hour a week; (2) that the firm has to pay contributions to FGTS (8 percent), social security and other programs (24.5 percent), SENAI (1 percent), SESI (1.5 percent), and SEBRAE (0.4 percent), totaling 34.5 percent of the amount paid to the worker; and (3) that 90 percent of the hours paid are effectively worked. Hence, given the monthly wage information provided by workers surveyed (U.S.x), hourly compensation is given by $(x/202)*(1.345)*(1.11)$.

Figure 7-3. *Hourly Compensation, Greater São Paulo, 1985–94*[a]

U.S. dollars

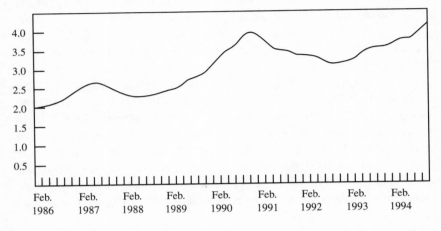

Source: Authors' calculations based on DIEESE.
a. Twelve-month moving averages.

Minimum Wages, Payroll Taxes, and the Informal Sector

It is usually thought that the presence of minimum wages and payroll taxes reduces employment or increases the size of the informal sector. Besides payroll taxes, firms also have to pay workers mandatory benefits, such as annual bonuses and contributions to forced saving funds.

Competitive Labor Markets

The argument behind the premise that minimum wages and payroll taxes have adverse effects is straightforward: mandatory benefits and a minimum wage reduce profit maximizing employment by firms in a competitive labor market if the law is enforced, and lead firms to establish informal labor relations if the law is not enforced.

Consider, initially, the case in which workers see both mandatory benefits and contributions to social security as part of their wages. That is, the utility to a worker of each dollar is the same, whether in the form of direct pay, mandatory benefits, or contributions to social security.[6] Thus

6. Three assumptions would make this hypothesis plausible: life cycle behavior on the part of workers, an absence of credit constraints, and negligible intertemporal preference.

it does not matter to a worker when in his or her lifetime the payment is received.

Let S be the hourly direct wage paid by a firm, W the legal minimum hourly wage, and F the rate of payroll taxes and mandated benefits. Hence in a formal wage contract, F^*W is the minimum hourly compensation.

Let Z_f be the equilibrium hourly compensation in the competitive labor market for workers with certain characteristics. In a competitive labor market, firms take the wage Z_f as given and set the level of employment by equating the wage to the marginal revenue product (MRP). In such a market, labor contracts will be formal if the minimum hourly compensation is smaller than the equilibrium wage, that is, if $Z_f > F^*W$.

Under these conditions, firms will have no reason to evade taxes and mandatory benefits. Since the wage is equal to or greater than F^*W, and workers do not care about the relative composition of total hourly compensation in terms of instantaneous and deferred payments, the firm can always set the direct payment for hours worked (S) such that $F^*S = Z_f \geq F^*W$. This case is shown in the top panel of figure 7-4.

The lower panel of figure 7-4 depicts another competitive market, in which the equilibrium wage Z_i is smaller than the minimum hourly compensation. In this case, firms will evade taxes and mandatory benefits and engage in informal contracts. Hence, the condition for evasion under these conditions is

$$Z_i < F^*W.$$

Now consider the case in which, although $Z_f > F^*W$, workers have a nonnegligible rate of intertemporal preference. That is, workers prefer instantaneous payments over deferred payments. In such a case, workers might be prepared not to enforce total payment of benefits and social security contributions if, in exchange, the firm is willing to increase their direct pay. Depending on the cost of evasion, the firm may be willing to agree to such a bargain. Hence, if $Z_f > F^*W$, the condition for evasion is given by

$$S' + C < F^*W < Z_f,$$

where S' is the instantaneous hourly wage acceptable to workers and C is a measure of the cost of evasion. This case is illustrated in the top panel of figure 7-4. Per hour worked, workers get $S < S' < F^*W$ and firms save $F^*W - S'$. The cost of evasion is given by the probability of

Figure 7-4. *Hourly Compensation in Competitive Markets*

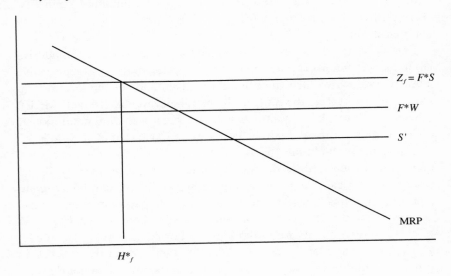

Minimum hourly compensation less than equilibrium wage

Hourly compensation (Z)

$Z_f = F*S$

$F*W$

S'

MRP

H^*_f

Equilibrium wage less than minimum hourly compensation

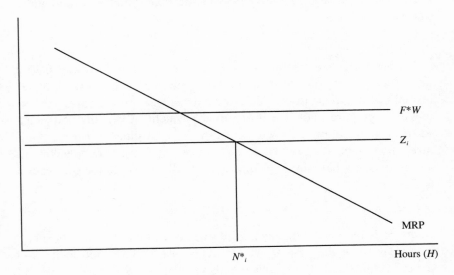

$F*W$

Z_i

MRP

N^*_i Hours (H)

Source: Authors' model, as described in text.

being caught when evading, which, in turn, depends on the level of enforcement of the law. Note that if some firms and their workers choose to evade, there will be an increase in aggregate employment ($H_i^* > H_f^*$ in the top panel of figure 7-4) and an increase in the degree of informality of employment.

In sum, in competitive labor markets, firms will have incentives to evade taxes and mandatory benefits if the equilibrium wage is smaller than the minimum hourly compensation or, even when the equilibrium wage is greater than the minimum hourly compensation, if workers have a strong preference for instantaneous payment and the cost of evasion is low.

The Damage Potential of Workers

The preceding analysis considers cases in which firms do not distinguish between workers. Workers can differ two ways. They can be different because of their backgrounds, as measured, for example, by education or experience. And even if they have similar backgrounds, differences in the characteristics of the firms in which they work make them "different."

The efficiency wage literature argues that two workers with the same human capital characteristics earn different wages because of differences in the technologies used by their firms. The wage paid by a firm depends on the cost to the firm of workers shirking and the cost of monitoring workers. Shirking is defined as a worker's deliberate decision to reduce effort. When the cost of shirking is high and monitoring is both difficult and costly, firms will be prepared to pay higher wages in order to reduce shirking.

R. Ramaswamy and R. Rowthorn introduce the concept of the "damage potential" of workers.[7] The greater the cost to a firm of shirking, the greater the workers' damage potential. But even if the costs of shirking were the same across firms, wages could be different if the damage potential of workers depended on "performance." Performance encompasses "a wide array of attributes which determine the effectiveness of work. . . . For instance, performance can depend upon how intensely workers concentrate on their jobs [and] upon factors such as the willingness of workers to take initiative and function flexibly."[8]

7. Ramaswamy and Rowthorn (1991).
8. Ramaswamy and Rowthorn (1991, p. 509).

The model that Ramaswamy and Rowthorn develop to explore the notion of damage potential is a generalization of Robert Solow's classical model of efficiency wages. They propose a production function in which standard labor input (that is, hours of work) and effort (or performance) are not multiplicative, but enter the function separately. This implies that hours of work and effort (or performance) are not perfect substitutes. Their function is as follows:

$$y = f(H, e(Z)), \text{ with } e' > 0, e'' < 0, fH > 0, \text{ and } Fe > 0,$$

where H is hours of work, e is effort (or performance), Z is real hourly compensation, and y is output. Profits are defined as $\Pi = y - ZH$. Profit maximization gives rise to the following equations:

$$\sigma\Pi/\sigma Z = f_e \, e(Z) - H = 0$$

and

$$\sigma\Pi/\sigma H = f_H - Z = 0.$$

Solving these equations yields the following effort-wage elasticity:

$$E_Z = [e'(Z^*) \, Z^*]/e(Z^*) = \epsilon_H/\epsilon_e,$$

where $\epsilon_H = (H/y)/(\sigma y/\sigma H)$ and $\epsilon_e = (e/y)/(\sigma y/\sigma e)$.

The size of E_Z depends on the characteristics of the firm. For firms in which hours of work and effort (or performance) are substitutes, ϵ_H and ϵ_e are more or less of the same size. For firms in which hours of work cannot replace performance, $\epsilon_e > \epsilon_H$. Hence E_Z will be lower in the latter case than in the former.

The first conclusion, then, is that E_Z is inversely related to the damage potential of workers, as determined by the importance attributed to performance by different firms. The second point to note is that in classical efficiency wage models—based on production functions in which H and e are multiplicative—the following (Solow) condition applies:

$$E_Z = 1.$$

The Ramaswamy and Rowthorn model, however, shows that when H and e enter the production function separately, E_Z can be smaller than one. Hence the so-called Solow condition becomes a special case.

Finally, first- and second-order conditions of profit maximization imply that if E_Z can vary across firms,

$$\sigma E_Z/\sigma Z^* < 0.$$

That is, workers who have greater damage potential (smaller E_Z) for their firms receive higher wages. Figure 7-5 depicts the determination of the equilibrium wage (Z^*) and of the equilibrium demand for labor (H^*). Note that the smaller is E_Z, the greater is the equilibrium wage and the smaller the equilibrium demand for labor.

Damage Potential, the Minimum Wage, and Informality

Figure 7-6 compares two representative firms that have demand for workers who are indistinguishable in terms of human capital. In firm 1, E_e is close to zero (damage potential is negligible), which implies that E_Z is very high. Without regard for the possibility of shirking, this firm hires the hours of work of workers with a given set of human capital characteristics. The firm takes the hourly wage (Z_i) of these workers as given by supply and demand at the industry level and fixes the level of employment by equating this wage with the marginal revenue of labor (H_i). In firm 2, E_e is positive and therefore E_Z is small. The greater is E_e, the smaller is E_Z. The wage decreases with E_Z.

Assume that these are the only two types of firm in the economy. For the sake of analysis, assume that the minimum hourly compensation lies between Z_i and Z^* (that is, $Z_i < F^*Z < Z^*$), so that workers in firm 1 have informal contracts and workers in firm 2 have formal contracts.

Let the level of aggregate employment (as measured by the total number of hours) be given at H. Once the equilibrium wage in firm 2 has been determined according to the profit maximization procedure described above, the level of employment (H_f) can be determined. It is assumed that the level of employment in firm 1 is determined as a residual lying between the aggregate level of employment and the level of employment in firm 2:

$$H_i = H - H_f.$$

Thus the smaller is the level of employment in firm 2, the greater is the level of employment in firm 1. Since we assume full employment, the equilibrium wage in firm 1 must accommodate to the excess supply of labor, given the level of employment in firm 2:

$$Z_i = \alpha_0 - \alpha_1 [H - H_f(Z^*)]$$

Figure 7-5. *Effect of Workers' Damage Potential on Equilibrium Wage and Equilibrium Demand for Labor*

Equilibrium wage

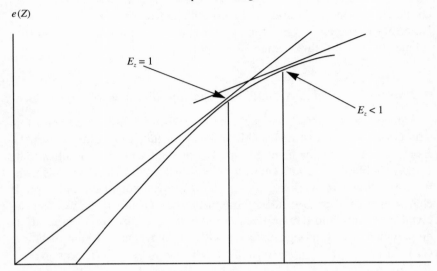

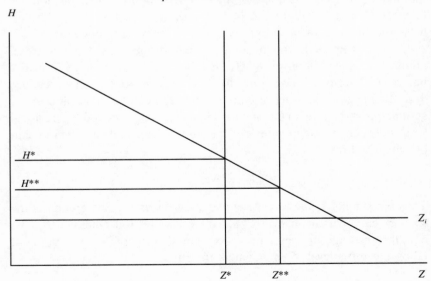

Figure 7-6. *The Determination of the Number of Formal (H*) and Informal Workers (H_i)*

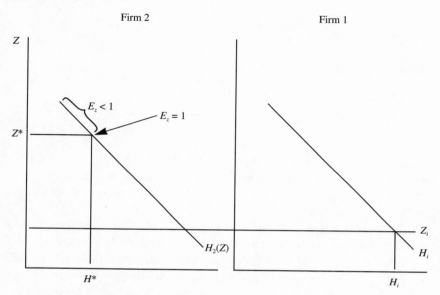

Source: Authors' model, as described in text.

where $H_f' < 0$, so that $\sigma Z_i/\sigma Z^* < 0$. That is, the greater is the wage in firm 2, the smaller is the wage in firm 1. Hence the wage differential between workers in the two types of firms is given by

$$Z^*/Z_i = Z^*/[\alpha_0 - \alpha_1 [H - H_f(Z^*)]]$$

so that $\sigma(Z^*/Z_i)/\sigma Z^* > 0$.

Finally, the degree of formality is given by

$$h_f = H_f/H,$$

so that $\sigma h_f/\sigma Z^* < 0$.

From this simple model it can be seen that for a given minimum hourly compensation (as long as $Z_i < F^*Z < Z^*$), the level of formality will depend on the determinants of Z^*. If, for some technological reason—for example, the introduction of numerical control—the damage potential of workers increases and there is a reduction in E_Z, the equilibrium wage in firm 2 will increase. Consequently employment in firm 2 will fall and there will be excess labor supply for firm 1, leading to lower wages in firm 1, a greater wage differential between the two types of firm, and

Table 7-3. *Effect of Preferences on Sectoral Demand*

	Employment	Wage (dollars)	Wage bill (dollars)	Output	Price = unit labor cost (dollars)
Situation 1					
Firm 1	5	1	5	5	1
Firm 2	5	2	10	5	2
Situation 2					
Firm 1	6	0.83	5	5	1
Firm 2	4	2.5	10	4	2.5

Source: Authors' model, as described in text.

a lower level of formality. Note that the degree of formality changes according to the minimum hourly compensation. Hence the degree of formality depends both on the level of the minimum hourly compensation and on the determinants of Z^*.

Demand has not yet played a role in this model. Assume that the firms have a given size, as measured by the level of output. In particular, firm 2 produces $y2^* = f[H^*(Z^*), e(Z^*)]$. The number of firms of type 2 producing $y2^*$ will depend on the demand for the goods produced by these firms. The same is true for firms of type 1, which each produce $y1^* = g(H_i)$.

Per capita income and preferences can affect the sectoral distribution of demand. In a very poor society, the demand for type 2 goods might be zero, in which case they will not be produced. As per capita income increases—assuming that the income elasticity of demand for type 1 goods is smaller than one—demand for type 2 goods will emerge. Assuming that $F^*Z > Z_i$, so that employment in firm 1 is informal, the emergence of demand for type 2 goods will give rise to a "formal sector" and wage differentials.

To consider the effect of preferences, assume that there are ten people in the economy: five employed in firms of type 1, earning $1 each, and five employed in firms of type 2, earning $2 each. The wage bills are, respectively, $5 and $10. Aggregate income is $15. The productivity of labor in both sectors is one (that is, $y/H = 1$). Hence the output of firms in both sectors is five units. Assume that profits are zero, so that the price of each good is equal to the unit labor cost. Producers consume only the types of goods they produce. Table 7-3 summarizes these assumptions.

Now assume that preferences change, so that the rich (who earn $2 working for firms of type 2) decide to demand greater quality in type 2 goods. The demand for greater quality will increase the damage potential of workers in firms of type 2. This will increase the wage in these firms and reduce employment. In this situation, four people employed in firms of type 2, each earning $2.5, would demand four units of type 2 goods— now of higher quality. There will be an excess supply of labor, thus increasing employment and reducing wages in firms of type 1. Workers employed in firms of type 1 became less productive and poorer. Table 7-3 summarizes a possible outcome. In this example, a change in preferences—represented by increased demand for quality in type 2 goods— leads to increased informality and a wider wage differential. Again, minimum hourly compensation is taken as a parameter.

The Brazilian Case

For the reasons mentioned above, it is very difficult to identify the determinants of informality. The degree of informality depends on minimum hourly compensation (the minimum wage and mandatory benefits), but also on the technology, preferences, per capita income, and income distribution. In the following analysis, we use various data sets to identify the likely determinants of changes in the level of informality in Brazil.

The first data set is taken from the DIEESE household survey in greater São Paulo. It provides the average real wage of workers in the informal sector. Figure 7-7 compares this wage with the minimum wage, using the same deflator. It shows that between 1985 and 1994, with a few exceptions at the beginning of the period, the average wage in the informal sector was at least twice as great as the minimum wage. In principle, this is evidence that firms in the informal sector could pay a smaller direct wage and establish formal labor contracts. If they do not, the previous analysis would argue that either workers have strong preferences for informal contracts or the law is not enforced. Indeed, both could be true simultaneously. However, the fact that the data refer to the average wage in the informal sector reduces the force of these conclusions. Depending on the quality of the sample, the average wage could be biased upward, in which case it would not be of much relevance. Hence the results should be interpreted with caution.

Figure 7-7. *Minimum Wage and Average Real Informal Sector Wage,*
São Paulo, 1985–94

Constant Brazilian real, October 1994

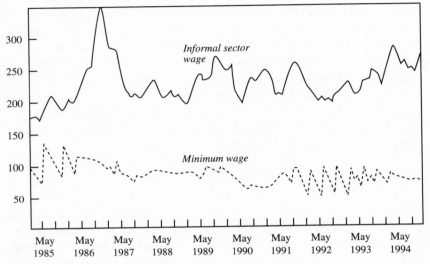

Source: Authors' calculations based on DIEESE.

A second data set, taken from the IBGE's Pesquisa Nacional de
Amostra por Domicilio (PNAD, a national household survey), shows
that 30 percent of the informal workers (wage earners without a formal
contract) in the Brazilian labor force earn more than twice the minimum
wage (see table 7-4). A third data set, based on the IBGE's Pesquisa
Mensal de Emprego (monthly employment survey) (PME), which covers
metropolitan workers, shows that on average almost 50 percent of wage
earners without a formal contract earn more than twice the minimum
wage. In the most developed metropolitan areas, such as São Paulo, the
proportion reaches 54 percent (see table 7-5).

Recall that the contribution to social security plus mandated benefits
amounts to approximately 100 percent of the direct wage. Hence the
minimum hourly compensation is around twice the minimum wage. As
a result, firms that pay wages greater than twice the minimum wage could
afford to formalize their labor contracts. If they do not, it is either
because the cost of evasion is low or because—as is often true—the
workers themselves prefer an informal relationship.

Table 7-4. *Wage Distribution of Formal and Imformal Sector Workers, Brazil*

Percent

Wage bracket[a]	Sector	
	Formal	Informal
< 0.5	0	7
0.5–1	16	29
1–2	24	25
2–3	14	10
3–5	18	9
5–10	15	9
10–20	7	3
> 20	5	2

Source: IBGE (1990).
a. Relative to minimum wage.

These figures show very clearly that minimum hourly compensation cannot be the sole determinant of the degree of informality in Brazil. Indeed, in urban areas—where 75 percent of the active population lives—minimum hourly compensation is not a binding constraint on the formalization of labor relations in almost 50 percent of cases.

Using the PNAD, Barros, R. Mello, and V. Pero find that workers in the formal sector earn wages 45 percent greater than identical workers (same age, gender, geographical region, sector of the economy) in the informal sector.[9] This means that firms in the formal sector not only pay a higher direct wage, but also pay the contribution to social security and

Table 7-5. *Wage Distribution of Urban Informal Sector Workers, Brazil*
Percent

Metropolitan area	Wage level[a]	
	≤2	>2
Belo Horizonte	61.78	38.22
Porto Alegre	45.11	54.89
Recife	75.18	24.82
Rio de Janeiro	57.57	42.43
Salvador	76.16	23.84
São Paulo	45.78	54.22
Total (average)	53.09	46.91

Source: IBGE, *Pesquisa Mensal de Emprego* (1992).
a. Relative to minimum wage.

9. Barros, Mello, and Pero (1993).

Figure 7-8. *Minimum Wages and the Informal Sector, Brazil, 1983–94*

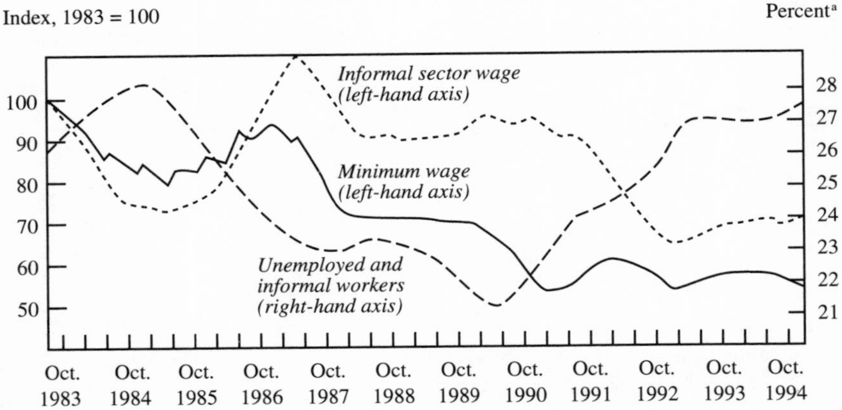

Index, 1983 = 100   Percent[a]

Source: IBGE, *PME* (various years).
a. Share of urban labor force.

all the mandated benefits (which together amount to 100 percent of the direct wage). Hence assuming that there is no significant difference in the number of hours worked by workers in the formal and informal sectors, hourly compensation in the formal sector is on average 2.9 times greater than that in the informal sector.

If there were no difference in structure between markets in the formal and informal sectors, hourly compensation would have to be the same in the two markets. Since firms in the formal sector pay approximately 100 percent of wages in the form of mandated benefits and social security contributions, the equalization of pay between firms in the two markets would imply a formal market direct wage that was 50 percent lower than that in the informal market, not 45 percent higher. Hence the difference in direct pay is clear evidence that firms in the two sectors operate in markets with different structures. In consequence, all the conclusions discussed above concerning the effects of fixing a minimum wage or increasing the minimum wage apply. In particular, the effect of an increase in the minimum wage on the degree of informality is ambiguous.

Finally, it is important to look at the relative movements of the minimum wage and the wage in the informal sector over time. Unfortunately, there is no reliable series of absolute values for the informal sector wage. What is available is the evolution over time of an index number (1983 = 100). Figure 7-8 shows the evolution of the real minimum wage, the real

Table 7-6. *Wages and Informality, Brazil, 1983–94*

		Percentage change in		
Period	Cycle	Informal sector wage	Real minimum wage	Share of informal and unemployed workers
1984–87	Boom	49	15	− 18
1987–89	Downturn and stagnation	− 14	− 30	− 6
1989–93	Recession	− 32	− 22	25
1983–94	. . .	− 30	− 45	5

Source: IBGE, *PME* (various years).
a. Calculated using twelve-month moving averages over the given period.

wage in the informal sector, and the share of informal plus unemployed workers in the labor force over the period 1983–94. The table 7-6 summarizes the evolution of the series.

The first point of note is that the real minimum wage has shown enormous flexibility since the early 1980s. Second, the minimum wage fell by 45 percent over the whole period, reaching its lowest value (around U.S.$65) in 1994. Third, during the 1984–87 boom and the 1989–94 recession, the minimum wage was less flexible than the informal sector wage. The latter increased by 49 percent in the boom and fell by 32 percent in the recession, while the minimum wage increased by 15 percent and fell by 22 percent during these periods, respectively.

Figure 7-8 shows clearly that both the share of informal plus unemployed workers and the level of informality fell continuously over the period 1986–89, whereas the informal sector wage initially fell and then remained stable. It is evident that the relation between the minimum wage and the informal sector wage became weaker. This can be seen as a factor in the reduction of the levels of informality and unemployment.

During the recession of 1989–93, the minimum wage fell less than the wage in the informal sector. Again, this can be seen as a factor in the growth of the share of informal plus unemployed workers.[10] In addition, the new constitution introduced in 1988 increased mandated benefits, thus increasing the value of minimum hourly compensation.

But there are probably other reasons for the growth of the informal sector. Among these, a reduction of around 25 percent in employment in

10. The share of informal plus unemployed workers increased by 6 percentage points, from 21.5 percent to 27.5 percent of the labor force, between 1989 and 1994. For each 1 percentage point reduction, the minimum wage fell by 3.7 percent.

the industrial sector is certainly very important. The level of informality in the industrial sector is considerably smaller than that in the services, trade, or construction sectors. It could be argued that this is due to the fact that, for technological reasons, the share of firms operating in an imperfectly competitive labor market (as discussed above) is greater in the industrial sector than in the others. Hence a reduction in the level of employment in the industrial sector would be associated with a reduction in the share of workers employed in high-wage firms, partially explaining the increase in informality.

Another possible reason for the growth of informality is related to the reduction in per capita income and the impoverishment of the population. As discussed above, this could lead to a reduction in the demand for quality, which, in turn, would reduce the share of firms operating in the imperfectly competitive segment of the labor market.

As was to be expected, therefore, it proves impossible to state definitively the causes of the growth in informality. There are various plausible reasons, but none can explain the phenomenon alone.

The Cost of Dismissal and Employment Flexibility

It is conventional wisdom that high firing costs prevent employment flexibility and reduce employment creation. In the face of shocks that alter the sectoral distribution of employment, if the cost of firing workers is high, transition to a new equilibrium will be slow and costly. Therefore, under such circumstances, firms should not be constrained in their decisions to fire and hire workers. Freedom to fire and hire allows a constant flow of workers from stagnant to more dynamic sectors. This is the essence of the concept of employment flexibility. Countries with high employment flexibility will be characterized by high frequencies of unemployment (that is, workers become unemployed more frequently) but also low rates of long-term unemployment (that is, the unemployed find jobs faster).

High costs of dismissal are also seen as a hindrance to job creation, for two reasons. First, they increase the bargaining power of employed workers, thus implying real wage rigidity. In the face of technological or negative demand shocks, downward wage rigidity will reduce the level of employment. The second reason is associated with the effect of firing costs on the cost of labor. Given the average level of labor turnover at a firm, the greater is the cost of dismissal, the greater is the average labor cost. For the firm, an increase in business cycle volatility (for example, due to increased international competition or rapid technological change) implies greater labor turnover, which, due to the high cost of dismissal, in turn implies a larger average labor cost. Hence the combination of high costs of dismissal and a more volatile business cycle implies an increase in the cost of labor. This seems to be the reason why employers all over the world demand the costs of dismissal be reduced. Thus there are good grounds to believe that reducing the costs of dismissal will increase employment flexibility—contributing to greater labor market flexibility—and increase job creation.

If the problem is looked at from another angle, one finds that it is also true that greater job stability enhances functional flexibility and labor productivity growth. The attitudes of firms and workers are not independent of their perceptions of stability or the duration of the employment relationship. From the point of view of the firm, durable relations induce investment in training and up-grading the workforce. From the point of view of the worker, durable relations increase commitment to the long-term objectives of the firm. These attitudes, in turn, enhance the capacity of workers to adapt to changes in technology and lines of production (if they are better qualified, they can learn new skills and adapt faster) and have a positive effect on productivity growth. Also, if the employment relationship is perceived as durable, workers and firms will tend to negotiate wage rates that are compatible with job stability in the event of shocks.

The notion underlying the negative assessment of costs of dismissal is that, if they did not exist, firms would hire and fire workers more frequently, hence increasing employment flexibility and wage flexibility, and ultimately reducing long-term unemployment. Where firing costs are high, firms facing environmental change are required to adjust their use of labor through changes in the number of hours or the abilities of workers, rather than changes in the level of employment. Yet since job stability has positive effects on functional flexibility and productivity growth, the net effect of inhibiting employment flexibility remains unclear. Indeed, the extent to which job security regulations have positive or negative effects should be a matter of continuous scrutiny.

Table 7-7 summarizes provisions for individual and collective dismissals in France, Germany, and Brazil in the late 1980s and early 1990s. In regard to individual dismissals, there is one important difference between

Table 7-7. *Selected Legal Provisions for Dismissal, France, Germany, and Brazil*[a]

Provision	France	Germany	Brazil
Individual dismissal			
Justification requirement	Yes	Yes	No
Advance notice	1 month for workers with less than 6 months tenure, 2 months for workers with more than 2 years.	2 weeks for workers with less than 5 years tenure, 1 month for workers with more than 5 years, 3 months for workers with more than 20 years.	1 month.
Compensation	1/10th of monthly pay per year of service plus 1/15 of monthly pay for each year over 10 years of service.	None	1/2 of monthly pay plus 40% of FGTS (equivalent to 40% of monthly wage for each year in service).
Collective dismissal			
Legal definition	2 or more employees within 30 days.	20% of labor force or more than 60 workers.	None
Notice and consultation requirements	Inform and consult with worker representative. Labor inspector must be informed if 10 or more workers dismissed.	Inform and consult with worker representative. Inform employment office.	None

Compensation	None	Social plan negotiated between work councils and management. Median settlement approximates 15 to 25 weeks pay for average blue-collar industrial worker.	None
Compensation system Unemployment benefit insurance	Yes	Yes	Yes
Amount of benefit	Government pays 65% of minimum wage for reduction in hours of work. Employer pays to raise short-time benefit to 50% of wages for reductions of less than 36 hours per week.	63–68% of net pay for hours not worked.	Value cannot be lower than minimum wage, is adjusted monthly to inflation, and is related to the worker's average wage in the last three months of the previous job.
Period of benefit	Maximum of 500 hours per year.	6 to 24 months.	4 months.
Funding	General revenues.	Non–experience-rated payroll tax.	General revenues.

Source: For Germany and France, Abraham and Housman (1993). For Brazil, Brazilian Labor Code and Brazilian Constitution.
a. Approximately 1988.

Brazil and the other two countries: Brazilian firms do not have to justify a dismissal either to workers' representatives or to public officials. In all three countries, firms must give workers advance notice that they will be dismissed; for workers with less than five years of tenure, the notice period is shortest in Germany. Compensation for dismissed workers is greater in Brazil than in France but does not exist in Germany. Unemployment benefits exist in all three countries and are much more generous in France and Germany than in Brazil.

As far as collective dismissals are concerned, the differences between Brazil and the other two countries are considerably greater than in the case of individual dismissals. There is no legal definition of collective dismissal in Brazil. Indeed, unless firms and unions specifically negotiate conditions for collective dismissals, they are treated as individual dismissals. In particular, there is no requirement that the firm consult with workers' representatives or government officials. In Germany, in contrast to Brazil and France, social plans (that is, benefits for workers who are dismissed) are negotiated between the firm and work councils.

In sum, there are two main differences between the provisions for dismissal in Brazil and the two European countries. First, in Brazil a firm may dismiss an individual worker without formal justification. And second, in Brazil, collective dismissals do not suffer any type of constraints; in particular, workers' representatives have no legal right to negotiate the terms of dismissals or compensation plans. As a result, the capacity of workers' representatives to influence and negotiate the process of dismissal is insignificant and the costs of collective dismissals are much smaller than in the other two countries.

A similar comparison between legal provisions for dismissal in the United States and other developed countries, including France and Germany, is striking. In the United States firms do not have to justify individual or collective dismissals, do not have to provide advance notice to workers, and do not have to give severance pay to workers who are laid off permanently. Moreover, the U.S. unemployment insurance system is "experience rated," which implies that layoffs increase the unemployment insurance tax liability of firms.

In terms of compensation, the U.S. system is probably more efficient than that of Brazil, since the tax imposed on firms to finance unemployment insurance inhibits firms from laying off workers. The Brazilian system is funded through a uniform tax on firms' revenues. Also, in the United States a firm can lay off a worker temporarily, thus establishing a long-term relationship with the unemployed worker. No such relationship exists in Brazil, and the dismissed worker has no advantage over other applicants when the firm decides to hire again.

Yet except for the funding of the unemployment insurance system and for severance payments, conditions of dismissal in Brazil are very similar to those in the United States; certainly, much closer than to those in Europe. The provisions of Brazil and the United States share the following characteristics: no obligation to justify individual dismissals, a negligible role for negotiations between the firm and workers' representatives or government officials, and no specific constraints on collective dismissals.

More important than constraints on dismissals, per se, is the fact that since workers' representatives do not have a legal right to negotiate dismissals, there is very little scope for bargaining reductions in hours against reductions in employment. In consequence, the incidence of layoffs is much greater in the United States than in Germany and France, where firms tend to adapt their use of labor through changes in the number of hours worked. Comparing the United States with Belgium, France, and Germany, K. Abraham and S. Housman conclude that "although the adjustment of employment to changes in output is much slower in the German, French, and Belgian manufacturing sectors than in the U.S. manufacturing sector, the adjustment of hours worked appears much more similar. . . . Compared to the United States, then, labor market institutions in these European countries seem to have encouraged relatively greater reliance on hours adjustment and correspondingly reduced reliance on hiring and firing to alter the level of employment."[11] Thus it could be argued that in these European countries, employment flexibility has, in part, been replaced by functional flexibility.

The Brazilian labor market data show a very significant level of employment flexibility. Figure 7-9 presents job security, as measured by length of tenure, in selected countries in the early 1990s. It shows that, of the total labor force, the share of workers with less than one year of service was 10 percent in Japan, 12 percent in Germany, 15 percent in France, and 28 percent in the United States. In the Brazilian manufacturing sector, the corresponding share was 33 percent. The share of workers with fewer than five years of service in the total labor force was 37 percent in Japan, 41 percent in Germany, 42 percent in France, 62 percent in the United States, and 71 percent in the Brazilian manufacturing

11. Abraham and Houseman (1993, pp. 24–25).

Figure 7-9. *Job Security, Measured by Length of Tenure, Selected Countries, Early 1990s*

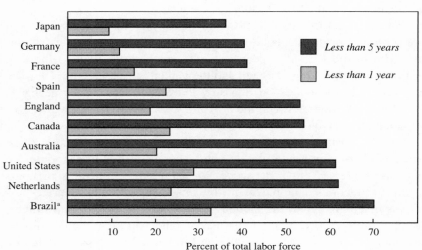

Source: IBGE (1990) and *Economist.*
a. Industrial labor force only.

sector. Thus job tenure is higher in Japan, Germany, and France than in the United States or Brazil.

Figure 7-10 presents data on the frequency and duration of unemployment in Brazil and selected OECD countries for the period around 1988.[12] Workers become unemployed frequently in Brazil and the United States, but very infrequently in Europe. In contrast, the periods of unemployment tend to be very short in Brazil and the United States and are considerably longer in Europe. In Japan the frequency and duration of unemployment are both relatively low.

Table 7-8 presents data on labor turnover in the Brazilian formal sector. It shows, for example, that in 1985 an average of 2.80 percent of the jobs in legally registered firms with more than five employees changed hands within one month. In 1989, 39.66 percent of such jobs changed hands within the year. Thus over the period 1989–93, 28 percent or more of jobs in these legally registered firms changed hands annually.

The data in figures 7-9 and 7-10 and table 7-8 show that Brazil and the United States have a remarkable degree of employment flexibility in

12. Although drawn from different sources, the Brazilian and OECD data are computed using comparable methodologies.

Figure 7-10. *Duration and Frequency of Unemployment, Selected Countries*[a]

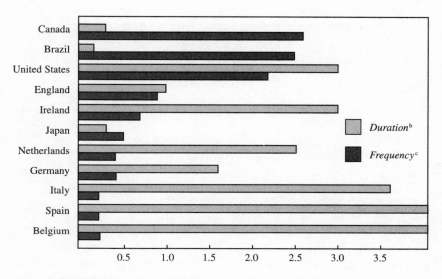

Source: For Brazil, Bivar (1993), and for the OECD countries, Layard, Nickell, and Jackman (1991).
a. Approximately 1988.
b. Unit is 0.1 month.
c. Average number of times a worker becomes unemployed over one year.

comparison with Europe. As noted above, Brazilian firms are required to give dismissed workers severance payments, which can create an incentive for workers to provoke dismissal. This is certainly a perverse incentive, since it tends to shorten the duration of labor contracts and negatively affect the attitudes of both firms and workers. Indeed, Amadeo and others argue that it is partly responsible for Brazil's high levels of labor turnover.[13] Hence it is reasonable to conclude that employment flexibility is excessive in Brazil.

Concluding Remarks

The preceding analysis provides evidence that the Brazilian labor market is very flexible. Indeed, the degree of wage flexibility is considerably greater than in any of the OECD countries considered by Blanchflower

13. Amadeo and others (1994).

Table 7-8. *Labor Turnover Rates in Formal Labor Market, Brazil,*
1985–93[a]

Percent

	Labor turnover	
Year	Monthly average	Annual
1985	2.80	. . .
1986	3.67	. . .
1987	3.72	. . .
1988	3.80	. . .
1989	3.49	39.66
1990	3.26	38.20
1991	2.69	35.75
1992	2.26	28.05
1993[b]	2.73	32.81

Source: Amadeo and others (1994), based on Law 4923 of the Brazilian Ministry of Labor.
a. Sample comprises legally registered firms with more than five employees.
b. January–October.

and Oswald. Conditions on the firing of workers are not important hindrances to employment flexibility, as measured by labor turnover or the frequency and duration of unemployment. In comparison with OECD countries, Brazilian employment flexibility is high. As for hourly compensation in Brazil, its structure does not differ from that in OECD countries, but in absolute value it is less than 20 percent of that in Japan, the United States, or Germany. Finally, it seems that besides the likely effect of the minimum wage and mandated benefits on the degree of informality, other factors also affect the creation of formal jobs in Brazil. Thus all the evidence points toward characterizing the Brazilian labor market as flexible; maybe too flexible (that is, for the wrong reasons).

One aspect of the Brazilian labor market that is worth further comment is the large size of the informal segment of the labor market. In 1990 about 30 percent of workers in the informal sector earned more than twice the minimum wage, implying that if labor laws were enforceable, their employer firms would be able to formalize their labor contracts. For the other 70 percent, we argue that the size of the minimum wage and of mandated benefits explains, at best, only part of the high degree of informality.

However, for the group of firms and their respective workers whose productivity is very low, the size of the minimum wage and of mandated benefits is an impediment to the formalization of labor relationships. Two issues arise in this context. First, to what extent is informality bad or undesirable? It is undesirable because these firms and workers do not contribute to the social security system, thus creating fiscal imbalances and causing the quality of the services provided by the system to deteriorate. Aside from this, it is possible to argue that the existence of the informal sector is not socially undesirable. If the workers in the informal sector were not employed there, they would be unemployed and demanding unemployment compensation from the government.

Second, it can be argued that if the minimum wage and mandated benefits were lower, these firms and workers would formalize the labor relationship and, depending on the level of enforceability, start contributing to the social security system. One solution would be to let employers and employees negotiate the level of benefits—given minimum standards, also negotiated at the industry level—in accordance with market conditions faced by firms. Indeed, the Brazilian labor market probably needs greater incentives for transparent negotiations between employers and employees. To create such incentives would require, on the one hand, making the labor code less encompassing, and on the other hand, developing institutions that would give workers' representatives greater capacity to negotiate over wages and employment.

References

Abraham, K. G., and S. Housman. 1993. "Does Employment Protection Inhibit Labor Market Flexibility?" Working Paper 4390. Cambridge, Mass.: National Bureau of Economic Research.

Amadeo, Edward J., and others. 1994. "Institutions, the Labor Market and the Informal Sector in Brazil." Unpublished paper. Pontificia Universidade Católica do Rio de Janeiro, Department of Economics.

Barros, R. P., and R. Mendonça. 1994. "Flexibilidade do Mercado de Trabalho Brasileiro: Uma Avalição Empírica." Unpublished paper. IPEA, Rio de Janeiro.

Barros, R. P., R. Mello, and V. Pero. 1993. "Informal Labor Contracts: A solution or a problem?" Discussion Paper 291. Rio de Janeiro, Brazil: IPEA.

Bivar, W. 1993. *Aspectos da Estrutura do Desemprego no Brasil: Composio por Sexo e Idade*. Rio de Janeiro, Brazil: BNDES.

Blanchflower, David G., and Andrew Oswald. 1990. "The Wage Curve." *Scandinavian Journal of Economics* 92(2): 215–35.

IBGE. 1990. *Pesquisa Nacional de Amostra por Domicilio*. Rio de Janeiro, Brazil: IBGE.

———. Various years. *Pesquisa Industrial Mensal*. Rio de Janeiro, Brazil: IBGE.

————. Various years. *Pesquisa Mensal de Emprego*. Rio de Janeiro, Brazil: IBGE.

Layard, R., S. Nickell, and R. Jackman. 1991. *Unemployment: Macroeconomic Performance and the Labor Market*. Oxford University Press.

Ramaswamy, R., and R. Rowthorn. 1991. "Efficiency Wages and Wage Dispersion." *Economica* 58 (November): 501–14.

U.S. Bureau of Labor Statistics. 1992. *International Comparisons of Hourly Compensation Costs for Production Workers in Manufacturing*. Department of Commerce.

CHAPTER EIGHT

Chile: The Evolution and Reform of the Labor Market

René Cortázar

LABOR MARKETS and their regulations have changed deeply during the last decades in Chile. Unemployment rates have varied tremendously, from less than 5 percent to more than 20 percent, and wages have fluctuated sharply with periods of strong contraction followed by others of systematic growth (figure 8-1, tables 8-1, 8-2, 8-3).

But these major variations have not been limited to outcomes. The institutions themselves, that is, the rules of the game, have been reformed several times in the past two decades. At first, as part of the policies of an authoritarian regime, the government tightly controlled the process of wage formation (1973–79); then, influenced by external pressure, it authorized unionization and collective bargaining but under restricted conditions (1979–89); and finally, with the reconstruction of democracy, the rules of the game changed again, so as to fully guarantee the right to unionize and the right to bargain (table 8-4).

In this paper I describe the three phases of labor policy of the last two decades and the changes that took place within the labor market. I argue that the evolution in labor policy, and in the institutions that were put in

Basic research for this paper was done as part of a CIEPLAN research program supported by the Ford Foundation. The comments by Juan Luis Burr, Pablo Gerchunov, and two anonymous referees are gratefully acknowledged. The views expressed here, of course, are the author's alone.

Figure 8-1. *Unemployment and Real Wages, 1974–94*

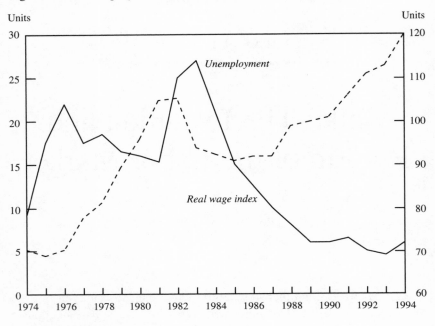

Source: See tables 8-1 and 8-3.

place, were the result of the "preferences" of the government and the other social and political actors, as well as of the "incentives" and "restrictions" faced by all of the players in the pursuit of their objectives. It was the strategic interaction among these different forces that gave rise to the results described below.[1]

Some of the common traits of these phases are also presented.

A Government-Controlled Labor Market: 1973–79

To understand the rules of the game imposed on the labor market after the military coup of September 1973, one has to start from a basic political fact. For political reasons, the military government decided to ban a great number of unions and suspend collective bargaining and the right to strike. It replaced decentralized negotiations between entrepre-

---

1. We will not build a formal model but refer to these preferences, incentives, and restrictions as plausible explanations of the results observed.

Table 8-1. *Real Wages and Growth, 1970–94*

	Average wage		Minimum wage		Labor	
Year	1989 = 100	Rate of growth (%)	1989 = 100	Rate of growth (%)	productivity growth rate (%)[a]	Growth of GDP (%)
1970	108.9	. . .	236.9	. . .	. . .	. . .
1971	133.6	22.7	264.1	11.5	5.5	9.0
1972	104.6	−21.7	227.7	−13.8	−2.2	−1.2
1973	87.6[b]	−16.3[b]	474.3[b]	108.3[b]	−3.8	−5.6
1974	70.8	−19.2	97.2	−79.5	1.1	1.0
1975	68.4	−3.3	95.4	−1.9	−7.9	−13.3
1976	71.0	3.7	98.8	3.6	−1.1	3.2
1977	77.6	9.3	106.4	7.6	−0.6	8.3
1978	82.5	6.4	125.5	18.0	3.1	7.8
1979	89.4	8.3	121.6	−3.1	4.9	7.1
1980	97.0	8.6	121.7	0.0	2.8	7.7
1981	105.7	9.0	140.6	15.6	2.9	6.7
1982	106.0	0.3	142.5	1.3	−4.3	−13.4
1983	94.4	−10.9	114.5	−19.6	−8.2	−3.5
1984	92.6	−2.0	98.1	−14.4	1.5	6.1
1985	90.5	−2.3	92.8	−5.3	−3.2	3.5
1986	92.2	2.0	89.5	−3.6	2.4	5.6
1987	92.1	−0.2	84.0	−6.1	3.1	6.6
1988	98.1	6.5	89.8	6.9	2.1	7.3
1989	100.0	1.9	100.0	11.3	4.6	9.9
1990	101.8	1.8	106.3	6.3	1.5	3.3
1991	106.8	4.9	116.2	9.3	6.3	7.3
1992	111.7	4.5	121.6	4.6	6.4	11.0
1993	113.8	1.9	127.6	4.9	0.9	6.3
1994	119.6	5.1	132.3	3.7	4.2	4.3

Sources: National Statistics Institute; and Cortázar and Marshall (1980).
a. Rate of growth of output per worker.
b. First eight months of 1973.

neurs and workers with a policy of wage readjustments determined by government authorities. These "preferences" of the government could not be offset by the "preferences" of other political and social actors, as a consequence of the extreme concentration of power in the hands of the military regime. The "incentives" and "restrictions" that conditioned the strategy applied by the government stemmed either from economic circumstances or from the internal politics of the regime, but not from a significant influence exerted by political parties or social sectors that opposed it.

As shown elsewhere the rate of variation of nominal wages (around their medium-term trend) throughout those years was basically an ex-

Table 8-2. *Employment in Chile, 1970–94*

Thousands

Year	Labor force	Wage earners	Employed	Unemployed
1970	2,890.4	1,398.6	2,719.9	170.5
1971	2,963.1	1,444.0	2,808.2	154.9
1972	2,955.7	1,458.3	2,836.0	119.7
1973	2,923.8	1,431.7	2,784.3	139.5
1974	3,059.6	1,429.6	2,780.3	279.3
1975	3,104.8	1,346.7	2,618.9	485.9
1976	3,279.8	1,380.4	2,732.4	547.4
1977	3,405.9	1,698.9	2,976.6	429.3
1978	3,655.6	1,783.8	3,111.3	544.3
1979	3,703.8	1,838.3	3,177.2	526.6
1980	3,802.4	1,874.3	3,331.0	471.3
1981	3,880.6	2,023.5	3,453.1	427.5
1982	3,871.4	1,720.1	3,124.0	747.4
1983	4,032.2	1,661.5	3,284.5	747.7
1984	4,094.9	1,831.7	3,433.4	661.5
1985	4,175.6	1,974.5	3,671.3	504.3
1986	4,238.1	2,129.4	3,785.5	452.6
1987	4,315.0	2,253.4	3,912.0	403.1
1988	4,476.7	2,448.6	4,112.1	364.6
1989	4,604.0	2,645.3	4,318.5	285.5
1990	4,675.0	2,723.2	4,395.0	280.0
1991	4,739.2	2,754.0	4,435.0	304.3
1992	4,876.5	2,892.4	4,627.0	249.5
1993	5,112.1	3,090.8	4,875.1	237.1
1994[a]	5,187.4	3,098.7	4,877.9	309.5

Source: National Statistics Institute. From 1970 to 1976, the data come from Jadresic (1986).
a. First three quarters.

ogenous variable determined by the central authorities.[2] Consequently, nominal wages were a policy instrument as were the nominal exchange rate or nominal public expenditure. Economic agents were unable to establish significant independence from official wage policies. On the one hand, workers were probably unable to do so because unemployment was over 17 percent during most of the period and unions had been weakened or disbanded. On the other hand, employers did not distance themselves from the official wage policies because they were fairly moderate, and

2. Cortázar (1983, pp. 112–18); and (1985, pp. 85–87). A highly conspicuous aspect of wage equations estimated for those years is that the unemployment rate does not appear to be a factor that influences the behavior of nominal wages. This is all the more surprising if one takes into account that unemployment varied a great deal over the period, with monthly rates going from 7 percent to 22 percent.

Table 8-3. *Employment in Chile, Rates of Change, 1970–94*

Year	Rate of change (%)			Rate of unemployment (%)	
	Labor force	Wage earners	Employed	Open	With PEM[a]
1970	. . .	. . .	. . .	5.9	5.9
1971	2.5	3.2	3.2	5.2	5.2
1972	−0.2	1.0	1.0	4.0	4.0
1973	−1.1	−1.8	−1.8	4.8	4.8
1974	4.6	−0.1	−0.1	9.1	9.1
1975	1.5	−5.8	−5.8	15.6	18.0
1976	5.6	2.5	4.3	16.7	21.9
1977	3.8	23.1	8.9	12.6	18.1
1978	7.3	5.0	4.5	14.9	18.9
1979	1.3	3.1	2.1	14.2	17.8
1980	2.7	2.0	4.8	12.4	17.4
1981	2.1	8.0	3.7	11.0	15.5
1982	−0.2	−15.0	−9.5	19.3	25.2
1983	4.2	−3.4	5.1	18.5	27.0
1984	1.6	10.2	4.5	16.2	20.2
1985	2.0	7.8	6.9	12.1	15.3
1986	1.5	7.8	3.1	10.7	12.6
1987	1.8	5.8	3.3	9.3	10.2
1988	3.7	8.7	5.1	8.1	8.3
1989	2.8	8.0	5.0	6.2	6.2
1990	1.5	2.9	1.8	6.0	6.0
1991	1.4	1.1	0.9	6.4	6.4
1992	2.9	5.0	4.3	5.1	5.1
1993	4.8	6.9	5.4	4.6	4.6
1994[b]	1.5	0.3	0.1	6.0	6.0

Source: National Statistics Institute. From 1970 to 1976, the data come from Jadresic (1986).
a. Unemployment includes the workers of the so-called Minimum Employment Plan (PEM), an emergency make-work program designed to alleviate the effects of massive unemployment. Workers of PEM are paid around one-third the minimum wage.
b. First three quarters.

severance payments made it expensive to fire and rehire workers as a way to avoid paying official wage adjustments.[3]

This hypothesis may be expressed in the following form:

(1) $$w = a + r$$

where w = percentage of growth in nominal wages in the period "t", and r = percentage wage readjustment decreed by the government in the same period "t." Therefore the rate of change in real wages may be expressed by:

---

3. Severance payments amounted to roughly one month's wages for each year of service.

Table 8-4. *Unionization in Chile, 1970–94*

Year	Number of unions	Number of workers affiliated	Average per union	Rate of growth of unionized workers	Affiliates/wage earners (%)
1970[a]	4,758	628,396	132	. . .	44.9
1971[a]	5,401	789,621	146	25.7	54.7
1972[a]	6,326	883,188	140	11.9	60.6
1973[a]	6,692	939,319	140	6.4	65.6
1980	4,597	386,910	84	. . .	20.6
1981	3,977	395,951	100	2.3	19.6
1982	4,048	347,470	86	−12.2	20.2
1983	4,401	320,903	73	−7.6	19.3
1984	4,714	343,329	73	7.0	18.7
1985	4,994	360,963	72	5.1	18.3
1986	5,391	386,987	72	7.2	18.2
1987	5,883	422,302	72	9.1	18.7
1988	6,446	446,194	69	5.7	18.2
1989	7,118	507,616	71	13.8	19.2
1990	8,861	606,812	68	19.5	22.3
1991	9,859	701,355	71	15.6	25.5
1992	10,758	723,496	67	3.2	25.0
1993	11,389	684,361	60	−5.4	22.1
1994	12,109	661,966	55	−3.3	21.4

Source: National Labor Administration Office.
a. In 1979 there was a change in legislation and registration procedures. These data are not comparable with the data of the following years.

(2) $$w - p = a + (r - p)$$

where p = rate of inflation in the period "t."

Hence, to explain the evolution of real wages during this period (table 8-1) we must compare the official wage adjustments with the rate of change of the CPI.

Equation (1) was estimated using monthly and quarterly data:

(3) $w = 0.0137 + 0.919\ r$ (monthly data, April 1976–July 1979)
          (6.06)   (41.12)

     $R^2 = 0.98$ DW = 1.90   N = 39

(4) $w = 0.0248 + 0.171D + 1.07\ r$ (quarterly data, IIQ74–IIIQ79)
          (1.94)   (8.15)   (22.4)

     $R^2 = 0.97$ DW = 2.65   N = 22

where D = a dummy for 1974.

In both cases support is found for the hypothesis described above. The quality of the econometric results is high, both regarding the efficiency of the estimations and regarding the overall adjustment.

Government authorities followed a very restrictive wage policy throughout the first three years (1973–76). Inflation had reached about 800 percent in 1973, and the government feared that wage adjustments would contribute to inflation and reduce the effectiveness of monetary and fiscal policies. Wage adjustments were below the officially measured inflation and, on the other hand, the 1973 CPI was subjected to tampering (the official inflation rate for 1973 was 508.1 percent, but the actual inflation rate was 813.6 percent).[4]

Throughout the next three years (1976–79), the government committed itself to following a 100 percent wage indexation policy. With inflation decelerating, real wages began a steady recovery (table 8-1).[5] Indexation was calculated on the basis of the CPI as computed by the National Statistics Institute (INE). But again, for the second time in this short period, the INE committed a serious "error" in computing the CPI. On this occasion, the "mistake" was made by underestimating the inflation rate for all months included in the period 1976–78.[6] But not only were nominal wages indexed to the official CPI, during most of this period the same was the case for the nominal exchange rate. Hence, as a consequence of this tampering operation the "true" inflation rate also diminished. Even if one takes into account the lower inflation that resulted as a consequence of these "statistical errors," real wages dropped by more than 15 percent, compared with what they would have been had the policy rules remained unchanged and had the INE computed the CPI accurately.[7]

Employment followed the fate of aggregate demand during this period. In the first years (1973–75), mainly as a consequence of the restrictive monetary, fiscal, and wage policies, the number of jobs dropped at about 3 percent a year, together with the fall in output. During the following years (1976–79), the trend reversed, and output and employment expanded, while at the same time wages grew at a very significant rate (table 8-3).

4. Cortázar and Marshall (1980, pp. 169–70).
5. Wages were adjusted four times in 1976 and, as inflation decelerated, three times a year in 1977 and 1978. See Cortázar (1983, p. 128).
6. Cortázar and Marshall (1980, pp. 170–72).
7. Cortázar (1983, pp. 205–07).

Restricted Liberalization of the Labor Market and
Social Security Reforms: 1979–89

By mid-1979, the Pinochet regime decided to legalize collective bargaining and eliminate a series of restrictions imposed on the labor movement. This policy change was triggered by the boycott with which the international labor movement threatened the Pinochet regime in late 1978.[8]

To understand the nature of the reforms that were introduced, one must consider the "preferences" of the government and the "incentives" and "constraints" it faced. The dominant view in the government was a neoconservative approach: government interventions, unions and collective bargaining were viewed with distrust, mostly as an interference with regard to the normal adjustments of markets.[9] However, something had to be done. Something that would reflect as much as possible the prevailing view on the workings of labor markets.

One could argue that other "players" had begun to influence the outcome. After all, the threat of an international boycott was partly induced by the domestic labor movement, which had found the support of the international labor movement. Hence, the "preferences" of other sectors began to play a role in determining the labor policy. But it is fair to say that power still was highly concentrated in the military regime. There was not a significant influence over the outcomes of the political parties or social actors that were in the opposition.

Reforming Labor Legislation

The government reformed labor legislation related to unions, collective bargaining, and individual contracts.

—Unions. It authorized the right to unionize, freedom of affiliation, democratic procedures for the election of union leaders, and freedom of association with very low quorums (this created the possibility of more than one union within companies or industries). But together with these opportunities, legal restrictions were imposed on certain aspects of the

8. Piñera (1990, pp. 11–14).
9. To talk about the "preferences" of a government is certainly a simplification. Most governments have more than one internal trend. In the case of the military regime the dominant trend, at this stage, was neoconservative but it coexisted with other, more corporatist, views. Piñera (1990, pp. 72–78).

right to unionize. For example, public sector workers and temporary agricultural workers were not allowed to unionize. National confederations of workers were not allowed legal existence. Legislation did not give adequate protection (against arbitrary dismissals) to union leaders and imposed a maximum amount of hours that elected officials could devote to union activities.

—Collective bargaining. The right to bargain was authorized. But collective bargaining could only take place within the firms. Even though, traditionally in Chile, collective bargaining had taken place within the firms themselves, the new legislation went beyond that tradition and declared invalid any agreement that covered workers of more than one company. It also forbade unions formed by temporary workers, as well as unions representing workers from more than one firm, to sign collective agreements. Hence if, say, a union of temporary workers from the construction industry signed a collective agreement with its employer, the contents would be invalid, even if both parties had agreed to it. Collective agreements covered the working conditions of workers who were directly represented in the collective contract. If a strike took place, workers could be replaced temporarily by the employer from the first day, and they could also, at any point in time, return to work individually under the conditions of the last offer made by the employer. After a strike had lasted sixty days, all workers could be permanently replaced. Employers could not offer less than the old collective agreement adjusted by inflation.[10] (This norm was maintained until mid-1982). Workers of firms that provide basic services, such as water, electricity, or gas, were not allowed to strike; and a system of final-offer arbitration was put in place.

The percentage of wage earners covered by collective agreements varied sharply during the 1980s and reached about 13.2 percent in 1989 (table 8-5). But one has to consider that in those firms where collective bargaining took place only about half of the workers, on average, participated in the bargaining process. Since it was a fairly common practice that the employer would "extend" the benefits of the collective agreement to the rest of the workers, the number of those effectively covered by collective aggreements is much higher than that registered in table 8-5.

---

10. Full wage indexation benefited all workers, including those that did not bargain collectively.

Table 8-5. *Collective Bargaining in Chile, 1970–94*

Year	Number of instruments	Workers covered by collective agreements	Employed (thousands)	Covered/ employed (%)	Covered/wage earners (%)
1970	5,295	316,280	2,720	11.6	22.6
1971	7,916	411,999	2,808	14.7	28.5
1972	8,098	396,792	2,836	14.0	27.2
1979	1,405	113,108	3,003	3.8	6.2
1980	1,824	265,633	3,257	8.2	14.2
1981	1,760	335,409	3,191	10.5	16.6
1982	932	264,480	2,825	9.4	15.4
1983	1,407	224,435	3,152	7.1	13.5
1984	1,030	228,739	3,130	7.3	12.5
1985	1,681	232,224	3,257	7.1	11.8
1986	1,179	262,144	3,896	6.7	12.3
1987	1,684	269,563	4,042	6.7	12.0
1988	1,405	282,256	4,266	6.6	11.5
1989	2,334	350,152	4,425	7.9	13.2
1990	2,399	406,195	4,460	9.1	14.9
1991	2,810	436,941	4,450	9.8	15.9
1992	2,809	508,663	4,773	10.7	17.6
1993	3,038	513,017	4,986	10.3	16.6
1994	2,697	532,338	4,878	10.9	17.2

Source: National Labor Administration Office. From 1973 to 1978 there was no collective bargaining.

—Individual contracts. A series of restrictions on individual contracts was suppressed. Before these reforms, those who wanted to work in many occupations, ranging from hairdressers to radio announcers, required prior authorization and registration; subcontracting could only take place in activities that were not the main output of the firm; and collective dismissals required prior authorization from the government. These regulations, among others, were eliminated.[11]

By mid-1978, legislation regarding job security had been reformed. Employers were allowed to dismiss workers without "just cause," with a severance payment amounting to one month's wage for each year of service. Previously, employers had to have just cause for dismissal, but when a judge ordered that a given worker be rehired, employers could avoid complying by paying a severance payment that generally amounted to one month per year of service. By mid-1981, severance payments were reduced to a maximum of five months.

11. Alamos (1987).

Reforming Social Security

In 1981 the social security system was changed from a government-run pay-as-you-go system to a privately managed contribution one. The new system basically consists of a mandatory savings program, managed by highly regulated private institutions, and a mechanism that, upon a worker's retirement, converts the funds accumulated in the savings account into indexed annuities.

The three main features of the new pension system are that it exchanged the benefit formula, that is, the central concept for calculating the value of the pension under the traditional social security system, for a contribution formula; the state guarantees a minimum pension for workers whose contributions are not enough to finance it directly; the funds are privately managed and there is free choice of providers (the Administradoras de Fondos Previsionales, AFPs).

All covered or "dependent" workers must deposit 10 percent of their monthly earnings in a savings account managed by a private specialized institution (the AFP).[12] The AFP charges the workers a fee, in addition to the mandatory 10 percent, in order to finance the disability and survivors insurance and the costs and profits of the AFPs. The fee, which is determined by the market, has fluctuated around 3 percent.[13] By late 1994, pension funds amounted to more than twenty billion dollars, that is, more than 40 percent of the GDP.

Some of the expected benefits of the new pension system are related to the workings of the labor market. The labor tax was reduced, a fact that must have helped to create employment and to increase wages. The reduced contribution, which came together with the reform, was induced in great part by an increase in the age of retirement for all workers, which had been imposed prior to the privatization of the social security system.[14] The high rates of return of the pension funds, which have averaged 14 percent in the last fifteen years, also contributed to this same end.

But the argument was extended beyond the drop in the labor tax. The use of individual accounts was supposed to make workers more conscious

12. Social security contributions for independent workers are voluntary. Dependent workers must deposit 10 percent of their monthly earnings with a maximum mandatory contribution of U.S. $150.

13. Workers also have to contribute 7 percent of their wages for health care insurance and employers pay a fee for occupational accident insurance (of slightly over 1.5 percent).

14. Arellano (1985, pp. 217–22).

of the connection between their contributions and the pensions that they would receive in future. This would reduce the tax component of the contributions to social security and, hence, reduce evasion and increase coverage. It would also favor employment creation. This effect, although conceptually correct, may not be as important empirically as it would seem at first glance, if one takes into account, first, that a significant number of workers will only enjoy the minimum pension that is guaranteed by the state; and second, that most workers, partly because of liquidity constraints, are subject to high rates of intertemporal discount. The fact is that this system has not caused significant changes in the number of workers, as a portion of total employment, who contribute to social security.

Wages and Employment

In the period 1979–81 wages grew at a fast pace, above the rate of productivity growth (table 8-1). Three variables may have influenced this trend: decreasing inflation with 100 percent indexation (recall that full wage indexation was established by law and that it benefited all workers, including those who did not bargain collectively), opportunities to do better than the indexed "floor" through collective bargaining, and a reduction in the unemployment rate.[15] After mid-1982 a sharp devaluation reduced the purchasing power of wages, legal indexation was suppressed, and unemployment rates rocketed sky high owing to the major recession of that year (the GDP dropped by more than 13 percent).

Unemployment rates varied dramatically during this period. In the first three years (1979–81) unemployment decreased, mainly as the result of rapid growth rates. This trend was reversed drastically in 1982 when, as a consequence of the sharp recession (induced mainly by the debt crisis of that year), unemployment rates soared once more to higher than 20 percent. From 1983 onward, the rates gradually began falling again, mainly because of the steady growth process that continued at a fast pace during the rest of this period.

About 20 percent of wage earners were unionized in 1980. That figure decreased slightly until 1988, with a partial recovery occurring in 1989 (table 8-4).[16]

15. Wage equations estimated for this period show a significant impact of reductions in the unemployment rate over wages. Jadresic (1992, pp. 21–29).

16. Figures for the period 1970–79 are much higher because the legislation regarding

Labor Policy under Democracy: 1990–94

Labor policy suffered yet another change in the early 1990s. March 1990 marked the beginning of the four-year administration of President Patricio Aylwin—the first democratic government after almost seventeen years of military rule. To understand the change in the behavior of poli-cymakers consider, once more, the "preferences" of the new governing coalition, as well as the "constraints" and "incentives" created by the new setting.

For preferences, the new coalition—ranging from the political center to the left—emphasized that, together with maintaining growth and sta-bility, a need existed for more equity and social participation in Chilean development.[17] A stronger social consensus would also need to be forged in a society that had been highly polarized during the previous decades. This view reserved a more important role for government intervention in labor policy than the neoconservative one. Social organizations were seen as an opportunity for, rather than a threat to, development. Unions could give a voice to workers at the firm level, which could contribute to better labor relations and higher productivity growth. At the national level worker confederations could contribute to consensus building. A shift occurred from an ideologically motivated government with a neoconser-vative view to an ideologically motivated government that believed in what was called the strategy of "growth with equity."

In looking at incentives, the government realized that equity and social participation, besides being objectives in themselves, were also a condi-tion for the social legitimacy of the rules of the game of the labor market, as well as essential for future stability. The government was aware that it faced two types of constraints: a positive relationship had to be main-tained with the labor movement[18] (this required a decided will to intro-duce labor reforms) and a constructive relationship was required with

---

unions was very different from that after 1979. For example, if over 50 percent of blue-collar workers of a firm belonged to the union then all of the rest of the blue-collar workers were automatically affiliated to that organization. The National Labor Administration Office did not have an accurate accounting of the unionized population (there is some evidence that when affiliation to a union diminshed, figures were not revised downward). These data were not comparable with the data of the following years.

17. GDP grew at over 6.5 percent during this period, and the investment rate reached over 25 percent of GDP. Inflation dropped from an annual rate of almost 30 percent to less than 10 percent. There was a fiscal, as well as a balance of payments, surplus.

18. Recall that this was a center-to-the-left coalition.

business—a crucial partner in the new social consensus that was needed—as well as with the right-wing opposition, which had a majority in the Senate and whose votes were necessary for any legal reform.

In this new stage several players could affect the results of labor policy through their preferences and through the incentives and restrictions that they could impose on the other actors. For example, the fact that, for political reasons, the government wanted to maintain a positive relationship with the labor movement gave that actor the capacity to influence, however indirectly, the labor policy agenda. The fact that the government wanted to maintain a constructive relationship with business gave that sector a say in those same issues. Sometimes these forces offset each other, creating more room for autonomous government policy. But the fact remains that in an open polity, government policy—especially in areas such as labor policy—should be viewed not as an autonomous act of government authorities reflecting only their preferences, but rather as the result of the interaction between those preferences with the incentives and restrictions that are influenced by the strategic interaction of the government with the other political and social actors.

To attain its objectives, the new government pursued five different labor policies: social dialogue and tripartite agreements, enactment of a new Labor Code, improved enforcement of labor legislation, implementation of a training program for young people, and an increase in pensions and improvements to the social security system.

Social Dialogue and Tripartite Agreements

A few weeks after its inauguration, the government invited the main national confederations of workers and employers to sign a national agreement on the principal aspects of development and labor policies. The agreement also included an adjustment of minimum wages and family allowances. Chile lacked previous experience in national tripartite agreements. These agreements were signed during each of the four years of President Aylwin's administration. To make the rise in minimum wages compatible with lower inflation and less unemployment, after a two-year recovery (1990–91), minimum wages were increased according to expected inflation plus the rate of growth of productivity. During the Aylwin government, minimum wages rose an average of 5.6 percent a year (table 8-1).

These agreements undoubtedly reflected the preference for equity, social participation, and consensus building of the new governing coalition. But they were also compatible with the preferences of the labor movement, which was searching for a protagonistic role in the new democratic environment. The tripartite agreements made the labor movement a partner in the implementation of significant increases in the minimum wage. Business confederations, which had been very close to the Pinochet regime, found in this type of agreement an effective way of playing a visible role in the new democracy and helping to avoid social polarization.[19]

Not only were preferences ripe for agreements of this type, but the restrictions also made them possible. The fact that the minimum wage had lagged behind the average wage and productivity growth for several years before the transition made this type of agreement indispensable for workers and possible for business (table 8-1).

This policy of consensus building contributed to social peace. According to the *Annual Report of the International Labor Organization* in 1992, "In Chile, thanks largely to the agreements reached with the new government in April 1990, restoration of democracy was not accompanied by social unrest, as had occurred in other countries, such as, among others, Argentina, Brazil and Uruguay."

The Enactment of a New Labor Code

The labor legislation had to be modified, according to the government, to assure more equity but also as a way to allow social organizations to play a more significant role. Furthermore, a crucial restriction was that the reforms, to be approved, required the votes of the opposition in the Senate.

The preference of the opposition was to avoid the reforms, but it finally accepted and reached an agreement with the government. The opposition faced the restriction of its electorate, which was mostly in favor of reforming the labor legislation. The opposition also had an incentive to reach an agreement with the government: an opportunity was arising to

19. The fact that the preferences of the different actors made these agreements possible does not mean that they were in any way inevitable. Agreements were not the only potential outcome of these tripartite negotiations. On some occasions, the consensus was reached at the eleventh hour. And during the first two years of the Frei government (1994, 1995) tripartite agreements were not reached.

give more stability to the rules of the game in the labor market and to develop a relationship of cooperation with the governing coalition. Such relationship was viewed by the majority of the opposition as a positive sum game. After a long period of confrontations that had sharply divided Chilean society, most of the electorate was in favor of cooperative political relationships. Some of the main reforms that finally materialized were the following:

—Unions. The new legislation enhanced the right to unionize, authorizing unions in the public sector as well as among temporary agricultural workers.[20] It also permitted the legal existence of national confederations of workers. Union leaders were more adequately protected against arbitrary dismissals, and the restrictions on the number of hours that elected officials could dedicate to union affairs were lifted.[21] More effective mechanisms for union financing were put in place.[22] These reforms of the labor legislation were complemented by other policies, such as the creation of a government-financed fund for the training programs of trade unions.

—Collective bargaining. It is the employers' "duty" to bargain at company level, but legal prohibitions forbidding bargaining for unions of temporary workers, unions representing workers from different firms, and federations were abolished.[23]

The right of employers to replace striking workers, on a permanent basis, was suppressed. Workers could be replaced temporarily only if the employer had offered at least the same benefits as those existing under

20. The law guaranteed the right of state-employed workers to set up the organizations they deem appropriate, without prior authorization. It also stipulates leave entitlements and job security for their leaders.

21. The previous legislation established that a union leader could devote up to four hours per week to these activities, if affiliates numbered less than 250, and up to six hours per week, if affiliates numbered 250 or more. The new legislation increased the number of hours from four to six and from six to eight. But these were not legal maximums but rather the minimum guaranteed by law. If unions and their employers agreed on a higher number of hours legislation would not prevent this.

22. If the employer extends the benefits of a collective agreement to nonunion workers, the employer must discount from their wages and hand over to the organization 75 percent of the regular contribution made by members to the union. This charge takes into account the fact that nonunion workers have received a service, or benefit, from that union (reduces "free riding"). If the majority of union workers decide, in a democratic election, that mandatory contributions must be made to their union, federation, or confederation, the employer has to discount that amount.

23. It is the employer's "duty" to bargain at company level when workers take the initiative to negotiate at that level.

the old collective agreement, adjusted for inflation. If that was the case, then workers could also return to their jobs individually, after fifteen days on strike. If the employer offered less than the old contract, adjusted by inflation, both dates were postponed by fifteen days.

The government would not intervene in the process of collective bargaining, which remained as a bipartite labor and business affair. Government interventions were very significant at the policy level (tripartite national agreements, reforms and enforcement of labor legislation, social security, and resources for training) but not at the level of labor relations within the company, even in the collective bargaining of state enterprises.[24]

The strength of the policy rule precluding the intervention of the government in the collective bargaining process is crucial for a bipartite bargaining system to work. Labor and business know that if they sit at a table with a government authority they will be hard-pressed to reach an "intermediate" solution. The government official, who knows little about the internal situation of the firm but wants to solve the problem, will try to moderate the position of both parties so as to reach an agreement. If that is the case, then both parties have an incentive to exaggerate their positions before they are called upon by the authority, so as to reach a reasonable result when they are asked by the government official to moderate their demands.

In contrast, a policy of nonintervention in collective bargaining induces both parties to moderate their positions at the outset. The fact that no one is going to come to the rescue makes it possible for labor and business to try to overcome their differences from the very first day. The result, in the case of Chile, was a very low level of strike activity. As argued below, during the 1990–94 period, an average of one hour per worker a year was lost as a result of strikes and labor disputes, less than the average of OECD countries.

The number of workers covered by collective agreements increased during this period to about 17 percent of wage earners (table 8-5). But,

24. One clear example was collective bargaining in the government-owned copper mines. The military regime had forbidden the right to strike in the largest Chilean copper mine. The new government had given back that right but made it very clear that collective bargaining was a bipartite affair. During a long strike in 1991 pressure mounted for the government to mediate in the conflict of this state-owned esterprise. The fact that the government did not give in to such pressures and that the conflict was solved by a direct agreement between the management and the union established a clear precedent that avoided any kind of future interventions.

as just mentioned, one must remember that in the firms in which collective bargaining took place, only about half of the workers participated in the bargaining process. Since it was fairly common for the employer to extend the benefits of the collective agreement to the rest of the workers, the number of workers effectively covered by collective agreements is much higher than those registered in table 8-5. Furthermore, starting in 1990, the government signed, every year, agreements with the associations of public sector workers, determining their wage readjustment and other benefits. If one considers these workers as covered by collective agreements, then the percentage of workers that bargain collectively would increase to another 5 to 6 percent of wage earners.

—Individual contracts. As a way to increase the equity of labor legislation, several discriminatory regulations regarding the maximum daily working hours, weekly rest, and the duration of vacations were reformed.[25] Regulations that contributed to a bias against hiring women were abolished. Regulations that intend to protect the family were approved (for example, permission for a working man to take a day off when his wife is having a baby, the use of maternity leave by the father if the wife dies during that period, improvement of maternity leave when a child is adopted). Regulations on job security were reformed: employers could only dismiss workers by invoking just cause and in the case of economic needs of the firm, the company had to pay one month per year of service up to a maximum of eleven months.[26] If the judge decided that the reason for dismissal did not involve a just cause, severance payments would be between 1.2 and 1.5 months a year, up to a maximum of eleven years. The new legislation permitted workers and employers, if they so agreed, to substitute a month of severance payments payable only in the event of dismissal for less than a month but also payable if the worker quit or retired.[27]

25. For example, workers whose forty-eight-hour working week was distributed over five days enjoyed a minimum vacation of three weeks a year, whereas workers who worked the same number of hours distributed over six days (normally blue-collar workers) had a minimum vacation of two and a half weeks a year. This was made uniform, that is, three weeks' annual vacation. The weekly rest for workers in trade, fishing, transportation, and construction was improved.

26. The economic needs of the firm were deemed to be just cause.

27. The alternative payment had to be of at least half a month a year, and the money was to be deposited in an account that belonged to the worker and that was administered by an AFP. Consider that about half of the cases of labor contracts that came to an end corresponded to dismissals because of "economic needs of the firm." This agreement could not take place for those severance payments corresponding to the first six years at a firm.

Improved Enforcement of Labor Legislation

As a way to improve equity, the government increased by 50 percent the amount of resources devoted to the enforcement of labor legislation.[28] The number of workers who benefited, and the number of companies inspected, increased by about 70 percent. Tripartite efforts to increase compliance with labor legislation, through campaigns via the mass media, were also implemented. Legislation expediting a more appropriate control of compliance with labor legislation, as well as regulations that provide a more effective access to the legal system to lower-income workers, were approved.[29]

Development of a Training Program for Young People

The number of workers, of any age, who participated in courses financed by the tax subsidy, increased by 40 percent.[30] But the most innovative effort was made in the training of the unemployed youth.

Youth unemployment in Chile is about three times the average unemployment rate. Even during periods of economic expansion, it is very difficult for youths from poor neighborhoods to find a job. The training program was intended to benefit unemployed and underemployed youths from low-income families. The goal was to benefit 100,000 people. Training was to be funded by the government but provided mainly by private institutions. The program combined instruction at training institutes with three months as trainees in firms (a dual system). The results were highly positive in terms of targeting (75 percent of the beneficiaries came from the 40 percent poorest families), access to a job (the rate of employment was more than 30 percent higher among beneficiaries in comparison to the control group), and quality of jobs (higher wage increases and a higher degree of formalization of labor relations than the control

---

Workers that labor at homes (mostly maids) did not have the right to severance payments. The new legislation gave them the right to receive half a month per year, payable not only in the case of dismissal but also if the worker quit or retired, and that was to be deposited in an account at the AFP.

28. This corresponds to the budget of the institution responsible for enforcing labor legislation, the National Labor Administration Office (Dirección Nacional del Trabajo). During the previous period (1979–89) and due to the prevailing neoconservative approach, the resources of the National Labor Administration Office had dropped sharply.

29. Cortázar (1993, pp. 115–16).

30. The state subsidized job training undertaken by companies for up to 1 percent of the payroll.

group).[31] The elements of the program that contributed to these positive results, and which I believe reflect some general principles that are useful for other types of training efforts, are the following: decentralization (training was offered by hundreds of private or public institutions competing for government funds. It is only possible at a local level to discover the type of training that firms require. This information cannot be generated at a centralized level); strong participation of the private sector in providing the training courses; and a close relationship between training and the needs of the firms (before resources were allocated to training institutions they had to prove that firms were willing to receive their students as trainees. The assumption is that firms, in general, do not accept trainees in areas in which they have no intention of hiring in the future. This is then a practical manner of linking the expected demand for labor with the contents and design of courses).

Increase in Pensions and Improvements to the Social Security System

Although the new pension system has been in force for more than a decade, still around 90 percent of the passive workers were covered by the old social security system. During this period the government maintained the indexation clauses for this sector and increased the real value of pensions under the old system by more than 10 percent. It also corrected some forms of discrimination of the old system against workers in the public sector.

In the new system, a mechanism for preliminary pension payments was created, cutting the time it took for a pensioner to receive his first pension payment from six months to not more than fifteen days. Better regulations for the private pension funds, which amount to more than 40 percent of GDP, were put in place. There has been a gradual expansion in the set of allowable assets (the percentage of pension funds invested in stocks increased from 11.3 percent in 1990 to 32.9 percent in 1994, and investment in foreign securities was authorized). A new law was passed to regulate conflicts of interest that arise in the management of these funds, such as the use of information about the investment strategies of the AFPs, the situation of intermediaries that are simultaneously trading on more than one account, the use of voting shares in firms, the way AFP directors are elected, and mechanisms for the internal control of the AFPs.

31. Cortázar (1993, pp. 85–100).

Wages and Employment

Unemployment increased during the second year of the Aylwin government (1991) as a result of a restrictive macroeconomic policy aimed at decelerating inflation. Then, gradually, over the next two years, unemployment began to drop, as a consequence of the recovery in growth. Wages grew at an annual real rate of almost 3.5 percent during those years. Five reasons lie behind these considerable wage rises: high rates of productivity growth (table 8-1), decelerating inflation (with relatively widespread indexation),[32] reductions in the unemployment rate (starting in mid-1991), generous increases in minimum wages and public sector wages, and a better bargaining position for workers thanks to the new legislation and to the new social and political environment.[33] As a consequence of these conditions the number of families below the poverty line dropped by over 25 percent.

The rate of unionization increased sharply during the period 1990–91 and then diminished a bit during the period 1993–94. But considering that public sector workers have associations, which for all practical purposes are unions, then the rate of unionization of wage earners has to be increased by about 6 percent, to around 27 percent. This rate of unionization of wage earners, even though lower than the one that existed in Chile in the past, is higher than that of France, the United States, or Spain.

This increased unionization and collective bargaining occurred in a context of very little social unrest. During the 1990–94 period an average of one hour per worker was lost as a result of strikes and labor disputes. This figure is less than the average of OECD countries and half the number of labor disputes recorded in Chile in the 1960s.

Continuity and Change

This chapter has emphasized the changes that took place between the period that was oriented by the perspective of "growth with equity" (1990–94), and the one I have characterized as dominated by the neo-

32. Jadresic (1992) was unable to reject the hypothesis that wages were determined by long-term contracts of two years with full indexation every six months.

33. Together with this improvement in wages and employment, government social expenditure (health, housing, education, and social security) grew more than 30 percent during this period.

conservative view (1979–1989). In this section the emphasis is put on the elements of continuity between both periods when contrasted with the dominant perspective that prevailed in most of Latin America in the previous decades.[34] From the crisis of the 1930s to the early 1970s, a certain consensus existed on labor policy in the region. This consensus, which I call the old consensus, was based on a view that emphasized the goal of equity and that gave to state intervention in labor issues a leading role. As the director general of the ILO pointed out in his *Annual Report to the 1992 American Regional Conference*, to refer to labor policy during this period was to refer to "the preeminence of the State as regulator and guarantor of the goals of employment, wages, and work conditions; this without paying that much attention to the market, and, in most cases, with only token participation by social partners."

The old consensus was consistent with the development strategy of import substitution, which permitted a much more significant role for government intervention. For example, the government could participate in collective bargaining by modifying tariffs, nontariff restrictions, or price controls, so as to permit firms to transfer to prices the higher costs induced by wage agreements. But the choice of an open economy and the degree of competition in the world economy have created a strong link between wages and productivity, and this connection is decisive when it comes to setting wages and determining the level of employment. Market forces have to play a more significant role. The state's method of intervention is also influenced and the kind of intervention that the government had in collective bargaining in the past is precluded.[35] The role of social actors has become crucial in the setting of wages and working conditions.

Both the growth with equity perspective and the neoconservative one favor a more important role of the market and a less active role of state intervention than the old consensus. But there is a change, when com-

34. The period 1973–79 is not mentioned in this discussion because the paradigm that oriented the labor policy was not as well formulated. The main traits of labor policy were conditioned by the need to excert control over social organizations as well as by the need to reduce very high inflation rates.

35. In a more closed economy, oriented toward import substitution, employment was more dependent on aggregate demand. Fiscal, monetary and wage policies were mechanisms through which the government could affect aggregate spending and employment. In the open economy employment is more dependent on the relation between wages and productivity. There is much less the government can do to affect employment levels in the short run.

pared with the old consensus, not only with respect to the intensity of the desired government intervention but also with respect to the nature of the policies applied.

The choice of an open economy, which requires the growth of wages to reflect productivity growth, favors a process of wage determination that takes place at a decentralized level, especially in countries that have a very heterogeneous productive structure.[36] During both periods (1979–89; 1990–94), the "duty to bargain" has remained only at the company level, as a means of consolidating a very decentralized collective bargaining structure.

The choice of an open economy, integrated to a very variable world economy, requires firms to rapidly adapt to change and to institute training policies that have mechanisms to closely follow the new needs in terms of skills and competencies. This has resulted, in both periods, in new policies that favor training at private institutions, with a close link between the content of training and the needs of firms. The choice of an open economy that requires competitive firms has favored a reduction of taxes on wages, which have been diminished to 20 percent. The social security reform, imposed in the first period (1981) and perfected during the second one, constitutes one of the means for attaining this goal.

Final Considerations

The role of government preferences, as well as that of the incentives and restrictions government faces, has been emphasized in explaining the design and application of labor policies in Chile. In this last section some of the thoughts on the views that lie behind those preferences in the three periods analyzed here (1973–79, 1979–89, 1990–94) are summarized. I argue that those preferences were the outcome of basically ideologically motivated governments.[37] I also argue that there is a need, in these types of analyses, for a political-economy perspective, so as to link the views of the government to the workings of the labor market and the behavior of social actors in civil society.

36. If the economy is to remain close to full employment.
37. Alesina (1988).

*Behind Government Preferences: The Relation between
the State, the Market, and Society*

The views on the relationship between the state and the market that
lie behind the preferences of the government during these three periods
differ greatly. In the first period, marked by government control over the
labor market (1973–79), the emphasis on restricting wages and controlling the behavior of social actors dominated the labor policy implemented
by the government.

In the second period (1979–89) a neoconservative ideology dominated
the view of the government. The state, it was thought, should intervene
as little as possible so as not to interfere with the workings of the market.
As the result of this perspective, among other things, minimum wages
dropped (table 8-1), and the capacity of the government to enforce labor
legislation also decreased sharply.

In the third period (1990–94), the new perspective of "growth with
equity" reserved a more important role for government intervention in
labor policy. The government was supposed to determine minimum wages
(which increased by more than 30 percent real during those four years),
reform and enforce labor legislation (the capacity of the government to
do so increased around 50 percent in this period), and improve the social
security system and promote tripartite national agreements. But collective bargaining would remain a strictly bipartite affair.

The main distinction of the three periods, however, probably lies in
the role played by society in labor policy. In the first period, the role of
society was reduced by the need for tight political control.

In the second period (1979–89), even though unions and collective
bargaining were authorized in response to the need to avert a boycott,
legal restrictions were imposed on certain aspects of the right to unionize,
and legislation did not provide adequate protection for union leaders. It
also imposed a limit on their activities. In a perspective that is consistent
with the neoconservative ideology, organized interests were seen as in-
terfering with the normal working of markets. Unions were viewed as
"monopolies" that pressed for higher wages of their affiliates at the
expense of less employment creation. At the national level, social con-
certation was generally catalogued as the participation of corporatist
interests that tended to distort the policy agenda. In this respect, one
could say that social organizations were seen as a threat to development.

A weaker society fostered the construction of a stronger economy and a stronger state.

In the third period (1990–94) a major shift took place in the evaluation of the role of social organizations. Such organizations were seen as an opportunity for, rather than a threat to, development. At the company level, productivity was viewed as being strongly influenced by the social climate prevailing in the firm. Creative and productive work—as well as the capacity of the firm to adapt to change—could be enhanced by the role of unions, which gave voice to company workers.[38] At the national level, social agreements could contribute to consensus building. Stronger consensus reduced the variance of future policy shifts and hence diminished the "country risk," thereby favoring investment. Basic consensus also promoted social peace, which fed back into the development process through higher productivity growth. A stronger society fostered the construction of a stronger economy and a stronger state.[39]

The Need for a Political-Economy Perspective

The importance of labor policies in the evolution of labor markets in Chile points to the need to understand these policy shifts. Once it is accepted that government policies are not the result of the action of exogenous social planners but the outcome of the strategic interaction of policymakers with certain objectives in mind (in the case of this period mainly ideologically motivated governments), which face restrictions and incentives, and the public and organized society, one inevitably has to develop a political-economy perspective. One must identify the preferences, restrictions, and incentives of the different players and try to describe the interactions that take place among them. This is the approach I have pursued in this chapter.

---

38. Freeman and Medoff (1984).

39. To assert the potential contributions of social organizations to a stronger economy or to a stronger state does not mean that the potential negative effects of unions—when they act as a monopoly or when they accumulate too much power and end up distorting the agenda—should be overlooked. But those negative effects are not seen as the necessary outcome of social participation.

References

Alamos, R. 1987. "La Modernización Laboral." *Estudios Públicos*, no. 26. Santiago: CEP.

Alesina, A. 1988. "Macroeconomics and Politics," edited by S. Fisher, 13–61. *NBER Macroeconmics Annual 1988*. MIT Press.

Arellano, J. P. 1985. *Políticas Sociales y Desarrollo. Chile 1924–1984*. Santiago: CIEPLAN.

Cortázar, R. 1983. "Wages in the Short Run: Chile, 1964–1981." *Notas Técnicas CIEPLAN*, no. 56, April.

―――. 1985. "Distributive Results in Chile: 1973–1982." In *The National Economic Policies of Chile*, edited by G. Walton, 79–105. London: JAI Press.

―――. 1993. *Política Laboral en el Chile Democrático*. Santiago: Ediciones Dolmen.

Cortázar, R., and J. Marshall. 1980. "Indice de Precios al Consumidor en Chile: 1970–1978." *Colección Estudios CIEPLAN*, no. 4. Santiago: CIEPLAN.

Freeman, R., and J. Medoff. 1984. *What Do Unions Do?* Basic Books.

Jadresic, E. 1986. "Evolución del Empleo y Desempleo en Chile, 1970–1975." *Colección Estudios CIEPLAN*, no. 20. Santiago: CIEPLAN.

―――. 1992. "Dinámica de Salarios y Contratos en Chile." In *Colección Estudios CIEPLAN*, no. 34, June.

Piñera, J. 1990. *La Revolución Laboral en Chile*. Santiago: Zig-Zag.

CHAPTER NINE

Colombia: The Evolution and Reform of the Labor Market

Eduardo Lora and Marta Luz Henao

LIKE MOST Latin American countries, during several decades, Colombia developed a complex system of government intervention in the labor market, which was aimed, in principle, at protecting workers' jobs and incomes, strengthening their bargaining position vis-à-vis the capitalists, and establishing an ambitious social security system. Most of the legislation and the institutions that laid the foundations for this state intervention in the labor market were established in the 1950s and 1960s and remained almost untouched until 1990.

A general feeling of disenchantment with these and other interventionist practices led César Gaviria's administration (1990–94) to introduce substantial reforms in the most important areas of economic and social policy. International trade, foreign investment and capital flows were liberalized, foreign exchange controls were lifted, the financial liberalization process was deepened and an independent Central Bank was established. The reforms to the labor regime were less far reaching and certainly mixed as will be shown in this chapter. This was partly a result

A revised version of this chapter was prepared for "Labor Markets: Growth and Poverty in Latin America," a conference sponsored by the Brookings Institution, Instituto di Tella, Universidad di Tella, and the World Bank, Buenos Aires, July 1995. The authors are grateful to Ernesto May, Carmen Pagés, and two anonymous referees for their useful comments and suggestions.

of the bargaining process of the reform package bill introduced into Congress in 1990, some of its components only being approved in 1993.[1]

This chapter describes these reforms and analyzes some of its effects. Its main conclusion is that the reform was a step in the right direction, but a very timid one. The reforms eased the restrictions to temporary labor, made severance payments more certain, and strengthened the link between contributions and benefits in the social security system. But dismissal costs and total social security contributions, which were among the highest in Latin America, were further increased. Not surprisingly, the reforms did not alter the functioning of the labor market significantly. Along with a prudent minimum wage policy, they may have made some contribution to the reduction of informality and to the leveling off of labor costs of factory workers. However, the reforms were unable to reduce labor turnover, nor did they alter the patterns of labor demand or the increasing trend of administrative labor costs. The major challenge lying ahead is the reduction of payroll taxes, which could facilitate formal employment and reduce unemployment.

Legislation Reforms

In its most salient aspects, the Labor Reform Law of 1990 (Ley 50) called for hiring and dismissal practices to be clarified and made more flexible and modernized the negotiation and labor conflict regime. Labor legislation was also affected by the social security reform passed in 1993 (Ley 100), which created the pension funds, opened social security to the private sector, and increased the contributions to the pension and health systems.

Hiring Conditions

Like most countries of the region, in the early 1990s, hiring practices in Colombia were too rigid and severely limited nontypical and temporary contracts.[2] Before the reform, the law called for indefinite terms with a two-month probation period. Temporary contracts were limited to a min-

---

1. A detailed recount of the discussion and bargaining of the reform is Posada de la Peña (1995).
2. See International Development Bank (IDB) (1996) for an international comparison of labor legislation in Latin America and the Caribbean.

imum period of one year, with a few exceptions, and were not covered by any benefits such as vacation allowance and social security. Temporary labor demands were supposed to be met by specialized firms, which were responsible for the payment of payroll taxes and social benefits of the workers. In practice, however, the firms could very well evade these taxes owing to high employee turnover and lack of adequate supervision from the Ministry of Labor. Labor reform lifted most restrictions to temporary contracts, while granting temporary workers the same benefits and social security rights of permanent workers. At the same time, it also made permanent contracts flexible by allowing any probation period agreed on between the firms and the entrant workers and by creating a new type of labor contract for workers earning more than ten times the minimum wage.

Severance Payments

Until 1990, workers with indefinite term contracts had the right, upon retirement, to an amount equal to one salary per year worked. This payment was not related to the cause of the termination of the labor relationship, even if that decision was made by the worker. During their permanence in the firm, workers had the option of cashing in advances on this payment (if they produced evidence the funds were to be used for housing or home improvements), which were deducted from the final payment amount with no inflation adjustment. Because of this accounting practice, which amounted to a "double retroactivity" of severance payments, the expenses incurred in those payments were quite high, given an average Colombian inflation of 25 percent.[3] Moreover, these expenses were highly uncertain, since they depended on the length of employment in the firm, salary increases, and especially the frequency of these withdrawals. For example, a worker could make a withdrawal eveiy year and retire at the fifth year, which would result in accumulated severance payments equal to 2.2 months of wages per year worked, whereas if he or she decided to retire at the tenth year, this amount would be equal to 3.3 months.[4] A 1986 industrial sector survey showed that severance payments were considered the biggest legal obstacle in job creation.[5]

3. Ocampo (1987).
4. Assuming nominal salary adjustments of 24 percent a year. See Ocampo (1987).
5. Kertzman (1987).

The reform established that severance funds were to be deposited annually in worker accounts at specialized financial entities created to this end, where these funds would receive a market return and where certain partial withdrawals were allowed. In this way, the uncertainty of this labor cost was eliminated, though only for new contracts. In fact, the law allowed for the old system to apply for existing contracts, except in the case of free renegotiations between workers and firms. By late 1994, only 82,000 workers of all sectors had adopted voluntarily this option. However, because of high worker turnover (see below), by mid-1994 only 20.7 percent of the manufacturing sector workers and 14.5 percent of the retail sector workers were still entitled to the old severance system.

The labor reform also created a new type of contract for workers earning more than ten times the minimum wage and who were willing to forsake all types of severance payments and other legal benefits (except vacation) for higher monthly earnings. By mid-1994 only 1.5 percent of the industrial sector workers and 0.6 percent of the retail sector had accepted such contracts.

Dismissal Conditions

To ensure job security, Colombian legislation allows for several restrictions to worker dismissals, which include a notification period, unemployment compensation, and other benefits for workers with more than ten years of employment.

The forty-five-day notification period for dismissal after the probation period was not modified with the labor reform. In practice, the notification period is paid but not worked and therefore constitutes another layoff expense.

The unemployment compensation payment is an increasing function of the worker's length of employment in the firm. Though, in principle, this payment only applies for unjustified layoffs, the law does not consider the firms' own economic considerations a just cause and makes it quite difficult for them to prove their case on performance or behavior grounds. The labor reform increased unemployment compensation payment amounts for workers with 10 or more years in the firm, from 10.5 to 13.5 months of salary. For workers with more that 15 years of employment the increase went from 15.5 to 20.2 months of salary (table 9-1). This decision was taken to compensate for the dismantling of certain security guaran-

Table 9-1. *Cost of Dismissal (as monthly wages)*

Years of tenure	Before law 50/1990	After law 50/1990
5	4.2	4.2
10	10.5	13.5
15	15.5	20.2
20	20.5	21.8

Source: Reyes (1991).

tees for workers with more than 10 years in the firm. In fact, before the reform, if dismissed, such workers could sue the firm at a labor court. If the firm could not prove just cause for the dismissal, as was often the case, it was forced to rehire the worker and pay the total amount of wages forgone during the proceedings. Additionally, any firm dismissing a worker with more than 10 years of employment at the firm was required to take over the worker's pension at the time of the worker's retirement. These provisions were eliminated.

Social Security Reforms in Pensions and Health

In a separate legislative decision, in 1993, the pension and health aspects of social security were reformed. In the pension reform, the central element consisted in granting the worker the choice between the traditional defined benefit pay-as-you-go system and the new system of individual capitalization in private funds. The contribution rate rose gradually from 6.5 percent to 13.5 percent, applicable also to the capitalization system. The reform reduced the benefits offered in the traditional system, but gave a clear advantage for workers 39 years or older that stayed in the system (25 years or older in the case of women).[6]

With respect to the health regime, the social security reform replaced the individual affiliation system with a unique public entity with a complex system. Its main features are that the contribution rate is 12 percent of the wage bill instead of 7 percent as in the previous system; affiliation is family and not individually oriented as was the case previously; contributions are paid to the health plan promoter (EPS) chosen at will by the worker (these promoters can be public, private, or cooperative, and their main goal is to promote enrollment and hire the services of health providers [IPS]); and part of the contribution is used to finance a subsi-

6. See Lora and Helmsdorff (1995).

dized system by which families in poverty will be covered.[7] Although this complex system has only been implemented partially, the 12 percent contribution rate has applied since July 1995.

Minimum Wages

Minimum wage legislation was not altered by the recent labor reform. Minimum wages have been in place in Colombia since 1950. Minimum wages are determined by the government on an annual basis and previous negotiation with representatives of the labor unions and the business organizations. Past and expected levels of inflation are the main variables considered in the negotiations, thus resulting in a remarkable stability of the minimum wage in real terms. Since the late 1980s the minimum wage has declined gradually and by early 1996 it was 8 percent less than seven years before.

For Latin American standards, the minimum wage plays a very important role as a determinant of labor earnings in Colombia. Fewer than 10 percent of the unskilled workers (up to 12 years of education) occupied in the formal sector earn below the minimum wage and a percentage as high as 44 percent earns between 1 and 1.2 times the minimum wage. Even among the unskilled workers of the informal sector the minimum wage exerts an important influence. Thus, although nearly 30 percent of the workers in this group earn below the minimum, another 30 percent earns between 1 and 1.2 times the minimum wage. Therefore, the concentration of earnings around the minimum wage is very high for the unskilled workers, who represent nearly 80 percent of the urban labor working force.[8]

Labor Conflict and Negotiation

Labor union affiliation has been historically low in Colombia. It rose from almost 5 percent of urban employment in the 1940s and 1950s to a peak of 13.4 percent in the mid-1970s, and it has been on the decline ever since.[9] This low affiliation could be in part a result of legal restrictions to the creation, recognition, and functioning of unions, especially

7. World Bank (1994, chap. 3).
8. World Bank (1994).
9. Furthermore, according to Misión de Empleo (1986) these calculations exaggerate unionization, which probably never reached 10 percent.

administrative discretion granted to the Ministry of Labor to recognize or cancel the legal existence of unions; the absence of regulations to prevent firms from discouraging worker unionization; and the required minimum number of workers to form a union.

The first two impediments were eliminated by the 1990 reform. The legal recognition of any union is carried out nowadays by the simple registration of its bylaws, and the ministry has no power whatsoever in interrupting or canceling its existence. The law also prohibits and levies stiff penalties on employer practices aimed at hindering unionization. Before 1978 an additional obstacle to unionization was the possibility the firms had of negotiating separately with unionized and nonunionized workers. Since 1978, this possibility is restricted to firms where unionized workers account for less than a third of the total. However, although this can stimulate the creation of new unions, in practice this could discourage unionization, since nonunionized workers receive the same labor benefits granted to unionized workers. This adverse effect was strengthened before 1990 by the fact that union contributions were mandatory only for unionized workers. For this reason, the Labor Reform Law extended this obligation to all workers in the firm that could benefit from the union's negotiations.

The procedure to call for a strike was also modified by the Labor Reform Law. Before, the procedure comprised three steps: an initial 15-day direct negotiation period (this could be extended to 25 days); a mediation period with the active participation of the Ministry of Labor, with a maximum of ten days; and a final 10-day period in which a decision was taken by secret vote and by an absolute majority of all unionized workers on the option of calling for a strike or requesting the appointment of a mediation tribunal. The Labor Reform Law eliminated the second step, which involved the government in the conflicts, and extended the direct negotiation period to 20 days (with an option of up to 40 days). For the final walkout decision, the law established that, when unionized workers are fewer than half the firm's workers, the decision must be taken by absolute majority. The Labor Reform Law also extended the maximum strike period from 40 to 60 days, after which mediation is mandatory.

Even before labor reform, the rights of firms and workers during walkouts were clearly established and imposed high costs on both sides: workers do not get paid and are not permitted back to work, whether unionized or not. Firms are not allowed to fire workers or to hire labor, except for essential maintenance. Strikes are illegal in the so-called public services, which include transportation, public utilities, health services, and other activities related to the production and distribution of basic foodstuffs.[10]

The Effects of Legislation Reforms

Legislation reforms affected nonwage labor costs, total labor costs in the manufacturing sector, labor demand, composition of the labor force, labor turnover, and unionization and labor conflicts.

Nonwage Labor Costs

The main labor costs additional to wages imposed by Colombian legislation comprise severance payments; unemployment compensation; social security contributions; other payroll taxes appropriated by public entities for labor training programs, social assistance and family subsidies; and vacation benefits and other half-yearly bonuses. The labor and social security reforms modified the first three. The total average amount of these costs combined went up, but its taxation character and the uncertainty about the actual amount of these costs were alleviated.

Severance payments, which represented an average of 13.5 percent of wage costs, were reduced to 9.3 percent for new indefinite-term contracts. The new integral salary contracts were exempt of this cost, while for temporary contracts severance payments became an additional cost. Weighted by the importance of each of these contracting practices, total severance payments costs remained practically without change in the manufacturing sector and were reduced from 11.6 percent to 9.9 percent of the wage bill in commerce (table 9-2). More important still, severance payments have evolved into a totally known cost for all new contracts, due annually and independent of the seniority of the worker in the firm and of the withdrawal option.

As discussed above, unemployment compensation increased, but reimbursement for workers with more than 10 years of employment was eliminated. No information is available to calculate the incidence of these costs on total labor cost.

10. Misión de Empleo (1986); Posada de la Peña (1995).

Table 9-2. *Main Nonwage Labor Costs (percent of wage)*

| Item | Regular permanent contracts | | | | Temporary contracts | | Weighted Averages[a] | | | |
| | Before reform | After reform | | | Before reform | After reform | Manufacturing sector | | Commerce | |
		Old contracts	New contracts with full benefits	New contracts with integral salaries			Before reform	After reform	Before reform	After reform
Severance payments	13.5	13.5	9.3	0.0	0.0	9.3	10.2	10.0	11.6	9.9
Social security contributions										
Pensions	6.5	13.5	13.5	14.5	0.0	13.5	4.9	13.5	5.6	13.5
(of which, paid by employee)	2.2	3.4	3.4	4.4	0.0	3.4	1.7	3.4	1.9	3.4
Health	7.0	12.0	12.0	12.0	0.0	12.0	5.3	12.0	6.0	12.0
(of which, paid by employee)	2.3	4.0	4.0	4.0	0.0	4.0	1.7	4.0	2.0	4.0
Payroll taxes										
Labor training	2.0	2.0	2.0	2.0	2.0	2.0	2.0	2.0	2.0	2.0
Social assistance programs	3.0	3.0	3.0	3.0	3.0	3.0	3.0	3.0	3.0	3.0
Family subsidy programs	4.0	4.0	4.0	4.0	4.0	4.0	4.0	4.0	4.0	4.0
Complementary benefits										
Vacations	6.7	6.7	6.7	6.7	0.0	6.7	5.1	6.7	5.8	6.7
Bonus	8.9	8.9	8.9	0.0	0.0	8.9	6.7	8.8	7.7	8.8
Total paid by firm	47.1	56.2	52.0	33.8	9.0	52.0	37.9	52.6	41.8	52.5
Total paid by employee	4.5	7.4	7.4	8.4	0.0	7.4	3.4	7.4	3.9	7.4
Addendum: Composition of contracts in 1994										
Manufacturing sector	NA	0.207	0.536	0.015	NA	0.243				
Commerce	NA	0.145	0.71	0.006	NA	0.139				

Source: Before reform figures come from Ocampo (1987). Other according with current legislation. Addendum items come from a survey conducted by Fedesarrollo in August, 1994.
a. Weighting by the composition of contracts in 1994, see addendum.

Total security contributions were increased from 13.5 percent to between 25.5 percent and 26.5 percent (depending on salary) for workers
with permanent contracts and from 0 percent to 25.5 percent for workers
with temporary contracts. Social security contributions for pensions
(which went from 6.5 percent to between 13.5 and 14 percent) were more
closely linked to benefits, especially for workers in the individual capitalization system (approximately 28 percent of the urban labor force or
45 percent of the salaried urban labor force by mid-1995). For workers
staying in the public pay-as-you-go system, this link is not as close and
therefore for all practical purposes these contributions can still be considered taxes. Health-related social security contributions (which rose
from 7 percent to 12 percent), which before constituted a kind of last-
resort individual health insurance (for poor workers and for high-cost
health care for higher-income workers), turned into a more strict prepayment, also covering families and providing a choice between services.
However, the rate implies a subsidy component across income groups,
which also introduces an element of taxation.

Additional payroll taxes equal 9 percent of wages and apply to all
types of labor contracts. Included here are two percentage points for the
National Apprenticeship Service, SENA, three points for the Colombian
Family Welfare Institute, ICBF, and four points for the family compensation funds that carry out a system of family subsidies and offer (usually
at subsidized rates) health, leisure, and merchandising services to their
affiliates and families. The labor and social security reforms did not
reduce any of these surcharges, despite that, at least partly, contributions
for the family compensation funds were aimed at covering health-related
family expenses that are covered in the new health social security system.
Almost all of these nine payroll surcharge points can be considered taxes,
since they are not closely related to individual benefits workers receive
from these entities.

In short, the total amount of labor costs additional to wages paid by
firms (not including unemployment compensation) rose from 37.9 percent
to 52.6 percent in the manufacturing sector and from 41.8 to 52.5 percent
in the retail sector. Uncertainty of these costs was reduced notably, owing
to the change in the severance payments regime. The taxation character of
these surcharges was also reduced, though only for pension contributions.

The effects that these nonwage labor cost increases may have had on
total labor costs in the manufacturing sector are discussed next. Although
total labor costs have gone up, the hypothesis that this rise has occurred

because of these increases can not be supported econometrically, which suggests that workers have assumed the extra costs.

Total Labor Costs in the Manufacturing Sector

Monthly statistics for the manufacturing sector show that, after a continuous upward trend initiated in 1991, labor costs per worker were 11.3 percent higher on average in 1995 than in 1990 and that the increase was larger in the case of administrative (24.3 percent) than factory workers (5 percent, see figure 9-1). Given the interplay of many factors, including other important structural reforms implemented in the early 1990s, these increases could not be solely attributed to the labor reform. We have attempted to establish the influence of time trends, the increased social security contributions, the policy of minimum wage, and the increased capital intensity in manufacturing production induced by the reduction in the user cost of capital because of the decline in interest rates, the reduction of tariffs and the appreciation of the exchange rate, especially between 1992 and 1994.[11] Appendix table 9A-1 presents regressions for the change in real labor costs per worker using a constant and changes in the explanatory variables. This procedure has been chosen in consideration of the characteristics of the time series. To avoid simultaneity problems between the dependent variable and the variable measuring capital intensity, we have used two-stage least squares with the list of instruments that appears in table 9A-1.

The results show that labor costs have been influenced by an upward trend equivalent to 2.6 percent a year in the case of administrative workers and 1.6 percent a year in the case of factory workers, both statistically significant (captured in the constant term, C). The results also show that minimum wage changes D (WMIN) have been the most important factor determining labor cost changes in the short run since 1980. The elasticity in the case of factory workers is close to 0.5 and that for administrative workers is 0.26, in both cases with high statistical significance. The increases of social security contributions (DCONTR) do not seem to have affected total labor costs per worker, which implies that the burden of the additional contributions has been assumed by the workers. This result is not totally surprising given the overriding influence of the minimum

---

11. For a detailed calculation of the user cost of capital in the manufacturing sector see Cárdenas and Gutiérrez (1996).

Figure 9-1. *Labor Costs, Manufacturing Sector*

1990 = 100

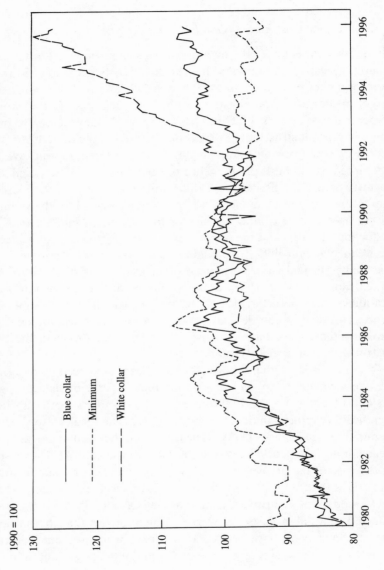

Source: Departamento Administrativo Nacional de Estadística (DANE), monthly surveys of the manufacturing sector. Series is de-seasonalized.

wage in determining wages, especially those of factory workers, and considering that the social security reform reinforced the link between contributions and personal benefits and implicitly reduced the tax component of the contributions. The changes in capital intensity (DLKPROD) are likely to have affected factory wages during the 1990s in a manner consistent with the results obtained by Mauricio Cárdenas and Catalina Gutiérrez, which are reported in the next section.[12] The use of more capital-intensive techniques possibly contributed to the relative stagnation of these wages owing to the substitutability between capital and unskilled labor. For administrative workers, the relation between capital intensity and labor costs appears to be weak and not statistically significant.

Therefore, although total labor costs in the manufacturing sector have increased in the 1990s, and especially so for administrative workers, our econometric results do not give support to the hypothesis that the increase was mainly because of the labor and social security reforms. This does not imply, as will be discussed below, that payroll tax reductions can not exert a beneficial effect on formal labor demand and on the economy as a whole. The upward trend of labor costs may be much more related to long-term trends that are left unspecified in these exercises. Higher capital intensity and the policy of marginal reductions of the real minimum wage may have helped to contain this trend, especially for factory workers. In the case of the administrative workers, where that trend is stronger, the influence of these two factors has been of less importance.

Effects on Labor Demand

The employment growth rate for the economy fell from an annual 4.9 percent between 1982 and 1991 to 2.6 percent afterward. Despite this deceleration, the urban unemployment rate dropped from 11 percent in 1990 to a historic low of 7.6 percent in the seven largest cities in September 1994—which roughly corresponds to a previous estimate of the structural unemployment rate[13]—and then increased again to 11.7 percent in mid-1996 (figure 9-2). The lower employment growth rate has come mainly from industry, commerce, and the so-called other services (personal and social, see table 9-3), but this occurrence has not been fully reflected in

12. Cárdenas and Gutiérrez (1996).
13. Misión (1986).

Figure 9-2. *Urban Unemployment and Labor Participation*

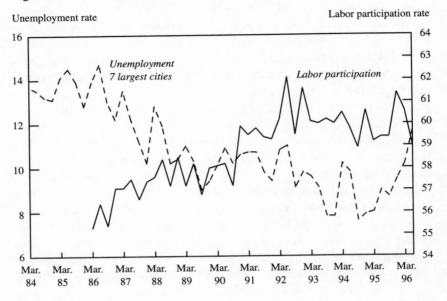

Source: DANE.

Table 9-3. *Average Annual Employment Growth*

	June 1982–December 91		December 1991–June 1995	
	Growth	Contribution	Growth	Contribution
Agriculture	6.74	0.08	−4.53	−0.05
Mining	7.01	0.03	−6.03	−0.02
Manufacturing	4.59	1.12	0.77	0.18
Electricity, gas, and water	4.97	0.03	−1.33	−0.01
Construction	2.25	0.14	11.22	0.7
Commerce	5.72	1.45	2.34	0.62
Transportation and communication	4.87	0.31	4.08	0.27
Financial services	4.64	0.32	7.89	0.58
Other services	5.11	1.44	1.3	0.36
Unspecified/uniformed	23.4	0.02	−6.12	−0.01
Total	4.95	4.95	2.61	2.61

Source: Cárdenas and Gutiérrez (1996). Based on DANE's household surveys.

an increase in the unemployment rates since participation rates have leveled off.

In view of the decline in employment growth, especially in the manufacturing sector, fears have arisen that the package of structural reforms, including the labor reform, may have caused a structural reduction of labor demand. This issue has been recently assessed by Cárdenas and Gutiérrez, who have estimated a generalized Leontieff cost function for the manufacturing sector with monthly data between 1980:01 and 1996:01, considering three factors of production: capital, factory workers, and administrative workers.[14] Their results indicate that the two types of labor are substitutes, and factory labor and capital are also substitutes, while capital and administrative labor are complements. They have found that factory labor and capital show an increasing degree of substitutability, which is consistent with our results reported in the previous section. They have also tested the hypothesis of structural change for the period after the reforms, for which they have found no support, thus showing that there has been no change in the way factor prices affect factor demands. Having also rejected the hypotheses of factor-augmenting technological progress and of economies of scale, they conclude that "changes in factor intensities have been the result of changes in factor prices alone." As discussed above, while real wages have increased, the reduction in interest rates and tariffs and the appreciation of the exchange rate have reduced the user cost of capital in the 1990s.

Composition of the Labor Force

Given the high nonwage expenses required by law, and the rigidities imposed on nontypical hiring practices, it is not surprising that informal employment has traditionally been a large component of total employment in Colombia. Before the reform, informal employment represented 57.1 percent of total urban employment, including the self-employed (22 percent), domestic service (5.6 percent), unpaid workers (2.6 percent) and salaried and microenterprise owners (21.1 percent and 5.6 percent, respectively) where enforcement of labor legislation is either low or nonexistent.[15] An alternative measure of informality is the lack of affiliation to the social security system. It is estimated that in 1988, 52.7 percent of all workers were not affiliated (table 9-4).

14. Cárdenas and Gutiérrez (1996, p. 13).
15. López (1989).

Table 9-4. *Composition of the Work Force, by Occupation*
Percent

| | Formal | | | | | Informal | | | | | |
| | Wage earners | | Managers of large firms | Professionals and technicians | Total | Microenterprises | | Self-employed | Household servants | Unpaid family workers | Total | Informality by social security |
Years	Large firms	Government				Wage earners	Managers					
1984	31.16	11.25	0.77	1.73	44.91	18.64	4.31	23.11	5.99	3.03	55.08	52
1986	31.13	10.91	0.76	1.61	44.41	20.45	4.71	21.34	6.33	2.75	55.59	53.8
1988	30.04	10.34	0.91	1.75	43.04	21.05	5.63	22.05	5.61	2.62	56.96	52.7
1992	32.94	9.23	0.99	1.93	45.09	20.46	6.18	20.96	5.16	2.16	54.92	51
1994	34.71	8.56	0.96	2.03	46.26	19.97	6.13	22.08	4.35	1.22	53.74	48.6

Source: Household surveys by DANE. Large firms are those with more than 10 workers; microenterprises, those with up to 10 workers.

These indicators of informality have been reduced after the reform. Informal employment was reduced three points between 1988 and 1994, and the lack of affiliation to social security fell four points in the same period. The reduction in informality was due only to a lesser extent to employment recomposition across sectors. In fact, with the sectoral composition of employment in 1988, the rate of informality would have dropped from 57.1 percent to 54 percent. The change in the sectoral composition would only account for an additional reduction of 0.2 points to 53.8 percent of informality in 1994. The greatest impact on the reduction of informality has come from commerce, where it dropped from 77.7 percent to 72.6 percent (representing 27.1 percent of employment in 1988 and 26.1 percent in 1994).

It has been argued that the recomposition of employment toward formal occupations could partly be attributed to the labor reform, as it made hiring conditions more flexible and labor costs more certain.[16] However, the decline of the real minimum wage could also be an important explanatory factor. In support of this assertion, table 9-5 presents some simulation results of a reduction of 10 percent in the nominal minimum wage, obtained with a computable general equilibrium model that allows for the presence of informality and unemployment as a result of wage rigidities and labor taxation.[17] The model is disaggregated into twenty-one sectors of production, which combine different types of inputs, unskilled labor, and skilled labor in varying proportions according to their relative prices and the technological possibilities of each sector. Unskilled labor used in each sector is a composite of formal and informal labor, where the proportions of use of each depend on their relative costs for the firms within certain limits of substitutability. The existence of a minimum wage and payroll taxes for formally employed unskilled workers contribute to unemployment and an informal segment of unskilled workers. Payroll taxes are also paid by all skilled workers. Unskilled workers may migrate (at certain cost) between the informal and the formal segments of the labor markets depending on the relative wages and the probability of unemployment. Prices in the urban sectors are determined by costs (plus a markup), and the quantities produced depend on domestic and net external demands, with imports being imperfect substitutes for domestic goods. The government receives payroll taxes and

16. Hommes, Montenegro, and Roda (1994).
17. A complete description of the model can be found in World Bank (1994, annex 2).

Table 9-5. *Macroeconomic Income and Employment Effects of a*
10 Percent Reduction in the Nominal Minimum Wage

Item	Percent change
Macroeconomic variables	
GDP	0.8
CPI	−3.6
Real exchange rate	3.5
Fiscal balance (change as percent of GDP)	−0.1
Real gross income	
Urban labor	
Unskilled formal (real wage per capita)	−6.1
Unskilled informal (real wage per capita)	−2.3
Skilled	−3.5
Rural labor, capitalists (by region)	2.9
Agriculture	2.1
Industry	1.6
Commerce	3.1
Urban income groups	
Lowest quintile	−0.5
Highest quintile	−0.3
Urban employment	
Unskilled formal	4.1
Unskilled informal	−1.1
Unemployment (change as percent of the working force)	−1.6

Source: Lora and Herrera (1993) using a computable general equilibrium model.

other taxes. Government expenditures and fixed private investment are given in real terms. Total savings must accommodate to close the model, and that is achieved through endogenous changes in private and public savings and a residual current account with the rest of the world.

The reduction of the nominal minimum wage by 10 percent results in a fall of 6 percent in the real wages received by the unskilled workers in the formal sector. Since the real minimum wage fell in reality 5.3 percent between 1988 and 1994, this simulation is a good indication of the magnitudes of the changes produced. In the labor market, that reduction in the minimum wage increases by 4.1 percent the number of unskilled workers in the formal sector, while reducing by 1.1 percent the number of informal workers and by 1.6 points the unemployment rate. Lower wages in the formal sectors translate into lower earnings for the informal workers owing to the high substitutability in production between the two. Those who benefit include all the capitalist groups and the rural workers. Interestingly, the GDP expands 0.8 percent as domestic demands have

Figure 9-3. *Evolution of Temporary Employment (Four Cities, 1977–94)*

Percent of total employment

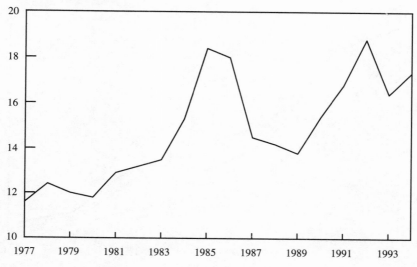

little change, but net exports increase as a result of the reduction in labor costs.

While informality has gone down since the labor reform, the importance of temporary labor has increased. Temporary labor averaged 17.3 percent of total employment in the period 1991–94, while it averaged 14.5 percent in the period 1987–90. However, this increase can not be directly attributed to the labor reform. Although temporary contracts were eased, they were made subject to the same nonwage costs of other contracts, and greater hiring and firing flexibility was granted to permanent contracts. Hence, it is not clear that the labor reform should have encouraged the demand for temporary labor. The recent increase seems to correspond to a long-term trend observed not only in Colombia (figure 9-3), but elsewhere in the world, in response both to a greater need for flexibility in the firms but also to the preferences of the workers. According to Stefano Farné and Andrés Nupia, a growing share of job seekers prefer temporary occupations, and a greater percentage of those in such occupations do not consider themselves underemployed.[18]

18. Farné and Nupia (1996).

Figure 9-4. *Job Survival Rates (Cumulative)*

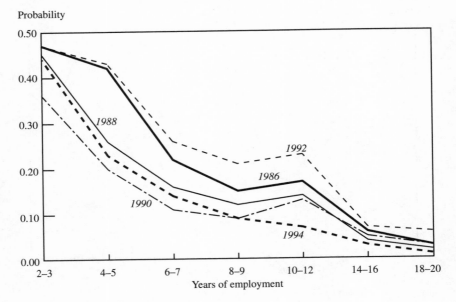

Source: Authors' calculations with DANE'S household surveys.

Labor Turnover

Some authors have pointed out that one of the main benefits of the reform has been an increase in job stability.[19] This assertion is based on the cursory observation that the percentage of workers with fewer than one or two years of employment was reduced since 1990. It is more adequate to analyze the effect of the reform on job security with more detailed information on labor survival rates obtained from the household surveys conducted by DANE (Colombia's Statistics Office). This information confirms the fact that labor turnover is quite high in Colombia: only about 40 percent of all workers remain in the same firm for two years; the probability of keeping the same job for four years is barely 15 percent and for nine years is less than 5 percent (figure 9-4). As a result, labor tenure expectancy in the same firm is quite low, although this varies substantially over time: between 2.7 and 4.4 years according to calculations based on data for 1986 and 1994 (figure 9-5). Labor survival rates

19. López (1993); Hommes, Montenegro, and Roda (1994).

Figure 9-5. *Job Tenure Expectancy and Employment Growth in Urban Areas*

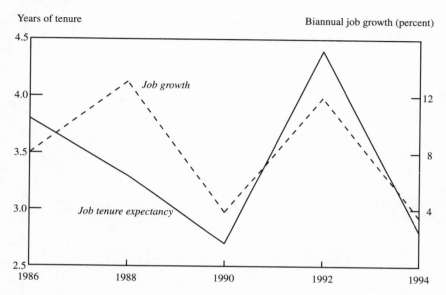

Years of tenure

Biannual job growth (percent)

Source: Authors' calculations with DANE's household surveys.

and labor expectancy rates in the same firm are quite sensitive to the economy's job creation rate, as suggested by figure 9-5, and as can be confirmed more rigorously by the regressions in Appendix table 9A-2. If this effect is isolated, the econometrics calculations show that the survival rates tend to increase with the years of employment at the firm, and these are significantly higher for the group with 8 to 10 years of employment (variable D8).[20] If the manufacturing sector is taken as the reference group, survival rates are found to be significantly greater in the public services sector (ELE) and to a lesser extent in the communal services sector (SOC), which includes the government. Survival rates are lower in the construction sector and in commerce, although not in a statistically significant way.

It cannot be argued that labor reform has altered any of these patterns in any significant way. If anything, the reform must have reduced survival rates. The total effect is not significant (see variable D90 of the first regression in Appendix table 9A-2), but the effect on the group with 8

20. Owing to the quality of the data, 10 was the highest number for years of employment in the firm used in the regression.

Figure 9-6. *Rates of Unionization*

Percent of urban employment

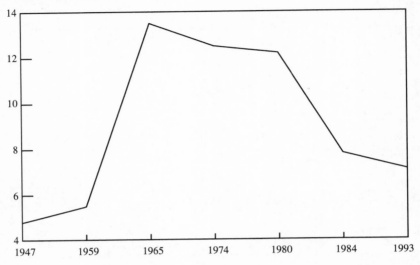

Source: Until 1984, Londoño, Grisales, and Delgado (1987), thereafter author's calculations based on data from the Ministry of Labor and DANE.

to 10 years of employment is clearly negative (D8D90 in the second regression), as well as in the public service group (ELE90), though the latter could be the result of public sector reforms more than labor reform. In short, there is no proof that labor reform has improved job stability.

Unionization and Labor Conflicts

In an effort to strengthen unionization, labor reform removed most legal restrictions to the creation, recognition, and functioning of unions. Nonetheless, the declining trend of unionization remained: in 1993, only 7 percent of the working force was unionized (figure 9-6). The labor reform introduced some minor changes to facilitate and expedite labor negotiations. The declining trend in the number of negotiations, which started in the mid-1970s, seems to have stopped after the reform, and the number of negotiations have recently varied between 600 and 800 per year (figure 9-7). Given the high costs imposed on both workers and firms, strikes are usually a last resort in the process of negotiation. Less than 5 percent of unions go on strike every year, and around two-thirds

Figure 9-7. *Labor Negotiations (Absolute Figure)*

Source: Ministry of Labor's records on labor negotiations.

of the strikes take place in the public services and the public education sector. Between 10 percent and 20 percent of labor negotiations end up in a strike, and this proportion does not seem to have changed significantly after the reform (figure 9-8).[21]

Looking Ahead

According to a survey performed among manufacturing and commerce firms in 1994, the main benefits of the labor reform were the greater certainty of labor costs and the changes introduced to the system of severance payments, whereas the so-called double retroactivity was eliminated (table 9-6). Other important benefits, according to the firms, were greater job stability and improved flexibility of contracts (the former is not confirmed by the statistics presented in this chapter).

Although the labor reform was a step in the right direction, the Colombian labor regime still has important deficiencies. According to the

21. Although this indicator seems to have gone up from percentages below 10 percent in the 1970s, it is probably overestimated by the inclusion of public illegal strikes, which are not preceded by negotiations.

Figure 9-8. *Strikes as a Percent of Labor Negotiations*

Percent

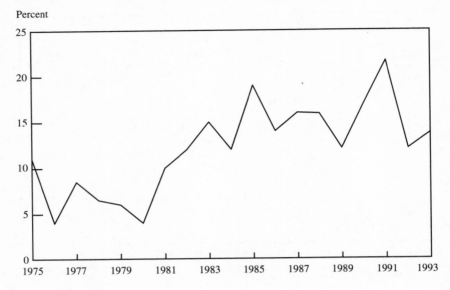

Source: Ministry of Labor and authors' calculations.

same survey, the contributions to the social security system and the dismissal costs are two of the main obstacles to the creation of employment (table 9-7). An international comparison shows why this is so. Among more than twenty countries in Latin America and the Caribbean, Colombia has the third highest level of social security contributions, the highest level of costs of dismissal for workers with 10 years of employment, and the seventh highest for workers with one year of employment. Furthermore, Colombia is the only case where dismissal costs for workers with 10 or more years in the firm have been increased since 1990 (as a com-

Table 9-6. *Benefits of the Labor Reform (Law 50/90)*

Percent of firms surveyed

Item	Industry	Commerce
Greater certainty of labor costs	32.9	34.2
Elimination of double retroactivity	37.2	31.8
Greater labor stability	13.4	12.6
Improved contract flexibility	11.6	8.8
Other	4.8	12.5
Total	100	100

Source: Encuesta de Opinion Empresarial, Fedesarrollo. Survey performed in July 1994 among 294 firms of the industrial sector and 138 firms of the commerce sector.

Table 9-7. *Main Remaining Obstacles to Labor Demand*

Percent of firms surveyed

Item	Manufacturing	Commerce
Contributions to social security	29.4	27.9
Dismissal costs	17.3	15.1
Fringe benefits due to labor negotiations	14.1	5.5
Other social benefits	13.3	10
All other reasons	25.9	41.5
Total	100	100

Source: Encuesta de Opinion Empresarial, Fedesarrollo. Survey performed in July 1994 among 294 firms for the industrial sector and 138 firms for the commerce sector.

pensation for the dismantling of security guarantees). The other few countries that have made labor reforms of importance in the 1990s (Argentina, Colombia, Guatemala, Panama, and Peru) either reduced or subjected these costs to caps.[22]

The fact that social security contributions were increased as a result of the recent reforms is especially worrisome, although in this respect the Colombian experience is not unique (contributions were also increased in Peru by the pension reform of 1993 and will go up in Mexico since 1997, though in this case the increase will be covered by the government).[23] The main reason for concern is that those contributions are additional to other payroll taxes that were originally established in order to finance different forms of social security, and they have not been reduced. As is often argued in public debates in Colombia, high nonwage labor costs reduce competitiveness of the labor intensive sectors, encourage informality, and increase unemployment. For these reasons, business union representatives and a number of analysts have clamored for a reduction in, if not a total dismantling of, the payroll taxes that finance SENA, ICBF, and the family compensation funds, which amount to 9 percent of the wage bill.

The effects of such decisions can be briefly discussed with the help of the computable general equilibrium model described in a previous section. Being a short-run, demand-driven model, tax reductions produce an expansionary effect on production and income. GDP would increase 2.18 percent if the 9 percent payroll taxes were eliminated (see table 9-8, column 1). Since unskilled labor is in excess supply at the current nominal

22. IDB (1996).
23. See IDB (1996).

Table 9-8. *Macroeconomic Income and Employment Effects of*
Elimination of Payroll Taxes

Percent changes

Item	No fiscal adjustment (1)	Value-added tax adjustment (2)	Personal tax adjustment (3)
Macroeconomic variables			
GDP	2.18	0.29	0.52
Consumption	3.56	−0.72	−0.45
Investment	0.38	0.54	0.93
Exports	0.40	1.37	1.55
Imports	1.85	−3.35	−3.00
Consumer Price Index	−0.69	−1.59	−3.74
Real exchange rate	0.42	1.47	3.69
Fiscal balance (changes as percent of GDP)	−0.86	0.37	0.32
Real incomes			
Urban workers			
Unskilled formal (real wage per capita)	0.39	1.34	3.35
Unskilled informal (real wage per capita)	0.30	−5.43	−2.91
Skilled	5.54	2.63	5.30
Rural workers, capitalists (by region)	8.62	0.29	4.26
Urban	1.37	−1.57	0.07
Rural	6.72	0.61	3.99
Urban income groups			
Lowest quintile	2.33	−1.33	1.11
Highest quintile	1.79	−0.53	−2.74
Urban employment			
Unskilled formal	10.40	2.50	3.50
Unskilled informal	−3.40	−0.63	−1.07
Unemployment (change as percent of working force)	−1.34	−0.29	−0.49

Source: Authors' calculations with the model described in World Bank (1994, annex 2).

minimum wage, the reduction of labor costs would increase formal employment of this type of labor by 10.4 percent, reducing both informality and unemployment, while leaving real wages of the unskilled virtually unchanged. Meanwhile, real wages of the skilled workers would increase by 5.54 percent as a result of larger demand for this full employed factor.

However, some of these effects are not just the result of fiscal expansion. Consider a case in which payroll tax reductions are compensated by a matching increase of value-added taxes (table 9-8, column 2). GDP would still increase 0.29 percent, and this would occur because of improved international competitiveness (exports would increase 1.37 percent and imports would fall 3.35 percent). Employment of unskilled workers in formal activities would increase 2.5 percent, largely at the expense of unemployment, and their real wages would increase 1.3 percent, owing to a reduction in the Consumer Price Index. Interestingly, however, informal real wages would decline 5.4 percent because of the reduction of formal labor costs and the high substitutability between formal and informal unskilled labor (an effect that was not apparent in the previous simulation owing to the stronger expansion of total labor demand). Therefore, although the reduction of payroll taxes would boost formal employment and would reduce unemployment, that would not necessarily benefit those in the informal sector. For these reasons, income distribution in the urban areas might also deteriorate slightly.[24]

A different fiscal compensation may alter some of these distributional effects, while leaving the direction of other variables unchanged (table 9-8, column 3). If the reduction of payroll taxes is compensated by higher personal income taxes, which are paid only by the top urban quintile, formal employment and incomes would increase further, informal earnings would fall less, and real incomes in the rural areas and in the rest of the urban quintiles would increase.

24. However, income distribution between the urban and the rural areas would improve as the value-added tax in Colombia is mainly levied on industrial goods. For a detailed analysis of the incidence of taxes in Colombia see Lora and Herrera (1994).

References

Cárdenas, Mauricio, and Catalina Gutiérrez. 1996. "Efficiency and Equity Effects of Structural Reform: The Case of Colombia." Mimeo. Fedesarrollo, Bogotá (July).

Farné, Stefano, and Oskar Andrés Nupia. 1996. "Aspectos Laborales y Sociales del Empleo Temporal en Colombia." Mimeo. Universidad Externado de Colombia, Facultad de Economía. (May).

Hommes, Rudolf, Armando Montenegro, and Pablo Roda. 1994. *Una Apertura Hacia el Futuro*. Ministerio de Hacienda y Crédito Público, Departamento Nacional de Planeación and Fondo Nacional de Desarrollo Económico. Bogotá.

Inter-American Development Bank (IDB). 1996. *Economic and Social Progress in Latin America*. Washington.

Kertzman, Fanny. 1987. "Obstáculos a la Creación de Empleo: El Punto de Vista de los Empresarios." In *El Problema Laboral Colombiano*, vol. 2, edited by J. A. Ocampo and M. Ramirez, 239–48. Bogotá: Contraloría General de la

Table 9A-1. *Determinants of Real Labor Costs in the Manufacturing Sector*

Variable[a]	Factory workers		Administrative workers	
	Coefficient	T-statistic	Coefficient	T-statistic
C	0.001354	1.94	0.00221	3.60
D(CONTR)	−0.14853	−0.86	−0.022115	−0.14
D(WMIN)	0.498961	5.72	0.258778	3.23
D(KPROD)	0.004491	0.12	−0.035851	−1.38
D(KPROD90)	−0.006792	−2.42	0.001232	0.50
AR(1)	−0.300818	−3.99	−0.478973	−7.14
Adjusted R^2	0.19122	. . .	0.20282	. . .
Durbin-Watson statistic	2.090156	. . .	1.988979	. . .
F-statistic	9.677351	. . .	10.91625	. . .
Addendum: Variable list				
D(.)	Change			
W	Real labor cost per worker (in logs, seasonally adjusted)			
CONTR	Contribution to social security (percent of wages)			
WMIN	Real minimum wage (in logs, seasonally adjusted)			
KPROD	Capital-output ratio (in logs, seasonally adjusted)			
KPROD90	Capital-output ratio since 1991:01, 0 otherwise (in logs, seasonally adjusted)			

Note: Regressions are two-stage least squares with the following instrumental variables: D(CONTR), D(WMIN), industrial production (in logs, seasonally adjusted, lagged one and two periods), and employment of administrative or factory workers for the first and the second regressions, respectively (in logs, seasonally adjusted, lagged one and two periods).

a. Dependent variable is D(W); number of observations, 186;1980:08–1996:02.

República, Departamento Nacional de Planeación and Servicio Nacional de Aprendizaje.

Londoño, Rocío, Orlando Grisales, and Alvaro Delgado. 1987. "Sindicalismo y Empleo en Colombia." In *El Problema Laboral Colombiano*, vol. 2, edited by J. A. Ocampo and M. Ramirez, 158–87. Bogotá: Contraloría General de la República. Departamento Nacional de Planeación and Servicio Nacional de Aprendizaje.

López, Hugo. 1993. "Contexto Macroeconómico, Mercado Laboral Urbano y Retos para una Política de Empleo." Mimeo. Fundación Friedrich Ebert de Colombia, Medellín.

Lora, Eduardo, and Loredana Helmsdorff. 1995. *El Futuro de la Reforma Pensional*. Bogotá: Fedesarrollo Asofondos.

Lora, Eduardo, and Ana María Herrera. 1993. "Macroeconomía del Salario Mínimo." In *Debates de Coyuntura Económica*, vol. 30, pp. 21–35. Bogotá: Fedesarrollo-Fescol.

———. 1994. "Tax Incidence in Colombia. A General Equilibrium Analysis." Fedesarrollo, Bogotá.

Misión de Empleo. 1986. "El Problema Laboral Colombiano: Diagnóstico, Perspectivas y Políticas," special issue of *Economía Colombiana*. Serie Documentos no. 10, August–September.

Table 9A-2. *Determinants of Labor Survival Rates*

Variable[a]	Model 1		Model 2		Model 3	
	Coefficient	*T-statistic*	*Coefficient*	*T-statistic*	*Coefficient*	*T-statistic*
C	0.4860287	12.09	0.4846338	11.23	0.4635083	10.08
RN	0.7984549	5.94	0.7985527	6.02	0.7145665	5.24
D4	0.0213933	0.63	-0.0042859	-0.10	0.0217310	0.63
D6	0.0359838	1.05	0.0269419	0.62	0.0363215	1.09
D8	0.2943055	8.62	0.3345821	7.69	0.2946433	8.86
D90	-0.0261772	-1.06	...	...	...	...
ELE	0.2508157	5.54	0.2508182	5.61	0.3548892	6.25
CNS	-0.0715283	-1.58	-0.0715304	-1.60	-0.0286480	-0.50
COM	-0.0323771	-0.71	-0.0323811	-0.72	-0.0104788	-0.18
TRA	0.0059629	0.13	0.0059587	0.13	0.1470260	0.26
FIN	0.0198501	0.48	0.0198472	0.44	0.0214266	0.38
SOC	0.0748376	1.65	0.0748355	1.68	0.0985728	1.73
D2D90	...	...	-0.0227051	-0.47	...	...
D4D90	...	...	0.0414919	0.85	...	...
D6D90	...	...	-0.0001015	-0.00	...	...
D8D90	...	...	-0.1223976	-2.54	...	...
IND90	...	...	...	...	0.0431877	0.68
ELE90	...	...	...	...	-0.2224057	-3.44
CNS90	...	...	...	...	-0.0594904	-0.92
COM90	...	...	...	...	-0.0031115	-0.05
TRA90	...	...	...	...	0.0302452	0.48
FIN90	...	...	...	...	0.0455599	0.71
SOC90	...	...	...	...	-0.0117986	-0.19
Adjusted R^2	...	0.55560	...	0.56650	...	0.57820
Durbin-Watson statistic	...	1.82756	...	1.77050	...	1.97124
F-Statistic	...	16.79799	...	13.97463	...	12.20831

Table 9A-2. (continued)

Addendum: Variable list

TS   Survival rate by tenure group and for each sector, calculated as the ratio between the number of workers in tenure group i in the year t and the number of workers in tenure group i-2 in the year t-2.

RN   Job creation rate by sector, calculated as the ratio between the number of jobs in period t and the number of jobs in t-2 minus 1.

Di   Dummy for the tenure groups. The tenure groups are as follows: from two to four, four to six, six to eight, and eight to ten years of tenure in the same firm.

D90   Dummy for the 1992 and 1994 observations

DiD90   Dummy for both Di and D90.

IND   Dummy for the manufacturing sector

ELE   Dummy for the utility sector

CNS   Dummy for the construction sector

COM   Dummy for retail (commerce) sector

TRA   Dummy for the transportation sector

FIN   Dummy for the financial sector

SOC   Dummy for the community services (including public administration). The suffix 90 indicates the intersection of these dummies and D90.

Note: The regressions evaluate changes in survival rates that occurred after 1990 by sector and years of employment in the firm, adjusted by the job creation rate in each sector. Data are obtained from the informal sector sections of the urban household surveys carried out every two years by DANE between 1984 and 1994.
a. Dependent variable is TS; number of observations, 140; 1984–94. The five-year panel data set starts in 1986, when the first survival rates were reported. It consists of four permanence groups and seven sectors for a total of 140 observations.

Ocampo, José Antonio. 1987. "El Régimen Prestacional del Sector Privado." In *El Problema Laboral Colombiano,* vol. 2, edited by J. A. Ocampo and M. Ramirez, 213–30. Bogotá: Contraloría General de la República, Departamento Nacional de Planeación and Servicio Nacional de Aprendizaje.

Posada de la Peña, Francisco. 1995. *Libertad para Trabajar.* Tercer Mundo Editores.

Reyes, Alvaro. 1991. "Algunos Lineamientos para el Análisis de la Reforma Laboral." Ministerio de Trabajo, ONU, OIT, Bogotá.

World Bank. 1994. *Poverty in Colombia.* Washington.

CHAPTER TEN

Mexico: The Evolution and Reform of the Labor Market

Enrique Rafael Dávila Capalleja

AS IS THE CASE in many developing countries (especially in Latin America), Mexico demonstrates a contrast between ambitious labor and social security laws and low levels of compliance with these laws. This contrast arises because many workers are located in nonsalaried jobs and because some firms evade compliance.

The presence of a large informal (or traditional or unprotected) sector[1] in developing countries (and Mexico in particular) is a phenomenon with numerous causes. Different authors have emphasized the following factors: the influence of economic development policies (and their failures);[2] the close ties between production and consumption decisions in family microenterprises;[3] noncompliance with excessive legal and regulatory

This chapter was translated by Gary Isaac Gordon, the Brookings Institution.

1. The terms and concepts utilized to categorize the labor market vary widely, as do their corresponding measurements. For a review centered on the case of Mexico, see Jusidman (1993).

2. See Márquez and Ros (1990) for the Mexican case.

3. Giner de los Ríos (1983, 1984). This is the only convincing reformulation, in my opinion, of the PREALC (1976, 1978) definition of the informal sector as the sum of activities characterized by a "different logic of production" focused on guaranteeing the subsistence of the family group rather than on capitalist accumulation. In the presentation of these documents at the ITAM-COLMEX seminar, some participants commented that the lack of efficient capital and labor markets is what impedes the separation of production

measures as a strategy on the part of microenterprises to keep costs low and thereby continue operating;[4] and the operating methods of enterprises in the formal (or modern or protected) sector which reduce costs by subcontracting to informal microenterprises.[5] At the same time, the formal sector maintains a stable nucleus of workers (who accumulate enterprise-specific human capital) by offering salaries higher than those found in the market.[6] In spite of their diversity, the majority of these views coincide in accepting, as a stylized fact, that individuals systematically prefer jobs in the formal sector,[7] at least as long as idiosyncratic or cultural factors, such as the personal desire to be one's own boss and make one's own work schedule, do not intervene.[8]

The claim that formal jobs are economically superior diverts attention from the gap that frequently exists between the cost incurred by the employer in order to comply with labor and social security legislation, and the benefit which the worker derives from this legislation.[9] This cost-benefit gap can constitute an important obstacle to formal sector employment growth[10] and to the adequate functioning of social security institutions (for example, by giving incentives to underdeclaration of income and adverse selection in affiliation). The economic analysis of this phenomenon takes on great importance in the case of Mexico, because of the magnitude of the distortions brought about by the laws currently on the books, and because one of the principal goals of the

---

and consumption decisions. Adding in the aversion to risk of poor individuals, this lack of efficient markets also provides a rational justification for "traditional" behaviors, such as the attachment demonstrated by many *campesinos* to diversified production for self-consumption (instead of specialization in commercial production, which offers greater earning potential).

4. Ozorio de Almeida and Graham, in their work on Argentina (1993) and Mexico (1994, with Alves), support this version, popularized by de Soto (1986).

5. Tockman (1978); for the case of Mexico see Beneria (1989).

6. See Akerlof and Yellen (1986), although their frame of reference is the labor market in developed countries.

7. This aspect has been perceptively emphasized by Maloney (1996).

8. The report of the results from the *Encuesta de Subempleados* (Survey of Underemployed) by Banamex (1983), conducted in Mexico City (during the second semester of 1982) emphasized the importance of this factor.

9. Concern over the distorting effects of this gap is the common thread in the works compiled by Márquez (1992).

10. This thesis is sustained, for Mexico, by Dávila, Levy, y López Calva (1996), who also emphasize distortions in nontradable sectors (energy, cargo transport, and telecommunications principally) and the high costs of transactions associated with overregulation in the economy in general.

recent social security reform (which will go into effect in 1997) was to reduce the cost-benefit gap.[11]

This chapter first presents an overview of the main characteristics of the Mexican labor market, then includes an analysis of the main regulations currently in effect concerning labor and social security: minimum wages, severance rules, medical services, and old age pensions. Finally, conclusions and recommendations are presented.

Overview of the Labor Market in Mexico

This section describes the current labor market conditions in Mexico, as well as of the recent evolution of the urban labor market. This overview is based on 1995 data from the *Encuesta Nacional de Empleo* (ENE), the national employment survey, and several years from the *Encuesta Nacional de Empleo Urbano* (ENEU), the national urban employment survey.

According to the 1995 national employment survey (ENE95), the total population of Mexico was 90.1 million inhabitants, divided in almost equal parts between men (49.1 percent) and women (50.9 percent). The population was also fairly well balanced between more urbanized areas (MUA, 100,000 or more inhabitants), with 44.5 percent, and less urbanized areas (LUA, less than 100,000 inhabitants) with 55.5 percent.[12] Of this total, the working age population (WAP), that is, the population 12 years old and older, represented 71.0 percent (63.9 million). This percentage has been increasing owing to the falling rate of fertility in recent decades.[13]

The economically active population (EAP) is defined as the sum of the employed population and the open unemployed population. The employed population consists of those who had worked at least one hour in

11. The analysis elaborated by the Mexican Institute of Social Security (IMSS, 1995) as a prelude to the social security reform underlines in some of its sections the disconnection between costs and benefits in various branches of social insurance.

12. Employment surveys in Mexico divide the population according to residence in MUA or LUA. This division contrasts with the more conventional one between urban and rural areas, which has a dividing line of 2,500 inhabitants.

13. The population 12 years old or older is considered, for statistical purposes, as the WAP in spite of the fact that, legally, the minimum working age is 14 years (with restrictions up until 16 years) and the Social Security Law, the *Ley de Seguro Social* (LSS), gives workers over 65 (who have worked for more than ten years) the right to a pension. The population of 16- to 54 year-olds was 53.3 million, or 59.1 percent of the total.

the week before they were surveyed. Those who did not work but were certain to return to a job or business, and those who were going to begin a new job in the next four weeks are also included. The open unemployed are those who did not work but were available to engage in some economic activity and actively sought to do so in the two months prior to the time of the survey. The EAP of the country numbered 35.6 million in 1995, according to the ENE.[14]

The average net participation rate (NPR) was 55.6 percent, although it was very different for men (78.2 percent) and women (34.5 percent). This rate evolves slowly over time, pulled by two opposite forces. On one side, economic and social development bring with them higher levels of participation by women in the labor force. On the other side, the same economic and social development give greater incentive to young people to stay in school, in order to better meet the requirements of a modern labor market. In the short term, an economic crisis also creates opposing pressures on the NPR. On one side, displaced workers can quickly become discouraged from seeking a job when faced with the low probability of finding an adequate one (above all in the case of spouses and children in families with medium or high income.) On the other, the fall in the real wage forces the poor to try to place formerly inactive family members in almost any available job in order to maintain family income at least at subsistence level.[15]

14. Nevertheless, the census data show substantially lower measurements of the EAP than those obtained by the employment surveys. The 1991 ENE estimates the EAP at 31.2 million, while the 1990 *Censo General de Población y Vivienda* (General Census of Population and Housing) indicates a figure of 24.1 million. This discrepancy is too large to be attributable to only one year of population and employment growth. At first glance it would appear reasonable to lean toward the data from the population census since they are based on an exhaustive head count and not on the expansion of a sample, as is the case with the data from the ENE. Nevertheless, upon checking the census questionnaire one finds that data on work status are gotten through a multiple choice question in which the interviewee is asked to indicate his or her primary activity during the previous week. Although the surveyors should explain that a response relating to economic activities (work and job hunting) is desired, it is reasonable to assume that many of those surveyed tended to report as their primary activity whichever activity they spent the most time doing in the previous week, whether economic or not. This factor, in addition to the greater depth of the interviews in the employment surveys (which contain a large number of recovery questions), makes the ENE preferable as a source of information.

15. Hernández (1989, 1996) and Fernández y Piñeiro (1994) present empirical evidence for Mexico showing periods of negative slope in individual and family labor supply, as is predicted by the Stone-Geary and Berzel-McDonald models.

The open unemployment rate (OUR) was 4.7 percent nationally, 6.3 percent for MUA, and 3.0 percent for LUA. The explanation for the apparent paradox of relatively low open unemployment rates in a country with both severe structural and short-run problems in its labor market lies in the definitions used (which, as was stated earlier, are based on international recommendations)[16] and in the very logic of the job hunting process at the individual level.

The existence of a large informal sector in Mexico permits job seekers to find employment easily, provided that they accept the going rate of remuneration. In Mexico workers lose nothing when they find a job, whereas in countries where unemployment insurance exists, its existence constitutes a strong marginal tax on employment.[17] Moreover, the low levels of income that predominate among Mexican workers lead to low levels of savings. This condition gives a disproportionate weight to the cost of a long job hunt, since workers do not have sufficient savings to afford one. In the case of heads of household and many spouses, the implicit costs of the job search force them to search only a short time for a "good" job. If they do not find one, they will then take the first available job, with the intention of continuing to look while they work.[18] In the case of children, other family members, and some spouses the explicit cost, although small, discourages searching (above all when little success in finding an adequate job is expected.) This means that job hunting is sporadic among these individuals, and they appear on panel surveys either as open unemployed or as inactive, depending on the moment at which the survey was taken.[19] Simply put, it can be said that *open un-employment is a luxury in which the large majority of Mexican workers cannot afford to indulge.*[20]

16. Measures of unemployment in Mexico are derived from household surveys, which are carefully taken using a solid sampling framework. This method is clearly superior to those used in some other countries, which are derived from administrative lists of unemployment insurance beneficiaries. The weakness of this practice lies in the possibility that workers, being rational, will try to combine the collection of unemployment benefits with an informal occupation that will provide them with additional income.

17. This effect can even distort the decision of spouses of unemployed workers to participate in the labor force, as is shown in Jaime García's (1986) analysis for Great Britain.

18. Employed workers seeking another job, whether it be a replacement or additional job, make up 4.8 percent of the working population at the national level: 3.6 percent in MUA, and 5.8 percent in LUA.

19. Revenga and Riboud (1992).

20. The quasi-voluntary character of open unemployment becomes patent upon analyzing its structure, since it is more common among individuals with medium levels of education than among those with lower levels of education, and it is much more prevalent

The *alternative open unemployment rate* (AOUR) has been defined by INEGI as the sum of the open unemployed, new job starters, and the hidden unemployed (inactive but available individuals who do not seek a job because they believe that they will not find one) with respect to the augmented EAP, which incorporates the hidden unemployed.[21] As expected the AOUR was higher than the open unemployment: 7.2 percent for the entire country, 8.6 percent for MUA, and 6.0 percent for LUA.

The employed population (EP) was 33.9 million persons. It was found that of this total: 45.6 percent live in MUA; 68.0 percent is male (but in LUA it was 71.2 percent, versus 64.1 percent in MUA); 24.7 percent is in agriculture; wage earners (including piece workers) represent only 57.3 percent;[22] 58.7 percent work in businesses with five or fewer employees;[23] 96.5 percent of the employed worked in the week prior to the survey interview;[24] and 13.0 percent of the employed population did not receive

---

among heads of household than among unmarried offspring. Hernández Gonzalo (1996) also estimates nonlabor income of individual workers and finds a positive relationship between nonlabor income and level of unemployment. Revenga and Riboud (1992) also report higher levels of unemployment among individuals with medium levels of education than among those with low levels, but they interpret this result as an anomaly which disappears when a broader definition of unemployment is used. This finding does not affect the arguments presented here, which refer to a strict definition of open unemployment.

21. The AOUR is one of the indicators proposed by INEGI to remedy the limitations of the OUR, along with others that are included in the analysis of the evolution of the labor market in MUA.

22. Although salaried workers were the decided majority in MUA (72.2 percent), they were the minority (44.8 percent) in LUA. The rest of the working population were freelance workers (25.3 percent of total employed population), unpaid workers (13.0 percent), employers (4.3 percent), and "others" (0.1 percent).

23. In contrast, enterprises with 51 or more employees accounted for only 26.2 percent of total employment, with an even more marked divergence between MUA (38.7 percent) and LUA (15.7 percent). Thus, the employment structure in more urbanized areas is clearly bipolar, with less than a fifth of employment in firms of intermediate size (6 to 50 employees). In LUA there is simply a predominance of microenterprises.

24. Of those who worked, 27.5 percent worked fewer than 35 hours (22.3 percent in MUA and 31.9 percent in LUA). On the other hand, 27.0 percent worked more than 48 hours (which was also nearly equal in MUA and LUA). The causes of the short work days have not yet been published for ENE95, but in ENE93 only 20.6 percent were attributed to labor market conditions (15.1 percent in MUA and 23.8 percent in LUA). In the 1995 ENEU this percentage was 12.3 percent. Based on this information it can be estimated that involuntary underemployment affected 5.2 percent of the employed (2.6 percent in MUA and 7.3 percent in LUA). In consequence, even when open unemployment, hidden unemployment, and involuntary underemployment are combined in an involuntary unemployment and underemployment rate (IUUR), this rate only reaches 12.0 percent (10.9 percent for MUA and 13.0 percent for LUA), a relatively modest level for an economy in crisis.

income, 19.1 percent earned less than the minimum wage, and 31.0 percent earned between one and two times the minimum wage.[25] Finally, with respect to access to labor benefits, 52.7 percent of the employed have no access, although in the more urbanized areas, the percentage is 43.7 percent and 60.2 percent in the less urbanized ones.[26] One can conclude that the most serious problems in the Mexican labor market are not, properly speaking, those of open unemployment, hidden unemployment, or involuntary underemployment, but rather of quality of employment: that is, low remuneration levels and limited access to labor benefits.[27]

25. If only the population that worked 40 or more hours per week is considered, the percentages of workers who did not receive income or earned less than the minimum wage go down to 7.5 percent (2.6 percent in MUA and 12.4 percent in LUA) and 13.1 percent (6.8 percent in MUA and 19.6 percent in LUA) respectively, while the percentage of those who earned between one and two times the minimum wage goes up to 36.8 percent (39.8 percent in MUA and 33.7 percent in LUA). From another perspective, a reasonable estimate puts the extreme poverty line for a family with an average of 4.9 members, at a total income of two times the 1995 minimum wage (mw). Of this income, 1.4 mw in urban areas and 1.2 mw in rural areas corresponds to monetary income. For this reason, a significant fraction of the employed cannot maintain a home by themselves although they work full time.

26. The design of the tables in ENE95 does not permit a calculation of the proportion of employed who claimed to have access to medical services at their job. For this reason, the most recent published information in this regard refers to 1993, when the figure was 34.0 percent for the entire country: 50.1 percent in MUA, and 19.8 percent in LUA. It should be mentioned that ENE93 reported the employed population with social security at (in absolute terms) 10.7 million workers, less than the sum of those directly insured by IMSS and ISSTE, let alone other insurance programs such as those for the armed forces and state governments. The possible sources for this discrepancy are the following: the expansion of the ENE is based on the 1990 census, but apparently it does not correct for undercounting, which would cause the number of employed with social security to be underestimated. Nevertheless, their percentage in the total number of employed would not be altered significantly since the number of workers without social security would also be underestimated. Individuals may be unaware of the programs to which their job entitles them, which would give rise to an absolute and relative underestimate of the number of employed with social security. This source of error cannot be discarded, but one would expect that it would not be very large since the question on the ENE survey specifically asks if the worker receives medical services and working families tend to be very aware of this information. In contrast, the IMSS and ISSTE figures may overestimate the covered population since they come from administrative registers that are not always well maintained. In any case, the simple summation of the population covered by social security requires a downward adjustment since individuals with two jobs would otherwise be counted twice, above all if the social security programs which cover these individuals are different.

27. This statement is not intended to imply that benefits are indispensable to workers' well-being (a lack of benefits can be compensated by a higher monetary income), but rather to indicate simply that (low) incomes are often a working family's only means of subsistence.

The evolution of the Mexican urban labor market can be traced with precision from 1987 onward. In that year the relevant survey, the ENEU, was redesigned to improve its statistical design and make its questionnaire more precise and detailed.[28] Table 10-1 shows the evolution of the most relevant indicators from 1987 to 1995.[29] It is apparent that in 1990 and 1991 the situation in the labor market was favorable, with low levels of unemployment, involuntary unemployment (RPELMR) and the so-called additional employment pressure (AEPR), and with a break in the tendency toward higher levels of informality (PWWB). In contrast, from 1992 to 1994 the indicators show signs of deterioration and in 1995 the effects of the economic crisis become manifest in the abrupt rise in unemployment and involuntary underemployment, as well as in the increase in informality and additional employment pressure.

Labor and Social Security: Legislation and Compliance

This section will analyze key elements of Mexico's labor laws (minimum wages and severance payments) and social security laws (medical services and the pension system), and comment on the available evidence on compliance.[30]

---

28. The most interesting indicators that can be derived from the ENEU are: net participation rate (NPR); open unemployment rate (OUR); alternative open unemployment rate (AOUR); additional employment pressure rate (AEPR: working job seekers / TEP); partial employment for labor market reasons (PELMR: employed who work less than 35 hours for labor market reasons / TEP); proportion of salaried workers (PSW: salaried workers / TEP); proportion of workers without benefits (PWWB: workers with no benefits / TEP).

29. There are minor differences from the data presented in "Minimum Wage," under "Labor Laws," which are basically attributable to the fact that the ENE95 data refer to a single survey while the data presented in this table are simple arithmetic averages of the four quarterly ENEU surveys.

30. A number of academic theses which the author had the privilege of advising as professor at ITAM were very useful in writing this section: Bueno (1985); Franco (1985); Moncada (1985); Schoch (1985); Díaz (1986); Marin (1986); Vergara (1987); Hernández (1989); Alvarez y Espinosa (1990); Andreu (1990); Nehmad (1990); Segovia (1990); Aburto (1991); Belmont (1992); Freyre y Vite (1993); Sanchezviesca (1993); Cejudo (1994); Fernández y Piñeiro (1994). An advantage of using this group of works is the fact that several use the same source, such as the fourth quarter survey of the 1987 ENEU (ENEU87IV) and the single survey (fourth quarter of 1976) of the Encuesta Complementaria a la Encuesta Continua sobre Ocupación (ECECSO). In addition, for the same source the data were processed with the same programs, which facilitates comparison of the results.

Table 10-1. *Selected Indicators for the Mexican Urban Labor Market*

Annual averages

Rate	1987	1988	1989	1990	1991	1992	1993	1994	1995
Net participation	51.8	52.6	51.8	51.8	53.3	53.8	55.2	54.6	55.0
Open unemployment	3.9	3.6	3.0	2.8	2.6	2.8	3.4	3.7	6.3
Alternative open unemployment	6.0	5.3	4.4	4.4	4.2	4.8	5.6	6.2	8.6
Additional economic employment pressure	3.6	3.6	2.9	2.4	2.3	2.8	3.3	3.0	3.7
Unemployment and partial employment, labor market reasons	2.8	2.6	2.4	2.2	2.3	2.6	3.0	2.7	2.4
Proportion of salaried workers	74.4	73.7	73.0	73.7	74.2	73.6	73.0	73.2	71.5
Proportion of workers with benefits	42.0	42.9	44.3	43.4	43.2	44.1	45.6	46.7	49.2

Source: Author's calculations using data published by Instituto Nacional de Estadística Geografía e Informática (INEGI).

Table 10-2. *Evolution of the General Minimum Wage*

Daily, annual national average in 1995 pesos

Year	General minimum wage	Year	General minimum wage
1975	48.76	1986	30.30
1976	54.33	1987	28.11
1977	54.32	1988	24.63
1978	52.50	1989	23.15
1979	51.26	1990	20.98
1980	47.66	1991	20.04
1981	48.35	1992	19.15
1982	42.73	1993	18.86
1983	35.42	1994	18.86
1984	33.22	1995	16.43
1985	32.76	. . .	. . .

Source: Informe de Gobierno, Mexico, 1994.

Labor Laws

MINIMUM WAGE. The Mexican constitution (Art. 123, apartado A, inciso VI) establishes the existence of general and trade-specific minimum wages. The former apply in a general way in one or several geographical areas and the latter apply to a specific type of economic activity or to special professions, trades, or work.[31] Table 10-2 shows the behavior of average general minimum wages in real terms. As can be observed, if 1976 and 1977 (when the minimum wage reached its historic peak) are taken as a point of reference, the 1987 level is a little over half and the 1995 level is less than a third of the reference level. The sharp drop in the real minimum wage is one of the most discussed phenomena in recent Mexican economic history. It is also one of the most misinterpreted, since many analysts jump to the conclusion that this drop implies a similar fall in the actual real wages paid to workers in the economy.[32]

31. Trade-specific minimum wages are related to a guild concept that denies the role of the labor market in orienting human capital investment decisions and that has become out of synch with rapidly changing demand for specialized labor. In addition, trade-specific minimum wages can create legal insecurity since paying the general minimum wage does not ensure that an employer is in compliance with the law—the employer must also make certain that the worker is not doing work that requires a trade-specific minimum wage.

32. Julio Bolvitnik, in a series of newspaper articles, has calculated the number of multiples of the minimum wage required to acquire the basket of essential goods and services postulated by COPLAMAR (1983). Bolvitnik then uses these calculations to support his opinion that the standard of living of workers has deteriorated proportionally.

Table 10-3. *Average Contractual Wage and Average Manufacturing Compensation*

Daily, annual averages in 1995 pesos

Year	Average contractual wage	Average manufacturing wage[a]
1975	61.17	164.90
1976	61.98	179.05
1977	53.13	180.88
1978	50.98	177.18
1979	62.36	175.56
1980	60.51	162.26
1981	61.83	169.11
1982	67.67	166.26
1983	49.09	127.66
1984	47.22	119.67
1985	47.43	121.50
1986	54.17	112.68
1987	67.89	112.93
1988	41.88	110.61
1989	40.47	120.44
1990	38.50	124.74
1991	38.92	132.13
1992	37.74	143.41
1993	37.72	149.50
1994	37.14	155.33
1995	29.76[b]	133.60

Source: Informe de Gobierno, Mexico, 1994.
a. Wages of workers, salaries of employees and total benefits divided by the total number of workers and salaried employees.
b. January–June.

In fact, the minimum wage is an institutional variable that does not necessarily reflect the evolution of actual real wages paid in the economy, even in the formal sector. Concerning remunerations in the formal sector, it is instructive to examine the two principal series available: that of average compensation in manufacturing industries and that of average contractual wages (table 10-3). As can be observed, the average compensation in manufacturing also reached a peak in 1976 and 1977, but its low point came in 1988 and its 1995 level was almost three quarters of its historic peak (instead of a third as in the case with the minimum wage). The average contractual wage reached its highest levels in 1982 and 1987 (curiously, also years of severe economic crisis) and in 1995 it stood at a little less than half of its 1976 level.

For the purposes of this chapter, the most important issue is the analysis of the gap between the minimum wage and the wage of an unskilled urban worker in the informal sector. This analysis must focus on wage-earners only—since owners and free-lance workers present a mixture of implicit returns to labor and capital in their income[33]—and adjust for hours worked (given that, as was pointed out earlier, the surveys capture many workers who do not work full time), controlling for the size of the business[34] and the personal characteristics of the worker.[35] Controlling for level of education turns out to be crucial, and it is also very important to consider sex and age.[36]

Table 10-4 shows average incomes per hour worked (expressed in terms of the minimum wage) for salaried workers in the fourth quarter of 1976, according to a double stratification (by levels of education and by size of establishment).[37] What stands out is that the expected wage of an uneducated worker in an establishment employing 1 to 5 people was half of the minimum wage. The wage only reached the level of the legal minimum in establishments employing more than 50 people, while a worker with 10 or 11 years of education in an establishment employing 1 to 5

33. Segovia (1990) and Pedraza (forthcoming publication) analyze compensation of free-lance workers using ENEU87IV, but this source does not allow them to control for indicators of capital reinvested in the business. For this reason, the best available evidence is still that of Franco (1985) who used data from ECECSO to compare income per hour worked, controlling for education level and business property ownership (owned, rented, or borrowed). For owners, Dávila (1986) and Nehmad (1990) used the number of workers in the enterprise as a key control variable.

34. Information on firm size was not captured by employment surveys before the redesign of the ENEU in 1986, but the one Encuesta Complementaria a la Encuesta Continua sobre Ocupación (ECECSO, Complementary Survey to the Continuous Employment Survey) that was carried out included size of establishment. These data cannot be exactly integrated with firm size since there are large firms that run chains of small establishments. Nevertheless, the large majority of small establishments are microenterprises. By a fortunate coincidence, it was carried out in the fourth quarter of 1976, precisely when the minimum wage was at its historic peak.

35. Even when the samples are very large, certain combinations of individual characteristics can be scantily represented, which results in cells containing few cases (for the analysis of subpopulation means) and in problems of multicolinearity (for regression analysis).

36. The studies which support the importance of these variables in the determination of expected individual incomes for the Mexican case are abundant and solid (for example, Vera y Diez-Canedo, 1977 and 1982). Limiting the scope to works closely related with this chapter, which refer to average income per hour worked for salaried workers, we have: the regression analysis of Moncada (1985) and the analysis of subpopulation means by Schoch (1985), both based on the ECECSO; the analysis of subpopulation means by Alvarez and Espinosa (1990) and the regression analysis by Cejudo (1994) based on the ENEU87IV; and the regression analysis of Freyre y Vite (1993) based on the 1989 *Encuesta Nacional de Ingresos y Gastos de los Hogares* (ENIGH).

37. Dávila (1986, 1989). Bueno (1985) calculated incomes per hour worked of uneducated salaried workers by size of establishment.

Table 10-4. *Average Income per Hour for Salaried Workers,*
Fourth Quarter, 1976

Multiples of the minimum wage

Schooling (years)	Establishment size (number of workers)				
	1 to 5	6 to 15	16 to 25	26 to 50	51 and above
0	.50[a]	.83[b]	.85[a]	.96[a]	1.09
1 to 5	.57[a]	.95[b]	1.01[b]	.99[a]	1.18
6	.71[a]	1.03[a]	1.10[a]	1.21[a]	1.33
7 to 8	.79[a]	1.11[a]	1.35[b]	1.42[b]	1.45
9	.91[a]	1.32[a]	1.55[b]	1.63[b]	1.77
10 to 11	1.11[a]	1.36[a]	2.67[b]	1.88[b]	2.32
12 or more	1.33[a]	2.17[b]	2.01[b]	2.59[a]	3.40

Source: Dávila (1986).
a. Significant difference at 90 percent confidence level.
b. Insignificant difference at 90 percent confidence level.

people barely surpassed the minimum wage. This indicates that the minimum wage was binding in 1976.

Naturally, all gaps between wages observed in small and large establishments cannot be attributed to the minimum wage since, if this were the case, the gaps would have been canceled out for those with at least 10 to 11 years of education (which does not occur). One may suppose that differences in uncontrolled variables, efficiency wages, and institutional factors other than the minimum wage came into play. An example is the influence of labor unions which (with greater success in larger enterprises) impose wage scales that increase as a function of skill level, but that have the minimum wage as a floor.

For the fourth quarter of 1987 Claudia Aburto calculated average incomes per hour of salaried workers, expressed in terms of the minimum wage, based on data from ENEU.[38] Aburto controlled for education level, age, sex, and firm size and compared the normalized average incomes with unity. Aburto found some significant and negative differences, but almost exclusively in microenterprises (1 to 5 employees), for very young men and women (12 to 15 years old) and for women with low levels of education (completed grade school at most). In consequence, it can be affirmed that in 1987 the minimum wage was no longer binding for large segments of the urban working population.[39] In spite of this

38. Aburto (1991).
39. Bell (1995), using data from the 1988 ENE, still finds an important percentage of urban workers who work full time and earn less than the minimum wage (table 9 of the article). A possible cause of this apparent discrepancy is that Bell's tables refer to workers

fact, there were significant differences between the average wage received by workers with similar characteristics according to firm size.

The same analysis was done for the first quarter of 1992 and average incomes below the minimum wage were only detected in isolated cases. These were very young individuals (12 to 14 years old) who worked in microenterprises. In addition, in no case were the differences significant. Thus, by 1992 the minimum wage was no longer binding in the Mexican urban labor market. Figures 10-1 and 10-2 show how for many of the categories analyzed average incomes surpassed the minimum wage by a wide margin.

An analogous analysis has not yet been done for 1995, but the percentage of workers in more urbanized areas who worked 40 or more hours and reported an income below the minimum wage was only 4.7 percent. Even though this figure was still higher than that for 1991 (3.9 percent) and 1993 (3.5 percent), it suggests that in spite of the economic crisis, the minimum wage does not represent a significant restriction in the Mexican urban labor market.[40] As for the less urbanized areas, even when the minimum wage is above the market wage (for unskilled workers), this barely has any practical effect given the limited capacity of the government to enforce labor laws in rural areas.

The nominal minimum wage is revised periodically, but there is no legal obligation to keep it fixed in real terms. Thus the real minimum wage can undergo substantial increases (such as the ones which brought it to its historic high) just as easily as significant and recurrent decreases (such as those which reduced it by more than two-thirds). It is worth pointing out that these decreases were caused by decisions induced by macroeconomic conditions and do not reflect a deliberate strategy to eliminate the restrictive character of the minimum wage. In fact, it would be desirable for the law to establish the obligation to periodically adjust the nominal minimum wage to keep up with variation in the general level

in general, not just salaried workers. The data therefore presumably include uncompensated workers. In addition, she compares income with "the minimum daily wage of 7,218 Mexican pesos," while the results referred to above are based on standardized income (in terms of the minimum wage in the region where the individual worked). Finally, wage dispersion within groups of workers with the same characteristics can mean that some of them earn less than the minimum wage although the mean is not significantly lower than the minimum wage.

40. In consequence, one of the key elements for generating a clear segmentation of the labor market is missing. Maloney (1996) finds (using the ENEU) relatively high levels of voluntary mobility between formal and informal jobs. This brings him to question the hypothesis of segmentation in the Mexican labor market in recent years.

Figure 10-1. *Wage Income per Hour, Education Level and Firm Size, Men*

Income

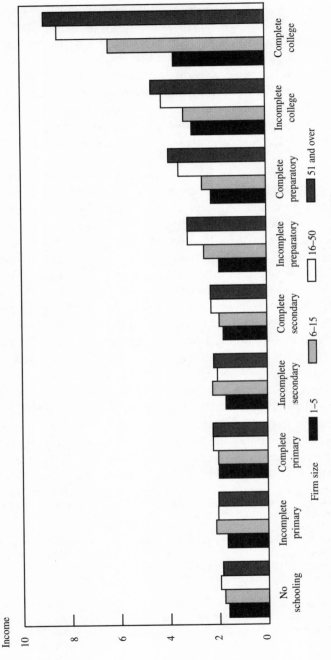

Source: Encuesta Nacional de Empleo Urbano (ENEU), 1st trimester 1992. Instituto Nacional de Estadística, Geografía e Informática (INEGI).

Figure 10-2. *Wage Income per Hour, Education Level and Firm Size, Women*

Income

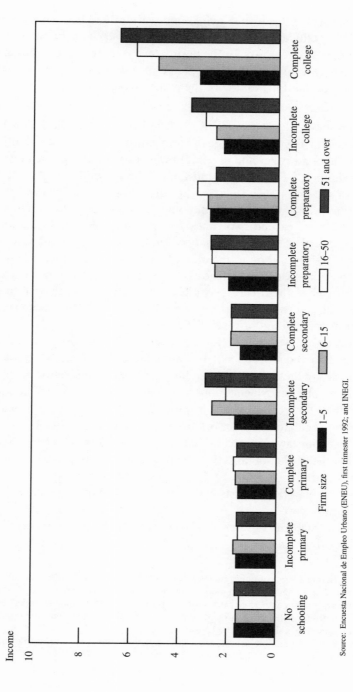

Source: Encuesta Nacional de Empleo Urbano (ENEU), first trimester 1992; and INEGI.

of prices, since this would give greater certainty to economic agents and avoid the political debates which accompany each adjustment of the nominal minimum wage. As for the desirable level of the real minimum wage, the current level offers the advantage of not presenting an effective restriction on the functioning of the labor market.[41]

DISMISSALS AND RESIGNATIONS. The Mexican Federal Labor Law establishes the payment of large indemnizations both in cases of unjustified dismissal of a worker and in cases in which a worker is given a just motive for resigning.[42] The payment must equal three months' salary plus twenty days of salary for each year worked, in addition to twelve days of service bonus for every year worked (although the base salary for calculating this bonus cannot exceed two times the minimum wage). In addition, the worker receives full compensation for the wage payments missed from the time of separation to the date of payment of the indemnization. The law also gives the worker the right to opt for reinstatement, except in certain well-defined cases. Workers who are fired with just cause and those who quit without just cause but have worked 15 or more years with the firm are entitled to receive the service bonus.

The only justifications for dismissal are those that can be directly imputed to the worker, but the abundance of subjective terms in the language of the law provides a large margin of discretion to labor authorities. This in turn encourages drawn out settlements and creates legal insecurity for economic agents. The high transaction costs associated with the regulatory framework are evident in the following:

—A labor lawyer typically charges between 30 percent and 40 percent of what the worker obtains through indemnization or private arrangement with the firm.

—The majority of suits end in private settlements owing to the long duration of cases.

—The majority of workers who consider themselves unjustly dismissed do not bring a legal suit.

41. Nevertheless, counterarguments such as those of Lustig and McLeod (1996) cannot be ignored. They find that high minimum wages tend to be accompanied by lower levels of poverty and examine possible causes for this phenomenon (for example, links between the formal and informal sectors through demand for products). Therefore, the optimum level of minimum wages should still be considered an open question.

42. For a more ample exposition of the regulations concerning dismissals and resignations and other aspects of labor law, see Dávila (1992).

In order to increase the flexibility of the labor market and reduce transaction costs the option of reinstatement should be eliminated. In its place a no-fault indemnization, which would favor the workers, should be established. Given the low probability of receiving the indemnizations which the law establishes in full (because they are very high) and the large magnitude of the transaction costs involved, a relatively small no-fault indemnization would be preferable for workers in view of the current situation. The service bonus could constitute the base for this no-fault indemnization. For this change it would be enough to eliminate the minimum time requirement (15 years to receive the service bonus in cases of resignation without due cause), and remove the ceiling on the salary used to calculate the bonus (two times the minimum wage).

To make this scheme operative it could be established that from the day of the dismissal or resignation the service bonus must be deposited by the employer in a subaccount of the worker's individual social security investment account. The worker could then withdraw amounts equal to those which he or she received as compensation until the funds ran out or the worker found a new job.

Social Security

BRANCHES, CONTRIBUTIONS, AND INSTITUTIONS. According to current laws, contributions to social security equal up to 30.5 percent of the base salary on which contributions are assessed (sbc), with an upper limit that goes from 10 to 25 times the minimum wage in the Federal District (mwDF). This includes: 8.5 percent for disability, old age, old age severance, and life insurance (IVCM); 2.0 percent for retirement insurance (R); 12.5 percent for sickness and maternity insurance (EyM); 2.5 percent for work hazard insurance (RT); 1.0 percent for day care center insurance (GHA); and 5 percent for the government housing program (INFONAVIT: Instituto Nacional del Fondo para la Vivienda de los Trabajadores). The federal government puts in 5 percent of the contributions for old age, sickness, and maternity leave. The Mexican Institute of Social Security administers the pensions, life insurance, work-related accidents compensation, sickness and maternity leaves, and day care centers. The INFONAVIT administers the housing fund.

Contributions for retirement and INFONAVIT are deposited in individual investment accounts in the banking system. The funds are channeled, respectively, to the Banco de México (thus constituting a public debt) and to INFONAVIT. In principle workers are also able to deposit their retirement contributions in investment funds known as the *Sistema de Ahorro para el Retiro* (SAR, Retirement Savings System). Although the SAR encountered severe operational problems, it represented the germ of the new system of old age pensions put forth in the social security reform that will go into effect in January 1997.[43]

DISABILITY, OLD AGE, OLD AGE SEVERANCE, AND LIFE INSURANCE. Contributions to this fund jointly finance disability and life insurance (3.0 percent of base salary), the medical expenses of retired workers, (1.5 percent), old age and old age severance pensions (3.0 percent), and even social benefit programs (0.4 percent). This distribution is the one that currently prevails, but it is not determined by law, which diminishes the transparency of the system.

The expected benefits of the IMSS old age pension system for the worker are in large measure delinked from the contributions made by the worker, the employer, and the state over the course of his or her working life. This situation is due as much to the specific rules that control the amount of pensions as to the fundamental inadequacy of a collective pension system in a country with a large informal labor market and with a female population that is not yet totally integrated into the labor market.

Among the principal specific rules that affect the determination of the real, effective amount of pensions are the following:

—Pensions depend on the base salary and the length of time that the worker is contributing, but according to a complex and arbitrary table. Workers who have put in 10 years (the established minimum) at levels of 1 to 6.5 the minimum wage receive the minimum pension (1 times the minimum wage [mw]). Those who have put in 10 years at levels above 6.5 the minimum wage (up to 10 mw) see their pension go up to 1.5 mw. For 40 years of contribution the pension equals 100 percent of the base salary. Thus the pension does not go up according to years put in for minimum wage workers, does so very slowly for low-wage workers, attains its most rapid growth for those earning 6.5 minimum wage, and then begins to slow down again.

43. An apparently trivial factor that turned out to be of critical importance is that Mexico has no single (or even predominant) system of registry numbers, unlike in countries like the United States (social security number) or Chile (Registro único Nacional).

—The base for calculating pensions is the average of nominal wages in the last five years. For this reason, if a worker retires during a period of high inflation, that individual will see his or her claim significantly reduced from what the law originally promised. If, for example, annual inflation reaches 100 percent the claims of a worker will be reduced to approximately one-third. Given that there is a minimum pension, the foregoing does not affect workers who contribute at the minimum level, but it tends to reduce the others to the minimum pension. Nevertheless, workers and employers frequently exploit this rule in their favor by underdeclaring wages during the majority of the employee's working life (reporting 1 times the mw [1 mw]) and overdeclaring wages in the last five years (declaring 10 mw).

—Pensions are indexed to the minimum wage, not to the cost of living, which means that reductions in the real minimum wage directly affect pensions. In addition, the possibility that the real minimum wage will go up abruptly in the future because of a political decision poses a grave financial risk to the pension system.

—The law grants the right to life insurance (with concomitant widow and orphan pensions) to retired workers who have a young spouse or small children, without a reduction in the base pension amounts. This arrangement tends to favor individuals who change partners at an advanced age. It also gives incentive to fraud since older workers can conduct fictitious weddings and register other people's children in order to will them a pension.

—The law limits the amount of pension benefits that can be accumulated by a person who is receiving a pension both in his or her own right and as a beneficiary of someone else. This limitation discriminates against wives who continue to work after marriage.

As has already been pointed out, IMSS old age pensions function on a collective basis. Specifically, in order to receive a pension a worker must continue to contribute up until the age of retirement (65 years) or reach the age of 65 years in the status known as "conservation of rights," in which an individual can stay one year for each 5 years of contribution in addition to accumulating the minimum number of years of contribution (10 years). Those who do not meet one of these requisites do not receive an old age pension.[44]

---

44. Even though they can receive an old age severance pension if they have contributed for 10 years and have done no paid work after the age of 60 years. The amount of the old

If the probability of continuing to contribute until the age of retirement were independent of personal characteristics the system would be equitable and not distorting. Nevertheless, there are clear differences associated with sex and education level, which derive from differences in employment permanence, differences in modalities of insertion in the labor market (that is, salaried employee, owner, free-lance worker, or unpaid worker), and from differing probabilities that a salaried worker will be located in the most formal segment of the labor market.[45]

Figures 10-3 and 10-4 show the percentage of contributors[46] by sex, education level, and age for the first quarter of 1992 (based on the ENEU), which gives an approximation of the respective probabilities of being a contributor. For men and women at each level of education we can estimate the upper-bound probability that they will continue to contribute until retirement. For each age group the upper bound can be taken as the probability of being a contributor at age 60 to 64 divided by the probability of being a contributor at other ages (since the effect of rotation is not incorporated). The drastic fall in the percentage of contributing women and contributing men of low education levels with increasing age show who are the losers in a pension system managed under the criteria of a collective fund.[47]

Finally, it is worth pointing out that in a healthy economic climate (with low inflation and interest rates and with good opportunity to find and keep a formal job) the pension benefits constitute an uncontrolled element in macroeconomic policy. This is because the IMSS, upon receiving contributions from the insured, assumes a contingent obligation. The expected present value of this obligation is substantially higher than the amount of the contributions on which it is based, such that each peso of cash flow is obtained at the cost of contracting public debt several times as large. For this reason the present value of the net financial position of the public sector deteriorates immediately. In effect,

—Life expectancy for 65-year-old men is an additional 19 years or more. According to estimates by the IMSS, an 84-year-old man (average

age severance pension is a fraction of that for an old age pension the size of which depends on the age at which the worker joins the scheme.

45. See appendix 10A-2.

46. Contributors, as distinct from beneficiaries (*derechohabientes*), are normally workers and, more specifically, salaried workers.

47. A former student of mine humorously called this phenomenon the "Hood Robin effect": the contrary of Robin Hood, robbing from the poor to give to the rich. Nevertheless, for those who are adversely affected by this situation, it is far from a laughing matter.

Figure 10-3. *Percentage of Contributors by Education Level and Age, Men*

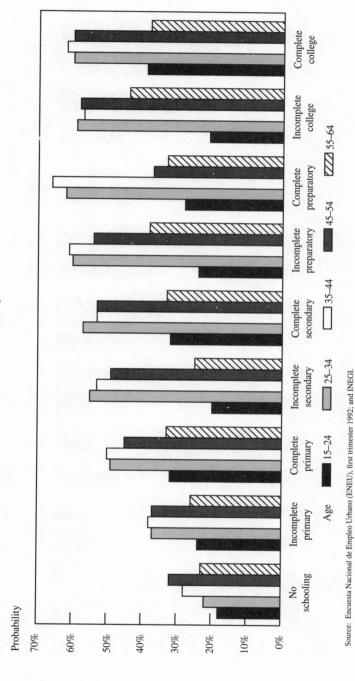

Source: Encuesta Nacional de Empleo Urbano (ENEU), first trimester 1992; and INEGI.

Figure 10-4. *Percentage of Contributors by Education Level and Age, Women*

Probability

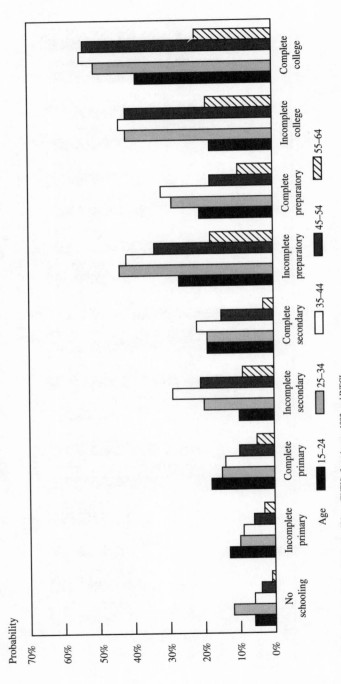

Source: Encuesta Nacional de Empleo Urbano (ENEU), first trimester 1992; and INEGI.

life expectancy beyond 65 years) has a 58.9 percent probability of leaving a widow, whose average age is 70 years. At that age, her life expectancy is an additional 17 years.

—At a real annual interest rate of 3 percent a fund equal to 14.5 times the annual minimum wage (amw) is required to pay the minimum pension (1 mw) to the covered individual during his expected life span. The widow will receive at least 0.9 mw from the time of death of the pensioner. A fund of 6.9 amw is required to pay this obligation. Once the probability that the covered individual will not leave a widow is taken into account, a fund of 18.6 amw is required to finance the minimum pensions (in the absence of orphans). If the pensioner is to receive a pension greater than the minimum, the fund required grows proportionately.

—With a real annual interest rate of 3 percent, and accumulating the whole 3 percent of the worker's annual wage that is applied to old age and old age severance, it turns out that the accumulated fund for a minimum wage worker is 0.3 amw if he or she contributes for 10 years and 1.8 amw if he or she contributes for 40 years. If the wage is higher than the minimum, the fund grows proportionately.

—In consequence, even if a worker contributes at the maximum level for 40 years, sufficient funds to finance a minimum pension for an average male will not be accumulated. A worker who contributes in this way will acquire, in the absence of inflation, a claim to a pension of 10 mw.

This confirms the contention that, up until now, the viability of the system has depended on two undesirable factors and one bound to change with the demographic transition. First, the loss of claims of those who do not continue to contribute up until the age of retirement (or have "conservation of rights" status) or who do not accumulate the minimum number of years of contribution required. Second, the confiscation of part of the claims of covered individuals owing to inflation. Finally, the lag between the number of pensioners and the number of contributors, which derives from the incomplete maturation of the system.

In this context, the change to a fully funded system with individual accounts permits significant improvement in the connection between costs and benefits (which gives rise to a better incentive structure). Such a change also simultaneously reduces the middle-run financial risk of the public sector. For these reasons, the system of accounts was one of the central elements in the social security reform, which will be discussed later.

SICKNESS AND MATERNITY INSURANCE (EyM). Contributions to EyM jointly finance benefits in cash and kind. Cash benefits are proportional to the worker's wage, but they barely reach 0.7 percent of the base salary, leaving 11.8 percent for benefits in kind. Benefits in kind are independent of the level of contribution of the covered individuals, leading to *cross subsidies by level of contribution* from workers with high declared wages toward those with low declared wages. The principal distortions introduced by cross subsidies by level of contribution are the following:

—There is a tax on salaries of higher-earning workers, who are also usually the most skilled. That is, this tax specifically targets human capital. This tends to distort the productive structure of the country and artificially induce the most skilled workers to work independently. It also encourages a type of adverse selection in which only the lowest-paid workers are fully affiliated employees of a business and the rest are paid through honoraria.

—Independent of how much the workers value benefits in kind from EyM, the fact that they can obtain them even if they only contribute at the level of the minimum wage causes them to perceive all contributions they make above this level as a pure tax. This situation encourages underdeclaration, whether open (above all in small businesses, owing to the low probability of a thorough audit) or legal (above all in medium and large firms that may take advantage of the fact that some types of compensation, such as food vouchers, bonuses for punctuality and attendance, savings fund, and so on, are excluded).

—Cross subsidies generate redistributions which are questionable from the point of view of strict equity, since these types of subsidies do not reach informal workers and do not capture resources from high-income individuals who receive honoraria, interest, dividends, and rents.

—The incorporation of free-lance workers is made difficult since their income has an important mixed element, incorporating implicit compensations for labor as well as capital.

—Cross subsidies create an obstacle to schemes that would remit contributions since such schemes would only be attractive to firms that pay high average wages. Permitting these firms to reclaim contributions freely would lead to the financial depletion of the system.

From another perspective, workers who prefer higher-quality services (above all in the nonmedical aspects of treatment, such as in the degree of luxury of hospital rooms) contribute without making use of IMSS services and only resort to IMSS facilities in cases of very severe or costly illnesses. This situation results in *cross subsidies by selection of medical services* from workers who prefer to use private medical services toward the rest of the contributors.

At each moment the expected value of benefits in kind depends on the number of beneficiaries covered at the same contribution level, and on their state of health, which is in turn crucially influenced by their age.

The fact that young individuals without families pay the same as middle-aged individuals with families and older individuals does not necessarily imply cross subsidies from a life-cycle perspective. Furthermore, the dominant practice in the private insurance market (charging an annual premium for medical insurance according to the age of the individual and the composition of his or her immediate family) is not optimal, since it reflects an imperfection of this market, namely, the difficulty of establishing long-term contracts which are sufficiently broad. In effect, an individual who has insurance against major medical expenses is normally not covered for catastrophic expenditures and runs the risk of being discriminated against by insurance companies from the moment it is known that he or she suffers from a serious health problem. In this context, it is efficient for individuals to be able to contract a fixed premium for their entire adult lives.

Thus cross subsidies will exist only to the degree that there are individuals who contribute only during the segments of their working lives in which they require more or less medical service than the average (*cross subsidies by permanence of affiliation*) and to the degree that certain families have consistently higher levels of dependency (that is, ratio of beneficiaries to contributors) than others (*cross subsidies by rates of dependency*). The appearance of these types of cross subsidies is encouraged by the following factors:

—Contributions to social security (and in particular to sickness and maternity insurance) do not diminish over the time during which a worker is contributing, nor does it diminish if he or she is the second contributor in the same family.

—Individuals can work legally without paying social security if they are employers, free-lance workers, or unpaid workers.

—The Department of Health operates a system of clinics and hospitals for the population that is not covered. In these facilities, fees are determined based on a case-by-case estimate of ability to pay and they are normally well below the cost of the services provided. This is due, among other reasons, to the fact that a large segment of the urban informal

Table 10-5. *Medical Services, Compliance by Firm Size*

Firm size (total number of individuals)	Compliance (%)
1 to 5	28.2
6 to 15	57.4
16 to 50	77.1
51 to 100	84.2
101 and above	92.2

Source: Aburto (1991).

population lacks the means to pay for a costly illness, although they may have the means to prepay (that is, they could afford an unsubsidized payment for health insurance).

The preceding factors encourage opportunistic behaviors, such as joining social security after starting a family, when one is already at an advanced age, or when one discovers a serious health problem. In addition, spouses of workers with social security prefer (or have less objection to) free-lance work, contract work on an honorarium basis, or employment in a firm that evades social security tax.

Cross subsidies by level of contribution can be eliminated through a uniform contribution (independent of declared salary). This would also facilitate remission of contributions, which is the ideal mechanism for reducing cross subsidies by selection of services. For this reason, the social security reform attempted to approach (to the degree permitted by the legal framework) the establishment of a single contribution.

FIRM SIZE AND COMPLIANCE WITH SOCIAL SECURITY OBLIGATIONS. Because of the disjuncture between social security contributions and benefits, payments are perceived fundamentally as a tax and not as the purchase of a service for workers. Under these circumstances, it can be expected that compliance patterns will behave according to a model of crime and punishment and will therefore depend directly on the size of the firm in question.

Table 10-5 shows the percentages of workers with medical coverage by firm size for the fourth quarter of 1987.[48] These figures can be taken as indicative of employers' compliance with their obligation to affiliate their workers with social security programs. It is apparent from the table that compliance is clearly an increasing function of firm size, as would be

48. Aburto (1991).

expected. Given that for 1987 the minimum wage was not restrictive for a large part of the urban work force, this result tends to confirm the existence of important cost-benefit gaps, which are perceived as such by workers and employers.

THE SOCIAL SECURITY REFORM. The reforms of the Social Security Law *(Ley de Seguro Social)*, which will go into effect at the beginning of 1997, deal with very diverse aspects of the law (for example, there is a new formula for calculating premiums for workplace hazard insurance), but two reforms eclipse the rest in importance: the switch to a system of individual investment accounts and the replacement of salary-based contributions to sickness and maternity by a (practically) single fee.

—Reform of the Financial Regime for Sickness and Maternity. The reform separates the financing of benefits in cash and kind in the following way: cash benefits are financed by a contribution of 1 percent of base salary, of which the federal government covers 5 percent (*Ley del Seguro Social*, article 107).

—Benefits in kind are financed (LSS, article 106 and 19th transitory article) with the following: an employer contribution, which will initially be 13.9 percent of mwDF (minimum wage in the Federal District) and which will rise over 10 years to 20.4 percent of mwDF; a worker/employer contribution paid on salaries above 3 mw, which will initially be 8 percent and will diminish over 10 years to 1.5 percent; a government contribution, fixed in real terms (indexed to the CPI), the value of which will be 13.9 percent of the current mwDF on the date the new LSS goes into effect.

Thus sickness and maternity benefits in kind will be financed in the long run by a uniform contribution (in that it is practically independent of the salary declared by the worker, although the fact that the employer contribution is indexed to the minimum wage and not to the CPI introduces an element of uncertainty concerning its future real level). It should be pointed out that these rates were set with an eye toward preserving the average income per contributor to IMSS (based on the fact that the average sbc of this population is about 3 mw).

From another angle, the government payment will increase substantially (from approximately 0.6 percent mw per contributor to 13.9 percent), which constitutes an aggressive policy of stimulus to formal employment.

Parallel to the reform of the obligatory program, a voluntary health insurance program was established with the same in-kind benefits as EyM (although without cash benefits). In the voluntary scheme the worker pays a contribution of 22.4 percent mwDF, and the federal government covers the same contribution as for the obligatory program. This represents an effort to incorporate free-lance workers and employers with the capacity for prepayment into the social security system on a voluntary basis.

—Reform of the Pension System. The reform implies that the following payments (in addition to the 5 percent sbc for INFONAVIT) be channeled to the individual accounts of workers: 6.275 percent sbc from worker/ employer contributions; 0.225 percent sbc from government contributions in proportion to salary; a government *social contribution*, independent of declared salary and fixed in real terms, the value of which will be 5.5 percent of the current mwDF on the date the new LSS goes into effect.

On reaching 65 years of age the contributing worker will be able to access the balance of his or her individual account in order to acquire a pension for the worker and his or her spouse and minor children. If the worker has contributed for 1,250 weeks he or she will have the right to a *guaranteed pension,*which is fixed in real terms (1 mwDF at the time the reform goes into effect).[49] After the death of the contributor, dependents will be able to receive widow and orphan pensions analogous to those in the current law.

The social contribution is an important innovation which reduces incentive problems associated with a combined system that includes pensions based on individual accounts and a guaranteed pension.

In effect, in a system with a guaranteed pension individuals can obtain a pension even though they only comply with the minimum requisites— a minimum contribution, based on a declared minimum salary for the minimum time period. The net present value of the savings accumulated by such a minimum contribution is normally less than the expected net present value of the guaranteed pension. Therefore, over a more or less lengthy interval the individual faces a 100 percent marginal tax on his or her savings, since each unit of additional savings (whether from a longer period of contribution or from a higher declared salary) gives rise to an equivalent reduction in the amount paid in by the state in order to reach the minimum pension. This constitutes an incentive for underdeclaration and impermanence as a contributor.[50]

49. This guarantee is also applicable in cases of old age severance (using the same definition as the current law).

50. This phenomenon helps explain the problems in the Chilean pension system pointed out by Bonilla (1994).

In this context, the social contribution encourages permanence on the contribution rolls and provides a proportionally greater benefit to low-income workers without creating inducements to distort declared salaries (as happens with a salary-based contribution or, in the opposite direction, with a subsidy inversely proportional to salary.)

As for the transition, the decision was made to respect the acquired claims (and even the expected claims) of workers, as well as the principle that workers cannot renounce their labor rights (*irenunciabilidad*). This led to a gradualist scheme: anyone who has contributed before the reform will have the option of calculating his or her pension according to the old system. If this amount is greater than the individual's accumulated fund, he or she can ask the federal government to make up the difference (LSS, third and fourth transitory articles.)

Naturally, during the first years of operation of the system the accumulated amounts in the individual accounts will be low. Therefore, individuals who have met the requirements for an old age pension (or old age severance pension) will do so under the conditions in the current law. Nevertheless, individuals who do not yet meet these requirements will begin to benefit from the new system as soon as it goes into effect.

Finally, it is worth mentioning that the transition does not provide for a recognition bond for individuals who renounce claims (or expected claims) generated under the current law, since these claims cannot be renounced under a strict interpretation of Mexican labor law.

Conclusions

The main conclusions that can be derived from the analyses presented here are the following. First, open unemployment, in the strict sense of the term, does not represent a problem in the Mexican labor market. Even the so-called hidden unemployment and involuntary underemployment have a relatively low presence, even in the current macroeconomic situation. The most serious problem in the Mexican labor market is the low quality and remuneration of employment, above all for less-skilled workers.

Second, the substantial reduction in the real minimum wage in the last two decades has resulted in a situation in which the minimum wage no longer represents a restriction in the Mexican labor market.

Finally, affiliation with the social security system continues to be achieved, in large measure, by coercive mechanisms. Social security institutions confront severe problems of underreporting of wages owing to the gap between the amount of contributions paid and the benefits derived from them. The recent reform of the social security laws tends to close or even reverse this cost/benefit gap through better design of incentives and a higher contribution on the part of the federal government. For this reason the reform may contribute significantly to the formalization of the Mexican labor market.

Appendix 10A-1: Glossary of Acronyms and Their Translations

AEEPR (Additional Economic Employment Pressure Rate) = TPEA (Tasa de Presión Económica Adicional)

AEPR (Additional Employment Pressure Rate) = TPA (Tasa de Presión Adicional)

AOUR (Alternative Open Unemployment Rate) = TDAA (Tasa de Desempleo Abierto Alternativa)

APEPR (Additional Preferential Employment Pressure Rate) = TPPA (Tasa de Presión Preferencial Adicional)

CECR (Critical Employment Conditions Rate) = TCCO (Tasa de Condiciones Críticas de Ocupación)

EAP (Economically Active Population) = PEA (Población Economicamente Activa)

EEEPR (Effective Economic Employment Pressure Rate) = TPEE (Tasa de Presión Efectiva Económica)

GEPR (General Employment Pressure Rate) = TPG (Tasa de Presión General)

IIR (Insufficient Income Rate) = TII (Tasa de Ingresos Insuficientes)

IIUR (Insufficient Income and Unemployment Rate) = TIID (Tasa de Ingresos Insuficientes y Desocupación)

IUUR (Involuntary Unemployment and Underemployment Rate) = TDSI (Tasa de Desempleo y Subempleo Involuntario)

LUA (Less Urbanized Areas) = Z − U (Zonas Menos Urbanizadas)

MUA (More Urbanized Areas) = Z + U (Zonas Más Urbanizadas)

NPR (Net Participation Rate) = TNP (Tasa Neta de Participación)

OUR (Open Unemployment Rate) = TDA (Tasa de Desempleo Abierto)

PEEPR (Preferential Effective Employment Pressure Rate) = TPEP (Tasa de Presión Efectiva Preferencial)

PER1 (Partial Employment Rate) = TOP1 (Tasa de Ocupación Parcial)

PER2 (Partial Employment (less than 35 hours per week) Rate) = TOP2 (Tasa de Ocupación Parcial)

PEUR1 (Partial Employment and Unemployment Rate) = TOPD1 (Tasa de Ocupación Parcial y Desocupación)
PEUR2 (Partial Employment (less than 35 hours per week) and Unemployment Rate) = TOPD2 (Tasa de Ocupación Parcial y Desocupación)
PSW (Proportion of Salaried Workers) = PA (Proporción de Asalariados)
PWWB (Proportion of Workers without Benefits) = PTSP (Proporción de Trabajadores sin Prestaciones)
RPELMR (Rate of Partial Employment for Labor Market Reasons) = TOPRM (Tasa de Ocupación Parcial por Razones de Mercado)
RUPELMR (Rate of Unemployment and Partial Employment for Labor Market Reasons) = TOPRMD (Tasa de Ocupación Parcial por Razones de Mercado y Desocupación)
TEP (Total Employed Population) = OT (Ocupación Total)
WAP (Working Age Population) = PET (Población en Edad de Trabajar)

Appendix 10A-2: Personal Characteristics and Insertion in the Labor Market

This appendix gives a brief discussion of the influence of personal characteristics (principally sex, age, and education) on the probability of insertion in the labor market and on specific modalities of insertion. The discussion is limited to MUA and is based on the first quarter 1992 ENEU.

The following conclusions may be drawn concerning male and female representation in the WAP according to age and education:

—The probability of being employed is systematically higher for men than for women of the same age and education categories. Nevertheless, the gaps are noticeably greater for uneducated individuals than for those with a college degree.

—The probability of being employed tends to first increase with age, and then decrease. In general, this pattern is more regular for men than for women, and the differences in probabilities from age group to age group tend to be less accentuated for men.

—The probability of being employed is lower for individuals with no education and higher for individuals with a college degree. Nevertheless, at intermediate levels of education the effect of schooling is not as clear.

—Married men have a higher probability of being employed than unmarried men, but married women have a lower probability of being employed than unmarried women.

An analysis of the different occupational categories (salaried workers, employers, free-lance workers, and unpaid workers) by sex, age, and education permits the following conclusions:

—Women and younger individuals are more strongly represented in the category of unpaid workers than in other categories.

—Conversely, the proportion of free-lance workers who are female is clearly lower than the proportion of salaried workers who are female.

—The lowest age strata account for a greater proportion of salaried workers than of free-lance workers. This result is due in large measure to two complementary, but very different, effects: Voluntary departure from a salaried job: once an individual has accumulated work experience and some savings he or she may decide to work independently, with the intention of later becoming an employer. Or involuntary departure from a salaried job: an individual who has been without salaried work and who is no longer young may not be able to find a willing employer and may therefore be obligated to work independently.

An analysis of the probability that a worker is employed at a private (or public) firm employing 51 or more workers reveals that

—The probability tends to be lower for less-educated individuals.

—The probability tends to rise at first with age, but then falls.

—The probability is greater, in general, for men than for women.

Finally, the patterns discussed in this appendix, together with the tendency of smaller firms to evade social security obligations, mean that the probability of being covered:

—Is lower, in general, for women than for men.

—Tends to be lower for less-educated individuals.

—Rises at first with age, but then decreases substantially, especially for women.

References

Aburto, Claudia. 1991. "Ingresos y Prestaciones de los Asalariados: El Efecto del Tamaño de la Empresa." Mexico City: Tesis ITAM.

Akerlof, G., and J. Yellen. 1986. *Efficiency Wage Models of the Labor Market*. Cambridge University Press.

Alvarez, Genoveva, e Irla Espinosa. 1990. "Tasas de Participación e Ingresos Salariales para Hombres y Mujeres: México 1987." Mexico City: Tesis ITAM.

Andreu, Miguel Angel. 1990. "La Influencia del Nivel Socioeconómico Familiar Sobre los Ingresos de los Hijos: México. 1987." Mexico City: Tesis ITAM.
Banco Nacional de México. 1983. *Encuesta de Subempleados*. Estudios Sociales, edited by Banamex. Mexico City.
Bell A., Linda. 1995. "The Impact of Minimum Wages in Mexico and Colombia." Mimeo. Paper prepared for the Conference on Labor Markets in Developing Countries. Washington, 1994 (revised version).
Belmont, Arlette. 1992. "Características Personales e Inserción en el Mercado Laboral en México: Un Modelo Log-Lineal." Mexico City: Tesis ITAM.
Beneria, L. 1989. "Subcontracting and Employment Dynamics in Mexico City." In *The Informal Economy*, edited by Portes and others. Johns Hopkins University Press.
Bonilla Alejandro y Gillion. 1992. "La Privatización de un Régimen Nacional de Pensiones: El Caso Chileno." *Revista Internacional de Trabajo* 2(2): 192–221.
Bueno, Marta. 1985. "Un Enfoque de Crimen y Castigo Aplicado al Pago del Salario Mínimo Legal: El Efecto del Tamaño del Establecimiento." Mexico City: Tesis ITAM.
Cejudo, Nora. 1994. "Los Ingresos de los Asalariados: Un Análisis de Regresión." Mexico City: Tesis ITAM.
COPLAMAR. 1983. *Necesidades Esenciales en México: Situación Actual y Perspectivas al Año 2000*. Mexico City: Editorial Siglo XXI.
Dávila, Enrique. 1986. "Investigación Sobre el Mercado de Trabajo Informal: Resumen de los Resultados Empíricos y Recomendaciones." Mimeo. Seminario ITAM-COLMEX.
———. 1989. *Ingresos y Prestaciones del Sector Informal*. Documentos de Trabajo, Fundación Friedrich Ebert (20), Mexico.
———. 1992. *Regulaciones Laborales y Mercado de Trabajo en México*. En *Regulación del Mercado de Trabajo en América Latina*, edited by Gustavo Márquez. *Centro Internacional para el Desarrollo Económico Ediciones IESA*.
Dávila, Enrique, Santiago Levy, y Luis López Calva. 1996. "Empleo Rural y Combate a la Pobreza: Una Propuesta de Política." *Economía Mexicana* 4 *Nueva Epoca: 313–53*.
De Soto, Hernando. 1986. *El otro sendero: La Revolución Informal*. Lima, Editorial El Barranco (Reeditado por Editorial Diana en 1987).
Díaz, Olivia. 1986. "Migración Interregional en México." Mexico City: Tesis ITAM.
Fernández, Cecilia, y Francesca Piñeiro. 1994. "Oferta Laboral para Salarios Bajos: El Caso de México en 1992." Mexico City: Tesis ITAM.
Franco, Midori. 1985. "Los Ingresos de los Trabajadores por Cuenta Propia: Un Análisis Empírico." Mexico City: Tesis ITAM.
Freyre, Rafael, y Norma Vite. 1993. "Capital Humano en un Modelo de Equilibrio General." Mexico City: Tesis ITAM.
García, Jaime. 1986. *Incentive and Welfare Effects of Reforming the British Benefit System*. A Simulation Study for the Wives of the Unemployed. W. P. 72.86.

Departament d'Economia i d' Història Econòmica. Facultat de Cincies Econòmiques i Empresarials. Universitat Autònoma de Barcelona. Bellaterra.

Giner de los Ríos, Francisco. 1983. "Una Tipología de Empresas Microindustriales y su Aplicación a Datos Censales." Mimeo. Seminario ITAM-Colmex, 8 de julio.

Hernández, Gonzalo. 1989. "Oferta Laboral de Familias de Escasos Recursos: Modelo Teórico y Evidencia Empírica para el Área Metropolitana de la Ciudad de México." Mexico City: Tesis ITAM.

———. 1996. "Efectos de la Pobreza Familiar sobre la Participacion en el Mercado Laboral, Las Horas Trabajadas y el Desempleo in Mexico." Tesis Doctoral. Wolfson College, Oxford University.

Instituto Mexicano del Seguro Social (IMSS). 1995. *Diagnóstico*. IMSS.

———. 1995. *Ley del Seguro Social*.

Jusidman, Clara. 1993. *El Sector Informal en México*. Cuadernos de Trabajo (2), Secretaría del Trabajo y Previsión Social, México.

Lustig, Nora, and Darryl McLeod. 1996. "Minimum Wages and Poverty: A Cross-National Analysis for Developing Countries." Mimeo.

Maloney, William. 1996. *Dualism and the Unprotected or Informal Labor Market in Mexico: A Dynamic Approach*. Office of Research Working Paper 96-0102. University of Illinois at Urbana-Champaign, College of Commerce and Business Administration.

Marin, Estela. 1986. *Ingresos de los Trabajadores Asalariados Migrantes: México 1976*. Mexico City: Tesis ITAM.

Márquez, Gustavo. 1992. *Regulación del Mercado de Trabajo en América Latina*. Centro Internacional para el Desarollo Económico. Mexico City: Ediciones IESA.

Márquez, Carlos y Jaime Ros. 1990. "Segmentación del Mercado de Trabajo y Desarrollo Económico en México." *El Trimestre Económico* 226 (Abril–Junio): 343–78.

Moncada, Elsa. 1985. "Ingresos Laborales y Capital Humano: Zonas Urbanas de México, 1976." Mexico City: Tesis ITAM.

Mundlak, Yair. 1978. "Occupational Migration Out of Agriculture. A Cross-Country Analysis." *Review of Economics and Statistics* (August): 392–98.

Nehmad, Marlyn. 1990. "Perfil e Ingresos de los Patrones." Mexico City: Tesis ITAM.

Ozorio de Almeida, Ana Luiza, and Scott Graham. 1993. "Employment Creation by Deregulation in the Informal Sector in Argentina." Mimeo. Washington.

Ozorio de Almeida, Ana Luiza, and Leandro Alves. 1994. "Poverty, Deregulation and Informal Employment in Mexico." Mimeo. Washington.

Pedraza, Raquel. Próxima Publicación. "Diferenciales de Ingresos entre Trabajadores por Cuenta Propia." Mexico City: Tesis ITAM.

Programa Regional de Empleo para América Latina y el Caribe (PREALC). 1976. *El Problema del Empleo en América Latina: Situación, Perspectivas y Políticas*. PREALC, Santiago de Chile.

———. 1978. *Sector Informal: Funcionamiento y Políticas*. PREALC, Santiago de Chile.

Rendón, Teresa. 1982. "El Empleo en México: Tendencias Recientes." *Investigación Económica UNAM* 161 (Julio–Septiembre): 157–81.

Revenga, Ana, and Michelle Riboud. 1992. "Unemployment in Mexico: An Analysis of Its Characteristics and Determinants." Mimeo.

Sanchezviesca, Marcela. 1993. "Factores Económicos que Determinan los Flujos Migratorios en los Estados Unidos Mexicanos." Mexico City: Tesis ITAM.

Schoch, Jacqueline. 1985. "Diferenciales de Salarios entre Hombres y Mujeres: Evidencia para las Zonas Urbanas de México en 1976." Mexico City: Tesis ITAM.

Segovia, Gabriela. 1990. "Diferenciales de Ingreso entre Hombres y Mujeres: El Caso de los Trabajadores por Cuenta Propia." Mexico City: Tesis ITAM.

Tockman, V. 1978. "Las Relaciones entre los Sectores Formal e Informal." *Revista de la CEPAL*, vol. 5 primer trimestre, Santiago de Chile, 103–11.

Vera, Gabriel, y Juan Diez-Canedo. 1977. *Distribución del Ingreso en México*. Banco de México. Mexico City.

Vergara, Cecilia. 1987. *Capital Humano. Estimaciones con Estadística Robusta*. Mexico City: Tesis ITAM.

Contributors*

Edward J. Amadeo, *Catholic University of Rio de Janeiro, Brazil*

José Márcio Camargo, *Catholic University of Rio de Janeiro, Brazil*

Enrique Rafael Dávila Capelleja, *Ministry of Finance, Mexico*

René Cortázar, CIEPLAN, *Santiago, Chile*

Alejandra Cox Edwards, *California State University, Long Beach*

Sebastian Edwards, *University of California, Los Angeles*

Marta Luz Henao, *FEDESARROLLO, Bogota, Colombia*

Hugo A. Hopenhayn, *University of Rochester and Universitat Pompeu Fabra, Spain*

Eduardo Lora, *Inter-American Development Bank, Washington, D.C., previously FEDESARROLLO, Bogota, Colombia*

Nora Claudia Lustig, Brookings Institution

Darryl McLeod, *Fordham University and Lehman Brothers*

Juan Pablo Nicolini, *Universidad di Tella, Buenos Aires, Argentina*

John Pencavel, *Stanford University*

Carola Pessino, *CEMA, Buenos Aires, Argentina*

*Affiliation at the time of the conference.

328

Index

Abraham, K., 229
Aburto, Claudia, 304
Administradoras de Fondos Previsionales (AFPs; Chile), 245, 254
AFPs. *See* Administradoras de Fondos Previsionales
Africa, 42, 50*n*37, 53, 57–58
Agriculture, 34–35, 72, 73
Aldao-Zapiola, Carlos, 192
Allende, Salvador, 45*n*32
America, North, 155, 156. *See also* United States
Analytical methods: census data (Mexico), 295*n*14, 296*n*26; data sources and availability, 28, 67, 68, 82, 87, 91; demand link model of minimum wage, 64*n*7, 65*n*11; determinants of labor issues, 288*t*, 289*t*; economic effects of payroll taxes, 285–87; employment effects of minimum wage, 210–13, 215–19, 277–79; Harris-Todaro model of minimum wage, 64, 65*n*11, 66; labor costs, 271, 273; labor market in Mexico, 294–99; optimal unemployment insurance contract model, 108–22; poverty and minimum wage, 67–81; poverty elasticities, 82–86; probit model of unemployment, 178, 193–99; rate of variation of wages, 237–41; study outcomes, 28; three-sector model of wage effects, 28–29; unemployment (Mexico), 296*n*16; wage curve, 13–14; worker damage potential, 214–19
Annual Report of the International Labor Organization, 249
Arbitration, 5, 56–57, 128. *See also* Disputes, labor; Collective bargaining; Unions

Argentina: collective bargaining, 131; cost of labor, 181–82, 185, 187*n*29, 189–90, 285; dispute resolution, 132; education, 166–67, 171–73, 178–80, 181*f*, 188; employment issues, 138–40, 152, 153, 155–59, 175–76; labor market reform, 2*n*3, 11–13, 20, 151–52, 153, 154, 184, 187–92; labor market trends, 11–3, 153–75; manufacturing and service sectors, 158–59, 162–63, 165–66, 171, 198–99; Mexican crisis, 159; payroll taxes, 188–89, 191, 192; pension reforms, 10, 144, 189; productivity, 184–87, 188; social security and benefits, 143, 175–77, 189–90; trade and tariff issues, 153, 159*n*4, 181–82; training programs, 146, 151, 192; underemployment, 169–73, 176; unemployment insurance, 106–08, 113–22, 169, 190–92; unions, 42, 51, 131, 189, 192; wages and earnings, 81*t*, 182–84, 188, 191, 192
Argentina, Convertibility Plan of *1991*: costs of labor, 185, 187*t*; economic issues, 153–54; education issues, 179; employment effects, 158–59, 175; labor trends, 11–13, 181–83, 187–88
Argentina, economic issues: benefits, 176; cost of labor, 154; education, 179–80; employment and labor issues, 11–12, 151–52, 153, 159–61; income and wages, 182–83*l*; productivity, 186–87; self-employment, 175
Argentina, unemployment: determinants, 178–80, 187–88; increases in, 11, 12–13, 105–06, 154; insurance, 114–16, 192; trends, 159–75; wages and, 152; of women, 198

329

DATE DUE			
JAN 0 9 2004			
JAN 1 0 2006			
JAN 1 1 2010			
MAY 1 1 2010			
GAYLORD			PRINTED IN U.S.A.